Preventative Law
for Business Professionals

Martin E. Segal

Revised Edition

New Age Publishing Co. P.O. Box 01-1549 - Miami, Florida 33101

Preventative Law for Business Professionals
Martin E. Segal

CONTENTS

INTRODUCTION

"The world is a place of business."

—Henry David Thoreau

"The best laid schemes o' mice and men . . . "

—Robert Burns

Why You Need this Book

We are all business managers in one form or another. Whether the form of our business is sole proprietorship or partnership or corporation, whether we are employee or chief operating officer or occupy some other position, we are still trying to manage our respective duties in as successful a manner as possible. But while we share this common goal, we also share a common predicament regardless of our age, prior experience, or station in life.

We are surrounded in the business marketplace by a complex web of legal rights and duties, most of which we are unfamiliar with until it's too late. And we live in an extremely litigious society. It seems the phone number dialed most frequently when a commercial transaction derails is 1-800-sue-everybody.

Wal-Mart is a prime example of a litigation target. It is both the world's largest retailer and its most frequently sued company. Current estimates are that over 5,000 lawsuits are filed against its "deep pockets" every year. Internet websites exist where plaintiffs' lawyers share their legal strategies and report on the results of pending cases.

Every business decision has legal implications. Proper management of the legal factor is crucial to success; yet business professionals often proceed blindly without an awareness of the hundreds of legal time bombs that may lie in their path, ready to blow up their deals. And when this happens, they come face-to-face with the dreaded four L's of a business transaction gone wrong – Lawsuits, Lawyers, Liability, and Loss.

The critical point in time to legally analyze a business transaction is before it has been finalized, rather than after something has gone wrong. Once the contract is made, the legal rights of the parties may have already been seriously compromised. And it all goes back to improper managing of the legal factor inherent in all our business interactions.

It happened to Elvis Presley. He promised to pay off the mortgage on his future mother-in-law's house but died before he could fulfill it. She sued his estate to enforce it. There was no dispute he had made the promise, but it was ruled to be a legally unenforceable gift and she lost.

She could have won by simply agreeing to bake Elvis a cake in exchange for his promise, so that the legal requirement of a bargained-for exchange of value was satisfied. You can look it up – it's in the book!

It happened to Elizabeth Taylor when she hired actress Cicely Tyson to appear in a Broadway play, and assured payment of $750,000 regardless of the show's financial success. When it closed early, Cicely sued to enforce her "play or pay" guarantee and won. Elizabeth could have avoided the legal problem with a contractual limitation of her financial obligation to the "lesser" of salary earned or show revenue produced. You can look it up – it's in the book!

And it happened to Empire Savings Bank when it paid $19 million for thirty-five real estate mortgage notes in an ill-fated transaction where it was prevented from enforcing them because it had neglected to "affix" transfer endorsements to each note. The bank right to collect would have been protected if it had simply stapled the endorsements to the notes. You can look it up – it's in the book!

My experiences as a lawyer, businessman, teacher, and legal risk management consultant convinced me that business managers needed a new and different approach to their old way of dealing with legal risks by "turning it over to legal" after problems arose. At that point legal expenses are maximized and net profits are correspondingly reduced. This is passive management and it doesn't work.

Why not be an active legal risk manager? Make an immediate change in your traditional executive decision-making process. Move away from your "after-the-fact" approach to one of "preventative advance planning," where you anticipate potential legal problems and develop winning strategies to fail-safe your commercial transaction in advance. This is your ultimate goal in effective risk management, and this book will help you to achieve it.

You can identify potential time bombs and defuse them before they blow you up. You can structure your business deal for success, and then finalize it with the assurance that it was planned well and can be safely completed. You can be a consistent winner by test-driving your proposed contracts or sales transaction vehicle using our map of success.

This book gives you all the tools you need. It tells you WHAT the legal rules that govern most commercial transactions are, WHERE the common legal time bombs that threaten their success are, and HOW to structure your deals to avoid these problems – using examples of actual cases involving well-known persons and companies whose transactions exploded because they weren't planned properly.

How the Book is Organized

The book is separated into the major business law areas of contracts and sales impacting most commercial transactions. It is organized in the same practical sequence that managerial business decisions need to be made in the marketplace.

We proceed, step by step, through the most common commercial transactions, highlighting the business law time bombs that may blow up into a typical dispute and the alternatives to minimize or avoid them.

One party's business law time bomb is another party's business opportunity. Ignore the problem or be unaware of it and you blow up financially. Avoid the problem or defuse it and you have a successful result.

There is a common thread woven throughout the world of business law disputes. One of the parties wants to enforce his contract because he believes it is a good business deal. The other party does not want to be legally bound because he believes he made a bad business deal. The respective motivations of the litigants are as basic as that. They each will argue the rules of law or exceptions to those rules that support their positions and are consistent with the outcome they desire. They will interpret the facts of their dispute in a way most favorable to their legal position.

The scales of justice that symbolize the legal system are a good visual metaphor to remind us that navigating successfully through the business marketplace is a daily balancing act. Imagine one of the scales holding a legal time bomb with its fuse lit and the other piled high with money. We constantly walk the tightrope between potential legal problems and financial success, trying to maintain an acceptable balance, constantly adjusting and readjusting our position. If we are not successful, we find ourselves and our company involved in litigation, and while this is to be avoided if possible, there are also dispute management strategies that can increase our chances for a favorable result.

Let's take a preliminary walk through the book's chapters as described in the table of contents:

Chapter 1 begins with a discussion of the Anticipatory Thinking Approach, which is the foundation of the Preventative Law Method, providing the opportunity for skillful planning of one's commercial transactions. It then examines the basic contract principles that are the foundation for all commercial agreements.

We next proceed chapter by chapter, to explore the perils, pitfalls, and planning skills involved in:

2. Creation of the contract – offer and acceptance
3. Enforceability of the contract – legal consideration
4. Legal ways to avoid contract liability – incapacity of parties, illegality of subject matter, lack of voluntary and knowing consent, verbal and written contracts, enforcement rights of outside parties, and other legal excuses for non-performance
5. Management of special contract rules – commercial sales of goods, product defects, and unique aspects of Internet law.

In Chapter 6 we examine and gain a realistic understanding of our legal system, just in case we are involved in a lawsuit. It answers important questions along the way, including:

- Why do we have laws?
- What are the sources of laws?
- To sue or not to sue? – alternative legal remedies, strategies of suing or defending in different courts, and the steps of a typical lawsuit
- How to hire, work with, or fire a lawyer

Each chapter contains a summary of the basic governing rules of business law. These are the legal rights and duties of which the public is usually unaware. Not complying with them creates the potential problems that cause most business disputes. These basic business law rules are explained and then illustrated with hypothetical examples of typical disputes.

Each chapter also highlights the business law time bombs that often trap the unsuspecting parties and sabotage their commercial transactions. They are identified, explained, and then illustrated with hypothetical examples of typical situations and how they might have been avoided by anticipatory planning.

The case study method of learning-analysis-problem solving is used throughout, with numerous examples and actual court cases that help bring these typical business disputes to life. Some of them involve well-known persons or companies, some are infamous disputes, and others are the everyday conflicts that are all too familiar in our daily lives in the commercial marketplace. Similar disputes are being heard and decided everyday in our courts.

The actual reasoning of the presiding judges is often presented, their direct quotations giving a voice to how cases are actually analyzed and decided based upon general rules of governing law and how the unique facts of the dispute fit into them. This gives the business manager a practical look into the legal implications of managerial decisions and assists in developing preventative law skills.

Analysis of the cases also often includes "defuse replays" that allow the legal time bombs that blew up a particular transaction to be illustrated, defused, and replayed. The manager is presented alternate ways the transaction could have been structured by the losing party to avoid the original explosive situation and achieve the desired result. This is Monday morning quarterbacking at its best, learning from the costly mistakes of others and using them in future for a better outcome.

How to Use the Book to Maximum Advantage

Underlying the unique factual patterns of each business dispute is a common underlying cause. One of the parties has made legally binding decisions in creating a contract to buy or sell goods or services without being fully aware of possible adverse legal consequences. In other words, they leaped before they looked.

So the skillful business professional needs to examine the red warning flags of potential legal time bombs, step by step, as the transaction is conceptualized, negotiated, and tentatively structured. The book will assist in the following areas:

- Project analysis for new matters
- Legal audits of pending contracts
- Reviews of past transactions
- Planning of future ventures

The book can also be used in a variety of ways, none of which is mutually exclusive:

1. As a template to manage transactional legal factors
2. As a checklist for the legal implications of executive decisions
3. As a desk reference guidebook for business managers and key employees
4. For individual initiatives, group discussion, and organizational brainstorming
5. To strategize contracts and sales negotiations
6. As a AAA reference guide for:

   • AWARENESS of the existence of potential legal problems
   • AVOIDANCE of them if possible
   • ASSESSMENT of damage and formulation of strategies to lessen adverse impact

7. In recruitment, training, and periodic review of impact personnel
8. Transactional financial analysis of legal gain/loss

Here are some suggestions to optimize your reading experience:

A. First, read the introduction; don't ignore it. It will give you the practical feel of the book and how properly using it can be of significant benefit.
B. Then look at the table of contents and view its areas of discussion in terms of your past, present, or future managerial business law problems.
C. Next read Chapter 1 carefully and digest the basic contract concepts which you probably take for granted when you make agreements, and try to absorb the anticipatory thinking approach that can save your business life.
D. Then read the other numbered chapters in the order of their presentation to get a flavor of the types of business law disputes you may encounter or have already experienced and the best ways to deal with them.
E. You will note sometimes in the chapters after text and illustrative court cases there are questions posed to the reader, as well as sections designated "Discussion Exercises." They are presented for the purpose of "brainstorming" common business problems. They can be very helpful in directing you to the anticipatory "what can go wrong?" thought process that will pay large dividends as you avoid or minimize potential business law problems.

   If they directly bear upon your present circumstances, digest them and use them for active discussion and problem solution. Otherwise, just allow them to be food for thought. We know you are no longer in school, and probably glad of it, but proper business management is an everyday assignment in our "college of practical knowledge."

   So please read on. Knowledge is power. Flex your business manager muscles, and don't delay. Your need for this book is probably just one transaction away. We wish you good fortune in all your business endeavors.

Martin E. Segal
Coral Gables, Florida
June 2014

CHAPTER 1

PROPER CONTRACT MANAGEMENT

A. THE PREVENTATIVE LAW METHOD: THE POWER OF ANTICIPATORY THINKING

"An Ounce of Prevention Is Worth a Pound of Cure"

—The Farmer's Almanac

The anticipatory thinking approach is the foundation of preventative law. It is also the basis of practical problem-solving in business. It enables us to evaluate the plus and minus factors involved in all types of commercial transactions, past, present, or future, and then act skillfully to preserve, protect, and plan.

We also use this approach all the time in our everyday lives. We ask ourselves, "What do I need to succeed?" If we can't accomplish our goal directly, perhaps we can do an end run to reach the finish line.

We are confronted with a potential problem – an apparently impassable situation – and we diagnose it and devise a strategy to solve it.

In fact, anticipating and preventing are two sides of the same coin. Webster's dictionary says:

Anticipate – to forestall
Prevent – to keep from happening

Simply stated, they both mean "look before you leap."

It sounds deceptively simple. But in order to legally anticipate we must know WHAT types of problems create liability time bombs that could sabotage our plans. And then we must know WHERE to locate them. And when we do find them we must know HOW to defuse them.

Everyone involved in a business transaction hopes it will be completed smoothly and profitably. But there always are potential perils and pitfalls that may jeopardize its success.

And a large part of our problem is the fact that we are poor contract shoppers when it comes to the due diligence needed to protect us. We would never buy a car without inspecting it and taking it for a test drive. But most of us enter into binding agreements every day without a clue as to our legal rights and duties.

Using anticipatory thinking to prevent legal problems will often allow us to successfully complete our commercial transactions – sometimes we can move in a straight line toward our goal and at other times we must zig-zag to skillfully dodge its hazards.

There are legal implications in every important business decision. Properly managing the legal factor bears a direct relationship to maximizing revenues by minimizing expenses, thus achieving greater net profits. And the converse is also true. Mismanagement usually occurs because affected parties are unaware or negligent in complying with the legal rules governing their transaction.

The more potential time bombs that can be exposed before the transaction is finalized, the greater chances we have for structuring it in a way that will avoid potential disputes and provide the best opportunity for a positive result.

The extent to which we make use of the Anticipatory Thinking Approach to prevent legal problems is our barometer of business success or failure.

In the initial structuring of any transaction we should routinely ask the following questions, which will highlight where in our path might lie potential business law time bombs:

1. What is my objective? What do I want to accomplish? What is the desired result? How do I propose to structure this transaction? (This is our own initial view of the deal, based upon whatever is our current level of experience and expertise.)
2. What could go wrong? What result do I want to avoid? What are the potential legal time bombs in my path? (This requires us to view the proposed transaction it its worst possible light. We exercise the power of negative thinking to identify our potential business law problems. But this critical step requires knowledge of the many rules that may create these obstacles, so this is where we must use this guidebook to identify the areas where we need to restructure our transaction.)
3. What are my alternative choices in changing the transaction? Will it have to be fully or partially revised? Will I be able to completely avoid the potential time bomb? Can I minimize its impact? What are the risks, rewards, and offsets involved in being able to finalize my business deal?

   Often the creation of needed detours around the business roadblocks that impede us requires quite a bit of give and take. We need to determine which aspects of our transaction are deal breakers, and thus non-negotiable, and which ones can be used as bargaining chips to still allow us to reach our desired destination.
4. What does my new transaction look like? Will my new map of the liability landscape realistically enable me to get from the points of inception to conclusion with minimal or no legal hazards? Does this new concept actually work? We may be able to enter into a similar transaction with a small amount at risk to test it, or use contract conditions to prevent loss.
5. But the best way to verify that our new plan of action is viable in our state is with the assistance of a legal professional. Although you may choose to proceed to complete your transaction without a lawyer, it is not recommended.
6. Can I be insulated from liability even if an unseen business law time bomb explodes? How can my potential business risks be further reduced? The legal form of organization used to conduct business is every bit as important as the nature of the business itself. There are simple ways to do business so

that our personal liability is limited just to the amount we have chosen to invest in the particular enterprise, rather than putting our total assets in jeopardy.

By training ourselves to ask these questions during the planning and negotiating phases of our commercial transactions, before binding business decisions have been made, we can completely avoid many business law time bombs, lessen the impact of many others, and in so doing, greatly increase our chances for success.

Court disputes illustrate to us how a lack of anticipatory planning can be financially disastrous. It is truly amazing how many times companies fall into the trap of failing to think about the legal consequences of their actions before they act. As we look at the next three cases, consider how you could have managed the situations better and avoided their adverse consequences.

In *City of Everett v. Mitchell, 631 P.2d 366 (Wash. 1981)*, an estate hired an auctioneer to sell some of the deceased's items. Included was a used safe that had an inside locked compartment which, for some reason, neither the executor nor the auctioneer opened before the sale. Mitchell bought the safe for $50 and hired a locksmith to open the inside compartment. Finding it contained over $32,000 in cash, the locksmith called the city police, who impounded the contents, pending a court determination of ownership. Mitchell won the case and kept the money.

"The Mitchells were aware of the rule of the auction that all sales were final. Furthermore, the auctioneer made no statement reserving rights to any contents of the safe to the Estate. Under these circumstances, we hold reasonable persons would conclude that the auctioneer manifested an objective intent to sell the safe and its contents and the parties mutually assented to enter into that sale of the safe and the contents of the locked compartment."

In *Dempsey v. Norwegian Cruise Line, 972 F.2d 998 (9th Cir. 1992)*, the plaintiff's passenger ticket reduced the standard three-year limitation period for filing personal injury lawsuits to one year, as allowed under the Federal Maritime Act. The ticket stated in bold letters, "Passengers are advised to read the terms and conditions of the Passenger Ticket Contract set forth below."

The plaintiff sued for an alleged injury on that cruise more than one year later, but within three years of the voyage. Summary judgment was entered for the defendant based upon the failure to sue within the one-year limitation period, and the appellate court affirmed.

"Congress has provided that vessels may contract for a one-year limitations period . . . Passengers like Dempsey who purchase tickets containing this limitation 'benefit in the form of reduced fares reflecting the savings that the cruise line enjoys.' Moreover, when a passenger is involved in an accident, it is reasonable to expect the passenger to consult his or her ticket or an attorney to determine his or her rights. The passenger can fully protect his or her rights by filing suit within one year of the injury."

In *Scott-Pontzer v. Liberty Mutual Insurance Co., 710 N.E.2d 1116 (Ohio 1999)*, the plaintiff's husband, Pontzer, was killed when a drunk driver collided with his vehicle. That driver's insurance only had minimum limits of liability. Prior to the accident, Pontzer was employed by Superior Dairy, which had a policy of commercial auto liability insurance written by the defendant containing a provision for underinsured motorist coverage as well as umbrella/excess liability coverage.

The plaintiff sued on behalf of her husband's estate, claiming coverage under the defendant's policy. It moved for summary judgment, claiming that under the policy, Pontzer was not a named insured because the policy was issued to a corporation, not an individual, and he was not operating a "covered" vehicle because the accident occurred when he was off duty. The trial court granted the defendant's motion.

The appellate court determined that "the policies in question were 'ambiguous as to the insureds' under the underinsured motorist coverages," and that Pontzer, "as an employee of Superior Dairy, was an insured under the policies issued by (the defendant)." But the court then affirmed because the insurance coverage "is available only to those employees injured while acting within the scope of their employment," and this excluded Pontzer.

The Ohio Supreme Court reversed the appellate court, and ruled for the plaintiff. It first agreed that Pontzer was "an insured for purposes of underinsured motorist coverage" due to the ambiguous wording of the policy. "Courts universally hold that policies of insurance, which are in language selected by the insurer and which are reasonably open to different interpretations, will be construed most favorably to the insured."

It then disagreed with the appellate court and ruled for the plaintiff, due to discrepant wording in the defendant's umbrella/excess and underinsured motorist policies:

"The Liberty Fire policy contains no language requiring that employees must be acting within the scope of their employment in order to receive underinsured motorist coverage. Thus, we find that appellant is entitled to underinsured motorist benefits under the Liberty Fire policy."

There were two dissenting opinions that suggested the decision was incorrect and that the specific language requirement of the majority was unnecessary.

"Despite the named insured ('you') being superior Dairy, the majority finds coverage for an off-duty employee driving his wife's car by saying that because UIM coverage protects persons and not vehicles, and because corporations cannot drive cars or sustain injuries, UIM coverage cannot protect a corporate entity. But, of course, a corporate entity has insurable interests for which countless policies are issued every day."

"This concept of Superior Dairy having corporate insurable interests defeats the majority's reasoning for extending coverage to the off-duty employee as an 'insured.' Though business entities like Superior Dairy operate through their employees, this employee was not acting for Superior Dairy at the time of the accident. So, there is no basis for saying he qualifies as an insured by virtue of his Superior Dairy employment."

The fallout from the majority opinion in Ohio has been tremendous. Most insurance policies did not have specific exclusionary language that limited recovery in these UIM claims only to that plaintiff's injured, "within the scope of their employment." Therefore, the case created a liability loophole through which many claimants have successfully sued for underinsured or uninsured motorist coverages.

A liability fund of almost $1 billion was set up by Ohio insurers to pay these so-called *Scott-Pontzer* claims, and they are still being decided in favor of plaintiffs. Now, in Ohio and other states that have witnessed the Ohio experience, liability policies are closely monitored to make sure they extend coverage, "only to officers, owners, or employees acting in the course and scope of employment."

Discussion Exercises

1. Discuss at least three examples of situations in your personal life where you used anticipatory thinking to provide a positive alternative to a problem that appeared to have no workable solution. Then discuss some examples of your failure to do so.

2. Discuss at least three examples of potential business problems you were able to identify in advance and avoid, solve, or re-structure for a successful outcome. Then discuss some examples of your failure to do so.

3. Discuss some of the advantages of using the preventative law approach in planning and evaluating commercial transactions.

4. Discuss some of the disadvantages of the preventative law approach.

5. Discuss and rank the top five obstacles to successful implementing of anticipatory thinking in your personal life.

6. Discuss and rank the top five obstacles to successfully implementing anticipatory thinking in your business.

Case Exercise 1

Failure to Renew a License almost Costs $34,000

The case of *Wilson v. Kealakekua Ranch, Ltd., 551 P.2d 525 (Hawaii 1976)* is a graphic example of a lack of anticipatory thinking that was almost disastrous.

Wilson was an architect who performed agreed architectural services totaling almost $34,000 for the defendant, and then sued for breach of contract when his bill was unpaid.

He had originally been licensed as required under Hawaii law, but neglected to pay his $15 annual renewal fee, causing his certificate of registration to expire until reinstated. He also failed to pay the $30 reinstatement fee. The services in question in this case were rendered during this period of license expiration.

Analysis

The trial court ruled that Wilson had violated a regulatory law and his contract was void. It cited the law that stated, "any person who practices architecture without having first registered in accordance with this chapter and without having a valid unexpired certificate of registration shall be fined not more than $500 . . ."

Fortunately for him, the appellate court reversed, holding that since he was originally licensed, the failure to renew only violated a revenue-raising law and did not invalidate his contract. It noted that "while the provisions of the statute requiring initial registration are clearly designed to protect the public from unfit and incompetent practitioners of architecture, we think that the provision requiring renewal, with which Wilson failed to comply, is purely for the purpose of raising revenues."

"Additional punishment (beyond the $500 fine), especially a disproportionate forfeiture (of up to $34,000) is not justified and could not have been intended by the legislature."

Defuse Replay

If the Hawaii law had stated, "and failure to comply with these provisions shall be deemed a violation of a regulatory law and invalidate any contracts made during a period of license suspension or expiration," Wilson would have lost his $34,000. A very expensive lesson, indeed.

Wilson could have insulated himself from this type of problem by including in his agreement to perform architectural services a provision that stated, "sums due hereunder for the rendition of valuable services rendered shall not be deducted or denied due to any inadvertent or negligent failure of Architect to comply with local license renewal laws."

Conclusion

Wilson almost blew himself up financially due to his failure to comply with the licensing law. Since all states always notify a licensee when renewal is due, he could easily have avoided the problem by prompt compliance. He could also have avoided it by prompt reinstatement. He did nothing, and was very fortunate.

A. Do you agree with the court's final decision? If not, why not?

B. Is the $500 fine for late renewal sufficient to teach Wilson a lesson?

Case Exercise 2

One Word in a Contract Offer Loses a Case

In *Osprey L.L.C. v. Kelly-Moore Paint Co., 984 P.2d 194 (Okla. 1999)*, the defendant, Kelly, entered into a fifteen-year commercial lease with the plaintiff. It had a six-month renewal clause that stated:

"NOTICES. All notices required to be given hereunder by Lessee or Lessor *shall* be given in writing and *may* be delivered either personally or by depositing the same in United States mail, first class postage prepaid, registered or certified mail, return receipt requested."

On the last day, Kelly faxed its renewal notice during the day and also sent a copy of that notice by Federal Express, which arrived the following day.

The plaintiff rejected the fax notice, claiming it was late because it didn't comply with the terms of the lease, and sued to remove Kelly from the premises. Kelly claimed its fax renewal was effective.

The case was the first time an Oklahoma court had been called upon to decide whether a faxed delivery of a written notice to renew a commercial lease is the same as "personal delivery."

Analysis

The trial court ruled in favor of Kelly, and the Court of Appeals reversed, determining that "the plain language of the lease required it be renewed by delivering notice either personally or by mail, and that Kelly-Moore had done neither."

The Oklahoma Supreme Court vacated the decision of its appellate court and affirmed the trial court, stating, "because the lease provision concerned uses the permissive "may" rather than the mandatory "shall" and refers to personal delivery or registered or certified mail, but does not require these methods of delivery, to the exclusion of other modes of transmission which serve the same purpose . . . a substituted method of notice which performs the same function and serves the same purpose as an authorized method of notice is not defective."

Defuse Replay

The landlord who offers lease renewal is "master of his offer" and can word it in any fashion to limit acceptance to its specific terms and to the time, method, or manner of acceptance.

Landlords also customarily draft the lease agreements they offer to prospective tenants, especially in commercial leases. Here, Osprey chose to use the word "may" when referring to the method of renewal notice, rather than the word "shall," and suffered the adverse legal consequences.

If Osprey had done a better job of anticipatory thinking when they drafted their lease form, they would have prevented the legal problem they encountered.

Conclusion

There is a trend that is emerging in various court decisions in cases such as this that is related to the numerous electronic and technological methods of legal communication that now exist.

Formerly, almost all decisions required strict adherence to the contract terms that specifically refer to a method of delivering notice of lease renewals or exercise of option contracts.

Now, a shift has occurred whereby a majority of courts have moved from the "strict compliance rule" to a more liberal "alternative method rule". It allows a substituted method if it is furnished in the same time frame. The practical philosophy here is "no damage, no foul."

A. Do you agree with the court's final decision? If not, why not?

B. Did the punishment suffered by Osprey fit his offense?

Here are two cases involving banks that may well be the most costly, yet easily preventable, examples of how the lack of an anticipatory thinking approach to preventative law can lead to financially disastrous results.

Case Exercise 3

Failure to "Affix" An Endorsement to a Promissory Note Costs the Buyer Bank $19 Million

In *Adams, et al v. Madison Realty & Development, Inc., et al, 853 F.2d 163 (3rd Cir. 1988)*, Empire, a federal savings bank in Deland, Florida, purchased thirty-five promissory notes for $19.5 million in the secondary market from Consolidated Mortgage Co. and Putnam Funding Co. as part of a bulk investment of negotiable instruments.

These notes were the debt instruments of separate investors in real estate partnerships that had been offered for sale to the public by Madison Partnerships. Approximately eighteen months later, a massive fraud by Madison was discovered and the investors sued to have their notes legally canceled.

Empire was the holder and owner by endorsement of these notes, whereby the endorsements on separate sheets of paper had not been stapled or otherwise attached to the notes ("affixed") as required by law, but rather had just been loosely inserted within each note. They claimed that since they had not participated in the fraud, they were still protected by the Negotiable Instrument Laws that insulate a holder in due course from any transactional problems of the party from whom they purchased the notes.

Analysis

The trial court ruled in favor of Empire. It acknowledged that the separate, unattached sheets of paper carrying the endorsements did not comply with the Uniform Commercial Code, which reads, "An indorsement must be written by or on behalf of the holder and on the instrument or on a paper so firmly affixed thereto as to become a part thereof."

But the trial court still ruled for the indorsee, saying that even if the indorsee had been exposed to some risks, "that is no reason to absolve the notemakers, who are in no way injured by the use of an unattached indorsement, of their obligations." The failure to properly attach the indorsements was excused as being "hypertechnical."

The appellate court reversed, vacating the lower court judgment. While admitting the affixation requirement was technical, the court also agreed with the argument that "the privileged status of holder in due course is also a technical creation bestowed only after strict compliance with the statutory prerequisites."

The appellate court was not sympathetic to the bank's self-imposed predicament, and took a position of insisting upon strict adherence to the governing law of the UCC:

"Financial institutions, noted for insisting on their customers' compliance with numerous ritualistic formalities, are not sympathetic petitioners in urging relaxation of an elementary business practice."

Defuse Replay

How could Empire have avoided this very costly problem?

The critical wording of the UCC provision required the endorsements to be "firmly affixed" to the promissory notes. "A purported indorsement on a mortgage or other separate paper pinned or clipped to an instrument is not sufficient for negotiation . . . the loose indorsement sheets accompanying Empire's notes would have been valid allonges had they been stapled or glued to the notes themselves."

By being "loosely inserted" with each note, the separate indorsements resulted in Empire not being a legal "holder" and therefore not entitled to the protective legal provisions of the UCC that allow a holder-assignee to take free of any transactional defenses that may be legally enforceable against their seller-assignor.

Conclusion

The law of negotiable instruments is highly technical in its requirements, because it affords special protection to the parties who purchase and seek to enforce their notes, drafts, and other types of commercial paper.

At first analysis, this clerical error of not physically attaching the indorsements to their corresponding promissory notes seems harmless. There was no question that Empire had bought them and was in possession of all the original documents.

But the technical nature of the law itself is exactly why Empire was duty bound to be meticulous in strict compliance. Compare the cost of thirty-five missing staples with the amount Empire had at risk. A $19 million mistake!

A. Do you agree with the court's final decision? If not, why not?

B. How could Empire avoid such problems in the future?

Case Exercise 4

Failure to Return Bad Checks on Time Costs Bank $25 Million

In *ChicagoTitle Insurance Company v. California Canadian Bank, 1 Cal. App. 4th 798 (Cal. App. 1991)*, a mortgage broker and its client used a title company to act as escrow agent in closing various real estate transactions.

They wrote checks totaling $17M payable to the title company, drawn on their account at the California Bank's San Mateo, California, branch. The title company deposited these checks for collection at its account at Bank of San Francisco, who sent the checks for payment to California Bank. The next day, California Bank sent the checks to its San Mateo, California, branch for payment, where they were dishonored due to insufficient funds.

Unfortunately, the mortgage broker and its client were engaged in a massive check fraud operation, where they had diverted the $17M to their own use before their fraud was discovered, with the title company paying funds out of its escrow account that were supposedly backed by these "good" checks.

The title company sued the bank, claiming it violated the usual banking procedures and statutory laws that established a "midnight deadline" rule to the effect that a bank that receives for collection a check of its account holder presented for payment at another bank must return dishonored items no later than midnight of the next business day, or be "accountable" for any losses.

The obvious purpose of the "midnight deadline" rule is to provide prompt notice of dishonor to check payees so they can protect themselves. The title company claimed it suffered the loss because of the bank's delay in returning the bad checks to their Bank of San Francisco.

Analysis

The trial court determined that the "midnight deadline" rule requires "a bank which performs bookkeeping at a computer center to *return* checks to the Clearing House by midnight of the day following receipt . . .," and entered judgment against California Bank for $25 million, which included accrued interest.

It also noted the bank's own internal policy and trade practice "to return checks by delivering them to a clearinghouse or the bank on which drawn prior to the 'midnight deadline.'"

The bank argued unsuccessfully that "it could somehow suspend the running of the midnight deadline by sending the checks to its own computer center, thereby getting them out of the bank branch proper before the deadline expired."

On appeal, the trial court's decision was affirmed. "Since the bank did not return the checks in question before the applicable midnight deadline, it is 'accountable' or strictly liable for the amount of the checks under (the California law)."

Defuse Replay

The "midnight deadline" rule is one of the basic principles of banking law. It requires banks that receive collection items to approve or dishonor them within the required one-business-day time limit, or suffer the financial consequences.

That rule is absolute, no matter how complex the internal routing structure of the bank in question is.

The testimony at the trial showed the internal practices of the bank were extremely sloppy. It admitted its returns of in-county checks were routinely late, "and that its own policy and procedure manual made no distinction between in-county and out-of-county checks." That manual stated:

"An office, regardless of its location . . . must return (dishonored checks) the same day."

Conclusion

The effect of this case was far-reaching on the California Bank in particular, and other banks across the country in general.

When the trial court decision was rendered, the bank realized this problem could repeat itself unless they drastically improved their internal procedures. They did this while their appeal was pending.

It was too late to save then from this loss, but there would be no repeats in the future. It was like locking the barn door after all the cattle had escaped.

When the appellate decision was widely reported, the entire banking industry took note. It reviewed, evaluated, and restructured its compliance procedures where necessary. The dramatic financial loss of California Bank served as an industry wake-up call.

A. Do you agree with the court's final decision? If not, why not?

B. Is the "midnight deadline" rule too strict?

C. How could California Bank avoid such problems in the future?

Probably the most well-known example of the adverse results from a failure to use the preventative law approach to risk management is the infamous McDonald's "hot coffee" case. *Liebeck v. McDonald's, CV-93-02419 (N.M.Dist. 1994).*

When it was originally reported in the standard fifteen-second media news flash format as "Woman spills hot coffee on herself and wins $2.9 million," the public was outraged by another seemingly bogus lawsuit and excessive damage award.

But here is what really happened as reported in the September 1, 1994, Wall Street Journal.

For years, McDonald's brewed their coffee at a super-hot 180 degrees, a temperature that could cause serious burns on exposed skin, and advertised it as "the hottest coffee around." Their training manuals said that temperature was necessary to fully extract the flavor and release coffee aromas. But none of its local competitors heated at more than 160 degrees for safety reasons. In the decade preceding this case, McDonald's had received more than 700 reports of coffee burns ranging from mild to severe, and had settled claims arising from scalding injuries out of court for more than $500,000.

Stella Liebeck was an 81-year-old woman who bought a forty-nine-cent cup of coffee at the drive-through window of an Albuquerque, New Mexico, McDonald's, and while removing the lid to add cream and sugar she spilled it on her lap, causing third-degree burns of the groin, inner thighs, and buttocks. She was hospitalized for seven days and had to receive painful skin grafts to repair the burns.

Mrs. Liebeck at first merely sought reimbursement from McDonald's for her considerable medical expenses, but when they refused she hired an attorney to sue them, claiming the coffee was "dangerously defective" because it was unreasonably hot. That attorney had also successfully sued McDonald's in a hot coffee case a few years earlier. As the trial date approached the attorney made a formal settlement offer of $30,000 and was prepared to settle for half that amount, but McDonald's again refused, denying any liability. Only days before the trial both sides were ordered to attend a mediation session and the mediator, a retired judge, recommended that McDonald's settle for $225,000, saying that a jury would likely award that amount. And once again McDonald's refused.

The trial lasted seven days. A doctor testifying for Mrs. Liebeck stated that lowering the serving temperature of the coffee twenty degrees would make a big difference in spills, because it would take about twenty seconds at 160 degrees to produce a third-degree burn, while at 180 degrees it would only take twelve to fifteen seconds.

The most damaging testimony to McDonald's was from their own witnesses:

(1) Their quality assurance manager testified that McDonald's knew its coffee sometimes caused serious burns but hadn't bothered to consult burn experts about it, had no plans to reduce the temperature of their coffee, and had decided not to warn their customers about the possibility of severe burns.

(2) Their human-factors engineer testified that hot coffee burns were statistically insignificant when compared to the billion cups of coffee McDonald's sells annually.

Jurors polled after the case said it appeared McDonald's had a "callous disregard for the safety of the people."

The jury awarded compensatory damages of $160,000 to reimburse the plaintiff for her medical and related expenses, and then found the conduct of McDonald's to be sufficiently willful, malicious, and reckless for them to award punitive damages of $2.7 million. The case was then settled, and no appeal took place.

An interesting postscript: One day after the verdict, a local reporter tested the coffee at the McDonald's that had served Mrs. Liebeck and found it to be a comparatively cool 158 degrees.

Discussion Exercises

A. What managerial strategies would you have used in the original policy decisions to superheat McDonald's coffee?

B. What managerial strategies would you have used when coffee spill burn claims began to be made to the company?

C. How would you have managed the Liebeck claim?

The anticipatory thinking approach to legal risk management is the future of modern business. And, in the words of the former great football coach George Allen, "The future is now."

B.   THE FUNCTION OF CONTRACTS

"All sensible people are selfish, and nature is tugging
at every contract to make the terms of it fair."

—Ralph Waldo Emerson

"To me, party platforms are contracts with the people."

—Harry S. Truman

Law Overview

The commercial transaction is the vehicle of business.

The engine that powers that vehicle in the business marketplace is the contract.

Contracts are created by the legally enforceable *agreements* of the parties to buy, sell, or trade goods and services.

The legal existence of any agreement depends upon whether or not the offeror has made a valid offer and the offeree has validly accepted it.

This formula is stated as: OFFER + ACCEPTANCE = AGREEMENT $(O + A = AG)$. Its significance to the world of business is similar to the importance of Einstein's $E = MC^2$ to the world of physics.

The legal definition of a contract is "an agreement between two or more parties that is legally enforceable in the event of a breach." Thus, the agreement forms the essential foundation of all contracts. (Enforceability depends upon Consideration, Capacity, Legality, and Written Form issues examined in later chapters.)

Notice the interconnectedness of the $O + A$ elements of the agreement.

If there is no valid offer, there is nothing to accept and there can be no agreement. If there is a valid offer but an invalid acceptance, there still is no agreement. In either situation, if there is no agreement, there can be no contract.

Even if there is a valid agreement, meaning that we have both legal offer and legal acceptance, that agreement must still be legally enforceable if one of the parties fails to properly perform.

Al calls Sylvia and says, "I offer to pick you up at eight for a date; I won't be late." Sylvia accepts, saying, "I can hardly wait." When Al fails to show up, he has breached their agreement. Sylvia is probably upset, but she has no legal recourse because social arrangements of this type have no legal remedy for the breach.

Many of our daily agreements fall in this category. A party may fail to do what they promised, or do something that they weren't supposed to do. In either case, it usually never occurs to us to question whether or not these broken agreements have legal consequences.

But if we can change the facts of the example just a bit, we reach an entirely different result as to the enforceability of the agreement.

Al calls Sylvia and says, "I offer to pick you up at eight *so you won't be late for your job interview.*" Sylvia accepts, saying, "I can hardly wait, *I'm relying on you.*" When Al fails to show up, *Sylvia loses the job to someone else not as qualified as she is.* Al's breach of their agreement is actionable under a contract fairness doctrine we'll talk about later called "promissory estoppel."

The key point in time for most agreements is when the parties progress beyond their preliminary negotiations and reach a mutual understanding that involves the exchange of their promises of performance.

"It is hornbook law that the existence of an enforceable contract is dependent upon agreement of the parties, or *meeting of the minds*, upon the terms of that contract." *Smith v. Hammons, 2002 WL 5694 (Mo.Ct.App. 2002).*

There are two basic sources of contract law:

- Common law – these are the legal rules or *precedents* that have been developed by the judiciary from federal, state, and local court decisions in contract disputes.
- Statutes – these are legislative enactments on the state and federal levels that relate to contract disputes.
- Uniform Commercial Code (UCC) – this is a body of specialized statutory law that applies to *sales of goods.* It attempts to assist the successful completion of commercial transactions and codifies the different contract laws of the various states in one *uniform* source, so there is uniformity and predictability of the probable outcome of such disputes, no matter where they occur. Every state has adopted it in whole or part.

It often provides a more flexible interpretation in promoting enforcement of contractual agreements than the common law rules, which tend to be more rigid and technical.

In many cases, the ultimate court decision will depend upon whether or not it is applicable. The UCC does not apply to:

1. sale of services
2. sale of real estate
3. sale of intangibles, such as stocks and bonds
4. gifts of goods

Most contract disputes are hybrid, mixing both goods and services. So how do the courts determine whether or not the UCC is applicable?

In *Pass v. Shelby Aviation, Inc., 2000 WL 388775 (Tenn.Ct.App.2000)*, the plaintiffs died in a crash of their private plane, and their estate sued the defendant, which had performed the annual inspection on the airplane, on a theory of breach of warranty. (Warranty recovery is a UCC concept where sellers of goods are legally responsible for defects.) The trial court denied the defendant's motion to dismiss, holding the matter to be a UCC warranty transaction. The appellate court reversed, holding the transaction to be predominantly the provision of a service, not the sale of goods.

"Most jurisdictions follow one of two different approaches to address the problem (of mixed transactions) . . . the first approach, sometimes called the 'gravamen test,' looks to that portion of the transaction upon which the complaint is based, to determine if it involved goods or services. The other approach, known as the 'predominant factor' or 'predominant purpose test,' looks at the transaction as a whole to determine whether its predominant purpose was the sale of goods or the provision of a service."

In adopting the "predominant purpose test" as the law of Tennessee, the court noted it used a weighing test and explained what factors it looks at to make its rulings:

"We examine the language of the parties' contract, the nature of the business of the supplier of the goods and services, the reason the parties entered into the contract (i.e. what each bargained to receive), and the respective amounts charged under the contract for goods and services."

This last factor of cost allocation is the easiest way for parties to identify their transaction as either a sale of goods or services.

Sonia goes to her dentist for a check up. He tells her she needs a gold inlay, and the cost will be $1,000. This is a typical mixed transaction. The inlay itself is goods, and its installation by her dentist is services. If this transaction is a sale of goods, Sonia has warranty protection. If it is services, warranty law does not apply. Normally, this type of professional services would not carry any warranties. However, if Sonia had the dentist allocate a majority of the price on her bill to the inlay ($550 for the gold and $450 for installation), she could create a "sale of goods" and have warranty protection just in case a problem arose.

Let's understand some general terminology of contracts:

- The Offeror makes the initial promise to do or not do something.
- The Offeree receives the offer, and can create an agreement by *acceptance*.
- The Offeree can also *reject* the offer, causing it to terminate.
- The Offeree can also make a *counteroffer*, reversing their roles.
- The Offeror can *revoke* the offer at any time before acceptance.
- An inquiry or question has no legal effect on contract negotiations.

Sam wants to sell his car for $5,000. He tells Herb the basic details. Herb asks if the car has a CD player and an alarm system. When Sam confirms, Herb proposes a price of $4,000. Sam refuses to sell for less than $4,500. While Herb is deciding whether or not to raise his price, Sam agrees to sell the car to Sally for $4,750. Then Herb agrees to pay the $4,000 and Sam tells him he's too late. Herb is mad and wants to sue for breach of contract. He asks your advice.

This is a typical scenario. All contracts start with preliminary negotiations between the parties. At some point they may ripen into a legal agreement (O + A), which, if legally enforceable, may be called a contract.

Let's identify what has happened. Sam and Herb were negotiating. Sam made the initial offer of $5,000. Herb's clarifying question has no legal effect. Herb's proposal of $4,000 is a counteroffer, which rejects the original offer and makes Herb the new offeror. Sam's agreement to sell the car to Sally is a revocation of his $4,500 offer to sell it to Herb. Herb has no legal rights.

There are two basic forms of contracts, depending upon what the offeree does in exchange for the offeror's promise:

- *Bilateral* form is the most common type of contract. It is best described as "a promise for a promise." The contract is formed when the promises are exchanged.

   Cynthia offers to sell her car to Rita for $5,000 cash. Rita accepts the offer. There is a bilateral contract formed when Rita agrees. The later actions of Cynthia delivering the car in exchange for Rita's payment of money are only relevant if either party fails to perform.

   In the case of *D.L. Peoples Group, Inc. v. Hawley, 2002 WL 63351 (Fla.App. 2002),* Hawley was hired by a Florida college to recruit students in Missouri. He had never visited Florida, but was offered the job on a recommendation. He signed the employment contract in Missouri, and then mailed it to Florida, where it was signed by the college president. While attempting to recruit a student in Missouri, Hawley was shot and killed. His heirs claimed he was entitled to receive Florida worker's compensation, but the trial judge denied the claim. It was reversed on appeal, the court ruling a bilateral contract existed, and that "a contract is created where the last act necessary to make a binding agreement takes place."

- *Unilateral* form occurs in those situations where the acceptance requires the offeree to complete the performance of an act, rather than just promise to perform. It is called "a promise for an act," and sometimes involves special rules when the parties have a dispute.

   Harold hires ABC, Inc. to paint his house. He says, "I offer to pay you $2,000 when you finish the job." This is unilateral form, where the acceptance is an action rather than a mere promise. The wording is critical. If ABC, Inc. had accepted Harold's ". . . promise to pay you $2,000 to paint my house," we would have a bilateral contract.

- Unless the language of the contract is clearly unilateral, it is presumed to be in bilateral form.

There are also certain classifications of contracts:

- Executed contract – fully completed by both offeror and offeree
- Executory contract – some required performance remains to be completed

   Sara and Ernest make a bilateral contract for Sara to buy Ernest's computer system for a fixed price, closing in one week. When Sara pays the agreed price and Ernest delivers the merchandise, the contract is executed. After the exchange of promises that creates the contract but before the time to close, it is still executory.

- Valid contract – legally enforceable by one or both of the parties
- Voidable contract – although it may be valid, one of the parties may have the legal right to elect to cancel it
- Void contract - has no legal effect and is not enforceable, such as a contract to commit a crime (discussed in a later chapter)

Contracts fall into three main types:

- EXPRESS contracts occur when all the essential facts are spelled out, either verbally or in writing. These details usually include a description of the subject matter, the price, payment time, terms such as cash or credit, the quantity and details of delivery if involving goods, and any other important terms.

> George goes to the local computer store. He sees a sign that states, "Zip diskettes on sale today." George asks the clerk, "Do you have any Zip 100 disks?" The clerk replies, "Yes sir, we have one six-pack left. You have to buy the whole pack and the price is $55. George says, "Sold," hands the cashier his credit card, and when the sale is completed the clerk puts the merchandise in a bag and tells George, "Bye now, have a nice day."

- IMPLIED contracts occur when some of the essential details of the transaction are not expressed, and must be inferred from the conduct of the parties, their past dealings, or the customs of the trade. These are known as "implied-in-fact" contracts. Written and spoken words have provided the essential terms.

> Harry wakes up with laryngitis, and slips in the shower, injuring his writing hand. He needs some 100 zip diskettes, so he drives to the local computer store. He walks in, locates the product, picks up a six-pack, goes to the cashier check-out and puts the diskettes down with a $100 bill. The cashier neither speaks nor writes anything as Harry's disks are put into a bag, he is handed his change, and as Harry leaves and the cashier waves goodbye. The essential terms are implied solely from the conduct of the parties – subject matter, quantity, price, terms, and delivery.
>
> In *Schism v. U.S., 2002 WL 109422 (3d Cir. 2001)*, the plaintiffs were retired veterans over 65 who each had more than twenty years of active military service. Their military recruiters had promised them free lifetime medical care benefits, which were later changed by Congress, moving them into Medicare, which is not free. They sued for breach of implied contract. The trial court rejected their claims, but the appellate court reversed, stating,
>
> "An implied-in-fact contract is one founded upon a meeting of minds which, although not embodied in an express contract, is inferred, as a fact, from the conduct of the parties showing, in the light of the circumstances, their tacit understanding."

- QUASI CONTRACTS are called "implied-in-law" because, unlike express or implied contract situations, the parties have no intended dealings with each other.

Normally this would prevent any contractual relationship, but in the interest of fairness to prevent one party from being unjustly enriched at the expense of the other, the law pretends they made a contract and requires payment of the fair value of the goods or services involved. These types of contracts are legal fictions that often arise when one party mistakenly confers a gratuitous benefit on another. The legal cause of action is called *quantum meruit*.

Mr. and Mrs. Jones have a nice home in a suburban housing development where the houses resemble each other. Their front driveway needs re-paving and they call Miami Asphalting Co. for an estimate. Its president, Ernest, offers to do the job for a fair price of $1,000, completion next Thursday, and they accept. On that date, Ernest forgets their address and starts to re-pave their neighbor Jerry's driveway by mistake. The houses look similar, and both driveways were in poor condition. In fact, Jerry was meaning to do re-paving but never got around to it. Jerry is inside the house when Ernest begins, watches him fully complete the job, and then admires his new driveway after Ernest leaves. Ernest sends his bill to Mr. and Mrs. Jones, they object, Ernest realizes his mistake, and sends his bill to Jerry. Jerry refuses to pay, claiming no contract exists. Ernest sues Jerry, claiming breach of quasi-contract. Who wins and why? Let's analyze this case.

There certainly was no express or implied contractual relationship between Jerry and Miami Asphalting Co. The key to this dispute is whether or not Jerry was "unjustly enriched." If he was, he is required by law to pay for the work done, even though he never ordered it. Unjust enrichment is another way of saying *unfair benefit*. Certainly Jerry received a benefit from Ernest's mistake. He now has a newly paved driveway. But that is only half the legal test – was it unfair, meaning could he reasonably have prevented the mistake from happening? In this case, the answer is yes. He should have stopped the work as soon as he realized it had started, rather than unfairly taking advantage of it.

If we change the facts of the case just a bit, however, we also reach a different result. What if Jerry wasn't home when Ernest re-paved his driveway?

Let's say he was at work in his downtown office, and arrived home to find a brand-new driveway. He probably smiled, looked up in the sky, and said, "Thank you. This is my lucky day." And it would be just that, because he could not have reasonably prevented the mistake, and therefore was not *unfairly* benefited. He has received a free benefit. This makes sense, because the problem was solely caused by the mistake, not enhanced by any conduct of Jerry.

There is a legal maxim that applies to these mistaken benefit cases. "Where one of two parties must bear a loss, it shall be the party who caused it, or who could have reasonably prevented it."

Quasi contract has also been described as the "garbage can" for losing claims because plaintiffs often raise it as a catch-all category of a fairness principle to try to justify their recovery. Courts apply this doctrine carefully, however, for that very reason, and try to limit its application only to proper cases.

In *Castillo v. Tyson, 701 N.Y.S.2d 423 (N.Y. App.Div. 2000)*, pay-per-viewers of the heavyweight championship boxing match between Mike Tyson and Evander Holyfield sued the fight promoters and telecasters for a refund of their money because Tyson was disqualified for biting off part of Holyfield's ear. They claimed various breach of contract theories, including unjust enrichment. The trial court dismissed the suit and the appellate court affirmed.

"Plaintiffs are not in contractual privity with any of the defendants, and their claims that they are third-party beneficiaries of one or more of the contracts that defendants entered into among themselves was aptly rejected by (the lower court) as contrived. Nothing in these contracts can be understood as promising a fight that did not end in a disqualification. The rules of the governing commission provide for disqualification, and it is a possibility that a fight fan can reasonably expect. The plaintiffs paid for what they got: 'the right to view whatever event transpired.' "

In *DCB Construction Company, Inc. v. Central City Development Co., 940 P.2d 958 (Colo.App. 1997)*, the plaintiff was a contractor that was hired by a lessee to do $300,000 worth of alteration to the building the lessee was leasing from the defendant. The defendant notified the plaintiff that it had no legal responsibility for the work. The lessee stopped paying rent, and was evicted by the defendant before it had paid the plaintiff. The plaintiff sued the defendant, claiming unjust enrichment for the work done to the defendant's building. The trial court awarded $280,000, but the appellate court reversed, saying, "The mere fact that a benefit has been bestowed on Development Co., and that it appreciated the benefit, is not enough to give rise to a claim for unjust enrichment."

To recover, the plaintiff must show that: 1) a benefit was conferred upon the defendant; 2) the defendant appreciated the benefit; and 3) the benefit was accepted by the defendant under such circumstances that it would be inequitable for it to be retained without payment of its value."

Examples of proper cases are:

- The plaintiff made valuable improvements to the defendant's bar and then was prohibited to operate it because she could not legally hold a liquor license. She had the right to recover the value of non-removable items. *Duncan v. Kasim, 2002 WL 125686 (Fla. App. 2002)*
- The plaintiff paid the defendant's real estate taxes due to an error by the tax assessor's office, and then sued to recover the amount of the over assessment on the theory of unjust enrichment. The trial court entered summary judgment for the plaintiff. *Partipilo v. Hallman, 510 N.E.2d 8 (Ill. App. 1987)*
- Wife and husband mutually agreed she would pay for his three years of law school and, when he finished, he would pay for her master's degree. She fulfilled her part of the agreement, but he then initiated divorce proceedings. She claimed entitlement to restitution in quantum meruit to prevent his unjust enrichment because of receiving his education at her expense. The

court awarded her reimbursement for the husband's living and educational expenses she had paid. *Pyeatte v. Pyeatte, 661 P.2d 196 (Az. App. 1982)*

A fourth type of contract category is PROMISSORY ESTOPPEL, which is another fairness doctrine that sometimes binds the parties when the three main types of contracts are not applicable. It applies in circumstances where:

1. the promisor makes a contract promise under circumstances where he knows, or reasonably should know, the promisee will rely upon it, and
2. the promisee does, in fact, reasonably rely upon the promisor's promise, by changing his position, and
3. the promisee suffers financial loss of some kind due to this detrimental reliance.

If all these elements are present, the promisor is *estopped* to deny the legal efficacy of his *promise.*

Like quasi contract, there is no real contractual relationship in promissory estoppel. Rather, the alleged unfairness is urged as the reason to create the fictional contractual transaction. Under these circumstances, although plaintiffs often try to raise it, courts allow its application sparingly.

This doctrine is used in appropriate cases throughout the law of contracts in any disputes where one party relies upon promises made by another. In *Charter Township of Ypsilanti v. General Motors Corporation, 506 N.W.2d 556 (Mich. App. 1993)*, the plaintiff awarded the defendant substantial property tax abatements at its local plant to attract their location and the creation and maintenance of the local employment they created. Four years after the last tax exemption award, the defendant decided to consolidate its operations because of economic necessity, and moved the operations to Texas. The plaintiff sued for breach of contract and promissory estoppel. While the trial court found the tax abatement did not create a contract between the parties, it did find the defendant was bound by promissory estoppel:

"There would be a gross inequity and patent unfairness if General Motors, having lulled the people of the Ypsilanti area into giving up millions of tax dollars which they so desperately need to educate their children and provide basic governmental services, is allowed to simply decide it will desert 4,500 workers and their families because it thinks it can make these cars cheaper somewhere else."

But the appellate court reversed, holding that "promissory estoppel requires an actual, clear, and definite promise," and that "the mere fact that a corporation solicits a tax abatement and persuades a municipality with assurances of jobs cannot be evidence of a promise."

Another key to this case, which at first glance seems to support promissory estoppel, is the failure of the plaintiff to "reasonably" rely upon the alleged promise not to relocate if tax exemptions were granted. There were no guarantees made by the defendant, but they could easily have been required by the plaintiff's inclusion of a clause in the tax abatement that read:

"In consideration for the tax exemptions granted herein, General Motors does hereby agree not to relocate the plant(s) for a period of _____ years, or reduce its local work force below _____ employees. Default in either of these assurances shall require General Motors to reimburse Ypsilanti Township for the full dollar amount of the tax abatements granted."

This clause would have protected the plaintiff, but would the defendant have agreed to it? Since the plaintiff never sought it in the negotiations between the parties, we'll never know.

This use of anticipatory thinking and preventative law could at the very least have produced some concessions from the defendant in exchange for the tax exemptions offered.

Discussion Exercises

1. Discuss examples of bilateral or unilateral express contracts.

2. Discuss your own example of an implied contract.

3. Discuss your own example of a quasi contract.

CHAPTER 2

CREATING THE CONTRACT

A.   IS THERE A VALID OFFER?

"I'll make him an offer he can't refuse."

—Mario Puzo: *The Godfather*

There is a negotiating dance the parties engage in preceding the creation of any offer. In the common purchase or sale transaction these dance steps consist of inquiries, preliminary discussions, invitations for offers, sales talk, soft and hard bargaining, and varied combinations of all of these. Ultimately, a legal offer must be made by the offeror before we proceed with the Acceptance side of the (O + A = Agreement) equation.

The legal disputes are typical. As in all contract cases, the plaintiff wants to enforce it because he thinks he made a good business deal, and claims breach of contract by the non-performing party. The defendant wants to avoid the legal consequences of the contract because he views the transaction as a bad deal, and asserts whatever legal grounds are available to cancel the contract or otherwise not be legally bound.

The Legal Requirements

The three required legal elements for a valid offer are:

1. intention to make a contract
2. definiteness in the required terms
3. communication to the offeree

Let's examine them one by one, since all three must be present.

1. There must be a current and immediate desire to enter into a contract. This "present intention" is not legally judged by the personal or subjective standard that relates only to the specific offeror. The actual intentions of the parties are irrelevant. Instead, modern contract theory requires the objective test, stated in terms of whether or not the particular facts as viewed through the eyes of a hypothetical reasonable *person* indicate it most likely that the offeror intends to be legally bound.

"A contract has, strictly speaking, nothing to do with the personal, or individual, intent of the parties. A contract is an obligation attached by the mere force of law to certain acts of the parties, usually words, which ordinarily accompany and represent a known intent.

</>

"If, however, it were proved by twenty bishops that either party, when he used the words, intended something else than the usual meaning which the law imposed on them, he would still be held, unless there were mutual mistake, or something else of the sort." Judge Learned Hand, speaking in *Hotchkiss v. National City Bank, 200 F. 287 (S.D.N.Y. 1911).*

Suppose Kim desires to buy a boat from Jim. Assume Jim's response to each of the following statements by Kim is, "I accept your offer." Let's see how the invisible line between preliminary negotiations and the actual offer typically fluctuates:

- "Is the boat for sale?" – no offer, just a beginning inquiry
- "I'd like to buy your boat." – again, just an inquiry in the negotiations
- "I can't pay more than $500." – sets a bargaining ceiling, but the parties are still dancing
- Jim replies, "I can't sell for less than $450." – sets a bargaining floor and the dance continues
- "I'll take it." – the dancing is over and we have an offer

2. The terms of the offer must be definite, clear, and unequivocal, so that the offeree can properly frame an appropriate response. Under the common law definiteness rules, there can be *no gaps* in the essential terms of the offer. These requirements are very strict. If any of the following are missing, there is no valid offer:

- Identity of the parties
- Description of the subject matter
- Price to be paid and terms of purchase
- Quantity
- Time of performance
- Place of delivery
- Special features

In *Gonzalez v. Don King Productions, Inc., 17 F.Supp.2d 313 (S.D.N.Y. 1998),* the plaintiff, a highly ranked professional boxer, sued to void a "promotional agreement" and a "bout agreement" between himself and the defendant for a boxing match with Julio Cesar Chavez on grounds that they lacked essential terms regarding compensation for future bouts after the Chavez fight, and were just "agreements to agree in the future".

The agreements were poorly drafted, but apparently provided that if the plaintiff won the Chavez match he would receive at least $75,000 for the next fight, and if he lost he would receive at least $25,000 for the next fight, "unless the parties of this Contract agree otherwise."

The Chavez match ended in a draw, and the plaintiff, who wanted to get out of having to deal with Don King, claimed the purse for subsequent matches could not be determined with sufficient certainty, and the contract was therefore unenforceable due to indefiniteness. The plaintiff moved for summary judgment.

The court denied the motion, agreeing with the defendant, who wanted to hold the plaintiff to the contracts, that, when read in context "could be interpreted as setting a default purse of $25,000 if the parties cannot agree."

"A price term may be sufficiently definite if the amount can be determined objectively without the need for new expressions by the parties; a method for reducing uncertainty to certainty might, for example, be found within the agreement or ascertained by reference to an extrinsic event, commercial practice, or trade usage."

An interesting side note to this case was that it was almost identical to a prior dispute Don King had with Buster Douglas after his surprise knockout of heavyweight champion Mike Tyson, when he had both under contract (*Don King Productions v. Douglas, 742 F.Supp 741 (S.D.N.Y. 1990).*

Under the Uniform Commercial Code (UCC), sales of goods transactions are treated more liberally as to required definiteness. The UCC will fill the gaps with what would be *reasonable* under the circumstances. While any missing terms would destroy the alleged offer under the common law, the UCC will keep the potential agreement viable and allow the offer to be valid.

3. The offeree must obviously be aware of the offer in order to respond to it with a question, a rejection, a counteroffer, or an acceptance. This awareness requires that the offer be properly communicated to the offeree. Communication can be direct and instantaneous, such as a face-to-face conversation or a phone call.

It also can be indirect, such as *receiving* the written offer by regular mail, electronic mail, fax, telegram, messenger, or carrier pigeon. The point is that it is not when the offer is sent that is critical; rather, it is the moment of receipt. And the communicator must be the offeror, or his authorized agent.

Herbert and John have been discussing John's proposed purchase of Herbert's house. John dictates a tentative offer to his secretary. She places it on his desk for review, where John's wife, Arleen, is awaiting his return from the bank. The phone rings and Arleen answers. Herbert is calling about the house deal, and Arleen reads him the offer. Herbert says, "I accept the offer." John then doesn't want to perform because his price is too high. Herbert likes the deal and demands performance. John claims no valid offer, because it wasn't properly communicated (by him) to Herbert. John wins the dispute because John's wife was acting on his behalf.

Another potential communications problem involves wording that is on the back of offers or is written in *fine print*. The typical dispute involves an offeree who claims not to be aware of certain portions of the offer and, of course, an offeror who claims they were binding.

Originally, the cases held that offerees were legally bound by all the terms of the written offer since they should reasonably have read everything before acceptance. However, as business became more intricate and fast-paced, and offers became more lengthy and complex, the original rules began to change as offerors often tried to take advantage of offerees by inserting provisions heavily weighted in their favor, hoping that the offeree wouldn't notice. Another fairness principle evolved.

Modern courts recognized this problem and remedied it by the rule that offerees are only legally bound by terms of the offer for which they had actual or reasonable notice. The UCC is similarly critical of non-obvious contract terms.

Special Situations

A. Statements made in anger, jest, or the heat of passion are not valid offers, because a reasonable offeree would understand that the offeror does not really intend to contract. Here we again apply the objective standard to evaluate.

Here's a true story. The author was attending a pro football game in Miami between the Miami Dolphins and Houston Oilers. The winner would clinch a spot in the playoffs. With five seconds to play, Miami was losing by four points, but had the ball on the Houston 1/2 yard line, and had time left for one more play. The ball was handed to the Miami fullback, who leaped into the end zone (hooray?) without the ball (oops!) because he had fumbled. Houston recovered the ball, time ran out, and Miami lost the game.

At that moment, one of the Miami fans (A) jumped up waving his next year's season tickets and yelled, "I've had it. Whoever gives me $20 for these tickets (face value $500) gets them." The fan next to him (B) pulled out a $20 bill and said, "I accept your offer." A then told B to forget about it, and B claimed there was a valid contract. If B had sued A for breach of agreement, no problem to pick the winner here. It would reasonably appear that A was not seriously intending to sell because he was angry and frustrated, and B should not have reasonably relied on A's statement as an offer to sell.

In *Leonard v. Pepsico, Inc., 88 F.Supp.2d 116 (S.D.N.Y. 1999)*, the plaintiff filed suit for specific performance based upon the defendant's Pepsi Stuff television commercial that encouraged consumers to collect "Pepsi Points" from specially marked packages of Pepsi or Diet Pepsi and redeem these points for merchandise.

The merchandise included a U.S. Marine Corps "Harrier Fighter (jet airplane for) 7,000,000 Pepsi Points."

The commercial began talking about basic merchandise that would appeal to "the Pepsi generation" such as t-shirts, leather jackets, and "cool" sunglasses, and then shifted to military music and a view of the jet plane, while a voiceover and print overlay stated, "Drink Pepsi – Get Stuff."

The plaintiff set out to perform the required actions to accept the offer by consuming Pepsi products, but "it soon became clear to him that he would not be able to buy (let alone drink) enough Pepsi to collect the necessary Pepsi Points fast enough."

The plaintiff then noted from the Pepsi gift catalogue that values of promotional merchandise were based upon monetary equivalents of $.10 per point, (it listed 53 items ranging from a jacket tattoo for fifteen points to a mountain bike for 3,300 points), so he raised the money to buy the necessary Pepsi Points and submitted a check for $700,000 to the defendant to purchase a new Harrier Jet, which would cost $23 million if purchased on the open market. That item was not shown in the catalog.

The defendant's motion for summary judgment was granted, on the basis that:

"First, the commercial was merely an advertisement, not a unilateral offer. Plaintiff's letter with the Order Form and the appropriate number of Pepsi Points, constituted the offer. There would be no enforceable contract until defendant accepted the Order Form and cashed the check.

"Second, the tongue-in-cheek attitude of the commercial would not cause a reasonable person to conclude that a soft drink company would be giving away fighter planes as a part of a promotion."

The court went on to state that the commercial was evidently done in jest. "The commercial is the embodiment of what defendant appropriately characterizes as 'zany humor.' The implication of the commercial is that Pepsi Stuff merchandise will inject drama and moment into hitherto unexceptional lives. A reasonable viewer would understand such advertisements as mere puffery, not as statements of fact."

B. Advertisements for the sale of goods are generally not considered to be offers, even if they say "special offer." They are regarded as only invitations for offers; a part of the sales dance in the usual situations involving print and visual media ads, mail order catalogues, ad circulars and handouts, price lists, and quotation sheets. The rationale for this general rule is based again on the objective standard, where it is not reasonable to believe a seller with limited quantities of goods intends to contract with every person who sees the ad.

Pete receives the Cycling USA catalogue that has on page 46 a "Special Offer for our newest 15-speed touring bike, only $175." He calls to accept the offer and pay with his credit card. The seller tells him, "Sorry, we're sold out, so we cannot accept *your offer to buy.*" Pete loses the dispute. He should reasonably know the seller would not fill every order.

But Pete is now an unhappy customer, so prudent sellers try to avoid this problem by stating in their ads, "quantities may be limited" or "product availability subject to prior sale."

Sellers also have to be careful of the consumer laws passed by most states which prohibit "bait and switch" advertising. This unlawful practice involves a seller who advertises an item at a very attractive price, knowing in advance that it is not available. Instead it is used as bait to get the customer into the store to try to sell him a more expensive item.

George reads a newspaper ad where Computer Associates offers to sell one of its Compaq Presario reconditioned computers at a terrific price. In truth, there are none available. When he arrives, the salesperson tells him they are sold out, but "while you're here, why don't you look at our new models that just arrived?"

As is the case with most of our general rules of law, there is a fairness exception that applies in factual situations where the ad in question is so definite that the specific item is identifiable, terms of sale are specified, or some special performance by the offeree is required. In both instances, a reasonable offeree would believe the offeror had the present intent to contract.

When Peter returns to his car in the parking garage, there is an ad flyer from Downtown Camera Co. on his windshield that offers for sale, "Kodak model 2200 digital camera, serial number #123456, black with silver trim, 1.23 lens, full read out and PC hookups, only $99, first 100 customers guaranteed sale, doors open tomorrow at 9am." Peter is the 50th customer (he waited in line and counted those ahead of him). If the seller refuses to sell, claiming the ad flyer just invited offers, they lose, because it was so specific that customers could reasonably rely on it.

There are cases that illustrate both the general rule and the exception:

- The advertisement mailed to plaintiffs from the United States Mint to purchase Statute of Liberty commemorative coins was ruled not an offer. "Generally, it is considered unreasonable for a person to believe that advertisements and solicitations are offers that bind the advertiser."

  "Otherwise, the advertiser could be bound by an excessive number of contracts requiring delivery of goods far in excess of amounts available." *Mesaros v. USA, 845 F.2d 1576 (Fed. Cir. 1988)*
- Kennel Club's advertisement to pay $25,000 to the party that picked six winners, which was erroneously printed by the newspaper as $825,000, was a binding offer. "If a member of the public buys a winning ticket on six races, he has accepted the offer and the parties have a contract." *Jackson v. Investment Corporation of Palm Beach, 585 So.2d 949 (Fla. App. 1991)*

C. Rewards for the return of lost items, or for information leading to the capture of criminals, fall into the category of unilateral form offers. They offer the promise of money or other value to be paid upon the completion by the offeree of the designated action. Disputes in this "promise for an act" type of case arise when the offeree peforms the required act to entitle him to the reward without knowing ahead of time of its existence.

Remember, communication of the offer to the offeree is one of the prerequisites for a valid offer. If the "an act" part of the unilateral offer is done without knowledge of the "promise for" part, most courts will not enforce payment of the reward. The law aside, most people will still "do the right thing" and honor their reward promises. They usually are so grateful that it is not a problem. But from a technical legality point of view, prior knowledge of the reward by the offeree is required.

Mrs. Magillicuddy is very upset because her cat, Henry, has run away. She posts a notice on her mailbox offering "a $100 reward to anyone who finds my dear tabby Henry and returns him to me." Susan is a jogger, and during her morning run she hears a loud meowing that seems to be coming from above. She looks up and sees an orange cat in a tree, apparently afraid to come down. She tries to do at least one good deed every day, so she climbs up and rescues the cat. It has a collar tag that says, "My name is Henry, and my mommy lives at 123 Main Street." Susan jogs over to that address, and returns the cat to the overjoyed owner. On her way back to the street she sees the reward notice, reads it, and then goes back to claim the reward. Mrs. Magillicuddy does not legally have to pay (but hopefully she will also do her daily good deed).

D. Auctions can be both enjoyable and profitable, if you know the legal rules that govern them. They are governed by the UCC. There are two types of auctions: "with reserve" and "without reserve." If the terms of the auction are not specified, it is considered to be "with reserve."

1. If with reserve, the "offer" of the auctioneer requesting bids on an item is really just an invitation for offers. The high bid is the offer. The auctioneer may legally refuse to honor it and withdraw the item if the price is too low.
2. If without reserve, the start of the auction by the auctioneer is a legal offer to sell the item, and the high bid, no matter how low, is a legal acceptance.

Here's another true story. When Ed was an active litigator, he would also handle his appellate arguments. They were heard either in Atlanta or New Orleans. On this occasion the argument was in New Orleans at 4 p.m. In those days, Bourbon Street was asleep during the day, except for a number of auction houses. To pass the time before his oral argument, he wandered into one of them. He noticed that an item to be auctioned was a large English Regulator wall clock, complete with mahogany cabinet and musical chimes. They sold at that time for over $500. When that item was "offered up for bids" by the auctioneer, he raised his hand to ask a question. "Would you please confirm that this auction is without reserve?" The auctioneer seemed confused and didn't respond. "This is an auction without reserve, isn't it?" Ed said again, nodding his head and smiling at the auctioneer. "Yes, sure it is," said the auctioneer.

The auction of the clock started and Ed bid $100. No other bids were made. "Come on, folks, this is a fine imported Regulator clock, it's worth much more than $100," said the auctioneer. He then began his countdown. "Going once, going twice, last call for any other bids. Sorry, we'll have to withdraw the item." Ed raised his hand again. "Excuse me, mine was the high bid, and you have to sell the clock to me." The auctioneer gave him quite a look. "What are you, a lawyer or something?" "Yes," Ed said. "Why don't you call a short recess and we'll talk about auctions without reserve." That clock still stands in the corner of his office, many years later, keeping perfect time as it chimes the hours.

Revocation of Offers – By the Offeror

The offeror is said to be *master of his offer.* The offeror not only decides to make the offer, but also determines its specific terms, can limit its duration to a specified time period or event, and can even require a particular method and manner of acceptance by the offeree.

If no duration is specified, the general rule is that the offeror has the legal right to withdraw it at any time before it has been legally accepted. This is called the offeror's *right to revoke.* This is an absolute right, and applies even if the offeror has specifically promised to hold the offer open for a stated period of time. The revocation is effective when actually communicated to the offeree, or under circumstances where he knows or reasonably should know it has been withdrawn.

Eva decides it's time to buy a new automobile. She goes to the local dealer, test drives a few models, and chooses her particular car. The salesperson, Frank, offers to sell it to her at a "special price," but she needs more time to decide. Frank tells her, "Take thirty days, little lady; the car will be here waiting for you." On day twenty, Louise sees the car, offers a higher price than the one quoted to Eva, and Frank sells it to her. On day twenty-two, Eva returns to the showroom to complete the purchase. She sees the car on the lot with a sign saying it's been sold to Louise. When Eva confronts Frank, he says, "Too bad, you shouldn't have waited so long." The car sale was a valid revocation of Frank's offer before Eva's acceptance.

In *Prenger v. Baumhoer, 914 S.W.2d 413 (Mo. App. 1996)*, the plaintiff sought to buy real estate from the defendant. After the parties and their attorneys met, the seller's counsel prepared a letter suggesting the parties had reached a "tentative agreement" about basic terms, including a price of $925,000 contingent upon financing, and "further contingencies."

The seller then contracted to sell the property to another buyer for $925,000 on an all-cash basis. The plaintiff obtained its financing approval, sued for injunctive relief to prevent the other sale, and requested specific performance of their contract.

The trial court granted the defendant's motion to dismiss, and the appellate court affirmed, stating, "The language itself imparts the notion that this letter was not a final agreement and that more terms needed to be agreed upon and realized." It "is at most an agreement to negotiate a future contract, with a tentative agreement upon some of the terms of the anticipated future contract."

The way an offeree can be protected against the general rule of revocation is to make the offer legally *irrevocable*. There are four major ways an offeree can skillfully do this, each of which shifts the decision-making power from the offeror to the offeree. We'll use the same factual example above to illustrate the first two of these exceptions to the general rule:

1. CREATE AN OPTION – This is a separate contract that has the legal effect of requiring the offeror to hold the offer open for the time specified. It can be verbal or written, has no limitation on its duration, and requires the offeree to pay the offeror something of value in consideration for its creation. The amount of value is immaterial as long as it is accepted by the offeror.

> Eva's factual situation is the same as above, to the point when Frank offers it to her at a "special price," but she needs more time to decide, and Frank tells her, "Take thirty days, little lady; the car will be here waiting for you."
>
> Eva starts to leave but then remembers her business law training, and says to Frank, "Do me a favor. I'm taking a course, so let's put this on a business basis; here's a shiny new penny to bind our deal." When Frank accepts the penny, an option is created, and he is legally prevented from revoking his offer for the agreed thirty days.
>
> When Eva decides to proceed, she, as the optionee, *exercises* her option. The amount paid for it is retained by the optionor as the price for the option contract, and not credited toward the purchase price unless the parties have agreed otherwise. If she passes on the deal, she has allowed her option to *lapse*. Again, the amount paid is forfeited unless the parties have agreed on a partial or full refund.

2. CREATE A UCC FIRM OFFER – This will also make the offer irrevocable, like an option, but differs in these aspects:

- It only applies to a sale of goods.
- The seller must be a merchant for these goods (his primary business).
- The offer must be in some type of signed written form.
- The maximum time period is ninety days.
- Nothing of value need be exchanged.

After Frank tells Eva, "Take thirty days, little lady; the car will be here waiting for you," she again offers to put the deal on a business basis with her tender of the shiny penny, hoping to create an option. However, Frank says, "I can't accept anything from you. Don't worry, we have a deal; don't you trust me?" Eva then says, "You know I have a terrible memory, and when I return to buy the car, which I'll probably do, I want you to get your sales commission for the sale, so do you have a business card? Please write on the back the car's description, the price and other terms, and my thirty days to think it over, and then sign or initial it." Once Frank does this and hands the card to Eva (and there's no reason for him to refuse), she has made the offer legally irrevocable for the thirty days, and it didn't cost her anything.

3. PROMISSORY ESTOPPEL – This is another fairness doctrine that applies when one party suffers damages because he changed his position by relying upon a promise that the other party originally made and now tries to revoke. The promisor is legally prevented (estopped) from withdrawing the promise if:

- The promisor makes the promise.
- The promisor knows the promisee intends to rely on it.
- The promisee does change position, relying on it.
- The promisee suffers legal detriment (damages).

Able General Contracting intends to bid on the University of Miami's new campus library project. It solicits bids from its subcontractors, telling them, "Give us your lowest bid offers so we can add our profit and overhead and make our final submittal to UM. If we get the job, your offer is accepted." Baker Plumbing gives its $50,000 bid offer to do all plumbing work, which Able puts into its final bid. UM announces to the press that Able is low bidder and will get the job. Before Able can accept the plumbing bid, Baker tries to revoke, relying on the general rule.

The law will not allow this. Baker is estopped to revoke its bid promise. Otherwise subcontract bidders could extort higher prices and take unfair advantage of the general contractors. This fairness principle is a relative of the Quasi Contract doctrine of "unjust enrichment" (unfair benefit) that we visited in a prior chapter.

4. UNILATERAL CONTRACT OFFERS – The potential for unfairness in "promise for an act" contracts is that the offeror may wait until 99% of the job is

completed, and then announce that he is revoking. He has the legal right to do this under the general rule, because acceptance requires *completion* of the promised action, and revocation is occurring before that occurs. So an exception was created to prevent such an injustice. It provides that once the offeree starts the required act, the offeror's power to revoke is legally suspended for the agreed time to perform. If no time is specified, the offeree must proceed in good faith for the time "reasonably necessary" to complete.

Sam offers to pay $1,000 to James, "upon your completion of covering my patio in one-foot-square Spanish tiles." James begins the job and is down to the last four tiles when Sam, realizing he is paying too much, tells James to stop the work because he is revoking his offer.

The inherent unfairness is obvious. Sam is trying to use the general rule of revocation to take advantage of James, who was acting in good faith. The law in this type of situation seeks to protect the innocent party.

Rejection of Offers – By the Offeree

Once a valid offer is made to the offeree, one possible response other than an inquiry or an outright acceptance is a *rejection*. It may be made expressly in verbal or written form ("no, not interested, forget about it"), or the result of the offeree's conduct (shake your head, walk away, ignore it). In either case, it must be communicated to the offeror to be effective.

Once rejected, the original offer is legally terminated, and can no longer be accepted. Any attempt to resurrect it by the original offeree is a counteroffer.

Jones has been looking at an oil painting done by Smith and asks, "How much?" Smith replies, "$5,000." Jones says, "Too high for my budget," and starts to walk away. Jones stops and says, "OK, you drive a hard bargain, but I'll pay your price; I accept your offer." Smith says, "Sorry, the painting is no longer for sale to you." Jones claims they made a legal agreement, and Smith claims no agreement because the offer was no longer on the table. Smith wins.

In *Papa v. New York Telephone Company, 528 N.E.2d 512 (N.Y.App. 1988)*, the plaintiff signed an order form to place its advertisement in the defendant's telephone yellow pages. The form provided that "Publication of any unit in any issue of the directory specified shall constitute acceptance of this order for such unit with respect to such issue only. The omission of a unit from any issue of the directory shall constitute a rejection by the Company..." The plaintiff sued for damages resulting from the defendant's failure to include its ad.

The trial court granted the defendant's motion to dismiss, and the appellate court affirmed, stating, "The order form therefore constituted a mere offer to make a unilateral offer." The defendant's not performing the required act of publication of the ad was a rejection of the plaintiff's offer, and no contractual obligation existed.

If the offeree's response to an offer is to add, eliminate, or modify in any material way the basic terms, it is a *counteroffer*. Counteroffers are legal rejections of the original offer and the creation of a new offer.

Jones has been looking at an oil painting done by Smith and asks, "How much?" Smith replies, "$5,000." Jones says, "I'll give you $4,000 for it." Smith does not reply. Later Smith agrees to sell it to another buyer for $3,750. Jones objects, and claims that Smith was legally obligated to sell to him. Wrong – Jones's counteroffer terminated the original offer and was never accepted by Smith.

Offer Termination by Operation of Law

Certain external circumstances may arise, having nothing to do with the conduct of the parties, which cause the offer to legally terminate:

1. Subsequent illegality – After a valid offer is communicated to the offeree, a law is passed making the subject matter illegal. (A offers to sell to B diet pills containing ephedrine, which are later declared a controlled substance by the FDA and banned from sale.)

2. Destruction of the subject matter – The merchandise offered is destroyed through no fault of either party. (A offers to sell his car to B, and a hurricane, tornado, earthquake, or other natural disaster destroys it.)

3. Death or disability of the offeror – In a personal service offer, the offeror becomes physically or mentally unable to perform due to accident or illness. (Tiger Woods offers to appear for a golf exhibition, and then is involved in an auto accident, which physically prevents him from performing.)

Discussion Exercises

1. Discuss how to determine when preliminary negotiations become the intention to make an offer.

2. Discuss how to determine the legal dividing line between fine print and the reasonable communication of an offer.

3. Discuss fairness exceptions that might allow you to claim a reward even though you did not have prior knowledge of it.

4. Discuss the fairness of allowing an offeror to revoke by selling to a higher offeree even though the offer states it will remain open.

5. Discuss whether the law should allow gap filling for missing terms in offers for the sale of goods.

Case Exercise 1

Self-Styled Tax Expert Gets Taught a Lesson

In *Newman v. Schiff, 778 F.2d 460 (8th Cir. 1985)*, the defendant was a tax rebel who called himself "America's leading untax expert." He espoused the view that there was no legal obligation to file income tax returns. He wrote books about this, appeared on numerous radio and television programs, and lectured in various cities. He claimed his activities caused over 100,000 people to no longer file or pay income taxes.

He appeared live on CBS News Nightwatch, a nighttime viewer participation phone-in television program, after having served four months in prison for failing to file federal income tax returns. He made this unilateral reward offer: "If anybody calls this show – I have the code – and cites any section of this code that says an individual is required to file a tax return, I will pay them $100,000."

The plaintiff, an attorney, did not view the live appearance, but saw a taped segment on a later rebroadcast on the CBS Morning News, believed the defendant's statements to be incorrect, researched the code, and then contacted CBS verbally and in a letter, stating that it represented "performance of the consideration requested by Mr. Schiff in exchange for his promise to pay $100,000."

The defendant claimed this was not proper acceptance of his offer, refused to pay, and the plaintiff sued for breach of contract.

Analysis

The trial court ruled in favor of Schiff by finding that Newman's acceptance was not timely. On appeal, that decision was affirmed. The appellate court noted:

"It is a basic legal principle that mutual assent is necessary for the formation of a contract.

"The present case concerns a special type of offer: an offer for a reward . . . In our view, if anyone had called the show and cited the code sections that Newman produced, a contract would have been formed and Schiff would have been obligated to pay the $100,000 reward, for his bluff would have been properly called.

"An offeror is the master of his offer and it is clear that Schiff by his words, 'If anybody calls this show . . ., limited his offer in time to remain open only until the conclusion of the live Nightwatch broadcast. A reasonable person listening to the news rebroadcast could not conclude that the above language – calls this show – constituted a new offer;

rather than what it actually was, a news report of the offer previously made, which had already expired."

Defuse Replay

The case illustrates the power an offeror has to control all aspects of a contemplated transaction. Schiff was "the master of his offer," and could specify all aspects of the necessary acceptance, including what acts would be acceptance, when they were required, and how they had to be completed.

This rule provides legal protection to an offeror to impose a personal, subjective aspect to his offer, so that the objective standard that would ordinarily bring in the outside judgments of hypothetical "reasonable persons" is limited by the offer's express terms.

It is immaterial if the terms of the offer are extreme, bizarre, or otherwise unusual. "I offer to pay you $100,000 if you can continuously stand on one foot for one hour, from 10 p.m. to 11 p.m. on October 1, 2003, at the top of the center span of the Golden Gate Bridge in San Francisco, California," is equally as valid as more conventional unilateral reward offers.

Newman's best strategy to legally obligate Schiff would have been to initiate a new conversation with him that would hopefully lead to a new offer being made by Schiff that stated, "If anyone can find any provision in the U.S. Tax Code making the payment of tax mandatory, I will pay that person $100,000." Notice there is no "call in this show" limitation, nor any time for acceptance limitation. The reward offer is more open-ended and, as such, much easier to legally accept. Given Schiff's talkativeness and sense of self-importance, this may have been easily accomplished.

Conclusion

Schiff's checkered career as a tax rebel came to an end shortly after this case, both because of increased pressure from IRS about his alleged tax evasion, and as a result of this wording from the court, which was widely reported in the media and cast him in a less favorable light to the public than he had previously projected:

"Although Newman has not 'won' his lawsuit in the traditional sense of recovering a reward that he sought, he has accomplished an important goal in the public interest of unmasking the 'blatant nonsense' dispensed by Schiff. For that he deserves great commendation from the public."

A. Do you agree with the court's final decision?

B. What do you think was Newman's real reason for suing?

C. Were the court's remarks about Schiff defamatory?

Case Exercise 2

Outlaw Jesse James Never Killed – $10,000 Says I'm Right

In *James v. Turilli, 473 S.W.2d 757 (Mo. App. 1971)*, the defendant who operated the Jesse James Museum in Stanton, Missouri, went on a nationally syndicated television show and made the following unilateral reward offer:

"The man shot, killed, and buried as Jesse James in 1882 was an imposter. In fact, Jesse James lived for many years thereafter under the alias J. Frank Dalton and last resided with me at my museum into the 1950s. I'll pay $10,000 to anyone who can prove me wrong."

The plaintiffs were the widow of Jesse James's son and her two daughters. They presented various affidavits of persons acquainted with the Jesse James family, each stating facts showing that Jesse W. James "was in fact killed as alleged in song and legend on April 3, 1882, by Robert Ford." They claimed the reward on the basis of acceptance of the reward offer, and, after the defendant refused to pay, alleging the offer was too indefinite to be enforceable, they filed suit.

Analysis

The trial jury ruled for the plaintiffs, and the defendant appealed. The appellate court affirmed, allowing the plaintiffs to collect the reward.

The appellate court stated, "The offer of a reward is a unilateral contract which becomes complete when accepted by performance of the act called for in the offer. A claimant to a reward needs only to show substantial performance."

The court noted that the defendant had virtually made a career out of his contentions, including his museum, publication of a book on the subject, and numerous appearances on radio and television. But he had lost an earlier case when he had tried to effect a name change for his "friend" J. Frank Dalton to Jesse James.

The case "hinges on the word 'prove,' a word of ordinary meaning. For present purposes, we accept defendant's own definition of the word, Under ordinary rules of construction, 'to prove' is to determine or persuade that a thing does or does not exist."

The jury felt that the plaintiff's proofs were sufficient, and the court said, "We may not upset the verdict unless it is so palpably unreasonable that reasonable minds can reach no other conclusion about it."

Defuse Replay

The wording the defendant chose for his reward offer doomed him to the adverse result. "By his alleged offer defendant did not say, as he could have, to whose satisfaction he should be proven wrong."

Conclusion

Note the different results in the *Newman* and *James* cases. In both, there were unilateral reward offers and, in both the defendant performed the required act. However, in the former, the plaintiff lost because he didn't call the live broadcast as required under the terms of the offer. In the latter, the plaintiffs won because there were no such limitations on how the offer was to be accepted.

Schiff was master of his offer and protected himself. Turilli was also master of his offer but failed to protect himself. We have a clear lesson in anticipatory thinking and preventive law.

B.   IS THERE A VALID ACCEPTANCE?

"The will for deed I do accept."

—DuBartas

The creation of an agreement is like watching a tennis match. The offeror serves up what looks like an offer. If it meets the three-pronged test of intention, definiteness, and communication, the ball is now in the offeree's court to respond.

- If the response is a question, everything remains suspended once it is answered, awaiting further action by the offeree.
- If the response is an outright rejection, the offer terminates.
- If the response attempts to change or vary any of the terms, it is a rejection of the original offer and a new counteroffer.
- If the response satisfies the legal requirements of an acceptance, a valid agreement is created.

The Legal Requirements

Acceptance has its own three-pronged test:

1. intention to make a contract
2. unconditional approval of all the offeror's terms
3. communication to the offeror

Let's examine them one by one, as we did for the validity of the offer.

1. Similar to the offer, there must be a current and immediate desire to make an agreement. It must also be definite, clear, and unconditional.

- "I agree to your terms, but I don't like them one bit." This is known as a "grumbling acceptance," which is still legally valid because the key is not why the offeree accepted, but the fact that he did.
- "I agree to your terms, but only if you give me a money-back guarantee." This is not a valid acceptance because there are conditions attached. It really is a rejection and a counteroffer.

The intent to accept is, like the offer, also judged by the objective standard. If it appears to a "reasonable person" that the offeree intends to be bound, the requirement is met.

This objective test is not necessary, however, if the offeror has specified the personal manner, method, or required details of the offeree's acceptance. As master of the offer, he can do this, and require the offeree to subjectively perform exactly as specified.

In *The Private Movie Company, Inc. v. Pamela Lee Anderson, Cal. Sup. Ct. (1997)*, the plaintiff sued the defendant, claiming she breached an oral and written contract to work on a movie project that contained nudity and simulated sexual content. The defendant claimed that while she had preliminary discussions with the plaintiff regarding the proposed film project, she never specifically agreed to the manner and method of presenting the sexual content.

In ruling for the defendant that no contractual relationship existed, the court said, "Consent is not mutual unless the parties all agree upon the same thing in the same sense. Ordinarily it is the outward expression of consent that is controlling. Mutual consent arises out of the reasonable meaning of the words and acts of the parties, and not from any secret or unexpressed intention or understanding."

2. All the terms of the offer, no matter how detailed or silly, must be accepted by the offeree. This is called the common-law *mirror image rule*. The acceptance must mirror the offer in all-important respects to be valid. While minor variations are permissible, any major differences in the essentials of the deal cause a rejection of the offer and create a new counteroffer.

An acceptance of an offer must be absolute and unconditional. All of the terms of the offer must be accepted without change or condition. A change in the terms set forth in the offer, or a conditional acceptance, is a rejection of the offer.

Phil owns a rental home and negotiates leasing it to Mary. He offers it to her for a monthly rental of $500, with a required security deposit of two months' rent. She responds, saying, "I accept your offer, and I'll pay you a one-month deposit. Here's my check." Phil returns her check and rents the house to Gale. Mary objects, claiming that the prior rental agreement was with her. She loses because her response changed the offer's terms regarding security deposits and violated the mirror image rule. She made a counteroffer that was rejected by Phil's conduct in renting to Gale.

"It is well settled in contract law that the failure to accept an offer on the terms proposed constitutes rejection of the offer, which is thereby terminated. Nothing more than a counteroffer, which rejects and terminates the (original) offer, is proposed where an offeree modifies or changes the terms of the offer." *Keryakos Textiles, Inc. v. CRA Development, Inc., 563 N.Y.S.2d 308 (N.Y.App. 1990)*

3. Communication of the acceptance is, like an offer, legally effective when actually received by the offeror. It can occur instantaneously, by dealings in person or on the phone. It can also be indirect, where there is a time delay between the transmittal of the offer and its receipt.

There is an alternative communication rule for indirect communication of the acceptance that can be quite dangerous for the offeror. It was originally known as "the mailbox rule," and provided that an acceptance of a mailed offer could be legally effective when *mailed,* if properly stamped, addressed, and dispatched in the mail − even if it was lost and never received by the offeror.

The obvious problem was that if the offeror sent the offer and had no response from the offeree, he would assume the offeree was not interested, and might then enter into a legal agreement with another party, impliedly revoking the offer, or otherwise expressly revoke the offer. Then the original offeree would appear with proof of mailing his acceptance, demanding performance of his agreement.

In *Casto v. State Farm Mutual Automobile Insurance Company, 594 N.E.2d 1004 (Ohio App. 1991),* the plaintiff insured two cars with the defendant, a Jaguar and a Porsche. She received two separate renewal notices by mail. She then placed payment checks in separate preaddressed envelopes and had them mailed to the defendant seven days before the stated policy cancellation date. The letter renewing the Porsche was delivered in a timely manner, but the Jaguar renewal was not. The plaintiff had an accident with her Jaguar after the policy cancellation date, and then the envelope for the Jaguar renewal was returned to her by the post office marked "Returned for Postage."

The defendant denied insurance coverage and the plaintiff filed a declaratory judgment action seeking a determination that her insurance policy was in effect as of the date of the accident. The trial court ruled for the defendant and the appellate court affirmed:

"The well-established general rule of contract formation is that an acceptance transmitted in a form invited by the offer is operative as soon as it is put out of the offeree's possession, regardless of whether it ever reached the offeror. This is the so-called 'mailbox rule' which states that in the absence of any limitation to the contrary in the offer, an acceptance is effective when mailed.

"To be effective upon mailing, however, the acceptance must be properly dispatched. The offeree must properly address the acceptance and take whatever other precautions as are ordinarily observed in the transmission of similar messages.

". . . the burden of proving coverage was upon the plaintiff and, consequently, plaintiff bore the burden of proving that the envelope was stamped when it was mailed."

In view of the numerous means of indirect communication that now exist, this rule has been updated and is now called "the reasonable medium rule." It allows acceptance to be legally effective when sent, *if* the method of communication used is reasonable under the facts of the case. A "reasonable medium" of acceptance is:

- one that is specified in the offer, or
- one that is the same way the offer was sent, or
- one that arrives as fast or faster than the offer.

Day 1: A mails an offer to B
Day 2: B receives the offer
Day 3: A mails a revocation to B
Day 4: B mails an acceptance to A
Day 5: B receives the revocation
Day 6: A receives the acceptance

The offer was legally communicated to B on Day 2. A's revocation is not effective until it was received by B on Day 5. If the mailing of an acceptance by B on Day 4 satisfies the "reasonable medium rule," it is then legally effective, and there is an agreement made before the revocation. If that mailing was not effective, the revocation occurs on Day 5, before the acceptance is received on Day 6. In this particular case B wins – the offer was dispatched by mail and the acceptance on Day 4 was sent via the same medium, so it is effective when sent on Day 4.

Day 1 11:59a.m.: A faxes an offer to B
Day 1 12:01p.m.: B receives the offer
Day 2:   B mails an acceptance to A
Day 3:   A calls B to revoke the offer
Day 4:   A receives the acceptance

The offer was legally communicated to B on Day 1 at 12:01p.m. The revocation by A is instantaneous when he calls B on Day 3. If B's mailing of the acceptance on Day 2 satisfies the "reasonable medium test," the agreement occurs as soon as it was mailed. If it doesn't, then A's revocation preceded receiving the acceptance on Day 4. In this case A wins – the acceptance was not sent the same way or faster than the offer, so it is not legally effective until it is actually received.

If the offeror specifies the required manner of communicating the acceptance, the offeree must strictly comply.

If the offer is not specific, but the parties had prior dealings or there is a trade practice for the way to communicate that method, it would be required. If none of these apply, then we use the "reasonable medium rule."

There really is no excuse for an offeror to be at the mercy of the rule. As "master of his offer" he can easily *unplug* it simply by stating that "acceptance of this offer is not legally effective until received." This is part of the anticipatory thinking approach to preventative law that is emphasized throughout the book.

Most modern decisions follow these "effective when mailed" rules, but some litigants who will benefit from the "effective when received" rule make the argument that the U.S. Postal Service has the legal right to recall mail, is therefore the agent of the sender, and that such right, coupled with a revocation of the offer prior to receipt of the acceptance, voids the acceptance.

In *Soldau v. Organon, Inc., 860 F.2d 355 (9th Cir. 1988)*, the plaintiff was fired by the defendant and received a letter in the mail that offered to pay him double normal severance pay in consideration for his signed release of all claims. He dated, signed, and deposited the properly stamped and addressed release in a mailbox outside the local post office. On returning home he received from the defendant the erroneously mailed severance check, returned to the post office and persuaded them to retrieve his release letter, and then cashed the severance check.

He then sued the defendant for alleged age discrimination, and the trial court granted summary judgment for the defendant, saying, "The release was deemed fully communicated to Organon, and a binding contract was formed, at the time plaintiff deposited the executed release in the mailbox."

Another communication dispute often involves a claim by one of the contracting parties that it is not legally bound by portions of the agreement if they are written in "fine print."

In *Littlefield v. Schaefer, 955 S.W.2d 272 (Sup. Ct. Tex. 1997)*, Walton was killed while participating in a motorcycle race when he struck an uncovered metal rail. Before the race, all participants had signed a "six paragraph release printed in miniscule typeface on the front of a one-page 'Release and Entry Form.'"

His widow sued the racetrack operator for wrongful death, and they defended based upon the release. The trial court dismissed the suit, but the appellate court reversed, "because the release is not conspicuous."

The court pointed out that risk-shifting clauses must satisfy two fair notice requirements:

"First, a party's intent to be released for all liability caused by its own future negligence must be expressed in unambiguous terms within the four corners of the contract. Second, the clause must be 'conspicuous' under the objective standards defined in the Uniform Commercial Code . . . when it is so written that a reasonable person against whom it is to operate ought to have noticed it."

Silence as Acceptance

As a general rule, if the offeree fails to respond to the offer within its required time or in its required manner, or in a reasonable time or manner if none is specified, there is a rejection.

In *Durick Insurance v. Andrus, 424 A.2d 249 (Vt. 1980)*, the defendant's old fire insurance policy was about to expire. The plaintiff sent the insured a new policy, which contained a provision that the insured could cancel the new policy by returning the old policy or a lost-policy receipt. Absent that action by the insured, the new policy would be deemed automatically accepted through inaction of the insured.

The insured did not respond, was then billed for unpaid premiums due on the new policy, refused to pay, and was sued by the insurance company. The trial court entered judgment against the insured in the amount of the premiums allegedly due.

The Court reversed, saying, "To constitute a contract . . . there must be a meeting of the minds of the parties; an offer by one . . . and an acceptance . . . by the other. The offeror cannot force the offeree to speak or be bound by his silence. Silence gives consent . . . only where there is a duty to speak."

But what if the offer states that the offeree's failure to respond constitutes an acceptance?

Victor wants to hire Gloria as a computer programmer. He tells her, "I offer to pay you $500 per week starting next Friday. If I don't hear from you to the contrary by 10 p.m. tonight, I will assume we have a deal." She listens, and then tells him, "I hear what you are saying." When she fails to appear for work on Friday, he claims breach of their agreement. She denies any acceptance of his offer. Gloria wins – the offeror cannot legally impose on the offeree a duty to respond to the offer.

However, the contrary result occurs if the offeree agrees to be bound by silence.

The same offer is made to Gloria as above. Her response is, "I hear what you are saying, and if I don't get back to you by 10 a.m. tomorrow, we have a deal." Here Victor wins – the offeree specified that her silence would be acceptance of his hiring offer.

There may also be other "silence as acceptance" disputes when unordered merchandise is received through the mail with an enclosed invoice requiring payment within a specified time. Sometimes the invoice includes a statement that, "unless the enclosed items are returned at our expense within fifteen days from receipt, you will be presumed to have accepted this payment obligation." The failure of the recipient to respond or return the items in these cases does not, as a general rule, create any contractual obligation.

In fact, the *Federal Postal Reorganization Act, Section 3009*, provides that whoever receives unordered mailed merchandise from a commercial sender has the right "to retain, use, discard, or dispose of it in any manner the recipient sees fit without any obligation whatsoever to the sender."

There are three other exceptions to the "silence is not acceptance" rule:

1. Book-of-the-month (or similar) memberships – "If you don't tell us no, we will send you this selection." The offeree has joined the club, and the membership contract expressly states that such a failure to respond is acceptance.
2. Prior dealings between the parties – Diamond merchants who for many months deliver a specific quantity and quality every Monday and pick up a check in payment every Wednesday. The customary conduct of the parties creates an implied acceptance.
3. Quasi-contract situations – A homeowner who watches the asphalting company mistakenly re-pave her driveway. Since she could reasonably have prevented the mistake but failed to do so, she has been "unjustly enriched" and must pay the fair value for the services performed. Her acceptance of the benefits activates her corresponding duty to pay.

The UCC Battle of the Forms

Most commercial transactions in the business marketplace are conducted by an exchange of pre-printed forms between sellers and buyers of goods. After the customary preliminary negotiations by the parties to reach agreement on the essential terms of their deal, the buyer usually sends out its *purchase order offer* (PO offer form).

All the basic negotiated terms of the deal are inserted on the front of this PO offer form as required by the offer rule of definiteness. They include the subject matter, price and terms, quantity, delivery, and other essentials.

On the reverse of the form are the pre-printed "boilerplate" provisions commonly used by that party. A buyer of goods would probably have the following terms:

- "All purchases carry full warranty protection in the event of any defects."
- "Buyer may cancel order within ten days due to labor strikes or adverse market conditions."
- "In the event of a default, buyer may sue in a court of law."

After the seller of the goods receives the PO offer form, it sends out its own form, which also has all the basics of the deal on the front and its own "boiler-plate" of seller's provisions on the reverse. The seller's acceptance form is the *order acknowledgement* (OA form), and it commonly has on its reverse these terms:

- "Sales are as-is; no express or implied warranties are given."
- "All sales are final."
- "In the event of a default, arbitration is the sole remedy."

Viewing the buyer's offer form and the seller's acceptance form from the standpoint of the common law "mirror-image" rule, there is no agreement because the acceptance has added different terms and caused a rejection of the original offer, thereby creating a new counteroffer.

But the drafters of the UCC wanted commerce to flourish, not to be interrupted by technical rules that invalidate agreements that are intended by the parties to be enforced. Modern business runs on this exchange of forms, which usually contain different terms in their "boilerplate" because the buying and selling parties have different goals to achieve. This is the *battle of the forms* – if the PO offer and OA acceptance do not mirror each other:

1. Do we have an agreement? If so,
2. Which of the conflicting terms in the offer and acceptance will govern?

1. Under the UCC, if the parties have agreed on the basic terms of their deal (the front of the forms), there is an agreement. Here, either there are no gaps so as to satisfy the common law rule of definiteness, or the gaps are filled under the UCC exceptions to that rule. The rationale is to not prevent the parties from completing a transaction they obviously desire to make.

2. Which of the conflicting provisions will govern is the area that creates the most difficulty. The UCC's explanation of how to handle this is overly complex, but reduced to its essentials it means that:

- If *both* parties are not merchants, the different terms in the second form are only *proposed additions* to the contract that are not binding unless accepted by the sender of the first form.
- If *both* parties are merchants, the different terms in the second form are again only proposed additions that must be accepted, so long as they are

"material" changes (important to the transaction). The first form (usually the purchase offer) again will govern unless the different terms in the second form are not material, in which event the second form governs. The three buyers' and sellers' examples above are all material, like most situations, since they could have a significant financial impact on the transaction.

While the UCC states that, "The additional terms contained in the offeree's form are treated as proposals for addition to the contract," the practical chances of the offeror accepting them are slim to none, because neither party usually reads all the reverse "boilerplate" of their forms, and even if the offeror did, there would be no agreement to different terms, because they would be disadvantageous.

The parties rarely sit down during the busyness of their days and compare the forms to see if they are identical. So the burden is on the offeree to make sure it reads the entire first form, because that is what it is usually legally accepting. The offeror is only concerned with "material" changes anyway, and the merchant-merchant rule that allows the second form to govern for non-material changes has no adverse effect on the offeror. Again, anticipatory thinking and appropriate action here will prevent later business problems.

Cancellation of the Acceptance

While offerors usually have the legal right to revoke their offers at any time before acceptance, offerees generally have no such right. The acceptance, once legally made, binds the offeree, even if he made a bad business deal or for other reasons wants to be relieved from the agreement.

There is, however, another of our fairness doctrines that will allow consumers – buyers of goods on credit – to withdraw their acceptances and not be legally bound if they do so within 72 hours of their purchase. This is known as the *three-day right to rescind*, and is created for consumers by the FTC (Fair Trade Commission).

This federal administrative agency requires installment sellers of goods for personal, family, or household purposes to place a conspicuous bold-faced legend in their contracts advising their customers of this right. Its purpose is to protect the public from impulse buying due to high-pressure sales.

Notice that a cash purchase has no such protection, only those sales where the buyer is financing the transaction by agreeing to pay the amount due plus interest over a stated time period.

Discussion Exercises

1. Discuss any additional legal tests you would use for a valid acceptance.

2. Discuss whether you agree or disagree with *Casto v. State Farm*. Did the insurer take unfair advantage of their insured?

3. Discuss the pros and cons on the "effective when sent" rule.

4. Discuss pros and cons of the "effective when received" rule.

5. Discuss any "battle of the forms" situations where differences between the forms are not "material."

Case Exercise 3

Hot Dog! Oscar Mayer Wieners Wins the Battle of the Forms

In *Union Carbide Corporation v. Oscar Mayer Foods Corporation, 947 F.2d 1333 (7th Cir. 1991)*, a suit for breach of contract was brought by the plaintiff claiming that the defendant was legally required to reimburse it for $88,000 in State of Illinois back sales taxes that the plaintiff had paid. The reimbursement obligation allegedly arose in a transaction where the defendant ordered plastic sausage casings from the plaintiff by standard purchase order form. There was an indemnity clause on the reverse side of the defendant's order acceptance form that read:

> "In addition to the purchase price, Buyer shall pay Seller the amount of all governmental taxes . . . that Seller may be required to pay with respect to the production, sale or transportation of any materials delivered hereunder."

After entering into their contract, another supplier of the sausage casings to Oscar Mayer began charging them a price one percent lower than Union Carbide's because they accepted orders at an office located outside Chicago and had decided they had no sales tax obligation to collect from their customers. When Oscar Mayer informed Union Carbide of this, the plaintiff instructed them to also send their orders to an address outside Chicago, and the plaintiff stopped paying the sales taxes and deleted them from the invoices it sent the defendant.

Eight years later, the State of Illinois decided that these sales taxes were due, assessed them. The plaintiff paid the amount required and then filed this suit.

Analysis

The trial court entered summary judgment in favor of Oscar Mayer, and the appellate court affirmed on the basis that the indemnity provision was a "material alteration" to the agreement of the parties, and was never agreed to by the defendant.

The court explained the "battle of the forms" provisions of the UCC:

> "Moreover, if it is a contract between 'merchants,' in the sense of 'pros,' as Union Carbide and Oscar Mayer are, the additional terms

become part of the contract. But not any additional terms; only those to which the offeror would be unlikely to object, because they fill out the contract in an expectable fashion, and hence do not alter it materially. If a term added by the offeree in his acceptance works a material alteration of the offer, the acceptance is still effective, but the term is not: that is the contract is enforceable minus the term the offeree tried to add."

It went on to discuss the standards to use to determine "materiality" of such contract changes:

"An alteration is material if consent to it cannot be presumed . . . what is expectable, hence unsurprising, is okay; what is unexpected, hence surprising, is not. Not infrequently, the test is said to be 'surprise or hardship.'"

Defuse Replay

As a practical matter, most of the "boilerplate" provisions on the reverse of the buyer and seller order forms are material to all parties concerned because they have significant financial consequences.

Perhaps they are as clear as having to pay $88,000 in back sales taxes.

Maybe they include more general areas of possible impact:

- remedy choices between litigation or arbitration

- the laws that will apply in event of default

- the forum that must hear such disputes

All are still "material," and therefore the sender of the second form that contains such clauses (usually the seller of the goods) is in danger of them not being legally binding.

The court points us to strategies that could be employed by both the buyer and seller of goods to avoid the adverse consequences of this UCC rule:

"To summarize, a term inserted by the offeree is ineffectual (1) if the offer expressly limits acceptance to the terms of the offer, or (2) if the new term (a) makes a material alteration, in the sense that consent to it cannot be presumed, and (b) there is no showing that the offeror in fact consented to the alteration – whether (i) expressly, or (ii) by silence against the background of a course of dealings."

Conclusion

The sender of the first form, usually the purchaser, can insulate itself from a "battle of the forms" dispute by inserting a provision that states, "We shall not be legally bound by any statements, clauses, provisions, and/or conditions of the (second form – offer or acceptance) which in any way, materially or otherwise, alter any of the terms of this (first form – offer or acceptance).

The sender of the second form, usually the seller, can protect itself if it will:

- Read carefully the first form to determine if there is a limitation of acceptance. If so, negotiate it away.

- Read carefully the first form to determine if there are any significant differences in "boilerplate" terms. If so, negotiate them away.

- Negotiate offeror consent to your "material" changes.

- Send the first form, and reverse the roles of the parties as well as the effects of the UCC rule.

A. Do you agree with the court's final decision?

B. How could Union Carbide have changed the result?

C. What could Oscar Mayer do better in the future?

CHAPTER 3

LEGAL ENFORCEABILITY OF THE CONTRACT

"Then in the marriage union, the independence of the husband and wife will be equal, dependence mutual, and their obligations reciprocal."

—Lucretia Mott

Law Overview

Consideration is the legal requirement that determines whether or not an agreement is legally binding upon its parties. This essential requirement of enforceability is often described as "whether or not the agreement is supported by legally sufficient consideration."

It commonly is viewed as the parties engaging in a mutually bargained-for exchange of "something of value," and impliedly saying to each other, "If you do this for me, I'll do that for you."

Even though there has to be a reciprocal exchange of valuable promises, the term "legally sufficient" does not mean the dollar amount of value has to be equivalent. As a general rule, courts will not inquire into the financial adequacy of an otherwise legally binding transaction. Their rationale in avoiding this "how much" analysis is sound – it is not the court's job to save one of the parties from making a bad business deal.

> Sophia has accumulated many items over her seventy-five years and decides to have a weekend yard sale. Arlene, a nurse, loves to spend her off days browsing at flea markets and garage sales. She looks through Sophia's items and notices a pastel painting that appeals to her. "How much?" she asks. "$10," says Sophia, to which Arlene says, "Sold." Arlene takes her purchase to be re-framed and is told there is a valuable under-canvas worth $5,000. Her good fortune is written up in the local paper. Sophia sees the article and sues to cancel the sale based upon inadequacy of consideration.
>
> Under this general rule, too bad for Sophia – she should have known what her property was worth and priced it accordingly.

However, if the facts of the case reflect that the defendant took unfair advantage of the plaintiff, and there is a wide disparity between the true value of the goods or services sold and the price paid, some courts will set aside the transaction.

In *O'Neill v. DeLaney, 415 N.E.2d 1260 (Ill. App. 1980)*, Mr. and Mrs. DeLaney were married in 1953, acquired a rare Rubens painting in 1958, and later in 1970, after he and the plaintiff had become close friends, Mr. DeLaney sold the painting to the plaintiff "for $10 and other good and valuable considerations," at a time when it was worth approximately $100,000, without the knowledge of Mrs. DeLaney. The painting remained for the most part in the home of the DeLaneys.

In 1974 Mrs. DeLaney instituted divorce proceedings, and claimed a special equity of ownership in the painting. The plaintiff sued for declaratory judgment that he was the owner of the painting. The trial court found the sale to the plaintiff to be legally unenforceable due to inadequate consideration, and the plaintiff appealed. The appellate court affirmed, saying, "Generally, courts will not inquire into the sufficiency of the consideration which supports a contract. However, where the amount of the consideration is so grossly inadequate as to shock the conscience of the court, the contract will fail."

The court noted the questionable circumstances under which the painting was allegedly "gifted" to the plaintiff. "Generally, a spouse has an absolute right to dispose of his or her property during marriage without the concurrence of the other spouse. Moreover, the spouse may do so even if the transfer is made for the express purpose of minimizing or defeating the marital interests of the surviving spouse. There is only one exception to this rule: when the transaction is merely 'colorable' or 'illusory' and is tantamount to fraud." (Here, the painting had been acquired by *both* spouses, not just the husband alone.)

Many contracts have standard legalese similar to the *O'Neill* case that states, "In consideration of the sum of ten dollars and other good and valuable considerations." Legal analysis of consideration usually focuses on the reciprocal interactions between the parties. But what if the nominal consideration of $10 is never paid? Does this, in and of itself, invalidate the transaction? The following case says no.

In *Bennett v. American Electric Power Service Corp., 2001 WL 1136150 (Ohio App. 2001)*, the defendant's employee signed a contract that, as a condition of employment, gave the defendant complete rights to all inventions made while on the job.

When the defendant patented the new invention, the employee would sign a document that read, "In consideration of the sum of One dollar (1.00), and of other good and valuable consideration paid to the undersigned Assignor, by the Assignee . . . the undersigned Assignor by these presents does hereby sell, assign, transfer and set over . . . unto (the defendant) the entire right, title and interest in and to that invention."

The plaintiff signed such a document relating to a profitable invention, the stated consideration was never paid, and the plaintiff sued to invalidate it on the basis of lack of consideration. The trial court and appellate court ruled for the defendant.

"Although ancient, the best authorities on the issue hold that nonpayment of such nominal consideration will not constitute breach, at least in instances where the actual value of the subject of the contract does not, in fact, correspond to the nominal consideration."

If the required consideration is present, it is said to be "legally sufficient" and the agreement is deemed to be "legally enforceable."

Since any agreement involves an exchange of promises by the parties (offer plus acceptance), the legal tests for consideration are based on the nature of these reciprocal promises:

A. Each party must receive (gain a benefit) and give up (suffer a detriment) something of value in order for the exchange of promises to be legally effective. The value exchanged is usually money or property, but can also be something less tangible like love, affection, or gratitude.

Albert and Jim mutually promise that Albert will buy Jim's car for $1,000. Albert's benefit is his new car and his detriment is his required payment. Jim's benefit is the payment and his detriment is giving up his car.

B. Value can also be the receiving or giving up of the legal right to do or not do something.

ABC law firm promises to pay Larry Litigator a salary bonus if he refrains from his dangerous skydiving hobby until he completes the important trial he is handling. ABC's benefit is Larry's assured presence at the trial and their detriment is the bonus they will pay. Larry's benefit is the bonus and his detriment is giving up his legal right to skydive.

In the unusual case of *Jennings v. Radio Station KSCS, 96.3 FM, Inc., 708 S.W.2d 60 (Tex. App. 1986)*, a penitentiary prisoner sued the defendant for breach of an alleged oral contract relating to the defendant's often-aired policy that they play "at least three in a row, or we pay you $25,000. No bull, more music on KSCS."

The plaintiff claimed the defendant breached this "contract" because it only played two songs, followed by a brief commercial, and then two songs, rather than "three in a row". He contacted the defendant and demanded the money, they refused, and he sued.

The trial court granted the defendant's motion for summary judgment, and on appeal that decision was reversed, and the case remanded for further proceedings:

"It is elementary contract law that a valuable and sufficient consideration for a contract may consist of either a benefit to the promisor or a loss or detriment to the promisee. Thus, when a promisee acts to his detriment in reliance upon a promise, there is sufficient consideration to bind the promisor to his promise.

"In the instant case, appellant's petition alleged he stopped listening to KSCS when appellee refused to pay him $25,000. Implicit in this statement is an allegation by appellant that he listened to KSCS because appellee promised to pay him $25,000 if he could catch the radio station playing fewer than three songs in a row. Appellant thus relied to his detriment."

Illusory Promises

The required "mutuality" of the obligations between the contracting parties, which is an essential element of legally sufficient consideration, requires that both must be bound, or neither will be bound.

In *E-Z Cash Advance, Inc. v. Harris, 60 S.W.3d 436 (Ark.2001)*, the business of E-Z was to provide cash loans to persons who presented personal checks that were to be held until the borrower's next payday. The loan agreement gave E-Z the option to sue debtors in court, but required debtors to go to arbitration if they had a dispute.

The defendant gave the plaintiff a check for $400 that it was to hold, and rather than paying her debt, she kept rolling over the loan and eventually was unable to repay it. She then sued, contending that E-Z's service charges were a hidden form of interest that violated the state's usury law and therefore prohibited them from collecting her debt.

E-Z moved to dismiss the lawsuit and compel arbitration. The trial court refused, and E-Z appealed. The appellate court affirmed, saying, "There is no mutuality of obligation where one party used an arbitration agreement to shield itself from litigation, while reserving to itself the ability to pursue relief through the court system.

Classic illusory promises lack mutuality because, even though they give the appearance that both parties are bound, the required mutual obligations are not present.

> Acme Technology hires Felipe as a computer programmer and the parties sign an employment contract that states in Paragraph 1, "We hire you for a term of three years." It also states in Paragraph 10, "Employer reserves the right to fire employee for any reason, at any time, upon fifteen days' notice."
>
> The hiring term is just smoke and mirrors. It presents the illusion of a binding definite three-year term, but really is not. The agreement is unenforceable.

These situations often arise in sale and purchase contracts between businesses when market conditions change after the agreement is made and one of the parties perceives they made a bad deal. While the courts allow a greater degree of latitude than in personal contracts, the parties often encounter illusory promise disputes that hinge upon specific wording:

- Output contracts – "I agree to sell you my entire production of widgets during 2003." By giving the seller a guaranteed market and the buyer a stable source of supply, these contracts are usually enforceable, since the implied wording is an exchange of promised based upon *need*.
- Requirements contracts – "I agree to purchase from you my entire 2003 production run of widgets." Again, the buyer has a uniform supply and the seller has reduced selling costs and an assured market.

However, if the express wording uses indefinite terms such as *desire, wish,* or *want,* the agreed performance is purely optional, the consideration illusory, and the agreement is not legally enforceable.

Gift Promises

The exchange of promises between the contracting parties requires a mutual bargain, where both gain a benefit and suffer a detriment. A gift promise is legally unenforceable, as a general rule, because the required element of detriment suffered by the promisee is missing.

> Herbert promises to pay Ann's past due credit card bill. If he then changes his mind and refuses, Ann has no legal recourse. Herbert's promise to pay her bill contains benefit (her gratitude) and detriment (his payment), but Ann is only receiving benefit without the required return detriment promise.

Another basis for non-enforceability of gift promises is that, although most donors honor the moral duty to fulfill their gift promises, donees should not, as a matter of law, reasonably rely on them.

There is an exception to this general rule of non-enforceability of gratuitous promises that applies to charitable pledges. Public policy encourages these gifts for the good of society. But there is a split of jurisdictions as to whether or not to enforce these gifts to charity:

> "Cases throughout the country clearly reflect a conflict between the desired goal of enforcing charitable subscriptions and the realities of contract law. The result has been strained reasoning which has been the subject of considerable criticism. This criticism is directed toward efforts by the courts to secure a substitute for consideration in charitable subscriptions. These efforts were thought necessary to bind the subscriber on a contract theory. Yet, in the nature of charitable subscriptions, it is presupposed the promise is made as a gift and not in return for consideration." *Salsbury v. Northwestern Bell Telephone Company, 221 N.W. 2d 609 (Iowa 1974) (The defendant's gift promise to help establish a college is held binding upon the pledgor.)*

- They are liberally construed by a majority of states to be legally binding based upon a legal fiction that presumes there is some element of exchanged detriment on the part of the donee.

    "A promise which the promisor should reasonably expect to induce action or forbearance on the part of the promisee or a third person . . . is binding if injustice can be avoided only by enforcement of the promise . . ." *Restatement of Contracts, Section 90*
- A minority of states take a strict construction that gift promises to charity are not legally enforceable unless there is a demonstrable showing of *reliance* by the charity on the promise, so as to activate the doctrine of promissory estoppel.

In *King v. Trustees of Boston University, 647 N.E.2d 1196 (Mass. 1995)*, Dr. Martin Luther King, Jr., named the defendant as the repository of all his papers by letter sent in 1964, delivered his files indexed through 1961, and then annually delivered to them his files of materials until his death. His widow, the plaintiff in this case, sued for return of all his papers, claiming his estate, not the defendant, had legal title because the donor's charitable gift promise was legally unenforceable due to lack of consideration.

The letter in question stated, "I intend each year to indicate a portion of the materials deposited with Boston University to become the absolute property of Boston University as an outright gift from me, until all shall have been given to the University. In the event of my death, all such materials deposited with the University shall become from that date the absolute property of Boston University."

The trial court jury ruled for the defendant on the basis that the gift promise was enforceable.

The appellate court affirmed, and while recognizing the strict requirements of the minority rule, found there to have been the required detrimental reliance on the gift promise by the donee-defendant. "The jury could conclude that certain actions of BU, including indexing of the papers, (and making them available to researchers, providing trained assistance staff, holding convocations to acknowledge receipt of papers) went beyond the obligations BU assumed as a bailee of the papers 'with scrupulous care' and constituted reliance or consideration for the promises Dr. King included in his letter to transfer ownership of all bailed papers to BU at some future date or at his death."

Promissory Estoppel

The fairness doctrine of "Promissory Estoppel" solves the problem of missing detriment in charitable gift promises, as we have seen. It also has an even broader application as a legal substitute for missing consideration, in cases involving some type of hardship or inequity, to make the promises of the advantaged party enforceable.

It applies to those disputes where the facts present a situation of "detrimental reliance."

Its elements are:

1. the promisor makes a gift promise where he knows or should know that the promisee will rely upon it,
2. the donee does in fact rely, and acts upon it, and
3. this reliance will cause the donee financial hardship.

Under these circumstances, the promisor is *estopped* to deny the validity or enforceability of his *promise*. To allow otherwise would cause injustice.

James agrees to give Martin an exclusive sales franchise in Miami if Martin sells his business in Orlando and relocates to Miami. Martin complies with the requirements but James refuses to honor his gift promise. James is legally prevented from denying the legal validity of his promise.

"Detrimental action or forbearance by the promisee in reliance on a gratuitous promise, within limits constitutes a substitute for consideration, or a sufficient reason for enforcement of the promise without consideration. This doctrine is known as promissory estoppel. A promisor who induces substantial change of position by the promisee in reliance on the promise is estopped to deny its enforceability as lacking consideration.

"The reason for the doctrine is to avoid an unjust result, and its reason defines its limits. No injustice results in refusal to enforce a gratuitous promise where the loss suffered in reliance is negligible, nor where the promisee's action in reliance was unreasonable or unjustified by the promise.

"The limits of promissory estoppel are: (1) the detriment suffered in reliance must be substantial in an economic sense; (2) the substantial loss to the promisee acting in reliance must have been foreseeable by the promisor; (3) the promisee must have acted reasonable in justifiable reliance on the promise as made." *Simpson, Law of Contracts, Section 61 (2d Ed. 1965)*

Past Consideration

The exchange of valuable promises by the parties must be new. It cannot be based on past actions.

> At the conclusion of Mary's retirement party, her employer promises, "Mary, in consideration for your fifteen years of faithful service just ended, we will issue you $25,000 worth of stock." If the employer does not honor the promise, Mary has no legal recourse.
>
> While the employer received benefit (Mary's gratitude) and suffered detriment (the payment), and Mary was benefited by the money, her detriment is lacking. She gave up nothing in order to receive the payment.
>
> If Mary had, for example, agreed to work one more hour, day, week, or month in exchange for her employer's promise, she could have legally enforced its performance.

In this respect, a promise based upon past consideration is similar to an unenforceable gift promise, and is governed by the same rules.

In *Dementas v. Estate of Tallas, 764 P.2d 628 (Utah App. 1988)*, the plaintiff was a close friend of Tallas, and had rendered various services for him over a period of fourteen years, including picking up his mail, driving him to errands, and assisting with the management of his rental properties. Subsequently, Tallas promised in a written memorandum written in his native Greek, that he owed the plaintiff $50,000 for his help over the years, and would change his will to provide for the plaintiff in that amount.

Tallas died one year later, had not changed his will as promised, and the plaintiff sued to enforce his probate claim for $50,000 based upon the decedent's promise. The trial court dismissed his claim on the grounds that it lacked consideration.

The appellate court affirmed, saying, "Even though the testimony showed that Dementas rendered at least some services for Tallas, the subsequent promise by Tallas to pay $50,000 for services *already performed* by Dementas is not a promise supported by legal consideration. Events which occur prior to the making of the promise and not with the purpose of inducing the promise in exchange are viewed as past consideration and are the legal equivalent of no consideration."

Notice how easily Dementas could have made the promise of Tallas enforceable if he had recognized this potential business law time bomb by creating a current exchange of a detriment promise by writing on the same memorandum, or in a separate writing, or in a provable verbal conversation:

"I will continue (for the next day, week, month, year, etc.) to provide mail, errands, management services," or "Here is my antique bouzouki you like so much, in exchange for your promise."

The past consideration rule is also ignored in situations where the payor makes: (1) a current promise to pay a debt barred in bankruptcy, or (2) a current promise to pay a debt barred by the statute of limitations.

Pre-Existing Duty Promises

A pre-existing duty promise is not legal consideration. It usually arises where the parties have made an agreement for the purchase/sale of goods or services at a fixed price, and later the seller wants to change it, for a variety of reasons, by increasing the price.

Even if the buyer agrees to the contract modification, only the original price need be paid if the seller's duty is to perform the same action it was previously bound to do, because there is no reciprocal exchange of a new detriment by the seller for the buyer's new detriment promise that benefits the seller.

> Mr. and Mrs. Jones hire Miami Catering to render all services for their upcoming 50th anniversary party at an agreed price of $2,000. One week before the event the caterer claims it miscalculated, and demands the price be doubled. The Joneses agree to pay the new price of $4,000. When the party is over and the bill is presented, only the original amount is paid. Miami Catering cannot recover the higher price.

Notice that when the caterer demanded the higher price, Mr. and Mrs. Jones did not refuse and threaten to sue for breach of the original contract. What identifies these pre-existing duty cases is that the response to the price adjustment is, "Yes, I agree to pay the higher amount!"

The rationale for the pre-existing duty rule's application in this type of case is to only require the performing party to honor its original promise, and prevent the unfairness of allowing a one-sided modification of previously existing contracts. If a new benefit is granted one party without a corresponding detriment being suffered by the same party, the promisor is, in essence, just making a gift. These cases often involve circumstances of coercion or extortion, like the Jones case, or other situations where the promisee has caused the problem that he seeks to be paid more for. We are on the legal and moral high ground by refusing to enforce these "tainted" promises.

In *Robert Chuckrow Construction Company v. Gough, 159 S.E.2d 469 (Ga. App. 1968)*, Gough was a subcontractor of Chuckrow on a construction job to build a

Kinney shoe store. The basic contract required Gough to perform carpentry work, including the assembly and erection of wooden trusses, which supported the roof deck on the building. After doing this work, thirty-two of the trusses collapsed, and Gough claimed there was an oral agreement with Chuckrow to pay extra for their removal, disassembly, rebuilding, and re-erection. Chuckrow refused, and Gough sued for breach of contract.

The trial court ruled for Gough, but the decision was reversed on appeal. The underlying contractual agreement between the parties stated, "Subcontractor hereby assumes entire responsibility and liability for any and all damage or injury of any kind or nature whatsoever . . . to all property caused by, resulting from, arising out of, or occurring in connection with the execution of the work provided for in this contract.

"An agreement on the part of one to do what he is already legally bound to do is not a sufficient consideration for the promise of another . . . Where one undertakes to perform for another service or labor for a given sum any amount (agreed to be) paid in excess of that sum, not based upon a new consideration is a mere gratuity."

But many times, parties who request contract modification are in a bind where they are less at fault, such as genuine miscalculations of the job and its location, honest mistakes in bidding or furnishing price quotes, and other situations that may arise after the contract that they have not caused.

There are four exceptions to the pre-existing duty rule which will allow the performing party to enforce a contract modification price adjustment:

1. The first relates to situations where the need for an upward price adjustment is caused by external conditions such as "acts of God," severe weather, labor strikes, wars, and other outside events that greatly increase the performing party's costs. In these cases, the agreed price increase may be justified as a fairness exception if the triggering event is an "unforeseen difficulty."

The legal test is again the objective standard. Would a hypothetical "reasonable person," under the same or similar circumstances as our situation, have anticipated the problem? If so, even though severe problems result that cause the actual costs of performance to greatly increase, it is NOT an event that allows the original contract price to be disregarded. It does not matter if the particular party didn't personally expect it to happen.

A legal test of "foreseeability" often used is, "Did this ever happen before?" The more often, the more recent, the more regular the occurrence – the more it should have been anticipated and taken into consideration when the original contract price was being negotiated.

Events that would be legally foreseeable:

- a severe earthquake in San Francisco
- a severe winter snowstorm in Montreal
- a hurricane in the Florida Keys
- another labor strike in the airline industry
- another war in the Middle East

Events that would be legally unforeseeable:

- an earthquake in Miami
- a snowstorm in Havana
- a war in Vatican City

The practical problem of reliance upon the "unforeseen difficulties" exception by the performing party is that "unforeseen" is an opinion, and reasonable decision makers may differ based upon the unique facts of each dispute. Why deal with such uncertainty? Most skillful navigators in the business marketplace insert a clause in their contracts called *force majeure*, which specifically allows the contract price to be modified upwards if specified outside events cause costly delays.

> "The parties agree that, should completion be delayed by more than ___days or construction costs increased by more than ___% by causes beyond the control of and through no fault of the parties, such as weather events, strikes, wars, acts of terrorism, or other similar unanticipated problems, the monies due and payable herein shall be adjusted accordingly."

Some states, when presented with such disputes, disregard this exception entirely as being too speculative or conjectural.

In *Crookham & Vessels, Inc. v. Larry Moyer Trucking, Inc., 699 S.W.2d 414 (Ark. App. 1985)*, a contract modification to pay a higher price for "extra ditching" was made in a construction project, because water would not properly drain out of the ditches due to clogged culvert drains, causing the original ditches to collapse. Although the trial court enforced the modification, the appellate court refused.

> "The appellee had the duty to acquaint himself before bidding with the conditions, nature, and extent of the work to be performed, and the condition of the culverts in question could have been taken into account. Where one agrees to do, for a fixed sum, a thing possible to be performed, he will not be excused or become entitled to additional compensation because unforeseen difficulties are encountered."

2. The original agreement is cancelled and a new one is entered into at the higher price, so there is nothing pre-existing.

> Using the Caterer v. Jones situation, when the higher price of $4,000 was agreed upon, the caterer could have said, "Let's make this simple. Why not just forget about the original $2,000 deal, and we'll just have this new deal for $4,000?" When the Joneses agreed, the new promise became legally enforceable.

3. The performing party does something new or different in exchange for the new promise to pay a higher price, thus furnishing the missing detriment to the promisee.

> When the caterer's demand for $4,000 was agreed upon, let's say a request was made that the Joneses cancel the old contract, but the request was

refused. When this happened, the caterer said, "Tell you what, I appreciate you agreeing to this, and to show my appreciation, I'll wash your car." When the Joneses agreed, the new promise became legally enforceable, notwithstanding the difference in value of the exchanged duties. Remember, all that is necessary is the exchange of "something of value." Since the caterer was not previously obligated to perform the new service, it is value.

4. The subject matter of the modified contract is a "sale of goods," so it falls within the Uniform Commercial Code provisions that require payment. Remember how tricky this can be, because most transactions involve both goods and services. If the majority aspect is tangible personal property, we have the required *goods* to satisfy this UCC exception.

> The catering contract made with the Joneses is basically a service agreement, even though it involves items of personalty such as the food, the silverware, the tables, etc. Suppose, however, that the caterer was skillful enough to have the contract allocate the total price: "$3,000 for all catering supplies and equipment, and $1,000 for labor." That would cause the UCC rules to apply, and protect the caterer against the pre-existing duty rule.

The UCC exception is further tempered by its corresponding legal requirement that the parties act in *good faith* so that their conduct is consistent with "reasonable commercial standards of fair dealing in the trade."

In *Roth Steel Products v. Sharon Steel Corporation, 705 F.2d 134 (6th Cir. 1983),* the defendant agreed to sell steel to the plaintiff at prices below its published book prices. Later, federal price controls to discourage foreign imports, as well as general market conditions, caused increased domestic and international demand for steel, resulting in substantial price increases.

The defendant advised the plaintiff that it was discontinuing all price discounts unless the plaintiff agreed to pay a higher price than originally agreed. The plaintiff agreed, and when a subsequent dispute arose between the parties over late deliveries and unfilled orders, the plaintiff sued for breach of the original contract, claiming the modification was unenforceable.

When the trial court ruled for the plaintiff, the defendant appealed. The appellate court affirmed, acknowledging the applicability of the UCC "sale of goods" exception that would otherwise enforce the contract modification, but ruled that the defendant had violated its obligation to act in good faith.

"We believe that the district court's conclusion that Sharon acted in bad faith by using coercive conduct to extract the price modification is not clearly erroneous.

"Therefore, we hold that Sharon's attempt to modify the November 1972 contract, in order to compensate for increased costs which made performance come to involve a loss, is ineffective because Sharon did not act in a manner consistent with Article 2's requirement of honesty in fact when it refused to perform its remaining obligations under the contract at 1972 prices."

Debt Settlement

The debt settlement cases are another type of pre-existing duty problem that frequently occurs in commercial settings. It arises when a debtor pays the creditor an amount less than invoiced, intending for it to be a release from any further financial obligation.

> Stanley hires Alan to perform architectural services for an agreed price of $1,000. Upon completion, Alan delivers his bill. Stanley sends Alan a check for $750 marked "payment in full" and Alan cashes the check.

Whether or not Alan can receive the $250 balance depends upon whether the debt is classified as liquidated (certain) or unliquidated (disputed).

If there is a good faith dispute about the debt communicated to the creditor before the debtor makes the payment, the tender of a check for less than the original agreed price with release language is an offer of settlement of the debt. When the creditor cashes the check, that offer has been accepted. An Accord and Satisfaction contract has now been created, which bars further payment to the creditor.

If however, there is no prior good faith dispute, the debtor's tendered release is viewed as a payment on account, and the creditor may recover the balance due.

In *F.H. Prince & Co., Inc. v. Towers Financial Corporation, 656 N.E.2d 142 (Ill. App. 1995)*, the plaintiff had a disputed claim against United Fire, a subsidiary of the defendant, for $1.6 million, which it compromised for $1.2 million by agreeing to release its right to sue United Fire in exchange for the defendant's guarantee of payment.

When the defendant refused to honor the guarantee claiming the settlement instruments were unenforceable for lack of consideration, the plaintiff sued for breach of contract and won a jury decision for almost $1 million that upheld the validity of the settlement.

The appellate court affirmed, saying, "The compromise of a disputed claim will serve as consideration as will a promise to forego legal action . . . the compromise of a disputed claim will provide consideration for the settlement agreement, even if the claim is shown to be invalid, as long as it is asserted in good faith."

Unconscionable Amount

As previously discussed, the courts will not usually inquire into the adequacy of the amount of exchanged benefits and detriments, as long as they involve "something of value."

However, on rare occasions the courts in some states will come to the rescue of the disadvantaged party, invoking a fairness exception that is sometimes applied if the circumstances involving the differential in amounts, relationship of the parties, and related factors may indicate that enforcement of the contract would "shock the conscience of the court."

This usually requires evidence that one of the parties has taken extreme unfair advantage of the other.

Let's go back to the garage sale case we discussed at the beginning of this chapter. Suppose that Arlene is not a nurse, but an art dealer. She goes to these homeowner sales hoping to "make a killing" on art that the owner knows little about. When she asked Sophia, "How much?" and was told "$10," Arlene's superior knowledge and special expertise required her not to take advantage of the situation.

If Sophia was also an art dealer and just sold her property too low, the court would not interfere. Similarly, if the amount paid, though low, is still within the guidelines of a hard bargain, the deal will stand.

Differing arguments are made in these situations.

Critics argue: A) If courts can inquire into the amount of value paid, we are disregarding the give and take of the commercial marketplace. No contract will ever be final because a party who made a bad business deal will always "take a shot" at litigation. The courts will be filled with these cases. B) Owners of property should be required to know its value, at their risk, no matter who the buyer is.

Proponents say there should not be hard-and-fast rules in this area. Review should be on a case-by-case basis to determine if the value exchanged and the circumstances surrounding the transaction require the court's assistance to right a wrong.

What do you think? Should the parties be allowed to make as good or bad a deal as they can negotiate, assuming that no unfair advantage was taken? Or should the court system be a watchdog, case by case, to make sure each transaction is "fair"?

What does fair or unfair really mean, except that reasonable persons may differ in their opinions?

Discussion Exercises

1. Discuss why courts allow minimal benefit but always demand detriment.

2. Discuss when you would require inquiry into the adequacy of consideration.

3. Discuss your view as to the enforceability of charitable gift promises.

4. Discuss your legal test for application of the unforeseen difficulty doctrine.

5. Discuss legal boundaries you would establish for use of promissory estoppel.

"Don't You Worry Bout a Thing, Cause I'm the King."

In *Alden v. Presley, 637 S.W.2d 862 (Tenn. 1982)*, the estate of Elvis Presley was sued by the mother of his fiancée to enforce his gift promise to pay off the remaining mortgage indebtedness on her house.

Elvis was engaged to the plaintiff's daughter, became aware of the plaintiff's desire to divorce her husband, and agreed to pay all her expenses, to furnish the money to purchase her husband's equity in their home, and to pay off the mortgage that encumbered it.

She then filed for divorce, and she and her husband signed a property settlement agreement on 8/1/77, subject to later court approval, whereby she would pay her husband $5,325 for his equity in return for a deed conveying her sole title to the house, and release him from any further liability on the mortgage debt, which was at that time $39,587.66. Elvis died suddenly on 8/16/77, and on 8/25/77 his estate advised the plaintiff it would not assume liability for the mortgage debt.

Analysis

The trial court ruled for the defendant on the grounds that his gift promise was legally unenforceable. "Plaintiff and her husband suffered no detriment as she 'wound up much better off after their association with Elvis A. Presley than either would have been if he had never made any promise to Jo Laverne Alden."

The appellate court reversed in the plaintiff's favor, applying the doctrine of promissory estoppel to hold that she "had foregone remedies available to her in the divorce petition *in reliance* upon the promise made to her by decedent."

The Tennessee Supreme Court affirmed the trial court's ruling for the defendant, because the "plaintiff has failed as a matter of law, to prove essential elements of promissory estoppel, *detrimental reliance*, and a loss suffered as a result of detrimental reliance."

Since the property settlement agreement was not binding until approved by the court and the estate had denied liability for Elvis's gift promise before it was submitted to the court, the "plaintiff's reliance on the promise after August 25, 1977, was not reasonably justified and she suffered no loss as a result of justifiable reliance."

Defuse Replay

How could Mrs. Alden have converted the non-enforceable gift promise made by Elvis into a legally binding obligation?

- Create an exchanged detriment by promising to do something for Elvis in exchange for his gift promise. "Thank you, Elvis; I'll bake you a cake."

- Create a promissory estoppel scenario. Suppose Mrs. Alden was working after hours to make her mortgage payments. In response to his gift promise, she says, "Thank you, Elvis, now I can quit my night job and spend more time with the family." All requirements of that doctrine would then be present: a promise, knowledge of it and reliance on it, and change of position to her detriment by the promissee.

Conclusion

There is no question Elvis would have honored his gift promise had he lived. His heirs, however, had a different agenda, as is the usual case in estates. The money to pay Mrs. Alden's mortgage would have come out of their pocket. It is therefore not surprising they refused to pay.

All of us will, hopefully, be in a situation at some time in our lives when a gift promise is made to us. At that moment, the proverbial lightbulb needs to be lit in our heads as we recognize this potential business law time bomb and act skillfully to defuse it.

A. Do you agree with the court's final decision?

B. Was it ethical for the estate to refuse to honor Elvis's promise?

C. Should provable gifts made by decedents be legally binding on their heirs?

Case Exercise 2

"Paid in Full" May Mean "Partially Paid"

In *Pierola v. Moschonas, 687 A.2d 942 (D.C. App. 1997),* the parties were business associates in the scraping and painting of bridges and other metal structures. They agreed to split profits 60% to Pierola and 40% to Moschonas, although Pierola claimed there was no such contract. They then had a heated disagreement, Moschonas walked off the job, and Pierola delivered to Moschonas a check marked "paid in full" for less than his 40% profit participation, which was cashed.

Then the payee sued for the balance due, Moschonas claiming that the check did not contain that release wording. Pierola raised the defense of accord and satisfaction.

Analysis

The trial court, "troubled by the lack of forthrightness of both litigants," ruled in favor of Moschonas and rejected the full payment defense raised by Pierola because his denial of the existence of the contractual agreement between the parties brought him outside the rule that "there must be a mutual acknowledgement of the underlying debt and a bona fide dispute as to its amount for the cashing of the check to operate as a settlement."

The appellate court reversed, holding that the trial court made a legal error. "It is not necessary for the parties to mutually acknowledge the underlying debt and to dispute only its amount for accord and satisfaction to operate. (It) can operate anytime the underlying claim is disputed *either* as 'to the amount due *or* as to the debtor's liability.' "

The court then considered whether there was a bona fide dispute, as required by law.

"The good faith requirement thus is concerned not so much with the subjective moral character of the debtor but rather the requirement of consideration. If there is an objective reasonable basis for the debtor's disputing his obligation to pay, whether in liability or amount, he is giving up something by making a part payment in full satisfaction of the disputed claim and thus provides objective consideration.

"The parties had had a heated disagreement regarding whether to sandblast or scrape the South Capitol Street Bridge, and as a result of that disagreement Moschonas had walked off the job before it was completed and not returned. These facts gave Pierola a legitimate basis to dispute Moschonas' claim to a flat 40% of the profits on both the bridge and tower contracts."

Both parties in the Pierola-Moschonas dispute had a problem telling the truth. The court said, "The requirement that a dispute be legitimate, bona fide or honest focuses not on the propensity of the parties to prevaricate, but rather on the basis for disputing the claim at the time the accord and satisfaction operates."

Defuse Replay

Debt settlement is a recurring problem in modern business transactions. Most parties assume that the debt is cancelled as soon as the check is cashed. Debtors thus are able to clear their accounts receivable balances, and creditors write them off and then abandon efforts to collect the balances. Creditors don't realize they may be able to treat such partial remittances as payments on account, and properly demand full payment.

The tricky area is the nature of the alleged good faith dispute. It has to be prior in time to the attempted tender. Merely writing on the check additional wording such as, "I dispute this debt," or self-serving words such as, "This payment relates to a prior dispute" will not suffice.

Even if there is a "prior" dispute, it must be legitimate, bona fide, or made in good faith. The debtor's mere refusal to pay does not constitute the required unliquidated debt if it is arbitrary or capricious, and has no legal basis.

> Anne hires lawyer John to draft some lengthy contracts for an agreed price of $500. Later she has lunch with her friend Susan, tells her about it, and Susan suggests that Anne is overpaying. Anne is taking a business law course and studies the debt settlement rule. She contacts John and pretends to disagree on the amount, trying to create the legal requirement of prior dispute. Later, after receiving the bill for $500, she sends him a check for $250 marked "paid in full," and it is deposited with his daily bill collections.

Anne should have to pay the balance due. She had no good faith dispute. This requirement protects creditors from being unfairly disadvantaged by a knowledgeable debtor trying to utilize this debt settlement rule to eliminate an otherwise valid debt.

Creditor's Perspective

Most debt settlement problems arise in busy offices where many invoices are sent to debtors, numerous payments arrive daily, and there is an automatic bookkeeping procedure to bank payment remittances the same day they are received. If the cashing of some of these payments would create a valid accord and satisfaction, the creditor may have forfeited substantial monies.

Businesses can initiate office procedures to protect themselves. These could include:

1. Monitor the daily banking procedure.

2. When the mail is opened, compare all payments to their invoice to determine if they are partial AND examine them for any "full release" or "payment in full" language.

3. Put the partial payments that contain release language aside, and do not deposit them until the question of whether there is a prior good faith dispute can be answered.

Debtor's Perspective

If you are the debtor in this situation, and otherwise qualify for binding debt settlement, a careful creditor that initiates the protective office procedures may thwart your efforts.

However, you may prevail by using a method of payment transmittal that bypasses the creditor's office, such as direct payment to the creditor's bank, certain wire transfers, or payments delivered to an assignee or other designated agent.

If the creditor has not thought ahead far enough to block these types of qualifying payments, you may be successful in discharging the debt.

Conclusion

Payments made to settle a debt must be closely monitored by both payor (debtor) and payee (creditor) to determine the possibility of the sequence of events creating a legally binding accord and satisfaction.

As doing business becomes more complex and the technology of e-commerce and instant communication grows, the parties need to be informed of and protect themselves from the danger of unintended cancellation of otherwise collectible account balances.

A. Do you agree with the court's final decision?

B. What if Moschonas had not walked off the job? Who wins then?

C. What if Pierola had bid on another lucrative job without telling Moschonas? Who wins then?

CHAPTER 4

AVOIDING CONTRACT LIABILITY

A. LEGAL CAPACITY OF THE PARTIES

"Contract defenses should be used as a protective shield,
not as a cutting sword."

—Legal Maxim

Law Overview

Disputes often arise after contracting parties have entered into an agreement that is supported by legally sufficient consideration, and is therefore deemed "enforceable."

Suppose one of the parties wants out of the deal they made, either because they miscalculated, market conditions have changed, or a variety of other reasons. Whether or not they will be legally extricated from their contractual agreement depends upon their ability to prove a legal defense to enforcement.

Like most legal disputes, the scales of justice swing back and forth depending upon the particular agenda of the parties: 1) The party who made the better bargain will always want his contract to be legally enforceable. That same party will sue for "breach of contract" if its terms are not performed. Defenses to enforcement based upon alleged lack of legal capacity will be vigorously opposed. 2) The party whose deal doesn't look as good as when the agreement was made may seek ways to legally be extricated from it. Can their agreement be cancelled, avoided, or disaffirmed? Can that party be allowed to withdraw with no adverse legal consequences?

The party who wants to be relieved of legal responsibilities has the burden of proof. These situations involve *voidable contracts*.

Note the focus of these disputes is on the legal status of the particular party who is seeking judicial permission not to have to perform, rather than the type of business transaction involved.

Even if one of the parties lacks legal capacity, the contract can still be valid and fully enforced by them, if they so desire. If, however, they are looking for a way out – their claim and proof of incapacity will free them from legal responsibility. It is their personal choice whether to accept the contract or seek to cancel it.

The legal remedy to cancel the contract is called *rescission*. The act of cancellation by the party who lacks legal capacity is called *disaffirmance*.

The lack of capacity cases usually involve these two types of situations:

- The plaintiff sues to cancel the contract and to require the return of the value paid to the defendant.
- The defendant is sued for breach of contract by the plaintiff and raises incapacity as a legal defense to its enforcement.

The two main areas of cases involving claims of lack of legal capacity are *mental impairment* and *minority*.

Mental Impairment

The legal test of mental impairment is whether or not the party in question is capable of understanding the legal effect of his contract at the time he enters into it. This is an objective test of cognition, whereby the law uses the "what is reasonable?" criteria to resolve disputes.

If the impaired party is allowed to legally cancel his contract, he has the corresponding legal duty to return any value he received, such as deposits or payments when the contract was made. The objective here is to balance the scales of justice again – to place the parties back into the *status quo* where they were before entering into the transaction.

Notice the law focuses on the moment in time when the contract is made, not before or after. Even if the allegedly impaired party was as "nutty as a fruitcake" just prior to making the contract or shortly thereafter, there might have been a *lucid interval* during which the contract was made. If so, the contract is enforceable, even if its terms are disadvantageous, as long as the unimpaired party did nothing wrong.

> Groovy was a child of the 1960s, and ingested a number of chemicals that cause flashbacks from time to time. When these incidents occur, he appears to be severely impaired. Groovy has been negotiating with Phil to buy a boat, and they enter into their contract on July 3. At the moment the contract is made, Groovy is clear, cogent, and fully aware of the nature and consequences of his actions, although shortly before and shortly after he is again in la-la land. Groovy now wants to rescind the contract, claiming incapacity. Phil should win – as long as it was an arms-length transaction. Remember, the marketplace is filled with good or bad deals, depending upon one's side in the transaction.

There are various valid ways that mental impairment disputes may arise:

A) Mental incapacity may legitimately occur due to impairment caused by actual instances of accident or illness such as concussions, brain tumors, neurological trauma or disease, senility, or other pathologies that impair judgment and cognition, short of a judicial determination of incapacity. These are readily proved by medical testimony, and are not usually litigated for that reason.

B) A legal adjudication of mental impairment may result if there has been a legal proceeding, commonly called guardianship, brought by family or friends to declare someone to be legally incompetent. If such a court order is entered, the person in question loses his legal rights to contract, and any such agreements made from its date forward are *void and unenforceable.* Only the court-appointed guardian has the right to contract on behalf of the incompetent. If the impaired party later recovers, his competency can be legally restored by another court order, and he is again free to enter into contracts.

C) Voluntary impairments such as drugs, alcohol, and allergic reactions to ingested food, drink, or medicine.

D) Situational impairments, such as inhalation of noxious fumes, atmospheric problems like smog or pollen that interfere with cognition, and severe emotional upsets that create imbalances in judgment.

But what if the party claiming mental impairment appears to be faking so as to avoid the bad contract bargain he made, or the tests for mental impairment are not so clear? These are the situations that cause most legal disputes, and often involve claims of "I was under the influence of . . ." alcohol or drugs or prescription medication, etc.

Originally, most states strictly construed the legal test for impairment, so that even if the complaining party's impairment were self-induced, he would still be allowed to rescind. The burden of proof was solely to convince the decision-maker that "he was legally incapable of understanding the contract at the moment it was created." The reason for his problem, and its surrounding circumstances, was immaterial.

However, parties began to abuse the rule in situations not so clear-cut as verifiable accident or illness and judicial incompetency. Judges became skeptical of their true motivations and whether they were acting in good faith. So the courts met this challenge by adding a fairness exception to the rule in these cases that requires complaining parties to prove that *unfair advantage* was taken – they were victimized by the non-impaired party. This is a fault versus no-fault test.

This has greatly reduced litigation in this area. Close cases can still occur where the alleged impairment was self-created, but there are mixed aspects of fault:

Sidney is an experienced businessman with an unusually high alcohol tolerance. He often uses this "gift" as a negotiating tactic as the parties sit around the table, having a few drinks. When the other party is sufficiently drunk, Sidney then completes the contract on very favorable business terms. Assume that Sidney has just completed such a contract with Karl, who also has business experience. Later, Karl claims mental impairment and seeks to have the contract cancelled. Sidney would argue:

- "Karl chose to drink himself into financial oblivion."
- "He should have thought about the consequences of his actions."
- "I didn't hold a gun to his head."
- "Business is business."

Karl would argue that Sidney didn't act in good faith, and victimized him by using his alcohol tolerance as a means to that end.

Under the old rule, Karl would probably win, since he could satisfy the legal test of impairment at the moment of contracting, and that was the sole factor to consider.

Under the new rule, Karl would lose unless he had some additional facts, such as, "When Karl went to the restroom between drinks, Sidney placed a drug capsule into his drink," so that he could prove that Sidney took unfair advantage of him, and was therefore at fault.

A case analysis of the "impairment" defense reflects how these rules are interpreted and implemented by the courts. Some analyze whether or not the facts of their particular dispute meet the "capable of understanding at the time of contract" test. Others, like the case below, allow enforcement by the non-impaired party, even if there was the legally required mental incapacity.

In *Hedgepeth v. Home Savings and Loan Association, 361 S.E.2d 888 (N.C. App. 1987)*, Cora Haith signed a power of attorney that authorized her son to sign for her a promissory note and deed of trust in favor of the defendant in connection with mortgage refinancing for the remodeling of her house. She was adjudicated incompetent *after* the papers were signed, and her daughter (the plaintiff) was appointed her guardian. The daughter then sued to invalidate the power of attorney and resulting papers due to the mother's alleged mental impairment at the time of signing.

The defendant argued the documents were legally valid, it had made previous loans to Mrs. Haith in which similar powers of attorney were used, and it was unaware of any problems with her mental state.

The trial court ruled for the defendant, upholding the validity of the note and deed of trust, despite the fact that the signer was mentally impaired. On appeal, the court affirmed, stating the applicable law:

"It is well established in our state that a contract by an incompetent prior to being so adjudicated, is voidable and not *void ab initio*. The party contracting with an incompetent may nevertheless enforce the agreement if the following requirements can be established: (1) ignorance of the party's mental incapacity; (2) lack of notice of the incapacity such as would indicate to a reasonably prudent person that inquiry should me made of the party's mental condition; (3) payment of a full and fair consideration; (4) that no unfair advantage was taken of the incompetent; and (5) that the incompetent had not restored and could not restore the consideration or make adequate compensation."

Notice how the plaintiff would first have the burden of proving mental incapacity at the time of signing the documents. That being done, the burden of proof would shift to the non-impaired party seeking enforcement of them to prove the five-pronged test of enforcement.

Other cases, often involving alleged intoxication, are decided on more traditional lines of whether or not there was mental impairment, and if so, did the impaired party demand cancellation in a timely manner.

In *First State Bank of Sinai v. Hyland, 399 N.W.2d 894 (S.D. 1987)*, the defendant's son borrowed money from the bank in the form of promissory notes. When they became past due, the bank required the defendant to co-sign as a condition to their renewal. The defendant did so in the son's presence, and also gave him a check for the past due loan interest of $900. The bank and the defendant had prior dealings over the last fifteen years in which the defendant had signed and paid off approximately sixty promissory notes.

When the note came due, the son filed for bankruptcy, and the defendant refused to pay, claiming he was "incapacitated through the use of liquor when he signed the note." The evidence showed that the defendant had been involuntarily committed to hospitals for his alcohol problems five times over the last few years. But it also showed he had transacted business with the bank between the periods of these commitments.

The trial court ruled for the defendant, and the bank appealed. In reversing the lower court's decision, the court enforced the defendant's note because "he did not show that he was entirely without understanding when he signed the note . . . and his subsequent failure to disaffirm (lack of rescission) and his payment of interest (ratification) then transformed the voidable contract into one that is fully binding upon him."

The conduct of the defendant was consistent with a legally enforceable obligation. He paid the interest arrearage. Why do this if he was allegedly alcohol-impaired when he signed the note? What if he also claimed, which he didn't, that he was impaired when he wrote out the interest check? Why not promptly notify the bank that he refused to be legally bound? Instead, he sat back and did nothing until the bank was forced to sue him for payment.

In *Diedrich v. Diedrich, 424 N.W.2d 580 (Minn. App. 1988)*, the marriage of the parties was dissolved in January 1981, and the court's judgment provided that the wife's remarriage would trigger a sale of the homestead which she occupied. In August 1981 the parties signed a post-judgment agreement contingent upon the wife's anticipated remarriage, which provided, among other things, that if she were divorced within five years, maintenance of $350 per month previously being paid by husband would be reinstated.

The wife remarried, was divorced within five years, and demanded enforcement of the maintenance payments under the post-judgment agreement. The husband opposed this demand, and "alleged he did not remember signing the agreement and that at the time of the signing, he had experienced blackouts due to alcoholism."

The trial court found the agreement valid, and the appellate court affirmed.

"Appellant took no action to have the agreement declared invalid for over five years. A contract is voidable but not automatically void if a party was too intoxicated to comprehend the terms of the agreement. In order to repudiate a contract entered while intoxicated, the party must act promptly."

The longer the alleged incompetent waits to assert his incapacity, the more it appears to the decision-maker that this is just another case of someone making a bad business deal and then wanting to be judicially rescued. Where the non-impaired party did nothing wrong, the contract will stand.

However, if the requisite "unfair advantage" is taken of the impaired party, the scales of justice are out of balance, and court assistance is necessary to prevent injustice.

In *Smith v. Williamson, 429 So.2d 598 (Ala. App. 1982)*, the plaintiff was an attorney who had previously successfully represented the defendant in an action to recover her residence, which had been conveyed to a party named Matthews when she lacked legal capacity due to her habitual alcoholism. When he learned of a threatened foreclosure against her, he appeared at her home and was hired to represent her again.

While in his office, where he was preparing to file this lawsuit, he "advanced $500 to Ms. Williamson and took back a note and mortgage on her home." When she later defaulted, he began foreclosure proceedings on her home, and she "obtained a temporary restraining order to prevent the attorney's actions."

The trial court invalidated the mortgage given to the plaintiff and prohibited him from foreclosing on it by permanent injunction. The appellate court affirmed, and questioned the conduct of the plaintiff:

"Smith appeared unsolicited at Ms. Williamson's home and assured her that he could help her with her legal problems . . . the record indicates that Ms. Williamson executed the note and mortgage on her home to Smith . . . the following morning. The record further shows that Ms. Williamson had consumed a pint of one hundred proof vodka and that she remained in an agitated state over the sale of her home. To hold that Ms. Williamson was incapable of understanding the nature of the transaction with the Matthewses and then to hold that she was able to comprehend the nature of her dealings with Smith would be to reach illogical results, especially in light of the facts presented at trial."

Minority

The law tries to protect underage parties from the legal consequences of their contracts on the theory that they lack sufficient maturity, education, and experience to protect themselves.

Under the common law, persons were classified and referred to as infants until they reached the age of twenty-one years.

"The dominant purpose of the law in permitting infants to disaffirm their contracts is to protect children and those of tender years from their own improvidence, or want of discretion, and from the wiles of designing men." *McCormick v. Crotts, 153 S.E. 152 (N.C. 1930)*

Most states have statutes that specify the age of eighteen, or older, as when people have attained *majority status*, and are treated as adults in their contracts and related business transactions.

Since the law presumes that adults have both the ability and the inclination to take advantage of minors, it declares most of their contracts to be *voidable* at their election.

1. The general rule, still followed by a majority of the states, is unchanged since earlier times, and causes adults to contract with minors at their peril.

It is very one-sided and allows a minor to rescind (cancel, disaffirm, avoid, withdraw from) his or her contracts at any time, and in any way whether verbally or in writing, as long as it takes place before reaching the age of eighteen, *plus a reasonable time thereafter.*

A) Adult's unlimited duty of restitution – Requires the competent party to return to the disaffirming party all the money or other value paid, with no deduction or offset for use, wear and tear, depreciation, or needed repairs due to non-intentional damage. The objective is to return the minor back to the pre-contract state.

B) Minor's limited duty of restoration – Requires only that the disaffirming minor return the property received from the adult in its then-existing condition. If the property has been totally destroyed, the minor need not return anything, but can still receive full restitution. If the damage or destruction of the property is caused, however, by the intentional acts of the minor, full reimbursement to the adult for these expenses is required.

2. A smaller number of states view the general rule as archaic in these more sophisticated times. They consider it too harsh on the adult that does not take advantage of the minor and where the terms of the business deal are reasonable and fair. They equate the minor's participation in the business marketplace with an acceptance of its adult rules.

While they allow the minor the same right to disaffirm as the general rule, they attempt to restore the status quo for *both* parties by requiring the minor to reimburse the adult for the reasonable use, wear and tear, and cost of repairs related to the period of the minor's ownership. This is usually deducted from the value originally paid, and the net amount is then returned to the minor.

Susan has just received $5,000 from her wealthy aunt for her seventeenth birthday. She lives in a state where the driving age is sixteen. Susan decides to buy a used car from Miami Motors. She chooses a red Ford because it looks "cool". She inquires of the salesperson, "How much?" and is asked in return, "How much do you have to spend?" When she tells about the money from her aunt, she is informed, "That certainly is an amazing coincidence, because you can drive that Ford out of here today for $5,000 cash." She buys the car. As she drives it off the lot, she turns the radio to her favorite music station, is distracted, and accidentally slams the car into a utility pole. She is not hurt but the car is totaled. She decides to disaffirm the transaction and requests her money back. The car dealer refuses. Who wins this dispute?

Susan prevails, since Florida is one of the majority rule states, Susan satisfied all the legal requirements, and is legally entitled to receive back her full $5,000:

- She was a minor at the time of the transaction.
- She cancelled before reaching age eighteen.
- She didn't intentionally cause the accident.
- She has nothing to return because the damage is total.

Assume that the facts are the same, except Susan drives the car away from the dealership and is on the road for six months. She drives north to Maine, west across the country to Washington, down to southern California, and then back east all the way to Miami. By the end of her trip, the car is dinged, dented, and dusty. She drives back into Miami Motors, declares her disaffirmance, again demands the return of her full $5,000 and the dealer again refuses. Same result – full restitution is required with no deduction for the usage or damage.

However, if this transaction had taken place in one of the "restore status-quo" states, Susan could still disaffirm, but would receive back the difference, if any. Between her $5,000 and the reasonable costs of repair, salvage, and/or replacement in the first example or the reasonable value of depreciation, wear and tear, and damage in the second.

3. The California rule attempts to re-balance the scales in favor of the innocent adult. It will refuse to allow disaffirmance by a minor in local cases where the minor has voluntarily contracted with an adult, there are no circumstances of unfair advantage taken, and now the minor seeks to use the minority doctrine *to victimize the adult.* "Nor should infants be allowed to turn that protective shield into a weapon to wield against fair dealing adults." *41 Indiana Law Journal 829 (1948)*

Walter has a produce trucking business in Bakersfield. His son, Tommy, is a seventeen-year-old high school junior, who keeps pestering him about learning the business. This reaches a point where Walter finally says, "OK, if you want to do this so bad, I'm going to give you the opportunity. I have bought you a truck and let's see how well you operate." To Walter's pleasant surprise, Tommy is a born entrepreneur, and is very successful. One of the contracts he makes is to buy fruit and vegetables at a current fixed price from Merle Farms for future delivery. Due to a crop surplus, that price is way above current market, so Tommy attempts to disaffirm the contract. Merle Farms objects. Who wins this dispute? Merle Farms is successful.

When Tommy placed himself into the world of adult commerce, its rights and duties bound him, and since Merle Farms is an innocent party that acted in good faith, they are protected and Tommy loses his legal right to use the minority doctrine.

4. Legal exceptions to the minor's right to disaffirm are also based upon fairness. The legal pendulum swings back and forth, using fairness doctrines to try to maintain the scales of justice in balance. There are four areas to discuss:

A) Under many state statutes, certain categories of transactions may not be disaffirmed by minors in the interests of public policy:

• Contracts made by a married minor
• Student loans
• Child support and alimony agreements
• Health, disability, and life insurance contracts
• Agreements to provide medical services

B) Ratification of the minor's contract occurs if it is not disaffirmed within the required time. That time, as we have seen under the general rule, is based upon the objective standard of "what is reasonable under the facts of the particular case." But can we be more precise than this when the disaffirmance occurs after age eighteen?

In various factual situations, a reasonable time period for disaffirmance can be the same day as the minor's eighteenth birthday, one day later, one week later, one month later, and in the most bizarre of possible scenarios – one year later:

> Remember our friend Susan, who bought her Ford at age seventeen for $5,000 cash? Suppose she was one day short of her eighteenth birthday when she drove her car off the lot, was distracted by her radio, and crashed into the utility pole, but she didn't walk away from the wreck. Let's assume Susan injured her head and is in a deep coma. Day after day in the hospital, surrounded by family and friends who try to summon her back into the world of consciousness with words of encouragement and love, she slumbers on. This continues for one year and one day. Then, as the family sings happy nineteenth birthday, Susan's eyelids start to flutter, her limbs begin to tremble, and she suddenly opens her eyes, sits up and says, "Mom, Dad, let's call Miami Motors so I can cancel my car purchase."
>
> Under the general rule, and these unique facts, this really was Susan's first reasonable opportunity to disaffirm. She would win the case.

In *In Re: The Score Board, Inc., 238 B.R. 585 (N.J. Dist. 1999)*, the federal bankruptcy court was presented with a dispute involving professional basketball player Kobe Bryant.

While seventeen, and before he achieved superstar status, he had signed a licensing contract with the debtor which obligated him to make personal appearances and sign autographs in exchange for $10,000 base compensation and other benefits. Three days after turning eighteen, he deposited the debtor's check for $10,000 and performed his contractual duties for about a year and a half, until he questioned the validity of the contract on grounds of infancy, and sent a "cease and desist" letter to stop the debtor from using his name, likeness, or other publicity rights.

The debtor went into Chapter 11 bankruptcy, and its valuable assets were ordered sold, including the Kobe Bryant contract. The plaintiff objected to no avail, as the bankruptcy judge ruled that "the parties subsequent conduct demonstrated their acceptance of the contractual obligation by performance, thereby creating an enforceable contract."

The appellate court affirmed. The right to disaffirm a contract is subject to the infant's conduct, which, upon reaching the age of majority, may amount to ratification. Performance of a contract's executory obligations can serve as acceptance even in the absence of any writing. Bryant's acceptance of the $10,000 check and the parties' subsequent performance were more than adequate to satisfy the offer and acceptance requirements of the contract formation.

C) Age misrepresentation by the minor, under traditional rules of law, still allows the minor to disaffirm the contract. Originally, there was not even a duty to restore the innocent adult back to the status quo. This evolved to the current rule of most states, which confers on the minor the right of disaffirmance but requires the corresponding duty of full restoration. Some states take a more extreme position and totally deny the right to cancel, viewing the minor's conduct in not being truthful about his age as a serious breach of duty.

What constitutes misrepresentation of age must also be judged by the objective reasonableness standard. Certain situations clearly violate the rule, such as furnishing false identification documents or lying when asked one's age.

For other verbal exchanges, there are no hard-and-fast yes or no guidelines. Each case is determinative. Let's assume that Rose is seventeen years old and has entered Acme Electronics to buy a laptop computer. The salesperson asks, "You are over eighteen, aren't you?" Rose's replies and their legal effect are the following:

- "How old do you think I am?" No misrepresentation
- "I hear you loud and clear." Probably no misrepresentation
- "Would I be paying you this money if I wasn't?" Misrepresentation

D) Necessaries are those items that are deemed essential to one's existence – food, shelter, clothing, and medical attention.

The minor's age, lifestyle, upbringing, and family background are considered in determining whether or not a particular item is a necessity or a luxury. This determination is determined by the unique facts of each case.

This difference in category is legally significant:

1. If the subject of the transaction is deemed a necessity of life, the minor must pay its fair market value under the related contract doctrine of quasi contract discussed in an earlier chapter. The law encourages adults to provide these necessities to minors and not be impeded by worries about possible disaffirmance of the transaction.

But the minor still receives protection under this law to the detriment of the adult, because most of the time the adult negotiates a contract price that exceeds the current fair market price, representing the profit margin. Even if the transaction is a necessity, the required payment by the minor merely covers the adult's marketplace cost.

2. If however, the subject of the transaction is deemed a luxury, the general rules of the minor's contracts apply and the adult is again at full risk of disaffirmance.

Examples for food: Basic food groups like breads and grains, vegetables, dairy, produce and beef, and the foods created from them are usually necessaries. Basic beverages like milk, tea, coffee, beer, and table wines are the same. The fancier the item or its preparation, and the higher its cost, the more it approaches the luxury category.

- Fried chicken vs. pheasant under glass
- Hamburger vs. filet mignon
- Fresh cherries vs. flaming cherries jubilee
- Fried eggs vs. eggs benedict
- House domestic wine vs. vintage imports

Examples for shelter: Harvey, seventeen, is orphaned when his parents are killed in a plane crash. The family had been living in a rental house whose lease expires in ten days. Harvey leases an apartment for an additional year. This is a necessity for him. If, however, his parents are alive, and while living at home he rents an apartment for romantic liaisons with his girlfriend, or runs away from home during a heated argument and has the right to return, it is a luxury.

Examples for clothing: There are basic articles of apparel, such as shoes, underclothing, shirts, trousers, dresses, blouses, ties, scarves, etc. that sell for reasonable prices and those that are specialty or expensive brands like Gucci, Versace, or Zegna. The former can be necessaries, while the latter are luxuries.

Examples for automobiles: Our friend Harvey needs a job to support himself. He is offered a job at a restaurant making home deliveries that requires him to use his own car. If he buys a reasonable means of transportation, the purchase is treated as a necessity. If, however, he is sold a top-of-the-line new and expensive sports car, the adult suffers the risks of the infancy doctrine.

3. A practical observation about the minority doctrine is appropriate. Businesses have done studies to determine what its real impact is. How often is a claim of rescission or disaffirmance made? How much in marketplace dollars is lost by adults when they are required to make restitution in a cancelled transaction? How much in sales is lost to competitors if a business refuses to do business with minors?

Most adults do not know their legal rights, and are unfamiliar with the doctrine and its intricacies. Most minors are in a similar predicament, with an added factor – even if they know their rights to disaffirm, few minors are skilled enough in communicating with adults and asserting themselves to complete a disaffirmance.

At the same time, the purchasing power of minors is substantial, and they will do business with whoever provides them the least complicated way to complete their transaction. The more roadblocks in their path in the form of identification/verification procedures regarding their age, the less likely they are to spend their money.

Try this practical exercise:

Picture the busiest shopping mall in your city. Every weekend hordes of teenagers descend to shop, their pockets bulging with cash. Notice the types of businesses. Music, books, clothing, electronics, toys, food – the variety is limitless. And most all stores in one end of the mall have direct competitors located at the other end of the mall. If you owned a store in the mall, what procedures, *if any*, would you implement to protect against the legal problems caused by the minority doctrine?

The possible negative financial impact of the minority doctrine increases in direct proportion to the price of the goods or services sold in your store. The more costly the transaction, the more you are at risk. But if you make it a "hassle" to shop in your store, the affluent teens will go to your competition. What should you do?

Many commercial organizations and business consultants suggest the best procedure is to do nothing to impede the underage customers.

This is good advice, up to a certain dollar amount of purchase. If all your items are relatively low ticket, like books, CDs, and DVDs, no problem. But what if you sell the more expensive items?

Various suggestions have been made that age verification procedures should apply to transactions of $300, $500, $1,000, or more. Would you draw a dollar line? If so, where would it be and how would you implement it?

Discussion Exercises

1. Discuss the criteria you would use to evaluate mental impairment defenses to contract enforcement.

2. Discuss any distinctions you would make between intoxication, drugs, injury, disease, or other types of mental impairment.

3. Discuss whether the minority doctrine is still necessary to protect underage contracting parties.

4. Discuss which of the minority doctrine rules you favor, and why.

5. Discuss your view of what sales situations for goods or service should constitute a necessity of life.

Case Exercise 1

Is the Minor Victim or Victimizer?

In *Dodson v. Shrader, 824 S.W.2d 545 (Tenn. 1992)*, the sixteen-year-old plaintiff paid the defendant $4,900 cash for a used truck he intended to use for recreational purposes. No inquiry of his age was made by the defendant, nor did the plaintiff make any age misrepresentations.

Nine months after the purchase, the truck developed mechanical problems, and after a mechanic advised the plaintiff that there appeared to be valve problems, he nevertheless continued to drive it until the engine blew up. He parked the vehicle in front of his parents' home and contacted the defendants to rescind his purchase, tendering the car and requesting a full refund. When they refused, he sued them.

Before the trial court could hear the case, the vehicle, still parked in his front yard, was struck by a hit-and-run driver, further reducing its value to $500 salvage.

The trial court granted rescission based upon the long-standing legal rules of a majority of the states allowing minors to cancel their contracts. The appellate court affirmed this decision.

Analysis

On further appeal to the state's highest court, the decision was reversed, and remanded to determine the proper amounts to be charged to the plaintiff for usage and damage liability, as well as the current fair market value of what was left.

In doing so, Tennessee adopted the so-called "restore status quo" rules of a minority of jurisdictions. These rules hold "that the minor's recovery of the full purchase price is subject to a deduction for the minor's 'use' of the consideration he or she received under the contract, or for the 'depreciation' or 'deterioration' of the consideration in his or her possession."

The court recognized how times have changed from the early days when the courts first created the minority doctrine.

"There is, however, a modern trend among the states, either by judicial action or by statute, in the approach to the problem of balancing the rights of minors against those of innocent merchants."

"This rule is best adapted to modern conditions under which minors are permitted to, and do in fact, transact a great deal of business for themselves, long before they have reached the age of legal majority . . . Further, it does not appear consistent with practice of proper moral influence upon young people, tend to encourage honesty and integrity, or lead them to a good and useful business future, if they are taught that they can make purchases with their own money, for their own benefit, and after paying for them, and using them until they are worn out and destroyed, go back and compel the vendor to return to them what they have paid upon the purchase price."

Defuse Replay

Comparing the conduct of the plaintiff and the defendant in this case unbalanced the scales of justice. The plaintiff was irresponsible and caused or contributed to the damage to the automobile. The defendants fit the legal profile of the "innocent merchant," and under the modern view adopted by the court, should be restored as much as possible to their business position prior to the sale.

The plaintiff could argue that the defendants could have protected themselves by determining his age and then either choosing not to do business with him, or more likely, requiring the joinder of a responsible adult. The traditional rule of minors' contracts makes the adult an insurer of the transaction, absent the presence of the legal exceptions that protect adults who deal with minors.

"This rule is based upon the underlying purpose of the 'infancy doctrine' which is to protect minors from their lack of judgment and from squandering their wealth through improvident contracts with crafty adults who would take advantage of them in the market-place."

The defendants would counter this argument by stating they had no legal obligation to make age inquiry, they were innocent and the minor was the party at fault, and the "restore status quo" rules by which they are benefited supply adequate legal protection for both parties.

"If there has been any fraud or imposition on the part of the seller or if the contract is unfair, or any unfair advantage has been taken of the minor inducing him to make the purchase, then the rule does not apply."

Conclusion

This case illustrates another area of our law that is evolving. Soon the majority of states will, no doubt, recognize some combination of the "status quo" and "benefit" rules in all cases where the adult is not attempting to take advantage of the minor.

The law will have come full cycle, to protecting the adult from the crafty minor, rather than vice-versa.

"At a time when we see young persons between eighteen and twenty-one years of age demanding and assuming more responsibilities in their daily lives; when we see such persons emancipated, married, and raising families . . . when we see such persons engaged in business and acting in almost all other respects as an adult, it seems timely to re-examine the case law pertaining to contractual rights and responsibilities of infants to see if the law as pronounced and applied by the courts should be redefined."

A. Do you agree with the court's final decision?

B. What are the advantages and disadvantages of the traditional rule?

C. What are the advantages and disadvantages of the modern rule?

Is an Employment Agency a Necessity or a Luxury?

In *Gastonia Personnel Corporation v. Rogers, 172 S.E.2d 19 (N.C. 1970)*, the nineteen-year-old defendant (minority under that state's law was twenty-one) was married, and his wife was expecting their first child. His wife was employed as a computer programmer and the couple was living in a rented apartment. He had graduated from high school and was close to obtaining his college degree in applied science, but had to quit school and go to work.

For assistance in obtaining suitable employment, he went to the plaintiff's office and signed a standard contract that provided, "If I accept employment offered me by an employer as a result of a lead from you within twelve (12) months of such lead even though it may not be the position originally discussed with you, I will be obligated to pay you as per the terms of the contract."

Under the contract, the defendant was free to seek employment on his own and was only obligated to the plaintiff for their employment referral. It further provided that he would pay a service charge of $295 if his annual starting salary exceeded $4,680.

The defendant was subsequently employed through the plaintiff's referral at a salary that obligated him to pay them the service charge. He refused to pay on the grounds that the contract was not enforceable against him due to the infancy doctrine. The plaintiff sued him for breach of contract, claiming the liability under the "necessity" rule.

Analysis

The trial court granted the defendant's motion for nonsuit at the conclusion of the plaintiff's evidence, holding that the minor's contract to be a "luxury" and thus fully cancelable. The first appellate court affirmed that decision. Then the North Carolina Supreme Court granted *certiorari* accepting jurisdiction, reversed, and remanded the case for submittal to a jury, because a genuine issue existed as to whether or not the contract in question was a "necessity," and therefore would require the defendant to pay the reasonable value of the services rendered.

"In general, our prior decisions are to the effect that the 'necessaries' of an infant, his wife and child, include only such necessities of life as food, clothing, shelter, medical attention, etc. In our view, the concept of 'necessaries' should be enlarged to include such articles of property and such services as are reasonably necessary to enable the infant to earn the money required to provide the necessities of life for himself and those who are legally dependent upon him."

The majority court took a "change the law if necessary" approach to this problem: "The nature of the common law requires that each time a rule of law is applied it be carefully scrutinized to make sure that the conditions and needs of the times have not so changed as to make further application of it the instrument of injustice."

Defuse Replay

There were two dissenting opinions favoring a "strict construction" of the law approach and questioning the propriety of the majority court expanding the legal definition of "necessaries" to include a contract for services of an employment agency.

"This is not my conception of the nature of the common law, nor is it my understanding of the authority conferred upon the Court by the people of North Carolina. The authority of the people, through their representatives in the State Government, to change the common law when conditions and needs have so changed as to render the law unjust or unwise is clear. They have, however, seen fit to vest this authority in the Legislature and not in us."

There was also a concern that the majority was creating a situation that would be harmful to minors in the future, because adults would be reluctant to deal with them.

"The reason for this rule (limiting 'necessaries' to the traditional categories) is the desire of the law to protect the infant. His liability to pay for necessaries is not imposed so as to protect an adult supplier against a shrewdly scheming infant. It is imposed solely because otherwise the infant, honest or not, might be unable to acquire that which he must have for the support of himself and his dependents."

Conclusion

One of the dissenting opinions also raised the obvious concern, whenever a long-established legal doctrine, like the definition of "necessaries," is broadened, that the courts would face a chaotic situation.

"Inferentially, this modification of the common law rule applies only to 'older minors,' although what age group this embraces is not clear . . . Thus with respect to contracts with minors, it now becomes impossible for the legal profession to advise clients with any degree of certainty. What is a 'necessary' in any given case is largely unknown until the jury speaks. Furthermore, what factual situation a trial judge should non-suit at the close of the evidence and what he should submit to the jury under appropriate instructions becomes a judicial game of chance."

A. Do you agree with the majority or dissenting opinions?

B. Under current business conditions, should the innocent adult face any legal restrictions in dealing with minors?

C. How would you handle the legal problems raised by this statement of one of the dissenting judges: "What was a necessary in 1770 may not be so in 1970, and vice versa."

D. Contrast the *Dodson* and *Gastonia* cases regarding their holdings that protect innocent adults.

B.   LEGALITY OF THE SUBJECT MATTER

"All the things I really like to do are either immoral, illegal, or fattening."

—Alexander Woollcott

Law Overview

Agreements are considered to be *void* and not legally enforceable if they (1) violate a statutory law, or (2) are contrary to public policy.

Unlike the prior section on capacity, where *voidable* contracts allow the affected party to choose whether or not to disaffirm, there is no choice process involved here. Courts usually refuse to enforce these contracts. They take a *hands-off* approach that leaves the parties exactly where it finds them and refuse to assist them in any way, because the parties are *in pari delicto* (having equal fault).

Therefore, in the usual cases of illegality, neither party can sue the other for breach, or recover any partial payments received or past performance rendered. The familiar contractual fairness doctrines of our legal system, such as quasi contract (unjust enrichment) and promissory estoppel (detrimental reliance) do not usually apply.

Non-enforcement language used in these cases often is, "Since the subject matter violates (the law in question), this transaction is declared void, illegal, and unenforceable."

The two categories of contracts contrary to law or public policy are related, because the laws enacted by the legislative bodies of various levels of government are presumably to protect the public and promote its general health, safety, and welfare.

The three major categories of disputes where the enforceability of a contract is in question because it allegedly violates a law are:

1. Licensing laws
2. Lending laws
3. Gambling laws

Often, disputes arise which, while not contrary to specific laws, are nevertheless governed by prevailing codes of conduct, acceptable behavior, and political considerations.

These are all lumped into a general title of the prevailing "public policy". This category often changes with the times we live in, but three major categories of these cases have become well-established law:

1. Non-competition agreements
2. Exculpatory clauses
3. Unconscionable contracts

Agreements that Violate a Law

The rules of acceptable conduct that govern our everyday lives and our transactions in the commercial marketplace are derived to a large extent from statutory sources. Each session of a state legislature yields new laws, changes some existing ones, or eliminates others that are no longer useful.

While most of these laws are relevant and contemporary, there are many laws still on the books in each state that are outmoded and rarely enforced. They serve as humorous footnotes of the past, and can be found on any web search engine under a heading of "crazy laws" or "weird laws." They include the following legal prohibitions:

- Alaska – it is illegal to provide alcoholic beverages to a moose
- California – it is illegal to ride a bicycle in a swimming pool
- Kentucky – it is illegal to carry an ice cream cone in your pocket
- Maine – it is illegal to exit an airplane while it is in flight
- Washington – moving goldfish in bowls may not ride city buses

The typical commercial dispute in this section arises when the subject matter of the contract the parties have entered into is prohibited by a particular law, one of the parties breaches the contract, and then the breaching party raises the violation of that statute as a defense to enforcement of their agreement on the grounds that it is void.

Licensing Laws

1. Revenue-raising laws are primarily for the purpose of collecting money for the local or state government that imposes them. They often are laws that require purchase of an occupational license before one can open a store in a particular location, or laws that require buying seasonal recreational licenses for hunting, fishing, or camping. Anyone who pays the fee is granted the license. But can the failure to obtain such a license by one of the contracting parties be used to invalidate the contract?

Brad leases a store for his new cellular phone business. The city has an occupational licensing law requiring payment of $100 before opening a business.

Before he is able to buy the license, his "grand opening sale" swamps him with customers. One of them, Craig, contracts to buy a complete phone planning system for his company for $1,000. Later, Craig realizes he overpaid, discovers that Brad was unlicensed at the time of the contract, and demands cancellation based upon violation of this licensing law.

Brad can still enforce the contract. Violation of a revenue-raising law does not invalidate contracts made by a non-complying party, because its primary purpose is the income it produces, rather than preventing harm to the public welfare. The only party allowed to complain is the licensing government, which usually imposes a fine for non-compliance.

2. Regulatory laws are the opposite of revenue-raising laws. They are laws that license various professions. Their primary purpose is the protection of the public. There is only an incidental collection of money to signify licensing compliance.

These laws are created so that unscrupulous or unqualified practitioners will not harm the general public. Such regulation is punitive, carrying criminal and civil sanctions. The offending parties can be fined or imprisoned, and they are legally prohibited from enforcing their contracts.

Harry is the top law student in his class, graduating with the highest GPA in the history of the school. He takes the bar examination required by his state and is sure he passed it, but is awaiting the results. Sally has a legal problem and seeks Harry's advice. He tells her not to worry; it is a matter he can solve for her, and "I'll only charge you $300 to handle it." She accepts his offer. He completes the work successfully and sends her a bill. She discovers he is not yet legally licensed as an attorney, and refuses to pay.

Sally wins – Harry cannot enforce his illegal contract and must suffer the consequences. If Sally complains to the bar, he might also be sanctioned for "unauthorized practice of law."

The annual bar dues that Harry must pay to remain licensed raise revenue for the state. But the contracts that Harry makes, even while in default of his duty to keep his annual dues current, are still valid. He runs the risk, however, of having his license to practice law revoked if the dues aren't paid by a certain date.

In *Gutfreund v. Demian, 642 N.Y.S.2d 294 (N.Y.App.Div. 1996)*, the plaintiff was acting as an unlicensed insurance broker who sought to receive from the defendant a percentage of insurance commissions earned for procuring new insurance carriers for the defendant's clients.

New York insurance law prohibited insurers from "paying any money or giving any other thing of value" to unlicensed brokers. The plaintiff sought to circumvent this law by having a friend of his, who was a licensed broker, send the bill for monies due, collect it, and then pay him.

The trial court granted the defendant's motion for summary judgment and the appellate court affirmed. "To allow plaintiff, as an unlicensed broker, to evade the statutory scheme by receiving payments from another broker, rather than directly from an insurance carrier, would violate the legislative intent. A party who contracts to violate a statute enacted for public protection may not sue for a breach thereof."

In *Hydrotech Systems, Ltd. v. Oasis Waterpark, 803 P.2d 370 (Cal. 1991)*, the plaintiff contracted with the defendant to design and construct a large "surfing pool" using their wave equipment. The total contract price was $850,000, and the defendant was allowed to hold back specified portions pending satisfactory completion and operation of the pool. After making full payment for the plaintiff's construction services, the defendant "retained" more than $110,000. The plaintiff sued for breach of contract and the defendant alleged it had no obligation to pay because the plaintiff lacked a California contractor's license.

The California statute provided that an unlicensed contractor could not "bring or maintain any action in a California court to recover compensation for the performance of any act or contract for which a (contractor's) license is required."

The trial court, appellate court, and Supreme Court all rejected the plaintiff's contract claims, which included promissory estoppel claims and allegations that the defendant had fraudulently induced them to perform while knowing they were unlicensed. "The purpose of the licensing law is to protect the public from incompetence and dishonesty in those who provide building and construction services . . . Thus, an unlicensed contractor cannot recover either for the agreed contract price or for the reasonable value of labor and materials . . . It follows that an unlicensed contractor may not circumvent the clear provisions and purposes of (the statute) simply by alleging that when the illegal contract was made, the other party had no intention of performing."

As a practical matter, Oasis could have refused to pay all or any portion of the contracted price and Hydrotech, as an unlicensed contractor, would have had no legal recourse.

Lending Laws

Lenders make money in their loan contracts by charging interest to their borrowers. State usury laws govern the allowable maximum rates of interest charged. A usurious loan is one that charges in excess of the allowable statutory rate.

The sanctions are severe for this unlawful contract in order to protect the public from being victimized and to deter lenders from engaging in such prohibited conduct in the future.

The maximum allowable interest rates and penalties for violation vary from state to state. There are often criminal penalties, as well as civil sanctions, depending upon the severity of the offense. Florida Statute Chapter 687 states:

"All contracts for the payment of interest . . . at a higher rate than 18 percent per annum simple interest are hereby declared usurious." However, if such ". . . obligation exceeds $500,000 in value, then no contract to pay interest thereon is usurious unless the rate of interest exceeds (25 percent per annum)."

Loan sharking is defined to mean extracting interest over 25% per year. Charging interest from 25% to 45% per year is a criminal misdemeanor, and taking interest over 45% per year is a felony.

"Any person, or any agent, officer or other representative of any person, willfully violating the provisions of s. 687.03 shall forfeit the entire interest so charged."

Florida's statute is typical. Other states are more severe, requiring a forfeiture of double the interest paid. A few states are totally punitive – they require the forfeiture of all interest *plus the entire principal*.

Jules desires to borrow $100,000 from Matthew. When Jules is told the only way the loan can be made is at maximum interest, he says, "That's fine. I need the money now and I don't care what interest rate I have to pay." Matthew sees the lack of resistance and charges interest of 2% per month for the two-year loan term. Jules agrees, and later refuses to pay, claiming usury.

Even though it looks like Jules might have induced Matthew into this position with his "no resistance" approach, the law is clear – the usurious lender is penalized to the extent of the laws of the state where the loan took place.

Gambling Laws

Wagering agreements are, as a general rule in all states, void, illegal, and unenforceable. They carry civil and criminal penalties.

We are not talking here about lawful risk transfers in the form of property, casualty, or liability insurance.

And we are also excluding the numerous revenue-raising exceptions such as the Florida pari-mutual industry that allows legal betting on horse racing, dog racing, and the game of Jai-Alai. Within the past ten years there has also been a huge increase nationwide in state-sponsored lotteries, scratch-off games, and related lawful gambling that raises needed revenue for their states of operation.

Gambling law prohibitions try to protect the public and deter offenses by allowing the participants in games of chance to legally refuse to honor their bets. This can impact both winners and losers in a betting dispute.

Ted, a Miami resident, wants to bet on the outcome of the 2003 World Cup soccer final. It is illegal in his home state, but legal under Nevada law in the city of Las Vegas, where his friend Bill lives. Ted asks Bill to bet $500 for him on Brazil to win the game, and says, "Don't worry about the money. When I win, you just get a bank check and send it to me, deducting the bet and your commission of 20%. If I lose, I'll reimburse you." When Ted loses the bet, he refuses to pay back the money that Bill advanced.

Bill is out of luck. The underlying transaction is a private gambling contract, void and unenforceable in both Florida and Nevada. Suppose Bill gets creative and claims this was really a loan agreement? No dice, Bill – again, a court would look to the true subject matter – the purpose of the loan – and reach the same result.

In *Ryno v. Tyra, 752 S.W.2d 148 (Tex. App. 1988)*, Ryno owned a BMW dealership and discussed a sale to Tyra of a 1980 M-1 auto for $125,000. When Tyra hesitated, Ryno suggested a "double-or-nothing coin flip." Tyra agreed, won the coin flip, and Ryno handed Tyra the car keys plus the title to the auto, and provided paper dealer's tags so it could be licensed for street use.

Later, Tyra was convinced by Ryno to loan the car back to the dealership for display at an auto show, and Ryno then took the car and sold it himself to a third party. Tyra sued for conversion of his property, and Ryno defended on the grounds that the original transaction was an illegal gambling contract.

The trial court jury awarded Tyra $125,000 conversion damages and $10,000 punitive damages. On appeal, the decision was affirmed.

"We agree with appellant that his wager with Tyra was unenforceable. The trial court could not have compelled Ryno to honor his wager by delivering the BMW to appellee. However, Ryno did deliver the BMW to appellee and the facts incident to that delivery are sufficient to establish a transfer by gift of the BMW from Ryno to the Tyras."

What about Internet gambling? Its proliferation in the last few years has been dramatic. Some states, like California, specifically prohibit it by statute, while others, like Florida, allow it until there is a legislative prohibition:

"The Internet is the first truly global communications network, utilizing both interstate and international wire communications to link users around the world. Therefore, any effort to regulate use of the Internet is better suited to federal regulations than to patchwork attention by the individual states. Evolving technology appears to be far outstripping the ability of government to regulate gambling activities on the Internet and of law enforcement to enforce such regulations. Thus, resolution of these matters must be addressed at the national, if not international level." *Florida Attorney General Opinion Number: AGO 95-70 (October 18, 1995)*

> Ted goes online to an offshore gambling site and deposits $500 to start making bets on sporting events with Cyberspace Gaming. He is very successful and builds a credit balance of $10,000. He then requests a check for $9,000 from his winnings, and Cyberspace refuses. Can Ted legally enforce this contract?

This collection problem rarely occurs due to the intense competition between Internet gambling sites and their need to maintain credibility. Their advertisements provide a large source of revenue for local media, and they are rated by gaming services as to their payout reliability. However, potential enforcement problems could certainly occur, since they legally do not have to pay these private gambling agreements under U.S. law.

Ted is probably out of luck. Even though millions of dollars are wagered online every day in similar transactions, if the gaming companies decided not to pay, there is nothing he could legally do. Firstly, his site and unpaid winnings are located offshore in a foreign jurisdiction. Secondly, even if a foreign lawsuit was filed and service of process legally made, the court deciding the case would apply the general rule and declare the gaming contract invalid. Thirdly, the time, expense, and stress of such litigation, as well as admitting to the world he had been gambling illegally, would probably cause Ted to walk away from the dispute and learn an expensive lesson. Internet gamblers beware!

The same type of practical collection problems arises in casino gambling. Aside from the non-legal aspects of whether a debtor would risk bodily harm by non-payment to the casino, and the public relations problems that would arise by a casino defaulting in its payment obligations, the same rules of non-enforceability of gambling contracts apply.

In *Metropolitan Creditors Service of Sacramento v. Sadri, 19 Cal. Rptr.2d 646 (Cal. App. 1993)*, the defendant incurred gambling debts of $22,000 at a Lake Tahoe, Nevada, casino.

He wrote the casino two personal checks for the amount, signed two matching promissory notes, received gambling chips in exchange, and lost all playing baccarat. He later stopped payment on the checks, which were drawn on his California bank.

A Nevada statute made credit instruments evidencing gambling debts owed to licensed casinos valid and enforceable. Caesar's Tahoe did not, however, sue the defendant on his debts. Instead they assigned them to the plaintiff for collection, and suit was filed against the defendant in California. The trial court ruled for the defendant under the established rules of non-enforceability of gambling debts in California. The appellate department affirmed and certified the case for transfer to the appellate court, where the judgment was affirmed.

The plaintiff contended that "Under the constitutional doctrine affording full faith and credit to the public acts, records, and judicial proceedings of other states, (the court was) required to enforce Sadri's gambling debts pursuant to the Nevada statute . . . "

The court said, "The pivotal question is whether such enforcement is against the public policy of the State of California . . . California has always had a strong public policy against judicial enforcement of gambling debts, going back virtually to the inception of statehood. This prohibition is deeply rooted in Anglo-American jurisprudence . . . "

The court then distinguished the proliferation of legalized gambling now present in California, and in most states, in the form of pari-mutuel racing, poker clubs, charitable bingo games, and the state lottery, from prohibited "gambling on credit."

"There is a special reason for treating gambling on credit differently from gambling itself. Gambling debts are characteristic of pathological gambling, a mental disorder which is recognized by the American Psychiatric Association and whose prevalence is estimated at 2 to 3 percent of the adult population. Characteristic problems include extensive indebtedness and consequent default on debts and other financial responsibilities, and financially motivated illegal activities to pay for gambling. Having lost his or her cash, the pathological gambler will continue to play on credit, if extended, in an attempt to win back the losses."

The plaintiff could not enforce the debt by a direct lawsuit in California, but the court told him what should he have done instead. "If a licensed owner of a Nevada casino wishes to recover on a check or memorandum of indebtedness given by a California resident under such circumstances, the owner will have to obtain a Nevada state court judgment, which will then be entitled to full faith and credit in California regardless of our public policy."

This legal time bomb exploded in the plaintiff's face because of the failure to employ anticipatory thinking and prevent a losing outcome.

Agreements that Violate Public Policy

Our courts have consistently recognized the importance of invalidating contracts that are adverse to the best interests of the general public and are considered to negatively impact society.

However, the judicial and legislative definitions of morality, acceptable conduct, and the public welfare have changed constantly over the years. So a book that may be declared pornographic in one era (Nathaniel Hawthorne's *The Scarlet Letter* or Henry Miller's *Tropic of Cancer*) may be recognized as a literary masterpiece in another time. The contract to publish that book would be unenforceable in the first instance, and perfectly valid in the latter.

Certain common business situations arise so frequently and are of such importance to commercial transactions that a body of law to govern them has grown from the many disputes that ripened into lawsuits decided by various courts. They involve the three areas of:

- Non-competition agreements
- Release of liability agreements
- Unconscionable agreements

Non-Competition Agreements

One of the oldest public policies we have is our common law principle that contracts in restraint of trade are unlawful because they limit the free competition that is the essence of our commercial marketplace.

Federal and state antitrust laws echo these sentiments. Nevertheless, two major types of contractual restraints on competition are skillfully used in everyday business, and are held to be valid and enforceable so long as they (1) serve to protect a legitimate business interest as part of an otherwise valid contract, (2) are not harmful to the general public, and (3) are reasonable in time restricted, geographic area involved, and scope of activity protected.

Purchase of an Existing Business

The value of a going business is primarily in the customers that shop there and produce its income stream. This is called goodwill. It applies to businesses that sell goods, and especially to those that are service-oriented.

When a prospective buyer is reviewing the flow of income the business currently produces and is projected to produce in the future, a key consideration is guaranteeing that the former owner will not open a competing business and lure away the former clientele.

The price paid for such a business is based upon that income, and a new owner needs transition time for existing customers to feel comfortable with the new management.

Nick has owned and operated the Mykonos restaurant for fifteen years in a South Miami Beach shopping center, growing from one storefront to the entire west side of the center. As that area has grown over the years, so has the restaurant. His customers are treated like family, and the food and service are consistently excellent. Nick decides it is time to retire, advertises the business for sale, and contracts to sell it to Neal and Mike. The purchase price is based upon a multiple of existing sales revenue. The buyers require a clause in the purchase contract that states, "Seller agrees not to enter into a competing restaurant or food service business in Miami Beach for three years." After the sale is completed and one year goes by, Nick is driving his wife crazy being around their house and opens a restaurant called Zorba's in North Miami Beach, twenty miles away from the old location. Neal and Mike claim breach of contract and sue for damages. Nick claims the non-compete is legally unenforceable.

Let's play judge and decide who should win. Firstly, the non-compete was a part of a valid contract to buy the restaurant, and serves a legitimate business purpose to protect the buyer's customer base. If the facts were different, and rather than buying Nick's business, Neal and Mike had an existing location and contracted to pay him not to expand into their area, such a restriction would be viewed as void and against public policy. The difficulty arises in deciding whether the critical terms of the non-compete are *reasonable*.

- Scope – This is a restaurant business that primarily serves Greek specialties. The restraint is therefore reasonable as to, "restaurant or food service." If it had said, "any restaurant serving any type of food," it would have been unduly restrictive, and unenforceable.
- Time – The restraint of three years seems reasonable. It will probably take the buyers at least one year to stabilize the new management situation, and at least another year to have everything running smoothly. If the duration of the non-compete exceeded five years, it probably would be excessive.
- Area – Herein lies the main problem. Miami Beach is a large city, spanning over twenty miles. Did most of Nick's customers come from the immediate area? If so, the restraint on the entire city seems too large.

    If however, the clientele came from all over due to the restaurant's reputation, status, and other factors, the area of non-compete would appear reasonable. The unique facts of each case will govern.

We may also have another practical problem with non-competes that involves the *no resistance* situation we looked at previously in usurious loans. What if Nick was desperate to sell his business, the buyers told him they would require the standard "reasonable" non-compete, and Nick had said, "Do whatever you like. I am burned out and have to get away from this place. I'll sign anything you put in front of me."

Let's suppose the non-compete he signed was for "any business involving food," "for ten years," in "all of southeastern Florida". The restrictive agreement is obviously unreasonably broad, void, and unenforceable as an illegal restraint. If Nick could have induced such an agreement, he could have opened a competing restaurant next door the day after his sale closed and effectively put the new buyers out of business.

Caveat emptor – let the buyer (of an existing business) beware!

In *Thermatool Corp. v. Borzym, 575 N.W.2d 334 (Mich. App. 1998)*, a case of first impression, the *defendant* sold his business to the plaintiff, and as a part of the sale, the buyer agreed to pay him 5% of annual sales above $2.5 million as a royalty "in return for assets such as good will, technological expertise, patents and trade names, as well as the agreement not to compete" for a period of five years after the sale. The seller collected in excess of $1 million royalties.

Before the end of the five-year term, the seller filed a declaratory judgment action claiming the agreement was unreasonable and therefore unenforceable. Thermatool counterclaimed that he had violated the agreement by forming a competing consulting company.

The trial court ruled that the non-competition agreement was reasonable and enforceable, and the buyer moved for a judgment awarding damages for Borzym's alleged breach of the agreement. The court agreed with the buyer, awarded damages of $30,040 and extended the term of the non-compete an additional eighteen months. Borzym appealed, and that aspect of the decision was affirmed:

"In cases where a party has flouted the terms of a non-competition agreement, the court should be able to fashion appropriate equitable relief despite the fact that the parties did not expressly provide for such relief in their agreement."

Thus, the court in effect rewrote the agreement for the parties, a result that is allowed in some states and not permitted in others. The critical factors usually involve the extent to which the seller of the business has breached its competition restriction and the resultant damage suffered by the buyer.

Employment Contracts

When people decide to buy a business they are making an investment. It is a calculated choice rather than a necessity. One's employment, however, is more of an emergency situation. Finding a job provides the financial resources for acquiring food, shelter, and clothing, as well as some luxuries if it succeeds. It pays the bills and allows the employee to survive and hopefully thrive in the world of work.

For this reason, the legal tests for the validity of an employment non-compete are stricter than those imposed by the sale of a business. The allowable scope, term, and area are smaller. People must be allowed to work.

1. The scope of restraint must be specific and not industry-wide.
2. The time of restraint should not exceed the term of the hire.
3. The prohibited territory should be reasonably limited.
4. The employee who leaves voluntarily or is fired with cause is usually not protected.

Many states treat employment non-competes as legally unenforceable, even if voluntarily created, unless the employer can show that the employee has access to or has been entrusted with trade secrets, technological details, and other valuable confidential information that would give a business rival (new employer) a distinct competitive advantage. In California they are totally prohibited by statute.

The more training and expertise possessed by the employee, or the higher up the ladder his position, the more reason exists to enforce his non-compete when he leaves employment. And this is especially true in this era of the Internet, because the downloading of a company's client or customer list and the transmission of trade secrets can take place literally in the blink of an electronic eye.

Courts may also refuse to enforce a violated employment non-compete and allow the breaching party to work for his new employer, but they can issue a permanent injunction to prevent disclosure and use of the trade secrets of the former employer.

Often the employee signs both an agreement not to compete and an agreement to maintain confidentiality of company information. These may also be separate clauses in the non-competition agreement.

Some employers that once limited non-competition covenants only to high-level executives, top salespersons, and research and development personnel are now routinely asking rank-and-file workers to also sign them as a condition of their employment because of the high-tech nature of many businesses and the current level of industrial espionage.

Disputes involving employment non-competes are not easily decided, and the law is in a state of flux.

- California bans employment non-competes. *California Civil Code sec. 16600*
- New York does not favor them, but will enforce them if reasonable and necessary to protect a valid business interest. But there is an important exception called the "employee choice doctrine": "New York courts will enforce a restrictive covenant without regard to its reasonableness if the employee has been afforded the choice between not competing (and thereby preserving his benefits) or competing (and thereby risking forfeiture). *Post v. Merrill Lynch, 397 N.E.2d 358 (N.Y. 1979)*
- A non-compete of a cardiovascular surgeon earning $300,000 who was within eighteen months to become an equal owner of the practice, "for a period of two years following the date of termination," "within a seventy-five-mile radius of Albany, Georgia," was upheld.

  "Keeley was to become an equal owner of CSA within 18 months, which means this covenant was not subject to the strict level of scrutiny accorded normal employment contracts, but to the middle level of reduced scrutiny accorded professional contracts where the parties are considered as having equal bargaining power." *Keeley v. Cardiovascular Surgical Associates, 510 S.E.2d 880 (Ga. App. 1999)*
- A non-compete of the general manager of a company engaged in the manufacture and sale of roofing and insulation products, "within three hundred (300) miles of Allentown, Pennsylvania," "for a period of three (3) years after the date of termination of Employee's employment hereunder," was held to be "both broader than necessary to protect the employer's business interests and unduly oppressive on the former employee." *Insulation Corporation of America v. Brobston, 667 A.2d 729 (Pa. Super. 1995)*

- A non-compete of a vice president employed "at-will," who was in charge of the content of the employer's websites was not upheld. Their business provided online products and services to information technology professionals who managed computer systems.

  The restraint that "prohibits Schlack from working for any person or entity that directly competes with EarthWeb for a period of twelve months after the termination of employment with EarthWeb," was ruled too broad.

  "As a threshold matter, this court finds that the one-year duration of Earth-Web's restrictive covenant is too long given the dynamic nature of this industry, its lack of geographical borders, and Schlack's former cutting-edge position with EarthWeb where his success depended on keeping abreast of daily changes in content on the internet ... When measured against ... the Internet environment, a one-year hiatus from the work force is several generations, if not an eternity." *EarthWeb v. Schlack, 2000 U.S. App. Lexis 11446 (2000)*

In *Gomez v. Texas Aries Medical Society Services, 814 S.W.2d 114 (Tex. App. 1991)*, a temporary injunction to prevent a former employee from competing with the employer's business of assisting hospitals in recovering money for medical services provided to indigent patients was dissolved, even though he was fired for alleged performance problems and as a result of the discovery of his plan to create a competing business.

His duties, which included soliciting hospitals to become customers of his employer, were deemed to be personal services, and under the state law the employer had the burden to prove that the restraint "contains reasonable limitations as to time, geographical area, and scope of activity to be restrained that do not impose a greater restraint than is necessary to protect the goodwill or other business interest of the promisee."

The non-competition covenant barred Gomez "from competing in an 'existing marketing area' and a 'future marketing area of the employer begun during employment.'"

"The covenant not to compete would cover virtually every major metropolitan area in the State of Texas. Non-competition covenants with such a broad geographic scope have generally been held unenforceable, particularly when no evidence establishes that the employee actually worked in all areas covered by the covenant."

In *Varsity Gold, Inc. v. Porzio, 45 P.3d 352 (Az. App. 2002)*, the plaintiff's business was to provide materials for fundraising programs used by schools throughout the United States, through a network of independent sales agents. The sales agents would contract with schools to provide "Gold Cards" entitling the holder to receive discounts at local businesses. The students would sell the cards to consumers, and the schools would keep a portion of the sales proceeds.

The defendant was hired on a month-to-month basis, and signed a "Sales Representative Agreement" that prohibited him "for a period of three years after termination of the agreement, from competing with Varsity in the State of Pennsylvania or any contiguous state." It also forbade him to solicit Varsity's customers or divert its business during the stated term.

The agreement further provided that "The court may reform the geographic area and time restrictions if it finds them to be unreasonable and unenforceable."

The defendant violated the terms of the agreement, and the plaintiff sued for breach of the covenant not to compete, an injunction, and money damages.

The trial court ruled that the covenant was unenforceable as written because the geographic area was too broad and the time constraint too lengthy. It then modified the restrictions, per the reformation clause, deciding "The covenant not to compete could be enforced in the south Pittsburgh area (where Porzio had worked) for a period of one year."

The appellate court reversed. "While Arizona courts may 'blue pencil' a restrictive covenant by eliminating grammatically severable, unreasonable terms, the court cannot add provisions or rewrite them." The attempted strategy of the plaintiffs in trying to cover themselves with a "safe-harbor" clause to allow judicial rewriting of an objectionable restriction failed. They should have been more careful in limiting the reach of their non-compete to only protect their legitimate business interests.

You try to be the judge on this one:

> Norman is hired by Kentucky Fried Chicken (KFC) as executive vice president in charge of their Atlanta, Georgia, regional office for a term of three years at an annual salary of $150,000. One of the conditions of his employment was his signing an agreement "not to enter into a competing business for five years anywhere in the southeastern United States." Two years later, Norman resigns and goes to work for Popeye's Chicken in Jacksonville, Florida, in a similar position for a comparable salary. KFC sues for breach of the non-compete agreement. Norman defends, claiming it is unreasonably broad and unenforceable.
>
> Certainly KFC's "secret seasonings" that make its taste unique are a valuable trade secret that requires protection. As an executive, Norman would have more access to such confidential information than a lower-level employee. Popeye's is in a related food enterprise and fits the definition of "a competing business."
>
> The time of the restraint of five years exceeds the three-year hire, and would therefore appear to be invalid, but this might be offset by the executive position and compensation received.
>
> The "southeastern United States" restriction appears on its face to be too broad. However, when considering the fact that KFC is a worldwide company, and both Atlanta and Jacksonville are within the restriction, this may not be the case.

Exculpatory Clauses

To exculpate is "to free from blame, liability, or responsibility." As our lives have become more complex and business relationships more litigious, it is almost essential for businesses to protect themselves against liability.

The use of an exculpatory clause with its customary language of *not responsible for loss or damage* covers the entire business spectrum, from damaged autos in parking garages and injured spectators at sporting events to liability claims for accidents in hazardous outdoor recreational activities.

Originally, such clauses were an absolute bar to recovery by the injured party under the legal theory of *volenti non fit injuria* – he who consents cannot be injured. This is the basis for the legal defense known as "assumption of the risk."

As our laws and their judicial interpretation turned more toward protecting the public, the blanket protection of these release clauses has changed to one that denies or allows enforcement based upon the following scenarios:

- A minority of states allow them to release ordinary negligence.
- A majority of states refuse to allow release of any negligent acts.
- Most states allow release of liability in athletic or sporting events for ordinary negligence, but not gross negligence.
- All states refuse to allow release of liability for intentional torts, willful misconduct, fraud, or acts of gross negligence.

Lois decides to go bungee jumping off the 200-foot Capilano Bridge in Vancouver, British Columbia. In order to participate, she is required to sign a form that states, "The undersigned agrees to release the operator from any and all liability for any and all claim, loss or damage suffered by me resulting from this activity." The employee strapping her into the elastic harness miscalculates her size and weight, and she hits her head on the riverbank at the bottom extension of her jump. She sues for damages, and the release form is offered as a defense to liability.

Most states would uphold the exculpatory agreement and rule in favor of the operator, if bungee jumping were considered an athletic or sporting event. Although the operator's breach of care caused the loss, the act in question was still within the bounds of ordinary or simple negligence.

If however, the injuries to Lois were caused by the bungee cord breaking, this would be gross negligence and invalidate the protection of the release.

Courts will also usually require that the exculpatory clause be clearly written and conspicuously placed in the contract, so that a "reasonable" person would be aware of its liability limitations. Also, if the party seeking to enforce the limitation has abused superior bargaining power and forced the limitation on the agreeing party, non-enforcement usually results.

California has gone the farthest in refusing to enforce exculpatory clauses:

- A residential tenant who tripped on a rock in a common stairway in his apartment building and was injured is not bound by a blanket exculpatory clause in his lease. The case was not decided on a theory of negligence, but rather a "public interest" ruling that "exculpatory clauses in residential leases violate public policy." *Henrioulle v. Marin Ventures, 573 P.2d 465 (Cal. 1978)*
- A hospital admission form that released liability for future negligence was invalid as an "exculpatory clause affecting the public interest." *Tunkl v. Regents of University of California, 383 P.2d 441 (Cal. 1963)*

- An auto repair order form contained the clause in bold letters: "Not responsible for loss or damage to cars or articles left in cars in case of fire, theft or any other cause beyond our control," which the court refused to enforce. A car owner's Porsche brought to his dealership for repair was stolen while parked at the repair garage. "The modern citizen lives – and all too frequently dies – by the automobile . . . An out-of-repair automobile is an unreliable means of transportation . . . It follows that clauses which exculpate repair firms for ordinary negligence in handling and securing vehicles under repair are invalid as contrary to public policy." *Gardner v. Downtown Porsche Audi, 180 Cal. App. 3d 713 (Cal. App. 1986)*

Other states are not so stringent, and will enforce exculpatory clauses in appropriate cases:

- A seventeen–year-old skydiver signed a covenant not to sue which included an exemption from liability that stated: "Whether such loss, damage, or injury results from the negligence of the Corporation, its officers, agents, servants, employees, or lessors or from some other cause," who was injured in an airplane crash due to alleged negligence, was not allowed to recover due to its specific terms. *Jones v. Dressel, 623 P.2d 370 (Colo. 1981)*
- ADT Security provided a fire alarm monitoring system for the plaintiff's plant, and extensive damage resulted due to alleged defects in the system. The contract, which specifically limited the liability of ADT to a maximum of $1,000, was upheld. "Both parties had equal bargaining power. Chicago Steel declined the opportunity to pay for an allocation of additional liability to the fire alarm service." *Chicago Steel Rule and Die Fabricators Co. v. ADT Security Systems, Inc., 763 N.E.2d 839 (Ill. App. 2002)*
- A health and fitness facility had members sign a standard exculpatory clause which included a negligence release. The plaintiff was injured while doing a series of tests to evaluate her physical condition. Summary judgment was granted in favor of the defendant based on the release clause. *Seigneur v. National Fitness Institute, Inc., 752 A.2d 631 (Md. App. 2000)*

Unconscionable Contracts

We previously discussed contracts that might "shock the conscience of the court" when we talked about the garage sale cases that raised the legal issue of whether or not the dollar equivalent amount of consideration paid was adequate. The key factor was if the buyer took unfair advantage of the seller. We were talking about exploitation.

We now revisit this concept. It is not to be used as a legal excuse for one party's bad bargain. Rather it is a balancing principle to prevent extreme unfairness or severe injustice.

If the following elements are proven, a contract will be declared void, illegal, and unenforceable on grounds of unconscionability:

1. There is a great disparity in the bargaining power between the parties.

2. The stronger party misuses its advantage to oppress the weaker party through extremely unfair contract terms.
3. The weaker party has no reasonable alternative.

In *Williams v. Walker-Thomas Furniture Company, 350 F.2d 445 (D.C. Dist. 1965)*, the plaintiff signed a contract requiring installment payments for the purchase of residential furniture where title and foreclosure remedies would be retained by the seller until the total of all payments for all items, even though individual items were paid in full. In refusing to enforce the contract, the court said, "Unconscionability has generally been recognized to include an absence of meaningful choice on the part of one of the parties together with contract terms which are unreasonably favorable to the other party.

"In many cases, the meaningfulness of the choice is negated by a gross inequality of bargaining power. The manner in which the contract was entered is also relevant to this consideration. Did each party to the contract, considering his obvious education or lack of it, have a reasonable opportunity to understand the terms of the contract, or were the important terms hidden in a maze of fine print and minimized by deceptive sales practices."

The following example is based on the case of *John Deere Leasing Company v. Blubaugh, 636 F. Supp. 1569 (D. Kan. 1986)*:

Jed is a wheat farmer with limited formal education. His crop is in the ground when his Caterpillar brand tractor dies. He needs a new one at once for his harvest. He goes to his local dealer and is presented a rental contract for a new tractor. He is told to "take it or leave it," with no modifications allowed.

It is printed on lightweight paper in complex, legalistic language, and the reverse has fine print which provides that if he defaults in payment, Caterpillar has the right to repossess the tractor, sell it, keep the sales proceeds, and still be able to recover from him a complex formula of termination damages. When he defaults after paying two annual payments that total $31,000, they seize the tractor, re-sell it for $42,000, and then sue him for an additional $12,000. He defends on the grounds that the default clauses were unconscionable.

Jed wins this case. Notice the telling factors that individually and collectively add up to the blatant unfairness of the lessor in exploiting their lessee. As we mark them off, one by one, we feel that Caterpillar should not be allowed to do this. It just isn't right. Public policy requires non-enforcement of the offending clauses.

These types of agreements are often called *contracts of adhesion*. They are preprinted on standardized forms that require the weaker party to "adhere" to their terms on a "take it or leave it" basis with no opportunity to negotiate, and the circumstances are such that they appear to be trapped with no reasonable way out of their predicament.

Parties who have made a poor business deal are often tempted to try to find a legal doctrine that will extricate them from their self-created problems. Unconscionability is often alleged in these commercial contract cases, but is rarely upheld by the courts unless the conduct complained of is extreme, way beyond the line of reasonable business conduct.

In *Iwen v. U.S. West Direct, 977 P.2d 989 (Mont. 1999)*, the plaintiff signed an order with the defendant for advertising in the telephone yellow pages. The order form prepared by the defendant was a standard preprinted form that read as follows:

"Any controversy or claim arising out of or relating to this Agreement, or breach thereof, *other than an action (at law) by Publisher for the collection of the amounts due under this Agreement, (emphasis added)* shall be settled by final, binding arbitration in accordance with the Commercial Arbitration Rules of the American Arbitration Association . . . "

When the directory was published the plaintiff noticed his phone number was incomplete and his address was missing. He advised the defendant he would not pay the bill until the parties had resolved the negligent errors. The defendant received a disconnect notice, and after several unsuccessful attempts to resolve the matter, he filed suit for damages. The defendant moved to stay litigation and compel arbitration per the clause in the advertising order.

The trial court ruled the arbitration provision valid and enforceable. The plaintiff appealed and the court reversed, holding "that the arbitration provision at issue in this case is unconscionable."

"Drafted as such, the weaker bargaining party has no choice but to settle all claims arising out of the contract through final and binding arbitration, whereas the more powerful bargaining party and drafter has the unilateral right to settle a dispute for collection of fees pursuant to the agreement in a court of law."

The legal claim of "unconscionability" also arises in situations where one party has signed a surgical medical release which either seeks to disclaim liability for malpractice or, more commonly, requires the patient to arbitrate a dispute before a medical board rather than litigate for personal injuries in a court of law.

In *Broemmer v. Abortion Services of Phoenix, Ltd., 840 P.2d 1013 (Az. 1992)*, the plaintiff was a twenty-one-year-old, unmarried high school graduate who was sixteen weeks pregnant, with a minimal $100 a week job and no medical benefits. The father-to-be insisted she have an abortion, her parents insisted she not have an abortion, and she was conflicted, confused, and emotionally upset.

The plaintiff's mother made an appointment with the defendant's clinic, and upon arrival the plaintiff was asked to complete a series of preprinted forms, one of which was an agreement to arbitrate, which stated, "Any dispute arising between the Parties as a result of the fees and/or services" would be settled by binding arbitration and "any arbitrators appointed by the AAA (American Arbitration Association) shall be licensed medical doctors who specialize in obstetrics/gynecology."

She completed the forms in five minutes without reading them, and the clinic staff made no attempt to explain them before or after she signed, nor was she provided copies. Her pregnancy termination procedure was scheduled the following morning, and unfortunately she suffered a punctured uterus, requiring separate medical treatment. She filed a malpractice complaint in a court of law and the defendant moved to dismiss based upon the agreement to arbitrate.

The trial court ruled for the defendant, holding that although the arbitration agreement was a contract of adhesion, it was not unconscionable and therefore was enforceable against the plaintiff. The appellate court affirmed, but the Arizona Supreme Court reversed.

"An adhesion contract is typically a standardized form offered to consumers of goods and services on a 'take it or leave it' basis without affording the consumer a realistic opportunity to bargain and under such conditions that the consumer cannot obtain the desired product or services except by acquiescing in the form contract.

"To determine whether this contract of adhesion is enforceable, we look to two factors: the reasonable expectations of the adhering party and whether the contract is unconscionable.

"Plaintiff was under a great deal of emotional stress, had only a high school education, was not experienced in commercial matters, and is still not sure 'what arbitration is.' "

Some text writers have suggested that all surgical medical releases are, by definition and surrounding circumstance, legally unconscionable. What do you think? Should distinctions be made based upon the severity of the patient's injury or illness and/or the medical risks of the contemplated procedure? What about cosmetic surgery? It is purely voluntary but can sometimes be very dangerous.

Special Situations

1. What if all or part of the purchase price is paid in an illegal contract? If the contract is not enforceable, does the paying party get his money or property back?

Perry buys a house in Coconut Grove that is surrounded by plants, trees, and all types of undergrowth. While exploring his property he notices that a large area of apparent weeds at the rear of his land is really marijuana. He is welcomed to the neighborhood by Duane, who makes him this business proposition: "Howdy, dude, you've got a cash crop growing in your back yard. I'll pay you $10,000 to harvest it tomorrow night at midnight. Here is $5,000 as a good faith deposit." Perry agrees and takes the money. When Duane returns, Perry refuses to allow him on the property and also refuses to return the money. Duane sues for breach of contract and Perry defends based on illegality.

The contract here is obviously void. But should Perry be allowed to profit? Under the general rule of illegal contracts, he would, because courts do not interfere with such contracts other than to refuse to enforce them. Should the fact that Perry did not grow the marijuana himself be a factor in his favor? What if he didn't even know the plant was growing on his property at the time Duane made his offer? Since Duane initiated the contract, should he suffer the greater loss? What if Duane's offer included the purchase of Perry's car for a fair price?

Notice how changing a fact or two in this dispute could change the persuasive arguments to be made.

When we talked about the types of contracts in an earlier chapter, we discussed the fairness concepts of quasi contract (unjust enrichment) and promissory estoppel (detrimental reliance). This isn't usually the case if the court adopts its "hands-off" policy in illegality cases and leaves the parties where it found them.

- The plaintiff, as a knowing and willing participant in a promotional stocks and bonds pyramid scheme of the defendant, was prohibited by New York law, could not recover any part of his investment. "It is the settled law of this State (and probably of every other State) that a party to an illegal contract cannot ask a court of law to help him carry out his illegal object. For no court should be required to serve as paymaster of the wages of crime, or referee between thieves." *Ford v. Henry, 598 N.Y.S.2d 660 (N.Y. App. 1993)*
- Employment contracts that guaranteed county employees salary merit increases violated the state's "pay as you go" law, and "any reliance on promises made by the county was unreasonable and could not form the basis for promissory estoppel." *Weese, et al v. Davis County Commission, 834 P.2d 1 (Utah 1992)*

While most states strictly enforce the illegality doctrine and refuse to assist either party to such a transaction, others are more lenient, and have created exceptions to the general rule in these situations:

a) The recovering party was less at fault than the other.
b) The recovering party was excusably ignorant of the governing law.
c) The illegal act was never performed.
d) The illegal act can be separated from the lawful activity.

2. What if illegality occurs or is discovered after the contract is created? In such a case, the parties have entered into a valid and enforceable agreement. The subsequent illegality prevents its enforcement and discharges the parties, but they should be restored to their prior status quo position or otherwise made whole.

In *Duncan v. Kasim, 2002 WL 125686 (Fla. App. 2002)*, the plaintiff contracted to run a bar owned by the defendant, made substantial improvements to the property, and then could no longer perform because she had failed to reveal she was a convicted felon, contrary to the liquor licensing law. She sued for unjust enrichment due to the value of the improvements she had made.

The trial court dismissed her case and she appealed. The appellate court reversed, recognizing that her contract to manage the bar was illegal, but this fact did not preclude her legal action.

"The fact that the contract is illegal does not mean that Kasim has the right to keep the property Duncan placed in the bar when she was in possession of it. Anything she brought to the premises she can remove. She also has the right to receive the value of fixtures not removable from the premises that enhance its value."

3. What if the parties have contractually agreed in advance as to the dollar amount of damages payable in the event of a breach? This is known as a *liquidated damages clause*. It is commonly used in construction agreements to prioritize the project and give the builder an added liability incentive to complete on time.

Similar to our discussion of non-competes, these damage agreements are a skillful way to transact one's business when it may be difficult to determine actual damages, and they are legally valid so long as the amount of the default damages are "reasonable." This has been interpreted to mean they must bear some proportionate relationship to the actual damages that would be suffered by the customer if the builder did not perform within the required time.

However, if the amount of agreed damages is unreasonably high, based on the facts of the case, they are deemed to be a *penalty*, and are void, illegal, and unenforceable on public policy grounds.

Here is another true story:

Martin is a young law school student in the 1960s. He and his wife contract with Southwest Construction (SC) to construct their new house for a total price of $24,000. (Yes, that's what it cost way back then.) Martin, whose wife is expecting their first child, discusses with the builder his desire to specify a date of completion and also to set a cost for each day of delay.

The builder approves the completion date, laughs, and says, "No problem, kid, put in any dollar amount you like; we always finish our jobs on time." Martin notices no resistance from the builder and puts the following clause in the contract: "SC agrees to complete this job in all respects, including issuance of certificate of occupancy by Dade County, no later than 7/1/61, and for every day SC is late in said completion it shall pay liquidated damages of $1,000 per day." SC completes ten days late. Martin wants to deduct $10,000 from his agreed purchase price.

Sorry, Martin – this clause is really a penalty because it is unreasonably high. Suppose the cost of renting a similar house in those days was $300 per month, and suppose there would be additional expenses to re-route furniture purchases, duplicate moving costs, and other damages directly caused by the delay of $500. The maximum allowable per day charge should have been $100. Martin was not as smart as he thought. (By the way, his wife never let him hear the end of it, either.)

In *Luminous Neon, Inc. v. Parscale, 836 P.2d 1201(Kan. App. 1992)*, the defendant leased outdoor advertising signs from the plaintiff which were custom-designed for her needs. The lease contained a liquidated damages clause that required her, in the event of a breach, to pay damages equal to 80% of the remaining payments due. She had originally been offered the signs for $5,600 on a purchase basis but declined. This computation was based upon the plaintiff's expenses incurred in manufacturing, installing, and financing the signs, plus their profit.

Later, street construction by the City of Topeka adversely affected the plaintiff's business and she was forced to close, at a time when forty-one monthly payments remained due under the lease, resulting in a computation of liquidated damages due of $6,951.04. The defendant refused to pay, so the plaintiff sued to collect it.

The trial court granted the plaintiff's motion for summary judgment and the appellate court affirmed, finding that there was a reasonable relationship between the expenses of the plaintiff and the amount charged the defendant.

"The contention that only the original sale price of the signs constitutes reasonable damages is not persuasive. There are advantages to be weighed when one considers leasing rather than purchasing an item . . . The damage clause of the lease was not a penalty."

The following case is controversial, since the computation of liquidated damages far exceeded actual damages and resulted in the recipient party receiving an apparent monetary windfall. What do you think?

California and Hawaiian Sugar Co. v. Sun Ship, Inc., 794 F.2d 1433 (9th Cir. 1986) involved a contract given by the plaintiff to the defendant to build for it a custom "integrated tug barge" for the shipping of the raw sugar it harvested from the islands during the six-month sugar season from Hawaii to its California refinery.

The contract price was $25,405,000, and provided that, "If 'Delivery of the Vessel' was not made on the 'Delivery Date' of June 30, 1981, Sun would pay C and H 'as per-day liquidated damages, and not as a penalty' $17,000 per day as a 'reasonable measure of damages.' "

Sun did not complete the vessel until March 16, 1982, thus triggering damages under the contract clause of $4,413,000. But during the 1981 season the plaintiff was able to arrange for purchasing another vessel for shipping the sugar crop, so that its actual damages were only $368,000.

C and H sued to collect the liquidated damages. Sun claimed they were a penalty "unreasonably disproportionate to the actual damages," and not due. The trial court upheld the contract clause and the appellate court affirmed:

"The anticipated damages were what might be expected if C and H could not transport the Hawaiian sugar crop at the height of the season. The damages were clearly before both parties . . .

"Given the anticipated impact on C and H's raw sugar and on C and H's ability to meet the demands of its grocery and industrial customers if the sugar could not be transported, liquidated damages of $17,000 a day were completely reasonable.

"Contracts are contracts because they contain enforceable promises, and absent some overriding public policy, those promises are to be enforced. 'Where each of the parties is content to take the risk of its turning out in a particular way' why should one be released from the contract, if there were no misrepresentations or other want of fair dealing? Promising to pay damages of a fixed amount, the parties normally have a much better sense of what damages can occur. Courts must be reluctant to override their judgment."

Strategic Planning

Notice that agreements that restrain trade, limit liability, require adherence to their terms, or specify damages in advance are all legally enforceable IF they are drawn and utilized properly. However, public policy considerations are increasingly used to question their enforcement, and the laws continually bend to assist the consumer or perceived weaker party in any bargain.

An improperly drafted agreement that goes beyond the bounds of reasonableness may be effective in intimidating the other party from violating it or seeking legal recourse to invalidate it. Most parties don't know their legal rights, and the express terms of these agreements bar any attack upon them.

However, more and more persons are questioning these agreements notwithstanding their terms, and the best strategy is to anticipate that they will be legally attacked and then prepare them in such a way that they are enforceable.

What should the drafting party do to help withstand a claim that the agreement or clause is "unreasonably restrictive?"

1. Non-competition agreements – Determine what at first appears to be the most conservative time, area, and scope of restraint, and then limit these areas even further to try and assure validity. There must be legitimate business concerns for reasonably worded restrictions, not arbitrary categories inflated by the other party's lack of resistance. In fact, that willingness to sign whatever the document says, "because I must have the job" or "because I have to sell the business," is a sure sign that perhaps the employer or purchaser is being set up for failure.

2. Exculpatory clauses – Recognize that one's own negligence or the negligence of one's agents cannot legally be waived.

Instead of wording that obviously overreaches, such as releasing "any and all acts of our negligence," the limitation should be directed more toward a dollar amount of recovery if negligence is proven.

3. Unconscionable contracts – Continue to use take-it-or-leave-it contracts of adhesion on preprinted forms, but make sure that the restrictive language is in bold type. There should also be an opportunity offered to the bound party both before and after signing for a full and complete explanation of the legal and practical effect of the document. Their clear choice then is to knowingly sign it or refuse the services or goods offered.

4. Liquidated damages – The same constraints of non-competition restrictions apply here. Don't be induced by non-resistance or enthusiastic acceptance to provide for payment of damages that will exceed actual loss. These clauses are not like punitive damages, and should be limited to the compensatory and consequential aspects of the loss suffered by delays in completion.

Discussion Exercises

1. Discuss what usury sanctions you think appropriate.

2. Discuss the advantages vs. disadvantages of the forms of legalized gambling that are available in your state.

3. Discuss the enforceability guidelines you would create for non-competes.

4. Discuss whether the California restrictions on use of exculpatory clauses should be followed or modified.

5. Discuss any other public policy arguments that should render contracts unenforceable.

Case Exercise 3

Future Employment Restricted without a Non-Competition Contract

In *Doubleclick, Inc. v. Henderson, Dickey and Alliance Interactive Networks, 1997 N.Y. Misc. LEXIS 577 (N.Y. 1997)*, Henderson was hired to an executive position in the plaintiff's business of selling Internet advertising through a network of websites. It agreed with the owners of the sites to sell advertising space and solicited advertisers to participate in its network. Customers would click on posted advertising banner links and learn about the advertiser's products.

When Henderson was hired as an executive to hire, train, and manage the plaintiff's sales force, he became their highest paid employee.

Like other executives, including Dickey, the person who recruited him, he signed a confidentiality agreement, but unlike the others who had signed one-year non-competes, he signed no such agreement.

After about one year, Henderson and Dickey were dissatisfied with the direction of the plaintiff, resolved to start their own company (Alliance), and began to draft a business plan and talk to some fellow employees about going with them. When the company president received a tip, he confronted them, and then the plaintiff brought suit to enjoin them from launching a new company or taking employment with a competitor, claiming (1) misappropriation of trade secrets, (2) breach of duty of loyalty, and (3) unfair competition.

Analysis

The court ruled against the defendants and granted injunctive relief to the plaintiff which was narrower than originally sought.

The plaintiff's initial injunction request was to "enjoin defendants for a period of at least twelve months from launching a competitive business or from working for a direct competitor of Doubleclick."

The court reviewed all the evidence and balanced the equities in favor of the plaintiff, finding that the defendants:

1. used Doubleclick's proprietary information to prepare for the launch of alliance and to position it to compete with Doubleclick,

2. worked on their plans for their new company during working hours at Doubleclick and used resources given to them by Doubleclick to do so, and

3. sought customers and financing for Alliance without regard to their duties to their current employer.

But the court felt the one-year time period was too long "given the speed with which the Internet advertising industry apparently changes," and ruled that:

"Defendants are enjoined, for a period of six months from the date of this opinion, from launching any company, or taking employment with any company, which competes with Doubleclick, where defendant's job description(s) or functions at said company or companies include providing any advice or information concerning any aspect of advertising on the Internet."

Defuse Replay

The decision can be attacked on two legal grounds:

1. The injunction seems to be a prohibited industry-wide restraint. Doubleclick's business is Internet advertising, the defendant's business tasks involved Internet advertising, and they are both prohibited from "launching any company or taking employment with any company" involving "any aspect of advertising on the Internet." What other field of work is available to them?

2. Dickey signed a non-competition agreement. It appears to be an unreasonable restraint upon him because it is overly broad as to scope, and thus unenforceable. As to Henderson, the argument is much stronger because *he never signed a non-competition agreement*. The court attempts to reform the confidentiality agreements signed by the defendants so that the usual prohibitions against disclosure of trade secrets while working for the new employer are broadened into a restraint against working at all for the next six months.

Conclusion

This case has had far-reaching implications in the everyday business world because it initiated a trend toward a more common usage of non-competition restraints among all workers, whether entry-level, midlevel, or executive/managerial.

Today's predominantly high-tech marketplace is an atmosphere of intense competition for the consumer dollar, predatory hiring practices to lure valuable employees and their intimate knowledge of the internal workings of competitors, and increasingly sophisticated techniques of industrial espionage.

But media reports indicate that non-competes are being required in many non-tech businesses, running the gamut from medicine, law, architecture, securities, and insurance to tattoo parlors, body-piercing shops, and your friendly neighborhood Starbucks restaurant. *Be loyal or see you in court, employers warn workers. U.S. News & World Report, December 18, 2000.*

Management strategy is to require non-competes from most all employees, even clerical staff. The restraints are drafted as broadly as possible and are legally unenforceable on their face. However, few employees faced with such restraints have the resources or inclination to challenge them. Strict compliance with the non-compete is the usual course of employee conduct.

They often obey these unreasonable contracts out of ignorance or the intimidation presented by this perceived threat to their jobs.

Even successful attacks may result in the plaintiff being perceived as a "litigious" person and cost them new job opportunities. The actual court proceedings are also so draining financially and emotionally that few employees are willing to file suit. The message to other employees is don't rock the boat.

And the impact of *Doubleclick* is to raise the stakes even higher, since employees whose conduct threatens company trade secrets are legally bound by non-competition restraints implied by the court, without the necessity of them signing a specific non-competition agreement.

C.   LEGAL CONSENT TO THE TRANSACTION

"It is true that you may fool all the people some of the time; You can even fool some of the people all the time; but You can't fool all of the people all the time."

—Abraham Lincoln

Law Overview

In the types of commercial disputes we have previously examined, one of the parties to the alleged contract seeks to avoid its enforcement by claiming that:

- no legal agreement was made because of lack of a legal offer or lack of a legal acceptance, or
- the agreement is not legally enforceable due to a failure of consideration, or
- even though the required agreement between the parties was reached and is supported by consideration, it is nevertheless legally unenforceable due to incapacity (voidable) or illegality (void).

Now we examine a new area of business disputes, where complaining parties agree that they made an otherwise legally enforceable agreement and do not claim incapacity or illegality, but still want to be legally excused from having to perform because of a claim that their consent given to the contract was not genuine.

They claim that there was a lack of voluntary and knowing assent due to the particular factual circumstances, and therefore the contract made should be legally cancelled.

Our commercial marketplace requires that contracting parties be able to enforce their contracts. But if that contract was obtained by threat or force or mistake or deception it should not, in fairness, be allowed to stand. The victimized party should be legally allowed to raise such unfair circumstances as a legal defense to enforcement.

This assumes that the offending party will receive an unfair benefit in the form of a more advantageous business deal than would have been otherwise available through an arms-length transaction. So equitable principles demand that the scales of justice be re-balanced to prevent one party from taking unfair advantage of the other.

Typically, the plaintiff sues for breach of the contract and the defendant seeks to have it cancelled and demands rescission based upon one of the following defenses:

1. Duress – coercion
2. Undue influence – persuasion
3. Mistake – error
4. Fraud – trickery

If rescission of the contract is granted, the reciprocal duties of restitution and restoration that we previously examined in the chapters on capacity and illegality apply. The party who is allowed to cancel is entitled to receive back anything of value previously given as consideration, but must correspondingly return anything received. This restores the parties to the status quo. If there is an imbalance in the valuations upon completing these rights and duties, courts will typically assess damages to equalize.

The complaining party has a further duty to act promptly. As soon as the offending circumstances occur, the decision must be made and announced in a clear and convincing way. Any unreasonable delay or attempt to retain the benefits of the contract while avoiding its burdens will be interpreted as a "ratification" of the contract and require its full enforcement.

Duress

Duress is wrongful coercion. One of the parties commits an unlawful act by which the other party is forced to enter into the contract against his will.

If this occurs, that contract is voidable at the option of the victimized party. Typical testimony in such a dispute is, "I was forced to sign the contract. I had no choice. He held a gun to my head, literally or figuratively."

The duress is actual force or, more commonly, the threat of force, and the victim is placed in a "no way out" situation, with no reasonable alternative other than agreeing to the proposed contract.

In these types of disputes, courts determine whether or not the plaintiff will prevail using the personal "subjective" standard. The fact that the conduct in question would or would not be actionable coercion to the hypothetical reasonable person of our law's "objective" standard is not applicable. The particular plaintiff is evaluated, with his existing background, station in life, level of experience, and unique personal characteristics, to ascertain if he may be excused from the agreement in question on grounds that it was procured by duress.

Clint, a six-foot-tall bodybuilder, wants to buy mild-mannered Gene's watch, and offers $100. Gene says, "I really am not interested in selling; sorry." Clint says in a menacing tone, "People usually don't refuse me, friend. My final offer is $150, and here is a bill of sale for you to sign." Again Gene says no deal. Then Clint grabs one of Gene's arms, twists it behind him, pulls the watch off his wrist, and says, "Sign the paper or I'll break your arm." Gene signs and then promptly sues to rescind the sale and recover his property.

This is a case of actual physical duress, a clear violation of the requirement of voluntary consent to the contract, and Gene would win. The contract here would be void because it was obtained illegally. Clint committed an offense of extortion and battery upon Gene. Often such conduct is met with criminal charges filed against the offender, as well as a civil action for contract rescission.

Duress disputes are usually much more subtle. These involve threats that induce the contractual agreement rather than actual physical contact.

Assume the same basic Clint and Gene transaction. When Gene says no deal, Clint pulls a gun from his coat, points it at Gene, and says, "This is a 357 magnum, the world's most powerful handgun, and unless you give me that watch and sign the paper right now I will blow you away." Gene complies and then promptly sues to cancel the sale.

Again this is clearly duress by Clint, and Gene would win. Although there was no physical force exerted, the circumstances clearly show lack of genuine assent by Gene, and Clint would still be subject to criminal charges for his unlawful actions.

Modern legal requirements for duress are more liberal. Rather than the threat situation having to involve conduct that is clearly illegal, most states allow duress claims in situations where the complainant successfully proves the contract was entered into "improperly." This is a matter of opinion that again is judged based upon the objective standard of reasonableness.

- The threat to file criminal charges is usually held to be duress.
- The threat to file a civil lawsuit is usually not duress.

The differences in the severity of penal vs. civil sanctions is given as the reason for these different results.

In addition to the conduct complained of by the victim being "improper" to the degree required by law, the victim must not have any reasonable "out," and thus be forced to comply.

Audrey needs repairs to her car, takes it to the dealer in the morning for an estimate, and is quoted $500 as the offer to perform the work. She accepts the offer and authorizes the work. When she returns to the dealership late that afternoon with a cashier's check for $500 to pick up her car, she is told at the cashier's desk that the bill is $750. When she objects she is told, "Sorry, miss, there is no one here at this hour but me, and unless you pay the charges I can't release your car to you." Audrey pays the additional cash and then demands return of the excess cost.

Audrey's claim of duress would be sustained. Although she technically "accepted" the higher contract, the mitigating circumstances would allow it to be cancelled.

A practical way that Audrey could avoid such a dispute is by paying with a credit card. Aside from the basic plastic money advantage of up to sixty days of "free money" – you buy the item on day one, are billed on day thirty, and don't have to pay until day sixty – Audrey is protected by consumer laws against improper deliveries, faulty workmanship, or breach of agreement.

She receives her car and then tries to work out the problem with the auto dealer. If unsuccessful, when she pays the credit card bill she just circles the disputed item on the front, writes her explanation on the back, and her vendor is then required to justify its item. If they can't, it is removed from Audrey's account, along with any finance charges incurred while the dispute was in process.

The raising of the duress defense in current business or commercial transactions is often known as *economic duress*. This occurs when the financial vested interest of one party is improperly threatened to force them to enter into a new contract, modify an existing one, or waive valuable contract rights.

Hurd v. Wildman, et al., 707 N.E.2d 609 (Ill. App. 1999), disallowed a claim of economic duress by a fired lawyer who signed a release and separation agreement to receive his last paycheck, and then sued for benefits due him under the law firm's partnership agreement. The court recited the basic law of duress:

"Economic duress is a condition where one is induced by a wrongful act or threat of another to make a contract under circumstances that deprive one of the exercise of one's own free will. To establish duress, one must demonstrate that the threat has left the individual 'bereft of the quality of mind essential to the making of a contract.' The acts or threats complained of must be wrongful; however, the term 'wrongful' is not limited to acts that are criminal, tortious, or in violation of a contractual duty. They must extend to acts that are wrongful in a moral sense as well.

"In terms of 'economic duress,' also known as 'business compulsion,' the defense cannot be predicated upon a demand that is lawful or upon doing or threatening to do that which a party has a legal right to do. Furthermore, it has long been held that where consent to an agreement is secured merely because of hard bargaining positions or financial pressures, duress does not exist."

Economic duress involves the traditional profile of a stronger party seizing an opportunity to take extreme unfair advantage of a weaker party that we have seen previously in the "take it or leave it" cases of unconscionable contracts.

CBZ Inc. is a small construction company that bids on a million-dollar apartment building project of Mega Corp. They are low bidder and get the job, which will be their biggest venture. As the job moves forward, they routinely submit their draw requests and receive progress payments. They then pay their subcontractors and suppliers from these funds.

They lack liquidity to carry their creditors more than thirty days. This is known to Mega Corp. CBZ Inc. completes construction and submits their final draw request for the $200,000 balance due. Mega Corp. never denies owing the money but plays games delaying payment, such as "the check is in the mail," "our computers are down," "we just lost our bookkeeper and our records are a mess." CBZ, Inc. is desperate. Its creditors are threatening lawsuits and worse.

Mega offers to pay $100,000 out of its petty cash, "as a favor to you, while we attempt to straighten out our financial records, so long as you sign a release indicating you are paid in full. Take it or leave it." CBZ, Inc. signs, receives the money, and then sues for the balance, claiming it signed the release under economic duress.

This is classic economic duress, a case of financial abuse of bargaining power, where Mega Corp. engaged in a predatory business practice once it sensed the vulnerable position of its adversary.

Mega Corp. will claim it was just engaged in "hard bargaining," which is an everyday fact of the commercial marketplace. This is an effective defense to a claim of duress, and modern courts are more prone to denying recovery in questionable cases because the basic motivation of the party raising this defense is to be relieved from what they perceive as a bad business deal. Courts will not usually substitute their judgment for the business risks assumed by the parties.

In *Strickland Tower Maintenance, Inc. (STM) v. AT&T Communications, Inc., 128 F.3d 1422 (10th Cir. 1997), (ATT)*, the plaintiff contracted with the defendant to provide supervision services in the burying of forty-six miles of fiber-optic cable, was to be paid a set percentage of the total project cost, and had management responsibility.

After the project began, the defendant demanded that they assume project management, and implied that if the plaintiff would not agree, the defendant would deny future business.

When a dispute arose about the computation of amounts due STM, it sued for breach of contract and "asserted that AT&T used economic duress to force STM to agree to use inspectors and hand control over the project to AT&T."

The trial jury awarded STM $470,601 in restitution damages on the economic duress claim. On appeal, that award was reversed. The court said, "A litigant cannot, therefore, make out a claim of economic duress by alleging merely that the opposing party took advantage of her weak negotiating position or because of 'business necessities.' The assertion of duress must be proven by evidence that the duress resulted from defendant's wrongful and oppressive conduct and not by plaintiff's necessities."

In *Aldrich & Company v. Donovan, 778 P.2d 397 (Mont. 1989)*, the defendant was a building contractor who purchased merchandise from the plaintiff and signed a promissory note for his open account debt. Due to nonpayment, the plaintiff sued.

"Donovan admits he executed the note, but asserts that he did so under economic duress. He alleges duress in that Aldrich would not extend him further credit unless he signed the note."

Summary judgment was entered against the defendant and, on appeal, the judgment was affirmed, because the court felt he was not forced to incur the debt.

"A claim of economic duress requires a showing that the contract at issue was made under circumstances evincing a lack of free will on the part of the contracting parties. It is not sufficient to show that consent was secured by the pressure of financial circumstances, or that one of the parties merely insisted on its legal right.

"The note at issue here evidenced an existing debt owed by Donovan to Aldrich . . . Aldrich had a legal right to require security of some sort before extending credit to Donovan. He was therefore 'pressured' only by his need for further credit, not by any duress imposed by Aldrich."

There are occasions, however, where a claim of economic duress will be sustained, often in situations where a release is signed in settlement of a disputed claim and the non-signer is the party who caused the dispute.

In *International Underwater Contractors, Inc. v. New England Telephone and Telegraph Company, 393 N.E.2d 968 (Mass. App. 1979)*, the plaintiff contracted with the defendant to assemble and install conduits under the Mystic River for a fixed price of approximately $150,000.

The defendant required major changes in the project to be done in the winter months, which caused delays in the work. This generated extras of over $800,000 that the defendant assured the plaintiff would be paid. When the defendant refused to honor its alleged promises, settlement discussions ensued and dragged on. The plaintiff by now had exhausted its bank credit, its cash position was overdrawn, and its creditors were demanding immediate payment. When the defendant offered $575,000, the plaintiff "was forced to take it 'on a take-it-or-leave-it basis.' "

The trial court entered summary judgment for the defendant on the economic duress issue, and the plaintiff appealed. The appellate court reversed, ruling that the issue should be fully litigated.

"A release signed under duress is not binding. Coercion sufficient to avoid a contract need not, of course, consist of physical force or threats of it. Social or economic pressure illegally or immorally applied may be sufficient.

"Merely taking advantage of another's financial difficulty is not duress. Rather, the person alleging financial difficulty must allege that it was contributed to or caused by the one accused of coercion. The assertion of duress must be proved by evidence that the duress resulted from defendant's wrongful and oppressive conduct and not by plaintiff's necessities.

"If the assertions of the plaintiff are true, the defendant did more than assert a legal right (settling the dispute instead of litigating), as its acts created the financial difficulties of the plaintiff, of which it then took advantage."

Undue Influence

Undue influence is closely related to duress. The difference in its disputes is that the abusive bargaining and wrongful pressure are exerted in a more subtle manner. Rather than outright coercive action, there is unfair persuasion of someone who, because of advanced age or illness or health conditions, is weak and vulnerable. The typical elements are:

- A special relationship of trust and confidence exists, such as legal fiduciary relationships of attorney-client and doctor-patient, or personal caretakers, nurses, or attendants.
- There is a strong party who has a dominant position over a weaker party.
- The strong party takes financial advantage of the weak party, usually in the form of asset transfers from them called "gifts."

Winifred is a ninety-year-old widow living alone in a large house. She is mentally alert but physically frail. Her needs are attended to by Cleo, her live-in companion and nurse. Winifred has a grown son and daughter who live in a distant city. Winifred owns a large Cadillac she no longer drives that is parked in her garage. One day Cleo tells her, "My car just died and I need a new one. Why don't you give me yours, since you no longer use it?" Cleo declines, saying, "Sorry, dear, but I'm saving it for my children." Then Cleo says, "If you don't sign over that car to me, I may forget to give you your medicine, or I may decide to leave you all alone tonight." Winifred is frightened and signs the title transfer.

Clearly this is undue influence, and the transfer can be cancelled. All the required elements of abuse of special relationship for personal advantage are present. Cleo's motives are clearly improper and we have no sympathy for her. But what if we change the facts just a bit?

After Cleo's initial request for the car, instead of making those threats, she merely asks Winifred to reconsider before declining. Winifred now says, "You know, dear, you are correct. You take such good care of me, and the children are far away and you need the car and they don't, so it is yours with my gratitude."

Here the transfer of the asset to Cleo is clearly voluntary, knowing, and Winifred obviously intends that the transfer occur.

But what if Winifred never tells the children about this gifting, and then dies? They expect it to be a part of their inheritance and when they find it was transferred to Cleo, they will suspect some impropriety. But they weren't present at the time of the transfer, so they really don't know Winifred's true intentions.

This is a practical dilemma that has caused most states to change the traditional burden of proof required in undue influence cases.

If Winifred wanted to cancel the gift transfer during her lifetime, she would seek rescission on the grounds of undue influence and testify as to the surrounding circumstances. She knows better than anyone whether her act was free and voluntary. She could easily sustain her burden of proving her lack of real consent with her personal assertions.

But when she dies and her heirs bring a rescission action to cancel the transfer because of their suspicions, they cannot sustain their burden of proving it was improper, because they have no personal knowledge of what actually occurred. Did Cleo abuse the personal relationship with Winifred for personal gain, or did Winifred voluntarily give the item in question to Cleo? There is the appearance of improper conduct, but the heirs don't really know.

Therefore, in undue influence actions, the complaining heirs need only prove that: (1) a special relationship of trust and confidence existed between the stronger and weaker parties, and (2) the stronger party received the so-called "gift" benefit. This raises a *presumption of undue influence* and the burden of proof shifts to the benefited party to prove that they *didn't commit undue influence*.

This is a total reversal of the usual proof requirements in the interests of fairness, because of circumstances that give the appearance that someone has taken unfair advantage of another.

A decision-maker in such a dispute must objectively evaluate the circumstances under the "reasonableness" test, without the benefit of personal subjective testimony of the alleged giver, and the shifting burden of proof is a great disadvantage to the recipient of the gift.

Rather than the criminal proof test of "innocent until proven guilty," the gift donee is faced with "guilty until you prove your innocence." And such proof is extremely difficult unless there were independent witnesses to the gift transfer, or other evidence of its voluntary nature.

"Where one party stands in relation of trust and confidence to the other, such as is here involved, attorney and client, trustee and cestue que trust, where the dominant party – and in this relation the attorney or trustee is regarded as the dominant party – receives or derives a benefit or advantage from a transaction during the existence of such relation, the party reposing the confidence, on seasonable application to a court of equity, may obtain relief from the burden of such transaction, by showing the transaction and the confidential relations, unless the person receiving the benefit overcomes the presumption of undue influence by evidence which reasonably satisfies the judicial mind that the transaction *was in every respect just, fair, and equitable*." *Verner v. Mosely, 127 So. 527 (Ala. 1930)*

This shift of the burden of proof in undue influence cases has had the practical effect of putting most situations of gifts between non-family members at legal risk. It requires an intended gift donee to anticipate the potential legal problems and try to create the necessary protective testimonies that the donor was not subjected to any unfair persuasion, the transfer was purely voluntary, and no improper advantage was taken. This is not an easy task, but it is essential to prevent unfair advantage being taken of susceptible donors.

Here are three types of typical undue influence court disputes:

1. Sometimes the plaintiff in an undue influence dispute is available to testify regarding whether or not the document in question, which usually transfers valuable property rights to another, was freely and voluntarily signed.

In *Goldman v. Bequai, 19 F.3d 666 (D.C. App. 1994)*, the plaintiff, an eighty–year-old widow, alleged that her attorney and long-time family friend had unduly influenced her to convey substantially all her property to him three months after her husband's death. She executed two transfer documents to her residence condominium and her partnership interest in a commercial property, creating joint tenancies with right of survivorship between herself and the defendant. The latter was later sold, and her proceeds were placed in a joint account with the defendant.

The plaintiff had been treated by a doctor with antidepressant drugs during her husband's last illness and thereafter, and had no legal counsel or independent advice when making the transfers. There were no witnesses to the transactions, and she also claimed the defendant did not fully explain the transactions to her.

The plaintiff stated that her "first inkling" that the defendant had "deceived" her came after she sold the commercial property. "He put his name on my half. His name was on everything I had: my checking account, my savings account. The other half he put in his name and his wife's name and I couldn't understand that."

After she had an argument with the defendant stemming from the transfers, she fired him as her attorney, but did not sue him to cancel the transfers until five years later when she sold the residence and learned she received only one-half of the proceeds. The defendant claimed no liability on the plaintiff's claims due to the running of the three-year statute of limitations. She asserted the statute was equitably tolled by the defendant's improper conduct.

The trial court rejected the plaintiff's claims, ruling by summary judgment that they were barred by the statute of limitations. It also noted that the plaintiff's psychiatrist testified she was not mentally incompetent.

The appellate court reversed and remanded for a trial on the merits, noting this was a case of first impression on the issue of whether or not, "if a plaintiff proves undue influence, the statute of limitations is equitably tolled so long as the influence continues."

"Undue influence is a contract doctrine which serves to equitably toll the statute of limitations. Appellant has presented evidence sufficient to raise a material question of fact as to this theory . . . undue influence in its essential elements has no real relation to mental incapacity.

"Undue influence is sometimes treated as a species of duress, as both doctrines address situations in which the will of one party to a contract is overcome by the improper acts of another party. Situations amounting to undue influence vary widely and are fact-specific, but in general undue influence may be found when 'a party in whom another reposes confidence misuses that confidence to gain his own advantage while the other has been made to feel that the party in question will not act against his welfare.'"

2. More often, a defense of undue influence is raised by the estate of an alleged lifetime transferor of valuable property, complaining about the appearance of improper conduct when a particular asset has been previously conveyed by the decedent and is no longer available for distribution to the heirs as an estate asset.

In *Rea v. Paulson, 887 P.2d 355 (Or. App. 1994)*, the plaintiff, as personal representative of his mother's estate, sued to set aside a deed conveying her former home to the defendant, who was the plaintiff's half-brother and the deceased's son by a second marriage.

The decedent died, leaving four children, including the plaintiff and the defendant. Her will left all her property to them in equal shares. During the last years of her life, she suffered from arthritis, renal failure, heart failure, and diabetes, was taking several strong medications, and was undergoing daily dialysis treatments.

The defendant did not originally reside near his mother, but one year before her death moved in with her, expressed admittedly false concerns to her that she was in danger of losing her house to the state due to improper Medicaid payments (although she did not receive Medicaid), and convinced her to transfer the house out of her name. The defendant did not mention the transaction to his half-sisters or half-brothers until months later, after they learned of her death, a fact that he had also not communicated to them.

He obtained a form warranty deed from a local title company and filled it out in his handwriting, conveying the residence to him. His mother had previously moved in with him in a rental residence, her former house was rented out, and the income it produced was deposited in her savings account, to which the defendant had power of attorney and did, in fact, use for his personal expenses.

The trial court ruled in favor of the estate, and the appellate court affirmed, concluding that the transfer in question "was the product of undue influence exerted by Larry on his mother . . . We conclude that there was a confidential relationship between decedent and Larry and that, under the circumstances, he held a position of dominance over her; he was, literally, in the driver's seat."

The court noted the various factual indicia of Larry's undue influence:

• She was completely dependent on him in her daily life.
• He helped with her finances and held her power of attorney.
• He wrote all her checks and signed her name for her.
• He drove a wedge between the rest of the family and the decedent.
• The rest of the family was not welcome in his house.
• He procured the deed, prepared it, and assisted in its signing.
• It was his false idea to transfer the house out of her name.
• She had no independent advice.

3. Sometimes, what appears to be voluntary valid gifting to charitable religious organizations is really the result of the donee taking unfair advantage of a wealthy and susceptible donor.

In *Dovydenas v. The Bible Speaks, 869 F.2d 628 (1st Cir. 1989)*, the plaintiff, the multimillionaire heir to the Dayton-Hudson department store fortune estimated at $19 million, moved with her husband to Massachusetts and joined the defendant's church, known as TBS. They attended services and after she left a very generous contribution of $500 in the collection plate, she was contacted by Carl Stevens, the fundamentalist preacher and founder of TBS.

The church had grown from a small group of fifty members in Maine to a large organization centered in Lenox, Massachusetts, having 1,300 members, a large campus with many outbuildings, and a radio and television ministry.

A series of private meetings with Stevens ensued, at which he asked for and received increasing donations for his church, until the plaintiff started attending bible classes, became a part of his inner circle of friends, was a devout member of TBS, abandoned her prior friends, and had little to do with her family.

The plaintiff testified she had daily private meetings with Stevens. "In these private meetings, she was given advice on religious, financial and personal matters. She was told she had to obey Stevens because he was the highest authority on earth. She was also told to listen to tapes of Stevens' speeches over and over and to take notes of all Stevens told her and then study those notes. She was to inundate her mind with Stevens' words. She disclosed her net worth to him, and he told her that her mission in life was to give and that her gifts could cause great events."

The plaintiff became friendly with Baum, Stevens' future wife, who suffered from migraine headaches and was concerned about their effect on their forthcoming marriage. Before the wedding, the plaintiff was driving with Stevens and heard a voice telling her to donate $1 million to TBS, which she did in Dayton–Hudson stock. She told him she was going to give TBS $1,000,000 and that she believed by doing so it would cure Baum's headaches. Stevens told her the headaches were cured after the gift, even though they continued, and the "plaintiff believed that large gifts from her to TBS could affect events on earth."

The plaintiff's husband opposed the $1 million gift, and after it was made, Stevens told him "he would not take any more money without Jonas' consent."

Later, she told Stevens she heard God tell her to give $5 million to TBS. He advised her not to tell her husband about it, and plotted a strategy for it to be paid by her company, whereby she signed a letter he had drafted which stated that "God had spoken to her, which was why she was making the gift, that no one from TBS had asked her for the gift or knew about it and that Stevens was to administer the gift."

The plaintiff also made another gift of $500,000 under similar questionable circumstances when she wrote a check on her brokerage account with a note attached that said she had been led by God to make the gift.

The plaintiff was subsequently tricked away from Stevens and the church by her relatives, deprogrammed from her "cult" experience, relieved of the "mind-control" to which she had been subjected, and then sued to rescind the gifts on the grounds of undue influence and fraud.

The trial court ruled in her favor and the defendant appealed. The appellate court ruled that the $1 million gift was valid, finding no undue influence when it was made, but invalidated the $5 million gift. "Any species of coercion, whether physical, mental or moral, which subverts the sound judgment and genuine desire of the individual, is enough to constitute undue influence. Its extent or degree is inconsequential so long as it is sufficient to substitute the dominating purpose of another for the free expression of the wishes of the person (who gives)."

"Because undue influence is often practiced in 'veiled and secret ways,' its existence may be inferred from such factors as disproportionate gifts made under unusual circumstances, the age and health of the donor, and the existence of a confidential relationship. Two other factors are also important under Massachusetts's case law. One, attempts by the recipient to isolate the donor from her former friends and relatives can be considered undue influence. Two, a court can also consider that she (the donor) acted without independent and disinterested advice."

Mistake

Defending enforcement of a contract on the basis of mistaken circumstances does not involve situations where there are claims of unfair advantage taken by one party at the expense of the other. Instead, after the contract is made, one of the parties wants to avoid it based upon allegations that there was a serious misunderstanding regarding material, existing facts that are essential to the bargain made.

A mutual or bilateral mistake of a material fact made by both parties allows either to rescind. If, however, the mistake was unilateral, where only one of the parties was mistaken, no rescission is allowed and the contract will stand, regardless of how disadvantageous its terms.

Therefore, the party who made a bad deal and wants out will claim "mutual mistake" and the party who has the economic advantage will defend on the basis of "unilateral mistake."

These types of disputes are complicated by the legal nature of what in fact is a legal mistake, and how courts should evaluate them:

- It is not a simple error in judgment or miscalculation.
- It is not a matter about which reasonable people would differ.
- It does not relate to facts that may arise in the future.
- It must involve fact(s) that are important to the transaction like existence, identity, quality, price, time, quantity, delivery, and the like.
- It must concern present facts, where reasonable people do not differ, such as the existence or identity or essential nature of the subject matter of the transaction.
- It cannot primarily relate to a matter of opinion – where reasonable people may differ – such as the value or inherent worth of the transaction, although value always underlies every business deal.

Vincent and Carlos go wilderness hiking. Carlos finds two amber stones along the bank of a river. Neither has any training in gemology. Carlos and Vincent both believe the stones to be topaz, semi-precious gems only worth about $30 each. Vincent offers Carlos $50 for them and Carlos accepts. When they return, Vincent shows the stones to his friend, who is a gem collector, and is informed they are really yellow diamonds worth $4,000. An article appears in the local paper about Vincent's good fortune, Carlos sees it, and sues to cancel the sale on the grounds of mutual mistake. Vincent defends the sale as an arms-length transaction, stating he did nothing wrong, and Carlos is just upset because he made a bad business deal.

Let's analyze the problem. One complication in these mistake cases is that value underlies all such disputes. Value is an opinion, not a fact, and therefore cannot be the basis of a rescission claim based upon mistake of fact. Carlos wants to rescind because he sold too low – but is the case really about value? No – both parties believed the stones to be a definite "something," topaz, and in actuality the stones were a different "something," diamonds. So they are mutually mistaken about the identity of the subject matter and therefore either party may cancel.

Same factual pattern, but neither party believes the stones to be anything other than yellow rocks. Since their identity is in fact what both parties believed them to be, there is no mistake and no cancellation is allowed.

Same basic factual pattern, but what if Carlos believes the stones to be topaz and Vincent believes them to be yellow diamonds? Unless Vincent has superior knowledge, like that of a gem expert, when Vincent's belief proves accurate he is allowed to profit. The unilateral mistake of Carlos does not allow cancellation.

In *North Grand Mall Associates, LLC v. Grand Center, Ltd., 278 F.3d 854 (8th Cir. 2002)*, the plaintiff leased rental space to the defendant.

The lease contained an option to buy the property, whose purchase price was to be computed by "dividing the average sum of the rent paid for the last three years prior to the purchase by seven percent."

A dispute arose after the defendant exercised its option to purchase, arriving at a purchase price of $500,000 based upon the average rent for the last three years of $35,000 divided by seven percent. The plaintiff sued, claiming the method of computation was based upon a mutual mistake and that such computations were usually done in a different way.

The trial court ruled for the plaintiff, and reformed the contract to result in a higher purchase price. The defendant appealed and the court reversed, saying, "The language in the lease, which even included an example, was unambiguous. The fact that industry custom is to use another method to establish commercial real estate prices is irrelevant since the parties to the original contract made their intention clear. The terms established by the contract do not indicate mutual mistake, so the contract stands."

Contrast the above case of no mutual mistake in a lease agreement with the following case of *Phil Bramsen Distributor, Inc. v. Mastroni, et al., 726 P.3d 610 (Az. App. 1986)*, where the opposite result occurred.

A commercial building was leased for twenty years, where the plaintiff was tenant and the defendants were landlord. The lease had a monthly base rental plus an escalation clause to be applied every five years based upon "the Consumer Price Index for Phoenix, Arizona." Unfortunately, there was no such index.

The defendants sought to invoke the escalation clause, and the plaintiff filed suit to enjoin its enforcement based upon mutual mistake. The trial court ruled for the defendants, reforming the rent escalation clause by replacing the faulty index with the "metropolitan Phoenix consumer price index prepared by the Bureau of Business and Economic Research, Arizona State University." Based on this reformation, the monthly rent would be increased from $4,150 to $6,848, and the court entered judgment for approximately $178,000 in back rent.

The plaintiff appealed, arguing, "There was no mutual mistake but rather a unilateral mistake on the part of appellees," because of the lack of the subject cost of living index. The court disagreed, and affirmed the reformation of the lease.

"In the present case, the parties agreed to an escalation clause based on the rate of inflation. It was a mistake of fact that caused the clause to fail. The draftsman, (the defendant's) attorney, inserted the term 'cost of living index for the city of Phoenix prepared by the Bureau of Labor Statistics.' There is no evidence that either appelles or appellants Bramsen had any independent knowledge of such an index or relied on anyone's word but the attorney's. Therefore, by mutual mistake the parties believed they had a workable formula."

What follows is another case of mutual mistake. As you read it, consider how easily the bank could have avoided the dispute, which fortunately for them was decided in their favor, if they had just properly inspected the estate residence before they sold it, or specified that the plaintiff could only keep "miscellaneous personal property having no significant monetary value."

In *Wilkin v. 1st Source Bank, 548 N.E.2d 170 (Ind. App. 1990)*, a world-famous artist and sculptor died, and the defendant was appointed personal representative of the estate. The defendant contracted to sell the deceased's residence to the plaintiff. The purchase and sale agreement included the real estate and its appliances, and standard built-ins, such as drapes, curtains, and sconces.

After the closing, the plaintiff complained that the premises had been left in cluttered condition, and requested a cleanup. The defendant proposed two options: it would retain a rubbish removal service or "Wilkins could clean the premises and keep any items of personal property they wanted." The plaintiff chose the latter, and during their clean-up efforts found eight drawings and a plaster sculpture made by the deceased, for which ownership was claimed. Even though neither party knew of the existence of the art, the defendant objected, and filed a petition with the probate court to determine title to the artwork.

The probate court determined the artwork was the property of the estate, and ordered the items returned to the bank. The plaintiff appealed and the court affirmed.

"Mutual assent is a prerequisite to the creation of a contract. Where both parties share a common assumption about a vital fact upon which they based their bargain, and that assumption is false, the transaction may be avoided if because of the mistake a quite different exchange of values occurs from the exchange of values contemplated by the parties. There is no contract, because the minds of the parties have in fact never met.

"The parties in the instant case shared a common presupposition as to the existence of certain facts that proved false. The Bank and the Wilkins considered the real estate which the Wilkins had purchased to be cluttered with items of personal property variously characterized as 'junk,' 'stuff' or 'trash'. Neither party suspected that works of art created by Ivan Mestrovic remained on the premises."

Cases of unilateral mistake usually result in the denial of requested cancellation of a contract unless the non-mistaken party has taken unfair advantage, but few have such a financial impact as *Wells Fargo Credit Corporation v. Martin, 605 So.2d 531 (Fla. App. 1992)*, which we'll call "The $100,000 Bidding Error."

Wells Fargo obtained a judgment of real estate mortgage foreclosure, and at the foreclosure sale, it was represented by its attorney's paralegal. She was experienced, having attended more than 1,000 of these sales. She brought a form instruction sheet to the sale that informed her to bid $115,500 for the property, which was its tax-appraised value. Martin attended the sale because his home had been destroyed by fire, and he needed a new residence. This was the first such foreclosure sale he had ever attended.

When the sale began, the paralegal misread her instruction form and opened the bidding at $15,500. Martin then bid $20,000. After giving ample time for any other bids, the clerk announced, "$20,000 going once, $20,000 going twice, sold to Harley —." At that point the paralegal screamed, "Stop, I'm sorry, I made a mistake!" The clerk took the matter to a judge, who ordered the clerk to issue title to Martin, as the high bidder.

Wells Fargo moved to set aside the sale, on grounds of mistake. The trial judge declined, finding that, "The $20,000.00 bid was grossly inadequate, but that there was no evidence of fraud or any type of misconduct on the part of Mr. Martin."

The appellate court affirmed. "We accept the trial court's conclusion that the amount of the sale was grossly inadequate. This inadequacy, however, occurred due to an avoidable, unilateral mistake by an agent of Wells Fargo. As between Wells Fargo and a good faith purchaser at the judicial sale, the trial court had the discretion to place the risk of this mistake upon Wells Fargo."

The court considered two prior Florida cases where bidding errors were made at foreclosure sales and the sales were set aside, but in one the mortgagee's agent failed to appear at the sale, and in the other the property owner's attorney was not present at the sale – both no-show situations being a result of alleged mistake. Those cases were distinguished by the court, "because the mortgagee never had an opportunity to bid at the sale, and because the prevailing bid was essentially nominal."

A. Was the court's decision too harsh on the bank?
B. Would your answer be different if the bank's paralegal had failed to appear?
C. Do you think the paralegal and/or her attorney-employer were fired by the bank as a result of this case?

Fraud

The relief granted in proper cases of duress, undue influence, and mistake is a cancellation of the contract made without real consent, and the attempt to restore the parties to their positions prior to the transaction. No money damages are usually allowed to punish wrongdoing.

Fraud, however, is a more serious matter, since its very nature involves an intentional act of deception. In addition to the contract remedy of rescission, the courts often award monetary damages for the non-contract tort of deceit to compensate the injured party for losses sustained. In the more severe cases that satisfy the textbook categories of conduct that is "willful, malicious, reckless, and outrageous," an award of significant punitive damages is often made to punish the wrongdoer.

The three most common fraud situations are:

1. Inducement – the fraud is *why you sign* the written contract or verbally enter into the transaction (consumer scams, sales of goods or services for unfairly inflated prices). These transactions are voidable.
2. Inception – the fraud relates to *what you sign,* and to the identity of the transaction (you sign a promissory note thinking it is an autograph). These transactions are void.
3. Nondisclosure – the fraud is in concealing valuable information that you have a legal duty to disclose (you buy a used car and are not told about its prior repairs that cause dangerous hidden defects). These transactions are also voidable.

There are four required legal elements that all must be proven to sustain a claim of fraud:

1. The defendant misrepresents a past or current fact that is important to his decision to enter into the contract.
2. The defendant knows that fact is false, thus intending to deceive.
3. The plaintiff reasonably relies on the misrepresentation.
4. The plaintiff suffers monetary damage as a direct result.

Many fraud cases arise regarding investment transactions. When they have adverse financial results, the losing party often cries, "I was defrauded," and seeks to cancel the transaction and recover their losses. Their complaints often fail, because they must not only prove damages, but also that the conduct of the defendant was intentional and not just a negligent failure of business judgment.

Hal is a securities salesperson who has gained a reputation as being able to make money for his clients with his stock picks. Josh is a young professional who decides to make his first market investments with him. Hal makes two statements to Josh: (1) "My sources tell me that Acme Radium is a terrific buy at its current values," and (2) My sources also tell me that Acme Radium should double in price within ninety days." Hal really has no information at all about Acme Radium. He just wants to unload his excess inventory of that stock. Josh buys $10,000 of the stock based upon Hal's recommendations. In thirty days, the price has dropped by half. Josh claims he was defrauded, and sues to cancel the transaction and recover his money.

Let's analyze the dispute for the required elements of fraud:

Hal did misrepresent the Acme Radium investment. He intended to deceive Josh to induce him to invest, and knew his statements were false. Josh relied upon both statements as a material inducement and suffered monetary loss. But were they statements of fact and did he reasonably rely?

Statement (1) is a present opinion, rather than a fact. Reasonable people could differ about it. The use of adjectives such as "terrific" is a sure sign of opinion rather than fact. Reasonable people do not normally rely upon opinions. However, there is a fairness exception for fraud cases when experts or those with superior knowledge, like Hal, state opinions. Utterances by such persons are treated the same as misstatements of fact and can be fraud. Courts inquire not only into *what* was said, but *who* said it.

Statement (2) looks like an opinion, but is really a prediction about the future. Under the law, reasonable persons never should rely upon predictions because of their unreliability, no matter who expresses them.

Therefore, Hal's (1) statement is fraud, but (2) is not.

There is also a long line of fraud cases involving dance studios that have sold their customers lessons that far exceed their ability and potential, with regard only to how much of their money can be spent.

In *Vokes v. Arthur Murray, Inc., 212 So.2d 906 (Fla. App. 1968)*, the plaintiff, a widow of fifty-one, lonely and without family, desired to be "an accomplished dancer" with the hopes of finding "a new interest in life." She attended a dance party at the defendant's local franchisee, where she was complimented on her grace and poise, and her future as "an excellent dancer." She signed up for eight half-hour dance lessons to be used within the next month.

She was then sold a total of fourteen "dance courses" in separate contracts, totaling an aggregate of 2,302 hours of dancing lessons for a total cash outlay of over $31,000. These contracts were procured by "false representations to her that she was improving in her dancing ability, that she had excellent potential, that she was responding to instructions in dancing grace, and that they were developing her into a beautiful dancer, whereas in truth and in fact she did not develop in her dancing ability, she had no 'dance aptitude,' and in fact had difficulty in 'hearing the musical beat.' "

She eventually sued to have the dance contracts declared null and void and cancelled based on fraud in the inducement. She also sought a recovery of damages in the dollar amount of her unused dance lessons. The defendant asserted that no fraud existed, because any statements and misrepresentations made were not "as to a material fact, (but) rather . . . an opinion, prediction or expectation, and (they) were in the category of 'trade puffing,' within its legal orbit."

The trial court dismissed her complaint for failure to state a cause of action, and she appealed. The appellate court reversed and remanded, stating that while "It is true that 'generally a misrepresentation, to be actionable, must be one of fact rather than opinion,' . . . it does not apply where there is a fiduciary relationship between the parties, or where there has been some artifice or trick employed by the representor, or where the parties do not in general deal at 'arm's length' as we understand the phrase, or where the representee does not have equal opportunity to become apprised."

"A statement of a party having superior knowledge may be regarded as a statement of fact although it would be considered as opinion if the parties were dealing on equal terms ... It could be reasonably supposed here that defendants had 'superior knowledge' as to whether plaintiff had 'dance potential' and as to whether she was noticeably improving in the art of Terpsichore ... Even in contractual situations where a party to a transaction owes no duty to disclose facts within his knowledge or to answer inquiries respecting such facts, the law is if he undertakes to do so he must disclose the *whole truth.*"

Here is another interesting fraud case; let's title it "Finding Your Guru – Inner Peace for You or Wealth for Him?" Notice the similarity to the *Dovydenas v. The Bible Speaks* case previously discussed in the section on undue influence.

In *Dushkin v. Desai, 18 F.Supp.2d 117 (D. Mass. 1998)*, fourteen former devotees of the self-proclaimed yoga guru Amrit Desai sued to recover losses suffered when he was revealed to be a charlatan.

They had resided for many years at the Kripalu Ashram, a 350-acre yoga retreat center in Lenox, Massachusetts.

It was here that the defendant presented himself as a "true and authentic guru, promoting a celibate and ascetic lifestyle with vows of poverty," and providing on a large scale a facility for the paying public "to relax, take yoga classes, meditate, have massages, and otherwise take a break from the routine of their daily lives."

The plaintiff's and others, some for as long as twenty years, had operated the facility, working for room and board and a small monthly stipend in exchange for the opportunity to live there as the defendant's "disciples." They also had, at the defendant's urging, donated literally all their material wealth and possessions to the ashram.

The plaintiff's alleged that the defendant, behind his carefully cultivated public image, was a fraud, and had entered into a series of privately lucrative contracts with the ashram as an independent contractor, providing him annually hundreds of thousands of dollars, and had also engaged in a series of secret sexual relationships with several female "disciples."

When there were public disclosures of the defendant's conduct, he resigned and moved to Florida. The plaintiff's suit included a count for fraud and misrepresentation. The defendant moved to dismiss for failure to state a cause of action, arguing that "His alleged misrepresentations did not concern matters of fact – that they were merely promissory in nature, or simple expressions of opinion – and therefore could not form the basis of an action for fraud."

The court allowed the fraud claims to continue, denying the defendant's motion. "In short, plaintiffs have offered sufficient allegations from which the court reasonably may infer that Desai made false representations with respect to his status with the intent to induce plaintiff's reliance, and that plaintiffs in fact relied on defendant's representations, as evidenced by their significant donations of time, labor and money to the facility."

The essence of fraud is a misrepresentation of material fact, as stated above. But what if the defendant says nothing? Can his silence be fraud? Rather than actively hiding important information the defendant fails to volunteer it. The issue here is whether or not the defendant has a duty to disclose information if not asked specifically about it.

The general rule of law followed by most states is that silence is usually not fraud, because defendants are not mind readers, and can't know what facts are important to the plaintiff unless they are asked specific questions. There are fairness exceptions, however, which create a duty to speak and require disclosure of hidden facts if:

- There is a fiduciary relationship between the parties
- Hidden defects may adversely affect the buyer's health or safety
- The private information may materially affect property value

Harriet goes to Gotham Motors looking for a good buy in a used car. She finds a late model Volvo that looks fine and meets her price range. She test drives it and is satisfied with its performance. She buys it, and later almost has a serious accident when the brakes fail coming down a hill. She discovers that the seller had the car repaired by the same mechanic she now uses, and there was a hidden leak inside the brake lining at the time she purchased that the seller did not disclose to her. She sues for fraud and wins.

What if the withheld information concerned a cosmetic problem, such as the original color of the car, rather than a mechanical defect? Probably not fraud, unless Harriet had discussed it as a part of her negotiations, such as, "I am assuming this dark blue is the original color." No response to her statement would reasonably be interpreted as an affirmation. If the color had been changed, it was obviously material to her, and nondisclosure of that fact by the seller would be fraud.

Here are two bizarre fraud cases, both of first impression, involving the alleged duty to disclose that residential real estate being sold: (1) was haunted by poltergeists, and (2) was the site of a multiple murder. With apologies to Charles Dickens, we will call this saga "A Tale of Two Houses."

In *Stambovsky v. Ackley, 572 N.Y.S.2d 672 (N.Y. App. Div. 1991)*, the plaintiff discovered after he had contracted to purchase a $650,000 house from the defendant in the village of Nyack, New York, that it was widely reputed to be haunted by poltergeists. When he learned of this set of facts prior to the closing, he sued to rescind the transaction on grounds of fraud, and sought return of his $32,500 down payment. The defendant moved to dismiss the complaint, and sought specific performance of the purchase agreement.

The trial court dismissed the complaint, but the appellate court reversed, holding that the plaintiff had a cause of action for cancellation. The court noted that the "defendant-seller deliberately fostered the public belief that her home was possessed," by widely reporting that fact, and had otherwise sought to capitalize on the attendant publicity.

The court went on to say, "Whether the source of the spectral apparitions seen by defendant seller are parapsychic or psychogenic, having reported their presence in both a national publication and the local press, defendant is estopped to deny their existence and, *as a matter of law, the house is haunted.*"

"However, with respect to transactions in real estate, New York adheres to the doctrine of caveat emptor and imposes no duty upon the vendor to disclose any information concerning the premises unless there is a confidential or fiduciary relationship between the parties or some conduct on the part of the seller which constitutes 'active concealment.'"

The court further noted that the doctrine of "let the buyer beware" deals with the physical condition of the premises, not the type of situation encountered in this case. "(The plaintiff) met his obligation to conduct an inspection of the premises and a search of the available public records with respect to title. It should be apparent, however, that the most meticulous inspection and the search would not reveal the presence of poltergeists at the premises or unearth the property's ghoulish reputation in the community."

"In an action seeking rescission of a contract to purchase a house widely reputed to be haunted, nondisclosure of that reputation constitutes a basis for relief as a matter of equity where the condition was created by the seller, it materially impairs the value of the contract, and it is peculiarly within the knowledge of the seller or is unlikely to be discovered by a prudent purchaser."

In *Reed v. King, 145 Cal. App.3d 261 (Cal. App. 1983),* the plaintiff purchased a house from the defendant, and learned from a neighbor after the sale that a woman and her four children were murdered there ten years earlier. Neither the seller nor his real estate agents had mentioned this prior to the closing.

The plaintiff sought to rescind her purchase and recover the purchase price. The trial court granted the defendant-seller's motion to dismiss. On appeal, judgment was reversed, and the plaintiff was allowed to proceed at law to prove her case of alleged fraud due to nondisclosure. "Reed paid $76,000, but the house is only worth $65,000 because of its past."

"Concealment is a term of art which includes mere nondisclosure when a party has a duty to disclose . . . In general, a seller of real property has a duty to disclose: 'where the seller knows of facts materially affecting the value or desirability of the property which are known or accessible only to him and also knows that such facts are not known to, or within the reach of the diligent attention and observation of the buyer, the seller is under a duty to disclose them to the buyer."

"The murder of innocents is highly unusual in its potential for so disturbing buyers that they may be unable to reside in a home where it has occurred. This fact may foreseeably deprive a buyer of the intended use of the purchase. Murder is not such a common occurrence that *buyers* should be charged with anticipating and discovering this disquieting possibility."

Even more bizarre, and worth noting in our contemporary society that values celebrity and sensationalism, was the quantifiable effect that murder had in raising, not lowering, the market value of two other houses:

- Lizzie Borden was tried and acquitted in 1892 for the alleged hatchet murders of her father and stepmother in the family home in Fall River, Massachusetts. The case attracted such attention that it was popularized in verse: "Lizzie Borden took an axe and gave her mother forty whacks, and then when all was said and done, she gave her father forty-one."

• Charles Manson and his "family" of followers have been serving life imprisonment for the brutal Tate/LaBianca murders that they committed in 1969 in actress Sharon Tate's Beverly Hills, California, residence. The case attracted worldwide attention, was described in detail by the prosecuting attorney Vincent Bugliosi in his book *Helter–Skelter*, and was the subject of a Beatles song of the same name.

Both of these houses were eventually sold for a premium over their current market value due to their notoriety, and are now sightseeing attractions operated on a bed-and-breakfast basis, with the rooms where the murders took place commanding the highest nightly rentals, especially on Halloween.

Fraud is also the basis of many consumer laws and is enforced by state and federal regulatory agencies. The legal requirements for a fraud prosecution are the same as those for rescinding a contract – their essence is the defendant's conduct of intentional deception that victimizes the complainant.

Discussion Exercises

1. Discuss how to separate valid claims of business duress from efforts to avoid the consequences of a bad business deal.

2. Discuss how you would protect yourself, as a gift donee, from a claim of undue influence.

3. Discuss how you would differentiate between the mistake liability rules.

4. Discuss whether you would assess higher damages for fraud by misrepresentation or nondisclosure.

5. Discuss whether punitive damages deter fraud.

Case Exercise 4

Gifts from Clients – "Accept" or "Reject"?

In *Klaskin v. Klepak, 534 N.E.2d 971 (Ill. 1989)*, the administrator of Woodruff's estate sued to recover title and remove the defendant from possession of a condominium unit which the decedent held in a land trust.

The trust had been created eleven years before his death, and provided that he reserved a life estate and the property would belong to the defendant, his long-time attorney and "special" friend at the time of his death, or to his estate if she predeceased him.

When Woodruff died at the age of fifty-four without a will, he had never married, had no children, and his only legal heirs were two maternal aunts and one maternal cousin.

The professional relationship of attorney-client between the decedent and the defendant began ten years before he bought the condominium, when she first represented him in a criminal misdemeanor matter. She continued to represent him thereafter in various business matters, and "although their relationship began as attorney and client, it developed into one of friendship. They dined, attended operas, and vacationed together. Klepak testified that she and Woodruff socialized about once a month until three years before Woodruff's death.

When Woodruff purchased the property, he relied upon the defendant to review the contract, she advised him to proceed, assisted in the creation of the land trust, personally loaned him money for the down payment, returned all the signed documents to the trustee bank, and performed all services to complete the sale, although she didn't personally attend the closing.

Although the defendant repeatedly denied that she legally represented Woodruff when he bought the condominium, she testified that, in addition to the above matters to assist in the transaction, the land trust was signed by Woodruff and notarized by the defendant while they dined at a restaurant.

Analysis

The trial court reviewed all the evidence, some conflicting, entered judgment in favor of the plaintiff, and ordered the defendant to assign her beneficial interest in the property to the estate, holding that the presumption of undue influence created by the deceased's transfer to his attorney was not successfully rebutted by the defendant.

On appeal, the judgment was reversed, basing its holding on evidence that Woodruff "was not enfeebled by age or health," thus not lacking mental capacity, and that "She and Woodruff shared a close relationship for seventeen years; that it was Woodruff's expressed intent to give her the trust as contingent beneficiary; and that the trust was in existence for eleven years prior to Woodruff's death."

The state's highest court reversed, affirming the trial court ruling that invalidated the transfer to the defendant due to her failure to overcome the legal presumption that it was obtained by her exercise of undue influence.

"Transactions between attorneys and clients are closely scrutinized. When an attorney engages in a transaction with a client and is benefited thereby, a presumption arises that the transaction proceeded from undue influence. Once a presumption is raised, the burden shifts to the attorney to come forward with evidence the transaction was fair, equitable and just and that the benefit did not proceed from undue influence.

Defuse Replay

What could, or should, the defendant, the gift grantee, have done to protect herself from the estate challenge that usually occurs when a decedent's estate does not contain property that was transferred to a fiduciary, friend, acquaintance, or other family member during the deceased's lifetime without the knowledge of the complaining heirs?

The court provides help. "Some of the factors which this court deems persuasive in determining whether the presumption of undue influence has been overcome include a showing by the attorney (1) that he or she made a full and frank disclosure of all relevant information; (2) that adequate consideration was given; and (3) that the client had independent advice before completing the transaction."

Some courts will also add the following additional requirement where, as in our case, there was no monetary consideration paid because the property transfer was a gift, "(4) that the legal document(s) to complete the transaction be signed in the presence of disinterested witnesses," to verify the transferor understands the nature and legal effect and proceeds voluntarily and knowingly.

Here is another practical suggestion for Ms. Klepak. Even if she failed to satisfy all the legal factors set forth above, since the presence of full monetary consideration removes much of the thrust of an undue influence claim, why not pay full value to Woodruff for the condominium by borrowing the money from him? She could have given him a demand promissory note secured by a first mortgage on the property, with a provision that "Any balances due and owing by my dear friend Ralla Klepak at the time of my death shall be forgiven."

Conclusion

Klepak argued that the presumption of undue influence should not apply where "the attorney has a close, personal relationship with the client." Notwithstanding the nature of their non-professional relationship, she should have known the perilous nature of this transaction. "An attorney who maintains a close advisory relationship with a client has a duty not to abuse that relationship and an obligation to avoid even the appearance of impropriety."

As a practical matter, most gift grantees, whether fiduciary or not, are not going to decline to accept an offered gift. The problem is what happens when the donor dies. Even if the three required legal elements of a completed gift are present,

- Intent to make a gift by the donor
- Delivery of the gifted property to the donee
- Acceptance of the gift by the donee

the mere fact that the property is missing from "Uncle Harry's" estate raises the suspicion that whoever received it did something wrong to induce its transfer.

The more evidence that is available to substantiate the willing, knowing, and voluntary aspects of these transactions, the better it is for all parties concerned.

1. Do you agree with the court's final decision?

2. Is the legally created presumption of undue influence too harsh on innocent gift grantees?

3. If you were to create exceptions to the presumption of undue influence rules in gift cases where there was a pre-existing "friendship" between the parties, would they apply to:

- Fiduciary relationships, like attorney-client, doctor-patient, financial advisor-customer, etc.?
- Non-intimate personal friendships? Of what duration?
- Intimate personal friendships? How intimate? Of what duration?
- Intra-family transfers?
- Transfers to health care providers or caretakers?
- Gifts to charities?
- Gifts to minors?

D.   WRITTEN FORM REQUIREMENTS

"A verbal agreement isn't worth the paper it's written on."

—Samuel Goldwyn

"An honest man's word is as good as his bond."

—Don Quixote

"Put it in writing!" These four words are one of the basic commandments of business law. If followed consistently in everyday commerce, they will insulate most transactions from serious legal problems, and lessen the situations where one of the contracting parties is provided an "out" if the business deal has become less attractive than originally negotiated.

1. The first reason to comply is practical:

We know by definition that a contract is the result of a series of negotiations between the parties that culminates in a final, legally enforceable agreement. The best and only way to preserve that agreement, with all its unique aspects, is by reducing it to written form.

The writing memorializes what the parties intended to say, and the rights and duties to which they agree to be bound. When the inevitable business dispute arises and one of the parties to the agreement wants to avoid its enforcement, it is interesting how that party's memory of the terms of a verbal contract suddenly becomes different than that of the party seeking to enforce it.

We are talking about financial self-interest here, and faulty recollections often become misunderstandings or outright lies when the stakes are high enough. Why allow any opportunity for faulty memory or perjured testimony? "Put it in writing," and there is a document at either party's disposal as a reminder, reference and, evidence as to what the agreement is, what performance is required, and where one's legal obligations lie.

2. The second reason to comply is legal:

THE STATUTE OF FRAUDS, passed in England in 1677, which has been adopted in one form or another by all states, requires certain types of contracts to be in written form to be legally enforceable. If a particular type of verbal agreement is "within" the statute, writing is required, and verbal form, even if proven by witnesses, may not be enforced. If it is "outside" the statute, verbal form is legally acceptable and enforceable.

Although it is advisable to put ALL one's agreements in writing so there will be no dispute as to essential terms, most verbal agreements are legally enforceable if their terms can be sufficiently proven. But the following five categories of transactions covered by the statute are deemed too susceptible to potential problems to be enforced in verbal form:

1. Contracts for the sale of any interest in real property (land and anything permanently affixed to the land)
2. Guaranty contracts to pay someone else's debt
3. Contracts for a definite performance term of one year or more
4. Contracts for the sale of goods for $500 or more
5. Special situations – promises to make a will, inheritance promises, finder's fee agreements, marriage contracts, real estate brokerage contracts, and certain service agreements such as assisting the completion of the sale of a business.

In *Whitman, Heffernan, Rhein & Co., Inc. v. Griffin Company, 557 N.Y.S.2d 342 (N.Y. App. 1990)*, the plaintiff was a financial advisor, assisting in the defendant's (Merv Griffin) acquisition of Resort's International, Inc. (Donald Trump), by analyzing and considering various alternatives in the proposed transaction and assisting in arranging necessary financing.

The parties verbally negotiated payment to the plaintiff of performance fees, including some based upon a percentage of the total purchase price. A draft agreement was prepared incorporating this agreement, but was never signed by the defendant. (Danger ahead for plaintiff!)

Once the defendant completed the purchase, it refused to pay the fees to the plaintiff, citing the New York Statute of Frauds, which "provides that an agreement is void, unless evidenced by a writing signed by the party to be charged, 'if the agreement is a contract to pay compensation for services rendered in negotiating the purchase of a business.' The term 'negotiating' includes assisting in the consummation of the transaction."

The plaintiff sued to enforce the verbal agreement and lost at the trial court level, and on appeal. "The services to be rendered by plaintiff, in assisting (the defendant) in evaluating and analyzing the proposed acquisition and providing consultant services, fall within the ambit of the Statute of Frauds, and plaintiff's claims are, therefore barred."

There is also a curious legal requirement regarding the signing of written contracts. Most people would automatically assume that all parties to the agreement must sign it. This is the best procedure, of course. But it is not required under the statute – if signed by less than all its parties, the contract must at least be properly signed by "the party to be charged," as stated in the New York law above.

This means the party against whom the contract is being enforced, which in all disputes is the defendant.

Sean wants to buy Tom's boat. The parties have been negotiating the terms of the deal, and have finally verbally agreed on all aspects, including the price of $50,000. Sean signs a confirming letter that repeats the terms of the transaction and sends it to Tom, requesting he sign and return it. Tom never signs it. Later there is a dispute when Sean realizes he has agreed to buy at a price far above market value, and he refuses to perform. Tom sues for breach of agreement. Sean claims non-compliance with the Statute of Frauds (sale of goods for $500 or more).

Tom wins the case. The confirming letter was the required writing, and the defendant, against whom it is being enforced, signed it.

Same facts, except the dispute occurs when Tom realizes he has agreed to buy at a price far below market value. He refuses to perform, and Sean sues for breach of contract. Tom claims non-compliance with the statute.

Sean loses the case. Even though we have the writing required by the statute, Tom, who is the party to be charged, did not sign it. This renders it legally unenforceable.

In addition to WHO must sign the writing, issues sometimes arise as to HOW one must sign. Any signature or mark that expresses the intention of a party to be bound is sufficient. This includes one's legal name, nickname, signatures with either hand, initials, a seal or stamp, a symbol or making one's mark (X), or having someone else sign for you as your agent. And any medium for signing can be used, such as pencil, pen, ashes, blood, or even crayon, as the next case suggests.

In *Rosenfeld v. Basquiat, 78 F.3d 84 (2nd Cir. 1996)*, the dispute centered around an alleged sales contract for three paintings made by neo-expressionist artist Jean-Michel Basquiat to the art dealer-plaintiff. Basquiat was talented and eccentric, rising to fame and a premature death at age twenty-seven. The plaintiff alleged she had visited the artist's apartment, agreed to buy the paintings for $4,000 each, and gave the artist a $1,000 cash deposit.

"When she asked for a receipt, he insisted on drawing up a 'contract,' got down on the floor and wrote it out in crayon on a large piece of paper, remarking that 'some day this contract will be worth money.'" The document listed the paintings and stated the terms, and she and the artist both signed it. She later returned to pick up the paintings, but claimed the artist convinced her to wait at least two years so he could show the paintings at exhibitions.

When the artist died, the plaintiff sued his estate for delivery of her paintings. It denied her ownership rights, claiming, among other grounds, that the alleged contract violated the New York Statute of Frauds because it lacked a delivery date.

After the trial jury ruled in the plaintiff's favor, the estate appealed, and even though the case was ordered retried due to certain discretionary evidence rulings by the trial judge, the contract written in crayon was validated.

"Any question regarding the Statute of Frauds is governed by the U.C.C.; section 2-201 contract for (sale of goods) $500 or more is unenforceable 'unless there is some writing sufficient to indicate that a contract for sale has been made between the parties and signed by the party (charged). Under the U.C.C., the only term that must appear in the writing is the quantity. Beyond that, 'all that is required is that the writing afford a basis for believing that the alleged oral evidence rests on a real transaction. The writing supplied by the plaintiff indicated the price, the date, the specific paintings involved, and that Rosenfeld paid a deposit. It also bore the signatures of the buyer and seller. Therefore, the writing satisfied the requirements of section 2-201."

Technological advances have also expanded the concept of what constitutes a signature, as noted in the controversial case of *Parma Tile, Mosaic & Marble Company, Inc. v. Estate of Short, 663 N.E.2d 633 (N.Y. App. 1996)*, where the plaintiff was a material supplier on a building project, and refused to deliver tile to a designated subcontractor unless the general contractor guaranteed payment.

The general contractor sent a two-page, unsigned fax that said, "MRLS would guarantee payment for goods delivered to the Nehemiah project in the event Sime Construction does not pay within terms." Its transmission was not preceded by or accompanied with any cover letter. The name MRLS was printed across the top of each page of the unsigned fax, together with its phone number and the date, time, and page number. The plaintiff then began furnishing quantities of tile to the subcontractor.

When the subcontractor, the plaintiff, sued in 1992 demanding payment under the guarantee, MLRS refused, arguing that a guarantee contract fell within the writing requirements of the Statute of Frauds, and since the writing was unsigned, it was not legally enforceable. The defendant also argued that the transmission was, at best, an unsigned guarantee proposal. The trial court entered summary judgment for the plaintiff and allowed enforcement of the unsigned guarantee, ruling that "the heading automatically imprinted by the fax machine on plaintiff's copy of the document satisfied the subscription requirement (of the statute) because an intent to be bound had been demonstrated."

"The Statute of Frauds was not meant to be utilized to evade an obligation intentionally incurred. MRLS should not be permitted to evade its obligation because of the current and extensive use of electronic transmissions in modern business transactions."

After the appellate division affirmed this ruling, leave for further appeal was granted. The Court of Appeals set aside the summary judgment, ruling that the defendant's mere sending of an unsigned guarantee document and its programming of its fax machine to automatically imprint its name across the top of all transmitted pages, "does not, by itself constitute a signing authenticating the contents of the document for Statute of Frauds purposes."

WHAT form must be used for the writing is equally flexible. Again we are seeking a lasting memorial of the terms of the transaction, so one can use almost anything: parchment, paper, a tee shirt, toilet tissue, the back of an envelope, or the bark of a tree. Any form is acceptable, so long as the writing is legible and lasting.

"Any signed memorandum is sufficient to satisfy the Statute of Frauds so long as it (1) identifies the subject matter of the agreement, (2) establishes that a contract has been made, and (3) states the essential terms with reasonable certainty. The memorandum may be written after the alleged oral promise occurred. It does not have to be a formal memorial of the agreement." *Busler v. D&H Manufacturing, Inc., 611 N.E.2d 352 (Ohio App. 1992)*

The legal disputes that occur in this chapter are typical of all contract disputes. They involve the parties entering into an oral agreement and then, when one of them perceives they made a bad business deal, seeking to avoid enforcement of the agreement on the legal ground of non-compliance with the writing requirements of the statute. This raises critical comments like the following, which comes from a case involving breach of an oral promise for lifetime employment:

"Whatever may be the fact with regard to the history of the statute, and whatever may have been the difficulties arising from proof that all sides agree brought about the enactment of the statute of frauds over 300 years ago, it is an anachronism today. The reasons that prompted its passage no longer exist. And, far from serving as a barrier to fraud – in the case of a genuinely aggrieved plaintiff barred from enforcing an oral contract – the statute may actually shield fraud." *O'Hanian v. Avis Rent A Car System, Inc., 779 F.2d 101 (2nd Cir. 1985)*

1. Contracts for the Sale of Any Interest in Real Property

Real estate contracts are treated with the highest degree of legal sanctity. Land has always been a traditional source of wealth and financial security. Real property transactions can involve vacant land, improved property with residential dwellings, commercial offices, mercantile shops, and any other permanent improvements that are made on or to the land.

In *Hoffman v. S V Company, Inc., 628 P.2d 218 (Idaho 1981)*, the court was faced with a dispute based upon the refusal of the defendant to convey real property under an alleged contract with the plaintiff. The real estate "writing" consisted of the plaintiff's signed letter confirming terms of their purchase negotiation, which the defendant did not sign, and the plaintiff's deposit check, which the defendant endorsed and deposited into its account.

In agreeing with the trial court that the agreement was not enforceable by the plaintiff, the majority of the court noted the rationale of the basic law regarding real property transactions, and the Idaho exception to the general rule that the defendant need only sign writings:

"The purpose of the statute is commonly thought to be the prevention of fraudulent assertions of oral contracts for the sale of land . . . The statute effectively insulates from litigation nearly all completely oral transactions involving the sale of land, thus contributing to the stability of title and marketability of land generally. The statute may also stimulate the use of formal written contracts, certainly an advisable practice for transactions as important as land sales.

"An agreement for the sale of real property is invalid unless the agreement or some note or memorandum thereof be in writing and subscribed by the party charged or his agent. Failure to comply with the statute of frauds renders an oral agreement unenforceable both in an action at law for damages and in a suit in equity for specific performance . . . Although the majority of jurisdictions require that the memorandum be signed only by the party against whom enforcement is sought, this Court (in a 1912 case) has construed the Idaho statute to require both parties to a bilateral contract to sign the memorandum."

Often there are disputes concerning whether a particular piece of property is real or personal because of how differently they are treated in our legal system:

- The UCC rules apply only to goods, tangible personal property – real property is specifically excluded.
- Municipalities raise the majority of their revenues by imposing taxes on one's real property. Certain types of personal property are taxed at much lower rates. Again, the laws and procedures differ.
- Owners of property often use it as collateral for borrowing. These loans are usually secured by a mortgage that encumbers the property and is foreclosed by the lender if the borrower defaults. Laws and procedures differ for real or personal property.

Fixtures

Items that are personal property, such as cabinets, bookcases, air conditioning units, and printing presses, can legally become part of the real estate where they are permanently attached. If so, they are called "fixtures" and lose their character as personalty. Often this requires a legal interpretation of the intention of the parties and what is reasonable under the circumstances.

What if a property owner borrows from two different secured lenders, one having a mortgage encumbering real property and the other encumbering personalty, and the borrower defaults? Often both lenders will claim the same item of property as a part of their mortgage lien, and the court must decide the priorities.

John and Marsha own a nice home in suburbia. They borrowed part of the purchase money from CityBank, which has a real estate first mortgage on the property, "and all items of personal property later permanently affixed to it." The owners later borrow additional sums from StateBank, securing that home contents loan with a personal property chattel first mortgage that states, "encumbering all tangible personalty located within the residence of the borrowers." Lining the walls of the home's living room are built-in bookshelves of fine Philippine mahogany that are bolted to the supporting struts of their load-bearing walls.

When John and Marsha default on both loans at the same time, both lenders seek to foreclose on the bookshelves.

An analysis of the case leads to a reasonable conclusion that it was the intention of the owners that the bookshelves become fixtures. Any type of personal property is removable, but the more difficult to remove or more damage to the surrounding property in accomplishing the removal, the more it appears that the item is a part of the realty. Bolting the bookshelves to the superstructure of the walls of the house is more consistent with a permanent attachment.

Real Property Interests Included

Verbal agreements involving the following transactions are within the statute and must be in required written form:

- Purchase or sale of any interest in real property
- Mortgages encumbering any interest in real property
- Easements that allow the use of one's real property
- Leases of real property for a term of one year or longer
- Real estate brokerage listing and commission payment agreements

Hank verbally agrees to sell Joe his farm property located on fifty acres of land, which includes (1) a five-bedroom house, (2) separate outbuildings including barn, silo, and livestock enclosures, (3) ten apple trees, (4) ten bushels of apples from the trees, and (5) one hundred chickens, for $150,000, and to (6) lease an additional ten acres of adjoining land for six months at a fixed price of $10,000. Joe wants out of the deal. What is the result?

Items 1, 2, and 3 are clearly real property, requiring a writing. Item 5 is clearly personal property, so the oral agreement is legally enforceable. Item 4 could be a bit tricky – we need more facts. If the apples are to remain attached to the trees, they retain the character of their source and remain part of the land. If, however, they are picked or have fallen on the ground, they are personalty. Item 6 is outside the statute and enforceable because the verbal lease is under one year.

Here are two cases where what appear to be verbal real estate contracts are ruled outside the statute, and enforceable:

In *Pardoe & Graham Real Estate, Inc. v. Schulz Home Corp., 525 S.E.2d 284 (Sup. Ct. Va. 2000)*, the defendant builder promised to pay the plaintiff real estate broker a 2.5% commission when he built a custom home on a lot already owned by the home buyer. This promise was in the form of an amendment to a written agreement, whereby the defendant agreed to pay the plaintiff a 6% commission on the sale of any speculative homes that they had built. The amendment was never signed by the defendant.

When a lot owner hired the defendant to build his home, the plaintiff claimed its 2.5% commission. The defendant refused to pay on the basis of failure to comply with the Statute of Frauds. The trial court ruled for the defendant-builder, and the plaintiff-broker appealed. The appellate court reversed.

"The Statute of Frauds covers a contract for the sale of real estate. Real estate does not include a building that is unattached to land. Since construction of the Carlton home had not begun at the time of the oral contract between Pardoe and Schulz, the home was not included in the definition of real estate under Virginia law."

The court viewed the oral agreement as one for the performance of services, and thus enforceable as being outside the statute.

"An oral contract providing for a sales commission is not subject to the statute of frauds when that contract is based on the sale of a house to be affixed to land that does not include a contemporaneous sale of the land to which the house will be attached."

In *Firth v. Lu, 49 P.3d 117 (Wash. 2002)*, the plaintiff verbally agreed to buy the stock ownership of the defendant in cooperative apartment unit #2 for $180,000, and paid a $3,000 deposit, with the closing to be in October. The defendant requested a three-month extension of time to close. The plaintiff demanded the original closing date and sued for specific performance. The defendant moved to dismiss on the basis of the failure of the alleged verbal real estate contract to satisfy the Statute of Frauds.

The trial court held the verbal agreement valid and ordered specific performance. The appeals court reversed. The Supreme Court reversed again, upholding the trial court decision based on the distinction between real estate such as a condominium where the property owned is real estate, and a cooperative where the ownership is personal property.

"The corporation owns the land and building that contains 19 apartments. Each apartment is associated with a block of shares in the corporation. The corporation rents the units to the shareholders under long-term leases. One may become a resident only by buying a block of stock associated with apartment 2.

"Stock in a corporation whose only asset is real property is not an interest in real property; it is ownership in a corporation."

The Part Performance Exception

Like most areas of business law, there are numerous fairness exceptions to the applicable general rules that seek to keep the scales of justice in balance. Part performance is an equitable doctrine that courts use to accomplish this in the area of real property contracts.

In an oral real estate sales contract, if the buyer has made partial payment of the agreed consideration, some states will take the agreement outside the statute and allow its enforcement.

Other states require additional facts that show the buyer has paid a deposit and has also been allowed by the seller to take early possession of the property.

The majority of states take a harder line before they will allow the part performance doctrine to enforce a verbal real estate contract. In addition to the part payment and the granting of occupancy, they also require facts that show the buyer has made valuable improvements to the seller's property with the seller's knowledge and consent. This is our old friend again in disguise, the fairness doctrine we call *promissory estoppel*.

Ross owns ten acres of fertile land in the Mississippi Delta. Amos is a poor, hardworking farmer who has always dreamed of owning his own property. The parties reach a verbal agreement whereby Amos will buy the land for $15,000, payable in five yearly installments of $3,000 from the sale of the crops he cultivates on the land. Amos pays a deposit of $100 and starts to clear the property and farm it. Six months later, Ross receives an offer from

Delta Sugar Co. to buy his ten acres for $50,000, accepts it, and tells Amos his oral purchase agreement has been cancelled.

You can almost feel the blatant unfairness of this situation if Ross is allowed to avoid the contract with Amos. Ross has a verbal agreement to sell to Amos, Amos has changed his position in reasonable reliance upon it by paying the deposit and improving the vacant land, and Ross should be legally prevented (estopped) to deny the legal enforceability of his verbal (promissory) contract.

What if no deposit was paid by Amos? What if he cleared the land, prepared it for planting, put the seeds into the ground, and grew some crops? Should Ross be allowed to escape liability because of the lack of this technical requirement? Probably not. Most states would create a legal fiction for fairness purposes by "pretending" that the work done by poor Amos that improved Ross's property was the same as an implied deposit.

In *Sutton v. Warner, 12 Cal. App. 4th 415 (Cal. App. 1993)*, Warner inherited a residence and some other properties. To afford the mortgage payments, Warner verbally agreed to allow Sutton to purchase the property by paying a $15,000 down payment toward the $185,000 purchase price and making all required mortgage and real estate tax payments. Sutton also made valuable improvements to the property, relying upon the oral purchase agreement.

When the market value of the property greatly increased, Warner offered to sell the property to Sutton for $250,000, following which Sutton sued for specific performance. The trial court ruled for Sutton on the grounds of the part performance exception, and the appellate court affirmed:

"The doctrine of part performance by the purchaser is a well-recognized exception to the statute of frauds as applied to contracts for the sale or lease of real property.

"Under the doctrine of part performance, the oral agreement for the transfer of an interest in real estate is enforced when the buyer has taken possession of the property *and either* makes a full or partial payment of the purchase price, *or* makes valuable and substantial improvements to the property."

The longer the period of allowed occupancy of the property under the verbal purchase agreement by the buyer, and the more improvements he makes that benefit the seller, the more likely courts are to uphold the buyer's rights under part performance.

2. Guaranty Contracts to Pay Someone Else's Debt

Your verbal promise to pay your own debt is a direct, original, and primary obligation that is outside the statute. It is legally enforceable against you by your creditor without legal writing requirements (unless required by another section of the statute).

A secondary, collateral, or guaranty promise is within the statute and must satisfy written form. It typically is a promise you make, not to initially obligate yourself to pay, but only to be responsible if the other party who has the primary obligation to pay fails to do so. The statute refers to these as "promises to pay the debts of another."

Len is a hard-working young man who needs a computer for his work. He and his best friend, Alan, a wealthy doctor, go to Miami Motors, where Alan is a long-time customer. Len chooses his purchase (let's assume it is under $500), but is short of cash to close the deal. Alan says, "Give my pal Len the item, send him your bill, don't worry about it; if he doesn't pay you, I will." Later, after Len fails to pay the bill for the computer, the seller demands payment from Alan on his verbal guarantee.

Alan does not have to pay. While Len's promise to pay was primary and verbally enforceable, Alan's is a secondary guarantee promise and within the statute. The lack of a writing prevents enforcement against Alan.

What if Alan's response after Len came up short of cash was, "Give Len the item, don't worry about it, put it on my bill." Now Alan is liable. He made a primary promise to pay.

Notice how easy it would be for the seller in the guarantee situation to protect itself if it were aware of this potential problem of enforcement. As soon as Alan made his verbal guarantee promise, the seller could have simply had Alan sign the purchase invoice or other written receipt for the transaction. That would be a sufficient writing to comply with the statute.

These disputes often involve insurance companies, such as in *Carter v. Allstate Insurance Company, 962 S.W.2d 268 (Tex. App. 1998)*, where the plaintiffs had an auto accident with the defendant's insured, and then sued the defendant for failure to honor an oral pre-suit settlement agreement.

The defendant claimed enforcement was barred by the Texas statute of frauds, under its "suretyship provision," as "a (secondary) promise by another person to answer for the debt, default, or miscarriage of another person."

The trial court granted summary judgment for the defendant, and the appellate court reversed, distinguishing the nature of Allstate's obligations:

"Had Allstate only assumed responsibility to pay damages whenever its insured became legally responsible, it would have assumed the role of a surety. When Allstate took the initiative to settle the claim for which its insured had not yet become legally responsible, however, it was settling not only its insured's potential liability but its own possible obligation to pay and its own duty to defend its insured."

The Main Benefit Exception

A verbal guaranty promise often benefits the guarantor as well as the primary obligor. In the guarantee example above, Alan was assisting Len, but he was also motivated by their friendship. At what point does the amount of benefit to the guarantor convert his non-binding verbal promise into a legally enforceable obligation?

If the guarantor will receive financial benefit from his verbal guarantee promise, it will be treated like a primary promise for enforcement purposes. How much benefit will tip the scales from incidental to significant? The state law involved and the facts of each dispute are critical – the guarantor will claim non-liability because of lack of written form, and the seller-creditor will claim this fairness exception. Again, the objective standard of reasonableness is used by the courts to resolve these disputes.

Let's assume that Len works as the general manager of a business for which he needs the computer. If Alan were an owner of that business, or Len's boss, even if he has no separate friendship with Len, the main purpose of the guarantee would appear to be to benefit the business. If so, Alan is liable.

In verbal guarantee cases, courts will usually ask and seek to answer three questions:

1. Who made the primary promise to pay?
2. Who made the guarantee of the primary promise?
3. What was the underlying purpose of the guarantee?

In *Power Entertainment, Inc. v. National Football League Properties, Inc., 151 F.3d 247 (5th Cir. 1998),* the plaintiff alleged that the defendant had verbally agreed to transfer it a license to sell its collectible cards. This was in return for the plaintiff's promise to assume an $800,000 debt for unpaid royalties from card sales owed to the defendant by its former licensee, which had filed for bankruptcy.

When the defendant refused to honor the oral agreement, the plaintiff sued for breach of contract. The trial court granted the defendant's motion to dismiss on the grounds of failure to comply with the statute of frauds writing requirements for the plaintiff's guarantee promise.

The appellate court reversed, since "The Texas courts have adopted the 'main purpose doctrine,' which, broadly speaking, removes an oral agreement to pay the debt of another from the statute of frauds 'wherever the main purpose and object of the promisor is not to answer for another, but to subserve some purpose of its own ...'"

Some states, like New York, claim they do not recognize this exception, but in actuality do the same thing on a type of estoppel exception when a verbal guaranty promise "is supported by a new consideration moving to the promisor and beneficial to him and that the promisor has become in the intention of the parties a principal debtor primarily liable." *Martin Roofing v. Goldstein, 469 N.Y.S.2d 595 (N.Y. 1983)*

The "guarantee" disputes that present the most problems of judicial interpretation are those involving promises of indemnity, such as in the case of *Feiler v. Rosenbloom, 416 A.2d 1345 (Md. App. 1980),* where the parties were directors of a corporation that manufactured buttons and needed additional financing to sustain itself.

The bank loaned it $250,000, and to assure repayment, the defendant and others signed as loan guarantors. The plaintiff did not want to sign, but he nevertheless orally agreed to be responsible for "a pro rata one-sixth share of the loan payable to the five signatory guarantors who would be required to pay in the event of default by the corporation," and the others signed in reliance upon his promise.

When the corporation defaulted on its debt to the bank, the guarantors were required to pay off the amounts due. They demanded the agreed share from the plaintiff, who refused to pay, and sued him to enforce his oral promise of indemnity. The trial court ruled against the plaintiff, entering judgment against him for $42,666.67 plus interest.

On appeal, the judgment was affirmed. "Feiler's promise to pay, by way of indemnity, was a contract with the appellees. No third party was involved, ergo, the Statute of Frauds, past or present, does not apply."

"The type of indemnity contract which has produced the divergence in cases is the four party situation in which it is alleged that the promisor induced the promise to become surety for P by promising to save him harmless or indemnifying him. The decided preponderance of judicial opinion is that a promise to indemnify is not within the statute." *Simpson, Handbook on the Law of Suretyship, sec. 39 (1950)*

"The first and most fundamental reason underlying the majority decisions is that it is a horrid injustice to let the defendant escape his duty to indemnify after inducing the plaintiff to undertake the suretyship obligation for another person." *Corbin, A Comprehensive Treatise on the Rules of Contract Law, sec. 385 (1950)*

3. Contracts for a Definite Performance Term of One Year or More

The resolution of these disputes is often complicated by the convoluted wording of the statute itself. The Massachusetts statute is typical:

"No action shall be brought . . . upon an agreement that is not to be performed within one year from the making thereof; unless the promise, contract or agreement upon which such action is brought, or some memorandum or note thereof, is in writing and signed by the party to be charged therewith or by some person thereunto by him lawfully authorized." *Doherty v. Doherty Insurance Agency, Inc., 878 F.2d 546 (1st Cir. 1989)*

What in the world does this mean? Reduced to its essence, if the verbal agreement has a stated time period for performance of anything less than one year, it is outside the statute and verbal form is enforceable. Conversely, a definite time period of one year or more requires written form.

Courts are only required to look at the literal wording of the agreement itself, NOT events that happen afterward or any surrounding circumstances, in computing whether or not the one-year-or-more term exists. The running of the required time begins at the inception of the contract.

Fortunately, it can be simplified as "the one-year rule." If the specific terms of the verbal agreement state a fixed duration of anything less than one year, it is outside the statute and verbal form is enforceable. Conversely, a definite time period of one year or more requires written form.

In *Iacono v. Lyons, 16 S.W.3d 92 (Tex. App. 2000)*, the plaintiff and the defendant were long-time friends. The defendant invited the plaintiff to join her on a trip to Las Vegas, and would also pay all expenses, including providing money for gambling, since the defendant believed the plaintiff was lucky. Before the trip, the plaintiff had a dream about winning the jackpot of a particular Las Vegas slot machine.

The defendant also offered "to split 50-50" any gambling winnings. The plaintiff accepted the offers and the parties went to Las Vegas, where they played slot machines at Caesar's Palace. After losing $47, the defendant wanted to leave, but the plaintiff begged her to stay. The defendant agreed, so long as she could put the coins into the machines because it took the plaintiff, who suffered from rheumatoid arthritis and was in a wheelchair, too long. The plaintiff agreed and noticed a $1 machine that looked like the one in her dream. They played it once with no payoff. On the second play, however, it hit a jackpot of $1,908,064, to be paid out over a period of twenty years to the winner.

The defendant told Caesar's she was the sole winner, denied her oral agreement to split the winnings with the plaintiff, and refused to share the winnings she received. The plaintiff sued for breach of contract, and the defendant moved for summary judgment. The trial court ruled for the defendant based upon failure to comply with the one-year rule.

On appeal, the case was reversed and the plaintiff's right to 50% of the winnings was enforced. The trial court mistakenly believed the agreement could not be performed within one year because of the twenty-year payout of winnings, rather than looking only at the specific terms of the agreement, which did not specify any duration.

"(The statute of frauds) does not apply if the contract, from its terms, could possibly be performed within a year – however improbable performance within one year may be . . . To determine the applicability of the statute of frauds with indefinite contracts, this Court may use any reasonably clear method of ascertaining the intended length of performance. The method is used to determine the parties' intentions at the time of contracting. The fact that the entire performance within one year is not required, or expected, will not bring an agreement within the statute."

Employment contracts are often the subject of these cases:

Disney hires Tom Cruise and Tom Hanks to work as actors in their movie studio under two separate verbal contracts. The Cruise contract states, "We hire you for a term of six months, with our option to renew for a term of one year." The Hanks contract states, "We hire you for a term of one year, subject to our right to cancel after 6 months." Cruise and Hanks both work at Disney for two years, and are then fired. They both sue for breach of contract. Disney defends, saying their verbal agreements are legally unenforceable.

This is not as complicated as it looks. The Cruise contract term was six months, so it is verbally enforceable. The fact he actually worked there longer than one year is immaterial.

If Disney verbally exercised its option and renewed for one year, that would violate the statute. The Hanks contract is really of six-month duration due to its limiting terms. It, like the Cruise contract, is verbally enforceable, regardless of how long Hanks was actually employed.

The "For Life" Contracts Exception

What if a verbal employment contract states, "We hire you for life," or words of similar import, indicating a promise of lifetime employment? Is this to be treated as governed by the statute's writing requirements or not? The test remains whether or not there is a "fixed period of one year or more."

A definite time period such as six months or six years leaves no room for speculation. The six-year contract is "not possible of performance within one year" because its express terms state otherwise. Its duration exceeds the one-year rule and therefore must be in writing.

But a "for life" contract can last one second or one hundred years. It is impossible to determine its ultimate duration from its stated terms. In almost all states, it is outside the statute and may be verbally enforced, the same as any other contingent agreement. Whether it states, "You are hired for the remainder of your life" or "the term of this agreement will continue until the Miami Dolphins win the Super Bowl," we still lack the required definitive term of one year or more to be apparent from the specific wording of the agreement.

Currently only a few states, including New York, require "lifetime employment" contracts to be in writing. They reason that this wording should be treated the same as if it referred to a lengthy specific term, because such situations are usually accompanied by circumstances of changing existing jobs, moving to different areas, or other instances of detrimental reliance.

The counter argument is more sensible. If you want to require a written agreement in these situations, simply specify a definite term of one year or more, and then keep renewing it until the end of the person's life.

In *Hodge v. Evans, 823 F.2d 559 (D.C. Cir. 1987)*, the plaintiff was hired as vice president and general counsel of the defendant's company, based on oral promises of lifetime employment arising from this dialogue:

Hodge: "No. 1, the job must be permanent. Because of my age, I have a great fear about going back into the marketplace again. I want to be here until I retire."

Evans: "I accept that condition."

The plaintiff moved from his former company in Pittsburgh, Pennsylvania, to Washington, D.C., and began work in September of 1980. He was fired in May of 1981. The plaintiff sued for breach of his verbal contract of permanent employment, and the defendant raised failure to comply with the one-year rule of the statute of frauds requiring written form.

After a jury trial and award to the plaintiff of $175,000 in damages for breach of the oral agreement, the defendant appealed. On the fact that the lifetime employment agreement in question was outside the statute of frauds, and enforceable without being in writing, the court affirmed:

"Hodge argues that . . . a permanent or lifetime employment contract does not fall within the statute because it is capable of full performance within one year if the employee were to die within that period. Hodge's view of the statute's applicability to lifetime or permanent employment contracts has, in fact, been accepted by an overwhelming majority of courts and commentators.

"The enforceability of a contract under the statute does not depend on the actual course of subsequent events or on the expectations of the parties. Instead, the statute applies only to those contracts whose performance could not possibly or conceivably be completed within one year. The statute of frauds is thus inapplicable if, at the time the contract is formed, any contingent event could complete the *terms* of the contract within one year."

4. Contracts for the Sale of Goods for $500 or More

This is by far the largest category of commercial transactions, and is governed by Section 2-201(1) of the UCC. All contracts for the sale (not gifts or leases) of goods (tangible personal property – not real property or personal services) that have an agreed price of $500 or more are within the statute and must be in writing to be legally enforceable:

"Except as otherwise provided in this section a contract for the sale of goods for the price of $500 or more is not enforceable by way of action or defense unless there is some writing sufficient to indicate that a contract for sale has been made between the parties and signed by the party against whom enforcement is sought or by his authorized agent or broker."

Efforts are made annually in various states to adjust the dollar limit upward to reflect the needs of the current commercial marketplace. It is argued that only "expensive" transactions should have to be the subject of written contracts, and that the protection of the consumer by a required writing is not needed for common transactions of a lesser amount. But what should be the dollar threshold?

What about $1,000 or more? $5,000 or more? So far, all states retain the $500 or more threshold.

> Diane and Jill are antique collectors with different specialties. Diane collects art pottery and Jill collects rare books. They verbally agree that Diane will buy Jill's twelve-volume set of Dickens for $600 and Jill will buy Diane's ten-piece Royal Doulton tea set for $1,000. When the required performance date arrives, either Diane or Jill declines because she believes she made a bad bargain.
>
> If both transactions are viewed as two separate oral contracts, neither is legally enforceable due to lack of the required writing. If, however, they are viewed as individual agreements to buy and sell each item in the set(s), with no individual items costing over $500, which is probably not likely in these facts, no writing is required. The specific wording of the agreements will be crucial to the outcome.

The Non-Signer Exception

We have previously discussed how the parties often follow their period of verbal negotiations with some form of writing that sets forth the essential terms of their agreement. It can be a formalized contract, but is often some type of confirming letter or memorandum that acknowledges their intention to be bound.

Though usually signed by all parties to the agreement, this contract writing need only be signed by the party against whom it is to be enforced (the defendant), to be legally enforceable against that party.

But what if enforcement of a transaction for the verbal sale of goods of $500 or more is sought against a non-signing party? It is usually not enforceable. However, we have another fairness exception under Section 2-201 (2) of the UCC:

"Between merchants, if within a reasonable time a writing in confirmation of the contract and sufficient against the sender is received and the party receiving it has reasons to know its contents, it satisfies the requirements of subsection (1) against such party unless written notice of objection to its contents is given within ten days after it is received."

Between merchants means they both specialize in the subject matter of the particular transaction, or it represents their primary business enterprise. The legal test involves whether or not a majority of their business time is spent in the particular activity.

- A rare book dealer who contracted to buy a car would not be considered a merchant in that matter, although the auto dealer selling the car would.
- A transaction between merchants for the purchase of a car would require that both seller and buyer be in the automobile business, in one form or another, as their main commercial enterprise.

If both S and B are contracting merchants, and S signs a confirming memorandum of the deal and sends it to B, and B receives it and does not object to its terms within ten days of receipt – B is legally bound even though he never signed it.

The reason for this exception to the signing rule is that merchants, by virtue of their experience and expertise, are held to a higher standard by the law. Sales of goods between them which are governed by the UCC are to be encouraged, rather than legally limited.

> Fun, Inc., a toy manufacturer, verbally agrees to sell 5,000 of its Mr. Macho action figures to Toys Miami, Inc., a toy retailer, for $1 each. Five days later, it personally delivers to the buyer its signed memo confirming the details of the sale, requesting the buyer's signature and return. Toys Miami, Inc., puts the memo in its file and does not sign it. Thirty days later they phone Fun, Inc., to cancel their order because Mr. Sensitivity figures are now the rage and Mr. Macho will not sell, and say, "Besides, we never signed anything." Fun, Inc., refuses to cancel and demands enforcement of the agreement.
>
> Fun, Inc., will win. Both parties are in the toy business. The signed confirming memo was received and not objected to by Toys Miami, Inc. As a merchant, they should have known about this exception to the general rule. Since they didn't protect themselves by a timely objection to the memo, they are bound by it.

In *Thomson Printing Machinery Co. v. B.F. Goodrich Co., 714 F.2d 744 (7th Cir. 1983)*, the plaintiff met with the defendant to discuss the purchase of used printing machinery for a price of $9,000. Four days later, the plaintiff sent the defendant a purchase order for the equipment with a $1,000 deposit check. Hearing no objection, the plaintiff called the defendant weeks later to arrange to remove the machines and was told they had been sold to someone else. The plaintiff then sued for breach of contract, asserting the applicability of the merchant non-signer rule.

The defendant asserted by way of defense that no contract had been formed, and "that in any event the alleged oral contract was unenforceable due to the Statute of Frauds. Thomson's writing in confirmation cannot qualify for the

2-201(2) exception because it was not received by anyone at Goodrich who had reason to know its contents."

"Goodrich claims that Thomson erred in not specifically designating on the envelope, check, or purchase order that the items were intended for Ingram Meyers or the surplus equipment department. Consequently, Goodrich contends, it was unable to 'find a home' for the check and purchase order despite attempts to do so . . ."

Notwithstanding a jury verdict for the plaintiff, the trial court entered judgment for the defendant based upon the plaintiff's failure to satisfy the Statute of Frauds "signed by the party to be charged" requirement. The appellate court reversed:

"Even if we go beyond the literal requirements of 2-201(2) and read into the 'receipt' requirement the 'receipt of notice' rule of 1-201(27)*, we still think Thomson Printing satisfied the 'merchants' exception.

"It is effective for a particular transaction . . . from the time when it would have been brought to (the attention of the individual conducting that transaction) if the organization had executed *due diligence.*"

Notice the court's wording, which clearly indicates that a business law time bomb exploded in the face of the defendant which they could easily have defused:

"If Goodrich had exercised due diligence in handling Thomson Printing's purchase order and check, these items would have reasonably promptly come to Ingram Meyers' attention. First, the purchase order on its face should have alerted the mailroom that the documents referred to a purchase of used printing equipment. Since Goodrich had only one surplus machinery department the documents 'home' should not have been difficult to find. Second, even if the mailroom would have had difficulty in immediately identifying the kind of transaction involved, the purchase order had Thomson Printing's phone number printed on it and we think a 'reasonable routine' in these particular circumstances would have involved at some point in the process a simple phone call to Thomson Printing. Thus, we think Goodrich's mailroom mishandled the confirmatory writings. This failure should not permit Goodrich to escape liability by pleading nonreceipt."

The Special Manufacture Exception

When the parties enter into a purely verbal sales agreement for the creation of a unique, specialized, or custom item costing $500 or more, another fairness exception applies which eliminates the writing requirements, under UCC 2-201(3)(a):

"If the goods (are) to be specially manufactured for the buyer and are not suitable for sale to others in the ordinary course of the seller's business and the seller, before notice of repudiation is received and under circumstances which reasonably indicate that the goods are for the buyer, has made either a substantial beginning of their manufacture or commitments for their procurement."

Once the seller substantially begins the manufacture of the specialty item, the buyer is estopped to cancel based on the statute because the item usually cannot be sold to anyone else. If the buyer could cancel due to lack of the required writing, injustice to the seller would result, since he would totally lose the time, effort, and costs expended.

Charles, a lawyer, verbally contracts with Miami Printing for all his customized office stationery for a total price of $700. The printer begins the job, has finished the business cards and envelopes, and is halfway through the print run of letterheads when Charles calls to cancel. He doesn't give a reason, but the printer suspects he founds someone to do the work at a lower price. The printer demands full payment for the finished work.

To allow cancellation by the buyer would result in a severe injustice. Miami Printing would be unable to find anyone else to assume payment of the job or purchase the specialty items because they are one of a kind.

Even if Charles argues that the transaction is really a sale of services rather than goods, and therefore not governed by the UCC or the statute, he still is faced with a legally enforceable verbal contract.

In *LTV Aerospace v. Bateman, 492 S.W.2d 703 (Tex. App. 1973),* LTV needed to buy a quantity of special export shipping crates to deliver a number of its all-terrain vehicles to Southeast Asia. It circulated a detailed sheet of specifications to prospective bidders, and Bateman's proposal exceeding $500 to sell 8,000 crates was accepted after extensive verbal discussions. Though there were written bid and purchase order communications exchanged by the parties, none were ever fully signed.

After Bateman had delivered approximately 653 crates, LTV's Tyler, Texas, plant closed and it refused to pay for any additional crates. Bateman sued for breach of contract and demanded damages for lost profits of $25,000.

The trial jury ruled for Bateman, and on appeal that decision was affirmed:

"These shipping crates or containers were manufactured by appellee to detailed specifications required by appellant, and they were to be used for shipping overseas an all-terrain vehicle manufactured by appellant. They were not suitable for sale to others in the ordinary course of appellee's business. The record discloses that appellee had made a substantial beginning in manufacture of the goods, and it was done for appellant's benefit before any notice of repudiation was given or received."

Notice that this exception allows enforcement of a verbal agreement for the sale of goods of $500 or more with no writing of any kind, not even a confirming letter or memorandum.

The Part Payment or Part Delivery Exception

This type of partial performance in a verbal sale of goods contract takes it outside the statute and allows enforcement because that conduct is a clear expression of the intention of the parties to be legally bound, under UCC 2-201(3)(c):

"With respect to goods for which payment has been made and accepted or which have been received and accepted."

Some states reason that such partial performance is a ratification of the contract; others use estoppel reasoning in allowing enforcement.

The Courtroom Admissions Exception

UCC 2-201(3)(b) also validates a contract that does not otherwise satisfy the "sale of goods of $500 or more" requirements of the statute:

"If the party against whom enforcement is sought admits in his pleading, testimony or otherwise in court that a contract for sale was made, but the contract is not enforceable under this provision beyond the quantity of goods admitted."

These situations of courtroom admissions of a contract are based upon the contract doctrines of waiver of defenses, ratification of otherwise legally invalid contracts, and estoppel to deny the enforceability of such agreements.

5. Special Situations

- A verbal promise to make or modify a will for the financial benefit of another must be written. Estate laws are highly technical, and the specific legal formalities surrounding the creation of testamentary documents are very detailed. There is too much risk of wrongdoing in allowing verbal inheritance agreements, because the party creating the contract is now dead and cannot state his true intentions.

- A verbal agreement to pay a fee to another contingent upon them finding a person or a business opportunity, or rewarding them for specific actions, or agreeing to compensate them for some required performance, must also be written. Again, any and all such unusual arrangements must be documented in written form to assure the intentions of the parties are followed.

    This also applies to fee-splitting agreements between attorneys, as was the case in *Chambers v. Kay, 2002 Cal. LEXIS 7396 (Cal. 2002)*, where Chambers was serving as a co-counsel in a sexual harassment action Kay had previously filed on behalf of his client, Rena Weeks. A dispute arose between the parties regarding settlement efforts, and Kay then sent a letter to Chambers removing him from the case.

    This letter also confirmed that he would receive the compensation previously agreed upon, "that is: in the event the case was settled before depositions, '16.5% of the attorney's fees called for under my agreement with (Weeks), which is 40% of the monies recovered'; thereafter, 'an increase to 28% of the fees specified under the agreement with Weeks; and reimbursement of the costs (Chambers) advanced to date." Chambers accepted the compensation.

    After the Weeks case resulted in a large award of compensatory and punitive damages for her, Kay offered to pay Chambers only $200 per hour for his rendered services. Chambers sued for breach of contract, the trial court granted summary judgment to Kay, Chambers appealed, and the appellate court affirmed:

    "(California Rule of Professional Conduct 2-200, patterned after the Statute of Frauds) provides: (A) a member shall not divide a fee for legal services with a lawyer who is not a partner of, associate of, or shareholder with the member unless: (1) The client has consented in writing thereto after a full disclosure has been made in writing that a division of fees will be made and the terms of such division."

Here is another liability time bomb that detonated, right in the wallet of attorney Chambers. All he had to do was confirm that Weeks had consented to his fee-splitting arrangement. She most certainly would have done so, since it had no effect on the total contingent fee she had agreed to pay.

• Agreements to marry were at one time common in this country, and still are in other venues. Because of their highly specialized nature and the sanctity of the relationship, written form is required. The same holds true for antenuptial and postnuptial agreements, where the parties agree before or after marriage on the financial arrangements to be made in the event of divorce or death.

The Equitable Estoppel Exception

In situations where the parties have made a verbal agreement that falls within any of the categories of the Statute of Frauds that require adherence to its writing and signing requirements, they may nevertheless be excused from this formality if they satisfy the elements of equitable estoppel:

As related to the party estopped, they are: "(1) conduct which amounts to a false representation or concealment of material facts, or, at least, which is calculated to convey the impression that the facts are otherwise than, and inconsistent with, those which the party subsequently attempts to assert; (2) intention, or at least expectation, that such conduct shall be acted upon by the other party; (3) knowledge, actual or constructive, of the real facts."

As related to the party claiming the estoppel, they are: "(1) lack of knowledge and of the means of knowledge of the truth as to the facts in question; (2) reliance upon the conduct of the party estopped; and (3) action based thereon of such a character as to change his position." *First Interstate Bank of Idaho, N.A. v. West, 693 P.2d 1053 (Idaho 1984)*

Interpreting Written Contracts

We know that "put it in writing" is the basic commandment of doing business successfully. Equally as important is "read it before you sign it." Parties are presumed to know the content and legal import of their contracts. Once you sign it, you are bound by its terms, good or bad.

THE PAROL EVIDENCE RULE encourages written agreements because it bars from legal consideration any prior written or verbal communications between the parties that seeks to alter, vary, or contradict their signed written contract. This law recognizes the inherent unfairness and potential danger of one of the parties trying to escape from a transaction and succeeding because they are more believable in the false story they concoct to justify such action.

The four corners of the writing are the best evidence of the final completed agreement of the parties, and it usually cannot be modified by outside matters, unless to explain prior dealings of the parties, supply missing information, clear ambiguities, or correct obvious clerical or typographical errors. All prior negotiations are deemed to be merged into the final contract. Thus, a fully integrated contract is the best evidence of what agreement was made and intended by the parties.

Robin applies for an employment position with Samaritan Hospital as a physical therapist. She signs a contract that states, "Employer may terminate employment at any time with or without cause by 14 days written notice," and begins work.

When she is fired six months later, she sues for breach of contract, claiming there were prior verbal discussions whereby the employer had said in response to her questions about job security, "You cannot be fired without cause, you are guaranteed a hearing, and even if fired it is not effective for 30 days." The employer denied this conversation.

Robin loses. The written contract is binding. It is presumed to include all prior negotiations. It is clear and unambiguous in this case. Robin could easily have protected herself by proofreading the written contract and continuing negotiations until it said exactly what she claimed the parties agreed. If you sign a writing without reading it, you usually do so at your peril.

Robin negotiates to buy Tina's car. A final written contract is signed by the parties which states that Robin "agrees to buy Tina's 1999 blue Chevrolet two-door sedan for $5,000, payable in cash no later than fifteen days from today." A dispute occurs because Tina has two blue Chevies, a Corvair and a Camaro. Robin claims she was buying the Camaro, and Tina claims she was selling the Corvair.

In this case, we have an ambiguity as to the subject matter of the transaction. Parol evidence of the prior negotiations or other outside circumstances may be introduced to resolve the dispute. The objective here is to help the court interpret the true contract intended by the parties, not to contradict it.

Ambiguity is the reason most commonly raised in cases to justify the judge looking beyond the four corners of a written agreement. The case of *Idaho Migrant Council, Inc. v. Warila, 890 P.2d 30 (Wyo. 1995)*, is typical. IMC leased property from Warila for use as a Migrant Head Start Center. The written lease agreement, prepared by IMC, contained a clause allowing IMC to terminate without penalty, under certain conditions.

One year after beginning the lease, IMC invoked the termination clause. The parties then attempted to negotiate a settlement of their differences through their attorneys, relating to whether or not the conditions for termination had in fact been reached. A verbal settlement was reached, a written agreement was prepared, but the Warilas refused to sign it.

IMC sued to enforce the oral settlement agreement that allowed it to terminate upon payment of two years' rent to the lessor. The trial court ruled the termination clause in the written lease to be ambiguous, construed it against IMC, and enforced the settlement. The appellate court affirmed, and noted, "We have repeatedly held that a contract will be construed most strongly against the party who drafted the contract."

"Contract interpretation is the process of ascertaining the meaning of the words used by the parties to express their intent. We generally look to the 'four corners' of an instrument to determine the intent of the parties. However, this rule is only applicable where the language clearly and unambiguously expresses the intent of the parties. If the meaning of a provision in a contract is not readily apparent, the court may resort to competent evidence of extraneous circumstances to explain the ambiguity."

Written agreements commonly have "integration clauses" at their conclusion, located immediately above the signatures of the parties, that literally caution the parties against seeking to alter the clear terms of the final agreement they have made.

A typical integration clause was present in *Malmstrom v. Kaiser Aluminum, 187 Cal. App.3d 299 (Cal. App. 1986)*, a case where Kaiser was granted a summary judgment in a dispute between it and a former employee about an alleged oral promise of lifetime employment that conflicted with a subsequent written contract that said the employment was terminable at will. It read as follows:

Paragraph 1 – "Employer employs and shall continue to employ Employee at such compensation and for such a length of time as shall be mutually agreeable to Employer and Employee."

Paragraph 6 – "This agreement shall supersede all previous agreements by and between Employer and Employee and shall be retroactive to the date on which Employee commenced his employment."

In *Leitz v. Thorson, 833 P.2d 343 (Or. 1992)*, the plaintiffs leased commercial space from the defendant to open a flower shop. Before the lease was signed, the defendant allegedly told the plaintiffs they could have a freestanding sign. The signed lease, however, had a standard clause that said, "Tenant shall not erect or install any signs or advertising media . . . without written consent of the Landlord," as well as an integration clause.

The plaintiffs later learned they could not place a sign along the highway to advertise their business, because the local zoning code allowed only one freestanding sign per property, and a sign advertising a business partly owned by the defendant was already in place.

The plaintiffs sued for breach of oral contract and fraud. The trial jury ruled for the plaintiffs, saying, "There are many appendixes that are referred to (in the lease), none of which were completed or attached to the document – that being the contract. Based on the testimony that I heard and I believe that this is not a fully integrated contract and that the additional evidence concerning the terms is not inconsistent with the written contract."

The defendant appealed, based in part upon a violation of the Parol Evidence Rule by the trial judge, admitting into evidence testimony about the oral signage agreement. The appellate court affirmed:

"No provision of this lease prohibits a freestanding sign. The disputed parol evidence was not inconsistent with the written agreement.

"If the parties did not intend the writing to represent their entire agreement, the agreement is only partially integrated, and prior consistent additional terms not evidenced by the writing may still form part of the entire agreement."

A. Do you believe the defendant intended to deceive the plaintiffs?
B. If the defendant was unaware of the prior sign, do you think the court would have allowed parol evidence of the prior oral signage promise?
C. Notice how courts sometimes reach a fair result by applying to the facts of the case the legal rule or legal exception that will accomplish it.

Some courts have differing interpretations of how the Parol Evidence Rule's "ambiguity" exception should be used. The traditional approach, followed by a majority of states and prohibiting reference to outside matters when the writing is clear and specific, is called the *plain meaning rule*.

A more recent approach called the *context rule*, which may signal a trend in the law, allows reference to outside sources for help in determining the intent of the parties even if there is no ambiguity.

In *Berg v. Hudesman, 801 P.2d 222 (Wash. 1990)*, the court allowed outside evidence to assist in understanding how to apply a rent payment clause in a lease ruled by the trial court not to be ambiguous. "We reject the plain meaning rule and expressly adopt the context rule as the applicable rule for ascertaining the parties' intent and interpreting written contracts."

"The Plain Meaning rule states that if a writing, or the term in question, appears to be plain and unambiguous on its face, its meaning must be determined from the four corners of the instrument without resort to extrinsic evidence of any nature.

"A trial court may, in interpreting contract language, consider the surrounding circumstances leading to execution of the agreement, including the subject matter of the contract as well as the subsequent conduct of the parties, not for the purpose of contradicting what is in the agreement, but for the purpose of determining the parties' intent."

A similar result to the *Berg* case took place in *This is Me, Inc. v. Taylor, 157 F.3d 139 (2nd Cir. 1998)*, where actress Cicely Tyson, through her personal service company, successfully sued to collect a $750,000 "play or pay" guarantee due her for the lead role in a Broadway play and later anticipated television tapings.

Actress Elizabeth Taylor and Broadway producer Zev Bufman had formed a theater group to produce live performances of plays on the legitimate stage and video and television versions of the same plays. Their second production, *The Corn is Green,*" cast Tyson in the lead role, but soon closed, and the video was never made.

Tyson, at the height of her career, had turned down other opportunities to do this project, and a series of contracts for the stage performances and the video performances guaranteed payment of $750,000 by the defendants if the show closed before she had earned that amount in salary.

"Considering all the circumstances, we believe that (A) the several agreements should be read together, and that (B), when they are so read in the light of all the evidence, they are capable of sustaining the jury's conclusion that Bufman and Taylor were bound by the $750,000 guarantee set forth in the video contract."

THE STANDARDS OF ANALYSIS RULES assist in determining what words, phrases, and terms the parties intended in their written contract if they are not available at the time of a dispute to testify. This non-availability, though sometimes voluntary, is usually in cases of accident, illness, disability, and, often, death. In a preprinted form agreement, there often are conflicts between the original content, added typewriting, and added handwriting. If the contracting parties are unavailable, the law presumes that the proper order of interpretation is:

1. handwriting
2. typewriting
3. preprinting

The rationale is that we are seeking the last expression of the intent of the parties. It is reasonable to assume that once the preprinted agreement is presented for signature, some additional changes may have been negotiated as reflected by the typewritten additions, and then at the final moment of completion the handwritten changes probably were inserted.

If the parties are members of a particular trade or profession, or the agreement concerns a specialized subject matter, the wording will be interpreted consistent with that specialty and the specific terminology used. For example, the number "86" has a special meaning in the restaurant and food business signifying cancellation. "Stet" in the printing business means let it stand. "Prima facie" in the legal profession means the fact is established. "Feed corn" means food for cattle.

Discussion Exercises

1. Discuss the advantages/disadvantages of a verbal one-year lease from the standpoint of the landlord. What about the tenant?

2. Discuss how you would determine when the main benefit exception to the guaranty contract rule should apply.

3. Discuss whether oral lifetime employment contracts should be enforced.

4. Discuss what dollar minimum you would require for a sale-of-goods writing requirement.

5. Discuss any additional statute of frauds exceptions you would implement, other than the ones already discussed.

Is the Ronettes' $15,000 Recording Contract of 1963 that Is Now Worth Millions Still Binding?

In *Greenfield, et al v. Philles Records, et al, 2002 N.Y. Lexis 3146 (N.Y. App. 2002)*, an unknown singing group known as The Ronettes met the legendary rock-and-roll producer and composer Phil Spector, who in 1963 signed them to a five-year "personal services" music recording contract with the defendant, his production company.

The agreement was a two-page contract, widely used in the 1960s by music producers signing new artists, and was signed by the plaintiffs without the benefit of counsel, and provided for the artists' transfer of full ownership rights to the master recordings of their musical performances for a cash advance of $15,000.

It specified defendants' "right to make phonograph records, tape recordings or other reproductions of the performances embodied in such recordings by any method now or hereafter known, and to sell and deal in the same . . . "

The Ronettes recorded twenty-eight songs for the defendant, including *Be My Baby*, which became a number-one hit and sold over one million copies. Despite the group's popularity, it disbanded in 1967, and no other monies were paid to the plaintiffs.

The defendants began to capitalize on a resurgence of public interest in 1960s music by using new recording technologies, non-existent at the time of the contract, to use master recordings of the Ronettes' vocal performances for "synchronization licensing" in the 1980s.

This was done in movies such as *Dirty Dancing* and *Goodfellas* and the television series *Moonlighting* to yield over $3 million in licensing proceeds, none of which was paid to the plaintiffs.

Analysis

The plaintiffs sued for breach of contract in 1987, alleging that the 1963 agreement did not grant the defendants the right to license their masters for the new synchronization process, and demanded the industry's standard 50% royalty fee.

The trial court ruled in their favor and awarded approximately $3 million in damages. The appellate division affirmed, "concluding that defendants' actions were not authorized by the agreement with plaintiffs because the contract did not specifically transfer the right to issue synchronization and third-party domestic distribution licenses."

The court of appeals accepted the case and ruled for the defendants, following the strict, plain meaning rule of contract interpretation:

"Despite the technological innovations that continue to revolutionize the recording industry, long-settled common-law contract rules still govern the interpretation of agreements between artists and their record producers. The fundamental, neutral precept of contract interpretation is that agreements are construed in accord with the party's intent. The best evidence of what parties to a written agreement intend is what they say in their writing. Thus, a written agreement that is complete, clear and unambiguous on its face must be enforced according to the plain meaning of its terms . . . Thus, if the agreement on its face is reasonably susceptible of only one meaning, a court is not free to alter the contract to reflect its personal notions of fairness and equity."

Defuse Replay

The court stated the central issue in this case: "Does the contract's silence on synchronization and domestic licensing create an ambiguity that opens the door to the admissibility of extrinsic evidence to determine the intent of the parties?"

Their answer was, "We conclude that it does not and, because there is no ambiguity in the terms of the Ronettes contract, defendants are entitled to exercise complete ownership rights, subject to payment of applicable royalties (at 3%, not 50%) due plaintiffs."

The author would respectfully suggest this ruling is wrong, from both a legal and ethical standpoint.

"AMBIGUOUS: 1. Having two or more possible meanings. 2. Not clear; uncertain or vague." *Webster's New World Dictionary(1969)*

There was most certainly an ambiguity in the 1963 agreement. The technology for synchronization licensing that produced the revenue in question was not in existence until well after it had expired in 1968. By definition, it was impossible to include in the agreement because these concepts were unheard of at the time. Therefore, outside evidence should be admissible, such as the current standard industry royalties paid for such types of licensing.

If we apply the context rule of interpretation, referred to in *Berg v. Hudesman, supra,* the existence or non-existence of an ambiguity is irrelevant, and all outside factors necessary to clarify the true intentions of the parties are admissible.

The trial court and appellate division rulings make more sense. How could the plaintiffs have protected themselves in the 1963 agreement against truly unforeseeable future events? Many fairness doctrines exist in our contract law to protect innocent parties from such a result. The plaintiffs are the victims, and the defendants the victimizers in the final court result.

Conclusion

This case had a number of other interesting aspects:

- Plaintiff Ronnie Greenfield, then known as Veronica Bennett, was married to Phil Spector from 1968 to 1974.

- The 1963 agreement did not restrict the ability of The Ronettes to earn income from appearances in concerts, on television, or in movies, and they re-formed briefly to do so after their renewed 1980s popularity.

- This litigation spanned a period of fifteen years until its final conclusion.

- The Recording Industry of America was a strong defendant's advocate during the case, as was the Recording Artists Coalition for the plaintiffs.

A. Do you agree with the court's final decision?

B. Does this case set a precedent to enforce all similar recording agreements from the 1950s, 1960s, and 1970s that are now significantly more valuable due to technological advances?

C. What legal standards would you use, and what factors would you consider to determine such disputes?

E.   ENFORCEMENT RIGHTS OF THIRD PARTIES

"Who is the third who walks always beside you?"

—T. S. Eliot

Legal Overview

We now shift our focus from disputes between the original contracting parties to situations where a third-party outsider to the contract claims legally enforceable rights. Let's look at the legal principles governing these situations, and then some actual cases that illustrate typical disputes.

The original contracting parties create their own legal bargain, with its unique terms and provisions. They usually are the only ones who have corresponding legal rights and duties. They are said to be in *privity of contract*. If one of the parties fails to properly perform its duties, the other has the legal right to enforce it by suing for breach of contract.

The early common law prohibited any transfer of contract rights or duties on the grounds that they were unique and personal to the original parties. There was little or no movement of capital beyond the real property-based economy. The extension of credit was viewed as a solemn bargain. In those days, the failure to pay one's debt was subject to possible incarceration in debtor's prison, because it was considered a form of theft.

As our society became more complex, the needs of the commercial marketplace required a broader-based system of obtaining credit and ways to trade in intangible assets such as debt obligations. Transfers of these obligations are encouraged in appropriate situations and assisted by the fact that they carry no legal writing or consideration requirements to be valid. As long as the intention of the parties to convey third-party rights or duties is clear, the courts will honor them.

There are three basic situations which grant to parties who were not part of the original contract the same rights of legal enforcement that belong to the original participants.

- Assignment transfers of legal rights (usually to collect debts)
- Delegation transfers of legal duties (usually to perform services)
- Third-party beneficiary cases – (no assignment or delegation made)

The legal effect of these exceptions is to cancel the rights and duties of the original performing parties to each other, and confer them instead upon the third-party outsider.

Direct Assignment of Third-Party Rights

The transfer of a legal right to another is called an *assignment*. The party who is legally obligated to perform is called the *obligor*, and owes this duty to the *obligee*. When the obligee transfers that right to receive the performance to a third-party outsider, the obligee-transferor is called the *assignor* and the third-party transferee is called the *assignee*.

The following diagram should be helpful. It illustrates a typical assignment situation, where the original creditor (A) assigns to a third party (C) its right to collect the obligation owed to it by the original debtor (B):

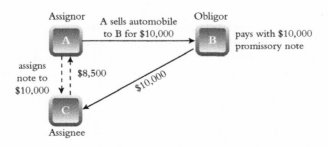

Though these assignment situations commonly involve loans of money or the creation of accounts receivable from the sale of goods to another, they may also take other factual forms.

There are also a number of reasons why the creditor (A) would transfer its right to collect to (C), rather than directly receive the funds due on the contract obligation:

- A owes C money on an unrelated matter and assigns this valuable contract right in full or partial payment.
- A desires to make a gift to C (perhaps a friend, family member, or charity) of this valuable contract right.
- A contracts with C to obtain financing for a project, and assigns this valuable contract right as its collateral security.

By far the most prevalent third-party assignment situation is one which is commonly known as *factoring*, or accounts receivable financing, which satisfies the needs of business to convert future pay assets into current cash:

- A sells goods or services to B on delayed payment basis (A gains an account receivable and B owes an account payable), needs current liquidity, and then sells it for cash to C at a discounted price.

There are a number of legal factors that determine whether or not the assignee can legally claim rights and enforce the obligations assigned.

In the typical dispute, a third-party outsider seeks to enforce rights against the obligor, who denies the validity of the assignment.

1. Does the contract itself prohibit assignments to third parties?

The wording of any contract determines the rights and duties of its parties. Under common law rules of most states, a contract is presumed assignable unless it specifically states otherwise. The UCC takes a different position regarding sales of goods, declaring that even though there is an antiassignment clause in the contract, it is binding as to delegation of duties but not as to assignments of rights.

There are good, practical reasons for these prohibitions against assignment in residential and commercial lease situations. The landlord has negotiated the deal with a particular tenant, and created the important lease terms that include rental payments, security deposits, and all other aspects of the transaction.

An antiassignment clause is designed to protect a landlord and the other tenants from undesirable new tenants who have bypassed whatever screening procedures are required before a lease is finalized. Sudden occupancy by strangers to the original lease contract is frowned upon by most states.

To allow the named tenant to assign (new party assumes the lease and pays the landlord) or sublease (new party pays directly to tenant) at any time they wish may seriously jeopardize the finances and security of the transaction and the property itself.

Jacob owns a twenty-four-unit apartment building near the local university. He enters into a lease agreement with student Emily, where he agrees, "to rent to Tenant unit number 12 for one year at a monthly rent of $500, first month and two months' security deposit payable in advance. No assignment or sublease allowed. Breach of lease entitles Landlord to declare immediate default and collect full remaining rental for entire term plus expenses and legal fees, if any." Emily is homesick after two months and decides to leave. Since her unit is the only one available in the vicinity, she is able to sublease it to Chad for $650 per month, thus making a $150 monthly profit for herself. Jacob finds out, demands Chad vacate, and sues Emily for the ten months of rent remaining under the lease.

The prohibition against transfer in this case raises another practical advantage to the landlord. The original lease may be a very good deal for the tenant due to a skilled negotiation or the supply and demand factors that change over time.

If Emily wants to assign or sublease in this case, she needs Jacob to give his consent, and their discussion will reveal the profit possibility that exists in a new rental.

Probably they will agree to share the profit in some mutually agreeable proportion, where in exchange for Jacob releasing Emily from any further lease obligations, he receives a larger share of the new rental. If the opposite situation exists, where Emily is unable to find a new tenant, she will negotiate a buy out of her lease obligations with Jacob. In either instance, Jacob makes a profit that would not exist if assignment were allowed.

Suppose Emily contracts to buy the apartment building from Jacob at the very low price of $250,000, due to a combination of her skilled negotiating, his desire to retire, and the fact she offers an all-cash deal with a sixty-day closing. Chad has been looking for this type of investment property, which he estimates is worth $350,000, finds out Emily has the contract right to buy at the low price, and contracts for her to assign her interest to him now for $100,000.

This assignment of rights situation is known in real estate terms as "flipping the contract." It highlights the respective practical interests of the original contracting parties. If you are a seller of real property, you always want to use an antiassignment clause to protect yourself against selling below the current market price. If you are a buyer, you always want to be allowed to assign just in case your deal has the potential for a market profit.

Most states, faced with a specific prohibition on transfer in a lease or sale of real property, will interpret it according to a rule-of-reason standard to say, "no assignment allowed without my consent, *but such consent shall not be unreasonably withheld.* Then each dispute is evaluated to determine what is reasonable using this objective test. Some of the relevant factors are the third parties' general reputation, credit rating, financial position, past history of similar dealings, effect on the property and/or its tenants, and profit or loss involved in granting or denying the assignment.

2. Is the assignment contrary to a law or public policy?

The legality of the assignment is sometimes at issue. Most states prohibit an assignment of future employment wages to protect against impulsive decisions created by illness or addiction, compulsive disorders such as gambling, and related situations.

Assignments for the benefit of particular creditors at the expense of others are also frowned upon, and often invalidated as unlawful preferential transfers.

The discounted cash sale of life insurance benefits by terminally ill policy holders, called "viatical settlements," caused such a legal problem when AIDS became an unfortunate part of our everyday reality. Most life insurance contracts at that time did not prohibit assignment. These transactions were initially viewed as beneficial to all parties. The seller received immediate cash to provide for medical and related expenses, allowing current gifting to loved ones as an accelerated inheritance. The third-party buyer was making a profitable short-term investment and assisting the seller with the funds paid. The insurance company was merely changing beneficiary to be paid upon death of their insured.

Publicity about these assignments raised public concern that insureds were being victimized by unscrupulous buyers who preyed upon their weakened physical and mental condition. The insurance companies were also criticized for allowing such transfers to take place.

As a result, new life insurance policies contained clauses prohibiting such assignments, even though many holders of policies publicly voiced their support for the financial flexibility these assignments allowed them. These conflicting positions became moot as the life expectancy of AIDS patients greatly increased due to improved treatment options. The uncertainty of when such life insurance policies will now "mature," and the negative public perception of them, has resulted in these assignments essentially disappearing from the marketplace.

Public policy arguments were also involved, as the reader will recall, in the chapter on illegal contracts, concerning the enforceability of non-competition agreements. Even if a particular non-compete satisfies the "reasonable" tests for time, area, and scope – is it assignable and enforceable?

In *Special Products Manufacturing, Inc. v. Douglass, 553 N.Y.S.2d 506 (N.Y. App. Div. 1990)*, the defendant was employed by Page-Wilson Corp. to service hardness-testing machinery pursuant to two employment contracts, one of which protected intellectual property and customer lists and one of which prohibited employment competition.

Canrad Corp bought all the assets of Page-Wilson, including the defendant's two employment agreements, and the plaintiff was their wholly-owned subsidiary, for whom the defendant worked until he resigned to work in a competing business that he established, violating the restrictions of his employment contract.

The plaintiff sued the defendant to enforce the non-compete, the defendant failed to respond on time, a default judgment was entered against him, and then his motion to extend the time to answer the complaint was denied by the trial court.

On appeal by the defendant, the appellate court affirmed:

"We perceive no merit in defendant's claims that the employment agreements are not binding because consideration therefor is lacking or not recited. Nor are we persuaded by the contention that because defendant entered into the agreements with Page-Wilson, they are unenforceable by plaintiff . . . Defendant's consent was not required to effectuate this transfer. When the original parties to an agreement so intend, a covenant not to compete is freely assignable." (unless it contains a non-assignment clause)

3. Is notice of the assignment required to be given to the obligor?

Michael loans Hannah $50,000 on July 1, payable in ninety days on October 1. Hannah signs a promissory note agreeing to these terms. Due to liquidity needs Michael sells the note to Xavier on August 1, receiving $40,000 cash in exchange for his assignment transfer. Michael tells Xavier, "Don't worry about contacting Hannah, I'll tell her to make all payments to you." Before Michael can notify Hannah, she calls him to say she wants to prepay her debt. He says, "Great, bring cash and I'll give you a paid-in-full receipt." She pays Michael on August 15; he never mentions the assignment, takes the money, and runs off to the jungles of Brazil. On October 1 Xavier calls Hannah requesting full payment of her note. She says, "I don't know you, and for your information I already paid it in full back on August 15. Leave me alone." Xavier sues Hannah to enforce the note.

Sorry, Xavier, you goofed. The law in this area clearly states that the validity of an assignment is not affected by the failure to give notice of it to the payment obligor. Hannah is obligated to pay someone at the due date, and whether the payee is the original creditor Michael or the assignee Xavier is immaterial. She is not prejudiced in any way by having to pay someone else.

From a practical standpoint, however, notifying the obligor of an assignment of her debt is of great importance in avoiding the predicament encountered by Xavier. He has lost $40,000, unless he can locate Michael, sue him for the loss, recover a judgment, and collect it. Hannah cannot be forced to pay her debt twice, unless it could be proven she was notified of Xavier's ownership interest before she paid Michael. The party who should notify the obligor is always the assignee, not the assignor, who may be a scoundrel in waiting like Michael in our example.

Disputes often arise in these notice situations because the parties confuse the obligatory *must notify* with the discretionary *should notify*. The assignee doesn't have to, but it certainly is the most skillful way to proceed.

4. Is the consent of the obligor to the assignment required?

There is no legal requirement, as a general rule, that the obligor must approve an assignment for it to be valid, especially when the obligation to be performed is the payment of money.

Suppose that notice of the assignment in the above example had been properly given to Hannah (obligor) by Michael (assignor), or more probably Xavier (assignee). Let's pretend that Hannah's response was, "I don't know you, Xavier, I signed a promissory note to Michael, and he is the only person I will pay. I don't consent to the sale of my note to you." Xavier says,

"I'm not asking for your consent, I'm just telling that you now are legally obligated to pay me on the due date."

Xavier is correct under the general rule. Hannah is not disadvantaged in any way by paying him instead of Michael.

There are some fairness exceptions where the prior consent or approval of the obligor is required for an assignment of his rights to be valid. They all relate to a legal test of whether or not the obligor is adversely affected in a significant way by the desired assignment. If it causes a "material hardship" on the obligor, consent is legally necessary.

- Legal claims of a personal nature – if I have a claim against you for alleged misconduct that injured me, it is not assignable to a stranger. Similarly, I cannot assign my insurance contract to a stranger without the consent of the insurer, who is obligated to pay for losses incurred under its terms.
- Personal service/relationship contracts – if I am hired as your personal physician or attorney, or your portrait painter or acting teacher – to perform specialized services for you, I may not legally transfer (delegate) them to a stranger who is less qualified or experienced.
- Personal employment situations – when employers sell a business, some of their significant assets that create value for the deal are their valuable employment contracts. When an employee is notified of the assignment of his contract, and is requested to report for work to the new owner, his response is often, "Heck no, I won't go." Are such contract rights assignable without the employee's consent?

Marlon is a talented actor under a ten-year employment contract with MGM Studios in Hollywood, California, where he has a house, a family, and children in school, and is a local city commissioner.

The MGM parent company sells its entertainment division to Disney Studios, based in Miami, Florida, in year seven, and assigns to them his contract. Disney notifies Marlon to report for work in ten days. He refuses, claiming he never approved the sale.

Marlon's consent is required. He would suffer financial hardship through moving expenses, relocation costs, and related monetary considerations. Even if Disney agreed to reimburse for these items, there are non-monetary hardships in having to adjust himself and his family to a new location, including personal associations, schooling, weather, population demographics, language and culture considerations, and related matters.

What if the move was from MGM in Hollywood to Universal Hollywood, located two miles away? Here Marlon could still argue hardship, citing emotional factors such as being uprooted from his long personal relationship with MGM, new surroundings, new personnel, possible changes in employment duties, and the like.

These employment cases rarely involve disputes in professional sports contracts, even though identical factors exist that would satisfy the prior consent test of hardship. This is because there are specific provisions in these contracts between owners and players that allow the purchase and sale of contracts without the employee's prior approval. Some sports have collective bargaining labor agreements that allow a player to veto a contract trade or sale after a required minimum number of years in the league, or for other special aspects of free agency.

The unique facts of each dispute will determine whether or not the obligor's consent to assignment is required:

- In *The Munchak Corporation v. Cunningham, 457 F.2d 721 (4th Cir. 1972)*, Billy Cunningham was under contract to play professional basketball for the Philadelphia 76ers during the late 1960s until his option year of 1970-1971, and signed a contract to play for the Carolina Cougars commencing when his prior contract ended. The new contract included a bonus to be paid him, part cash and part deferred, due in full before 10/1/71, which was his critical reserve clause date to either renew his 76ers contract or be paid at 75% of his last year's pay. In it he also agreed that the Cougars could "enjoin him from playing basketball for another team" during the contract term.

  When the note payment was not made he advised the new team that the contract was breached, and contracted with the 76ers for an additional five years at more than double the money to be paid him under the Cougars' contract. The plaintiffs (owners of the Carolina team) sued for an injunction to prevent him from violating his contract.

  The trial court denied the injunction, due to the "unclean hands" of the plaintiffs in luring the defendant away from his former team. On appeal, the decision was reversed, and remanded for entry and enforcement of the injunction prohibiting the defendant from playing for the 76ers.

  "Cunningham was under no obligation, option or restraint with respect to the 76ers after October 1, 1971, and the Cougars had a lawful right to bid and contract for his services to be rendered after that date."

  Notice the court's reasoning to remove contracts of athletes from the "consent rule," unless they specifically prohibit assignment. "The policy against assignability of certain personal service contracts is to prohibit an assignment of a contract in which the obligor undertakes to serve only the original obligee. This contract is not of that type . . ."

  (As an interesting sidelight, Cunningham was on the other side of the fence in later years as a part owner of the Miami Heat professional basketball team.)

- In *Aslakson v. Home Savings Association, 416 N.W.2d 786 (Minn. App. 1987)*, the purchase of the plaintiff's mobile home was contingent upon the buyers' assumption of their loan with the approval of the defendant. The defendant twice rejected the credit of two contract buyers from the plaintiff, thus preventing their sale from taking place.

  The plaintiff sued for the tort of "wrongful interference with contract," and the trial court granted summary judgment for the defendant. The appellate court affirmed, examining the applicable law regarding a party's right to delegate contractual duties, such as taking over the payments on a mortgage obligation:

"We believe the trial court correctly determined that a contract between appellants and a subsequent buyer could not arise absent performance of a condition precedent: respondent's approval of the subsequent buyer's assumption of the loan. Under the provisions of (the state's UCC law), which must govern here, appellants were prohibited from delegating their contractual duties if respondents had a substantial interest in having appellants perform or if an assignment would materially increase respondents' burden or risk or impair its chance of obtaining return performance."

One of the additional areas where the "consent" defense is raised pertains to efforts of an assignee of a guaranteed debt to enforce that guarantee after the primary obligor has defaulted.

Courts have made distinctions between the types of guarantees involved, factual situations where the assignment was made prior to or after default, and whether or not the assignee also extended credit to the obligor.

Notice the typical process of how courts analyze a complicated legal problem. In *New Holland, Inc. v. Trunk, et al, 579 So.2d 215 (Fla. App. 1991),* the *plaintiff* was the assignee of a contract from Sperry, the seller of equipment on credit to Trunkline. The defendant guaranteed payment of the specific Trunkline debt directly to Sperry. The assignment was made at a time that the debt was not in default, and the plaintiff continued to extend credit to Trunkline thereafter.

Later, when Trunkline defaulted, the plaintiff sued the defendant on its debt guarantee. The defendant claimed that it was a "special guaranty" that was not enforceable by the plaintiff because it was not activated by a default of the debtor prior to its assignment. The plaintiff claimed its assignment was valid, and its extension of credit created a type of estoppel that prevented the defendant from denying its claim.

The trial court ruled for the defendant, but the appellate court reversed in favor of the plaintiff, and discussed the legal principles involved, as well as the split of authority in different states on the question of whether a special guaranty was assignable:

"A 'general' guaranty is one addressed to all persons generally and may generally be enforced by anyone to whom it is presented who acts upon it. A 'special' guaranty is one addressed to a particular entity and under it ordinarily only the named or specifically described promisee acquires rights.

"Generally, contract rights can be assigned unless they involve obligations of a personal nature or there is some public policy against the assignment or such assignment is specifically prohibited by the contract.

"Under the common law which Florida follows, a general guaranty is assignable while a special guaranty is generally not assignable because extending credit constitutes the exercise of discretion and a guaranty agreement naming a particular creditor as promisee implies special trust and confidence placed by the guarantor in the named creditor and the assignment of the guaranty to another prospective creditor materially alters the guarantor's undertaking."

So at this point of the court's opinion, it looks like the trial court will be affirmed. But notice how the focus of reasoning is changed.

The court, after agreeing that a special guarantee is involved in this case, examines the four conflicting legal rules and then decides in favor of enforcing the special guarantee after all:

"Some courts hold that the assignment of a special guaranty is effective to collect obligations existing at the time of the assignment, others hold that whether a special guaranty can be enforced to collect debts accruing after the assignment is a question of fact to be resolved by reference to the intent of the parties, while still others hold that whether a special guaranty is assignable depends on whether the undertaking of the guarantor has been materially altered by the assignment. Others steadfastly adhere to the common law rule precluding assignment of special guaranties."

Now the court completes its analysis focusing on the distinction between original debt of the primary debtor that was guaranteed (enforceable) versus new debt created by the assignee's post-assignment advances (not enforceable):

"There is a principle of law that the assignment of a principal obligation also operates as an assignment of the guaranty of the obligation so that the guaranty is effective to collect the obligation which existed at the time of the assignment. This principle seems eminently fair, permitting an assignee to enforce the guarantor's obligation as it exists at the time of the assignment, but not subjecting the guarantor to liability for (additional) extensions of credit made by the assignee.

"The assignee of a special guaranty cannot enforce the special guarantee as to debt the assignee has created by extending credit to the debtor. An assignee of debt and of a special guaranty relating thereto can enforce the guaranty as to debt resulting from credit extended by the original creditor to the debtor, whether or not that assigned debt is due or past due at the time of the assignment."

5. What if the obligor has a legal defense to payment?

This raises the fundamental principle of third-party rights which is the basis of all sales of contract rights to an outsider. It is called the "stands in shoes" rule. Simply stated, it provides that the assignee stands in the shoes of his assignor, and takes subject to any and all claims or defenses that the obligor could assert against the assignor.

This rule makes it essential that a potential purchaser-assignee of an existing contract debt verify in writing with the *obligor-payor* the following matters after negotiating the financial terms of his deal with the obligee-assignor but *before* paying any of the agreed price:

- Is there an existing contract between the parties?
- What are its terms?
- Have there been any prior payments made?
- Are there any defenses to payment that may be raised?
- Are there any counter claims or set-offs due?
- Obligor will pay the assignee after being notified.
- Obligor will consent to the assignment.
- Obligor is solvent and able to pay.

Notice that the due diligence of the buyer-assignee is directed to the obligor, not his potential assignor. The assignor wants to sell the contract right and therefore has a financial agenda that may include bending the truth to suit his needs. The key party is the obligor, who will be ultimately called upon to pay. Once the obligor signs off on these matters, and the buyer has otherwise verified outside factors like the credit standing of the obligor, the purchase of the account may be completed.

Computers, Inc. sells $100,000 worth of laptops to Florida Stores (F) on a net-180, six-month payment basis, on March 1. It sells that account receivable to Southern Investors (S) shortly thereafter on March 15 for $80,000, and notifies (F) of the assignment to them. On the due date of September 1, (S) contacts (F) to arrange payment to it of the $80,000. The obligor says, "We will not pay you because after you notified us, we inspected all the laptops and they don't work. They are defective." The assignee demands payment, saying, "That's not our problem. Take it up with your seller."

This is a classic "stands-in-shoes" case, and Southern Investors loses. The account they bought from Computer, Inc. carries the right to collect its face amount but is also burdened with the risk of any valid defenses to payment. Faulty merchandise, deviation from contract specifications, and other transactional defenses that may be asserted against the assignor are also binding upon the assignee.

Southern Investors should not have completed their purchase of the account until *after* all verification was completed, including requiring the obligor to inspect the merchandise and waive any defects or other claims.

6. What if rights are assigned more than once?

Situations of successive multiple assignments are thankfully rare, but when disputes arise the courts are unable to agree how to handle them. This raises another potential problem to be avoided before it occurs.

These cases do not involve transfers of interests in real estate, mortgages, and other financing arrangements or accounts that are required to be recorded in the official records of the state involved.

When a prospective purchaser-assignee of such accounts does the necessary verifying, a search of the public records would reveal their existence and prior transfer to another, and he would decline to proceed.

But what if an unscrupulous obligee-assignor holds a valuable debt or account that is not customarily recorded, like most accounts receivable and unsecured promissory notes, and sells it more than once to unsuspecting assignees?

Assume the obligor agrees to the obligation and wants to pay somebody. But who has the payment priority as between multiple assignees?

Here is a typical dispute:

Scoundrel sells goods to Buyer-Obligor on open account, with payment due in ninety days. Scoundrel sells the account to 1st Assignee forty-five days later at a discount for cash. First Assignee does not notify Buyer-Obligor. Scoundrel then sells the same account again to Second Assignee fifteen days later, falsely certifying that there were no prior assignments. Second Assignee verifies with Buyer-Obligor that there was no prior notice of transfer of the account received from anyone. On the due date both Assignees demand payment. Buyer-Obligor pays the money due into the court registry saying, "Here is the money I owe to somebody; let the judge decide who gets it."

Most states follow the *American Rule*, which states that first-in-time wins, regardless of notice. Its reasoning is that a party can only transfer what he owns. Once Scoundrel sold the account to First Assignee there was nothing left for another sale. Its strict interpretation has been criticized as contrary to the numerous other fairness doctrines in our legal system, thus prompting some authorities to call it the "unfairness rule."

A growing number of states follow the *English Rule*, which states that the party first to notify wins. The second assignee who promptly notified and had no way to know of the prior assignment did everything required by the law, and in fairness should prevail. The first assignee could have prevented the situation if it had notified the buyer-obligor when it bought the account.

A compromise position is the *Symbolic Delivery Rule* that applies in cases where the contract right purchased has a tangible form, such as a promissory note, documentary draft, stock certificate, or bank account passbook. When the first assignee buys such an account, the physical delivery to him of the symbolic item establishes the legal right to receive payment. If, however, that token is not demanded by the first assignee and allowed to be transferred to a subsequent buyer who is also the first to notify, the later assignee wins.

Most business managers favor the English Rule due to its inherent fairness. It is hoped the law in this area will be soon codified with one rule of law that will lead to a predictable result in future disputes.

Direct Delegation of Third Party Duties

A contracting party may, as a general rule, designate someone else to perform required duties. Such a transfer is called a delegation of duties.

The original party owing the performance is called the delegator, and the new party who is to perform the services is called the delagatee. The promisee receives the services and is obligated to pay for them.

Notice in the diagram of a typical delegation of duties, the respective positions of the parties:

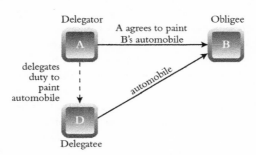

Similar to an assignment of legal rights, no writing or other legal formalities are required for creation. The intention of the parties is determined from the facts and surrounding circumstances of each case.

The parties may also specifically prohibit delegation in the wording of their contract. These clauses are legally treated the same as assignments, and are usually enforced, unless there is a highly personal relationship or the services to be performed are of a unique or specialized nature. Whether or not a duty is non-delegable depends upon similar considerations of relationship, hardship, and detriment as those found in the legal tests of "consent to assignment."

A few major differences between assignments of rights and delegation of duties do exist:

- The assignment of rights cancels the assignor's right to enforce the subject debt and transfers that right to the third party.
- The delegation of a duty does *not* cancel the continuing liability of the delegator in the event of a breach in the required performance by the delegatee.

Joshua and Madison are newlyweds who buy a three-bedroom, two-bath residence from Ram Builders. They pay 20% cash and the balance with a purchase money mortgage loan and promissory note with Local Bank. Three years later they sell the house to Jeanette, who assumes and agrees to pay the existing mortgage and note. Four years later she sells the house to Francine, with a similar assumption. Later, Francine defaults and declares bankruptcy.

Since the value of the property has substantially declined due to a changing neighborhood, Local Bank sues both of the prior owners for the remaining note indebtedness. They defend, saying they have no liability due to their sales to new owners and the resulting assumptions of the mortgage and note.

This is one of the least understood and most dangerous liability situations. Most persons who sell mortgaged property to another believe they are released from liability if their buyer legally takes over the payments. Not so! An assumption does not release the delegator-payor from liability unless there is a three-party *novation*, whereby the creditor-bank agrees to release the original debtors and substitute in their place the assuming party.

"An assignment is an expression of intention by the assignor that his duty shall immediately pass to the assignee. Many a debtor wishes that by such an expression he could get rid of his debts. Any debtor can express such an intention, but it is not operative to produce such a hoped-for result. It does not cause society to relax its compulsion against him and direct it toward the assignee as his substitute." *4 Corbin on Contracts sec. 866*

As we have discussed before, creditors hardly ever grant a novation and release a party from liability unless they are paid for this privilege, or it is part of the original negotiations for the first financing that creates the debt.

In *Rosenberg v. Son, Inc. and Pratt, 491 N.W.2d 71 (N.D. 1992)*, the plaintiffs contracted to sell their Dairy Queen business to Pratt for $10,000 cash and $52,000 installment payments due over a fifteen-year period. Pratt then assigned her rights and delegated her duties to Son, Inc. by assignment agreement, which obligated the assignee to assume all her obligations, as well as indemnify and hold her harmless, "against all claims, demands and actions by reason of the failure . . . to observe and perform the said agreement."

The plaintiffs then signed, at the defendant's request, a "consent to assignment" clause that read, "The undersigned, Harold Rosenberg and Gladys E. Rosenberg, sellers in the above described Contract of Sale, do hereby consent to the above assignment."

Son, Inc. then assigned the sales contract to Merit Corporation. There was no consent clause in that assignment, but the plaintiffs were aware of the assignment and later accepted a prepayment from Merit that reduced the outstanding debt to $25,000.

Ultimately Merit defaulted and went into bankruptcy, leaving an unpaid balance due the plaintiffs of approximately $17,000. The plaintiffs then filed this suit against the defendants to collect the indebtedness.

The trial court granted summary judgment for the defendants, ruling that "Once Pratt assigned her contract she became a guarantor," and was exonerated due to alterations in her original obligation.

The appellate court reversed, and remanded the case for a full trial:

"It is a well-established principle in the law of contracts that a contracting party cannot escape its liability on the contract by merely assigning its duties and rights under the contract to a third party . . . No delegation of performance relieves the party delegating of any duty to perform or any liability for breach . . .

This rule of law applies to all categories of contracts, including contracts for the sale or lease of real property, service contracts, and contracts for the sale of goods, which is present in the facts of this case.

"It is not however, a legal impossibility for a contracting party to rid itself of an obligation under a contract. It may seek the approval of the other original party for release, and substitute a new party in its place. In such an instance, the transaction is no longer called an assignment; instead it is called a novation."

Defendant Pratt claimed she was released from liability when the plaintiffs consented to her assignment to Son, Inc. She thought the consent was enough to free her from future problems. Wrong! The court reminded her of this legal time bomb, which had just exploded:

"The Rosenbergs did sign a consent to the assignment at the bottom of the agreement. However, by merely consenting to the assignment, the Rosenbergs did not consent to a discharge of the principal obligor – Pratt. Nothing in the language of the consent clause supports such an allegation. A creditor is free to consent to an assignment without releasing the original debtor."

Third-Party Beneficiary Cases

These are situations where there has been no specific assignment of rights or delegation of duties to the third-party outsider. If this direct linkage to outsiders is missing, their interest nevertheless derives in an indirect way from the facts and circumstances of the transaction that clearly shows they are its *intended beneficiary*.

If so, they have legally enforceable rights, though not the original contracting parties or specific assignees or delagatees.

Their beneficial interest is often shown by the fact they are identified as such by name in the contract. If not specifically identified by name, they may still occupy a class of persons who are clearly to receive the benefits of the agreement.

In *Cherry v. Crow et al, 845 F.Supp. 1520 (M.D. FL. 1994)*, Eddie Cherry was booked into the Polk County jail to begin serving a thirty-day sentence for drunk driving. He and his wife informed the authorities he was an alcoholic.

He had a history of delirium tremens, and repeatedly requested medical attention for symptoms related to alcohol withdrawal. When he was found in his cell hallucinating and shaking violently, he was taken to the infirmary and shackled to the bed. Later that night, he either walked or jumped off the bed and, because of the leg restraints, fell on his head, and died five days later.

His wife, as personal representative of his estate, sued the county and Prison Health Services, Inc., the medical contractor in charge of the county's prison system, for breach of contract and wrongful death based upon the negligence of county employees.

The contract between the county and the health provider stated:

"Whereas, the Sheriff, is desirous of contracting with PHS and PHS is desirous of contracting with the Sheriff to provide total health care services *for the inmates/detainees* (including federal and state prisoners) housed within the county correctional system facilities described above . . . "

The trial court denied the defendants' motions to dismiss and the appellate court affirmed, holding that "the Court finds sufficient evidence of an intended third party beneficiary relationship to withstand this motion to dismiss."

"Where, therefore, it is manifest from the nature or terms of a contract that the formal parties thereto intended its provisions to be for the benefit of a third party, as well as for the benefit of the formal parties themselves, the benefit to such third party being the direct and primary object of the contract, or amongst such objects, such third party may maintain an action on the contract even though he be a stranger to the consideration."

There are two basic categories of third-party beneficiary contracts:

1. Donee Beneficiary – the clear intent of one of the parties is to make a gift to the third-party outsider, who has legally enforceable rights in the event of default in receiving what is due them. The most common example is life insurance contracts.

Ann contracts with Dial Insurance Co. to buy a $100,000 life insurance policy, in which her friend Charlie is to receive the policy benefit upon her death. She perishes in a fire. The insurer fails or refuses to pay him, claiming he is not a blood relative. He sues to recover, asserting his legal status as an "intended third-party beneficiary" of the insurance contract.

Charlie wins the case. He did not pay anything because his interest is gratuitous. He is a donee beneficiary. He is its intended recipient because he is specifically named as such. The policy wording does not require any blood-relationship for his beneficial status. He has legally enforceable third-party rights.

2. Creditor Beneficiary – a party becomes a debtor by borrowing money from a third-party creditor to purchase some type of property. The creditor's lien encumbers the property. When the debtor later sells the property, the new buyer legally promises to pay the creditor. If he defaults, the creditor has legal rights to enforce it against him. The usual examples are "take over the payments" transfers of property.

The harder cases are those where plaintiffs claim legally enforceable third-party rights because, while not specifically named in the main contract by name or category of persons intended to be included, they will still receive some type of benefit from the contract performance. This potential "fall-out" benefit, they feel, gives them a legally enforceable right to sue in the event of default. Unfortunately for them, they occupy the legal status of *incidental or indirect beneficiaries*, and have no legal rights.

AA Corp. owns a small shopping center across the street from the local university. ZZ Corp. is a tenant in the center, operating a book and music store. AA Corp. contracts with McDonald's to lease to them the vacant corner of the center. ZZ corp. is delighted by this news, anticipates increased business at their site from the restaurant customers, and spends $20,000 to remodel its store. One month later, McDonald's decides not to proceed, and ZZ Corp. sues it for breach of the lease agreement with AA Corp., claiming rights as a third-party beneficiary of that contract.

ZZ Corp. has no legally enforceable rights. Though they would receive financial benefit from the increased customer traffic generated by the McDonald's lease, such advantage is merely incidental, a by-product of the lease, which was created for the primary benefit of the named landlord and tenant parties.

But what if we change the facts a bit to state that the lease had a clause that said, "All existing tenants of this center shall receive a 20% discount on all store purchases."? Now the case is not as clear.

ZZ Corp. could argue they are an "intended beneficiary" since they occupy the stated class of parties to be benefited. What do you think?

The cases that present claims for enforcement of contracts by third-party "incidental" beneficiaries involve some of the most novel requests for relief by obviously remote claimants. They cause the reader to question how in the world such bizarre cases were ever filed, and are a commentary on our litigious society:

- The Big Ten athletic conference hired Bain as a college basketball referee. He called a foul on a University of Iowa player, permitting the free throws that gave Purdue a last-second victory, and denied Iowa a championship. Gillispie operated a sports memorabilia store in Iowa City, and would have profited greatly by an Iowa victory. He sued for the alleged malpractice of Bain, claiming enforceable rights. The trial court and appellate court agreed that summary judgment was correct, denying the claim. "It is beyond credulity that Bain, while refereeing a game, must make his calls at all times perceiving that a wrong call will injure Gillispie's business or one similarly situated and subject him to liability. Heaven knows what uncharted morass a court would find itself in if it were to hold that an athletic official subjects himself to liability every time he might make a questionable call. The possibilities are mind boggling . . . There is no tortious doctrine of athletic official's malpractice . . . " *Bain v. Gillispie, 357 N.W.2d 47 (Ia. App. 1984)*

- The defendant had a contract with the owner of a Days Inn motel to treat it monthly for pests, including insects. When the plaintiff was bitten by a brown recluse spider while spending the night at the motel, she sued for negligence, claiming severe injuries and having beneficial rights under the contract. Both courts also granted summary judgment against the plaintiff. "The risk of being bitten by a spider is a general risk we all face . . . The motel's desire to reduce that risk by utilizing Admiral's pest control services does not create a negligence cause of action in favor of every guest at the motel." *Copeland v. Admiral Pest Control, Co., 933 P.2d 937 (Ok. App. 1996)*

- The plaintiff was injured when she slipped on an icy public sidewalk abutting Bank's property. Bank had contracted with Fox for snow and ice removal from the public sidewalk as required by local ordinance. The plaintiff sued for negligence as a third-party beneficiary of that contract, claiming it was "intended to benefit pedestrians who were using the public sidewalk to patronize Peoples' business establishment." Again summary judgment for the defendants was upheld. "There is no language in the contract before us to generate an issue of Peoples' intention to create in plaintiff enforceable rights as an intended beneficiary." *Denman v. Peoples Heritage Bank, Inc. and Fox, 704 A.2d 411 (Maine 1998)*

Discussion Exercises

1. Discuss assignment strategies of buyer and seller in real estate contracts.

2. Discuss due diligence strategies of a potential assignee.

3. Discuss boundary rules to determine when obligor consent to an assignment or delegation should be legally required.

4. Discuss boundary rules for differentiating between intended and incidental beneficiaries.

5. Discuss your preference of legal theories to govern the problem of multiple assignments.

Case Exercise 6

If You Stand in this Bank's Shoes, You Lose $50,000

In *Royal Bank Export Finance Company LTD. v. Bestways Distributing Co., 229 Cap. App.3d 764 (Cal. App. 1991)*, E.R.S. sold to Bestways ten "night Clerk" electronic units to be used in hotels and motels to register guests without the need for a clerk in attendance, at a unit price of $4,997, payable on a deferred basis as accounts payable.

E.R.S. then assigned these purchase order receivables to the bank as a means of raising financing capital. When the bank sued Bestways to collect the balances due, it declined payment on the grounds that the products they bought were defective and not merchantable. The bank claimed it purchased the accounts "free and clear of any defenses."

Analysis

The trial court entered judgment in favor of Bestways, based upon the conclusion that the accounts were non-negotiable instruments under the California UCC, and therefore "subject to any defenses Bestways had against E.R.S."

"(The trial court) determined that because of the failure of consideration by E.R.S., Bestways was not obligated to pay for the products."

The appellate court affirmed, based upon the "stands-in-shoes" rule of assignments:

"The question in this case is not whether there has been an effective transfer or assignment of the debt instruments from E.R.S. to Bank or whether Bank's title to the papers has priority over other claims of title.

"Rather, the issue in this case is whether the title transferred to Bank is subject to defenses Bestways has against the transferor.

"The assignment merely transfers the interest of the assignor. The assignee 'stands in the shoes' of the asignor, taking his rights and remedies, subject to *any defenses* which the *obligor* has against the assignor prior to notice of the assignment."

Defuse Replay

The court's last remarks highlight how incredibly inept the bank was in this case. Before any prospective assignee of accounts receivable purchases them from the original creditor, verification of the various due diligence factors previously mentioned is absolutely essential. Remember, "5. What if the obligor has a legal defense to payment?"

In addition, no bank that wishes to remain in business very long ever buys instruments that are non-negotiable, because they are by definition not protected from the "stands-in-shoes" rule. Purchasers of any types of commercial instruments would never provide the liquidity business demands if they had to worry about problems in the transactions that underlied the creation of those instruments.

That is the reason for the negotiable instruments provisions of the UCC, which provide that:

1. If an instrument is in *negotiable form,* and

2. If it is properly held by a *holder in due course,*

that holder-assignee circumvents the rule and takes free of all transactional defenses that may be otherwise asserted by the original debtor-obligor against the original creditor-assignor.

"A non-negotiable written contract for the payment of money or personal property may be transferred by indorsement, in like manner with negotiable instruments. Such indorsement shall transfer all the rights of the assignor under the instrument to the assignee, *subject to all equities and defenses existing in favor of the maker at the time of the indorsement."*

Conclusion

Investors in the factoring industry, who buy accounts receivable, and banks, insurers, and other purchasers of any types of commercial paper have basic rules that their financial lifeblood depends upon:

• Before completing the purchase, get written certifications of all facts from the debtor, including assurances that there are no transactional defenses.

• Verify negotiable form of any commercial instruments purchased.

• Verify legal ownership of commercial instruments as a true "holder" and "in due course" status.

A. Do you think the bank was aware of the legal distinctions between "stands in shoes" and "holder in due course"?

B. Why wasn't the bank aware of the problems with the goods experienced by Bestways?

C. What should the bank have done in this transaction to protect itself?

F.   OTHER LEGAL EXCUSES FOR NON-PERFORMANCE

"He who excuses himself accuses himself."

—Gabriel Meurier

*"I should have been clearer if I had desired to be excused from it,
as a thing against my conscience."*

—John Woolman

At the heart of contractual agreements is certain required performance by one or both of the parties. The timing of when this action must be completed distinguishes the two basic forms of contracts.

In the *unilateral* form, one party exchanges a promise (usually to pay) for the act of the other. The agreement itself is not legally made until performance of the act is completed.

In the *bilateral* form, the contract is formed when the parties exchange reciprocal promises, one to pay and one to perform an act. The agreement is legally made when the promises are given, prior to the actual performance of the designated act.

Disputes often arise when one of the contracting parties wants to be legally excused from having to perform and the other party demands strict adherence to the agreement. In cases of discharge by "breach," "operation of law," and "impossibility," the factual circumstances that surround the agreement determine whether or not adherence to it is legally required. In "discharge by agreement" and "conditional contracts," legal non-performance is based upon the wording of the agreement.

Discharge by Breach

A contract requires the parties to perform certain agreed actions. If there is a failure to do so by one party, they have breached.

The legal consequences of a minor breach are usually an award of money damages to compensate the non-breaching party for his loss. The required performance is still due from him, but it may be delayed until the breach is remedied. In construction contracts these are usually cosmetic touch-ups or other superficial deviations from the agreement.

If, however, there is a major deviation from the contract's requirements, called a *material breach*, the injured party can collect damages and is legally excused from his required performance.

Some states allow the breaching party to be paid the reasonable value of any partial performance that benefits the other party, while others deny any recovery to the breaching party. In construction contracts these are usually major structural problems.

Mr. and Mrs. Newlywed contract with Quality Builders to construct their new residence for $200,000. The construction contract is of the usual type, where the builder receives a 10% deposit at contract signing, submits draw requests for progress payments as the job moves through its stages of foundation, walls, roof, plumbing, electric, and finishing, and the owners hold back 20% until the final walk-through to assure that the job has been successfully completed. The final inspection reveals structural, non-cosmetic construction problems that would cost $25,000 to correct, plus an additional $5,000 for incidental expenses. The builder wants payment in full and the owners refuse.

In most states, the structural defects would be considered a material breach. The owners could deduct the actual repair costs plus the related expenses of completing the job from the contract price. Thus, the owners who have retained $40,000 as their holdback are discharged from any further payment obligations once they pay $10,000 to the builder.

Florida is one of the states with the highest dollar amount of new construction annually. It has numerous disputes between builders and their customers regarding their respective performance obligations. In determining what should be paid to a builder in cases where there are defects in construction, its courts often use a four-pronged computation formula based upon two factors:

A) If the defects are minor, the builder has substantially performed (SP). If the defects are major, there is (NO SP).
B) If the builder did the best he could, he has acted in good faith (GF). If the builder intentionally covered up problems or was grossly negligent, he has acted in bad faith (BF).

1) SP + GF = builder receives the contract price less the cost of repairs
2) SP + BF = builder receives the fair market value less repairs (assume the builder negotiated a higher price than similar marketplace comparables)
3) NO SP + GF = builder receives the reasonable value of what was properly completed
4) NO SP + BF = builder is penalized and receives nothing

Another form of material breach occurs when one of the contracting parties notifies the other, before the required date, that he will not perform.

This is called *anticipatory repudiation*, and while the non-breaching party is immediately discharged from performance, he also has a number of alternate remedies against the offending party that may include:

• Immediately declare a default and sue for breach of contract.
• Wait until the performance date to see if the other party will perform.
• Use the breach and threat of legal action to renegotiate a better deal.

In *Lucente v. International Business Machines, 2002 WL 31478458 (N.Y. App. 2002)*, the dispute between the parties was the violation of an employment non-competition covenant (discussed previously in the Illegality chapter), but also included allegations by the plaintiff of anticipatory repudiation, and the court presented a good summary of the applicable law:

"Anticipatory repudiation occurs when, before the time for performance has arisen, a party to a contract declares his intention not to fulfill a contractual duty.

When confronted with an anticipatory repudiation, the non-repudiating party has two mutually exclusive options. He may (a) elect to treat the repudiation as an anticipatory breach and seek damages for breach of contract, thereby terminating the contractual relation between the parties, or (b) he may continue to treat the contract as valid and await the designated time for performance before bringing suit."

Discharge by Operation of Law

Contracting parties can usually assume as a general rule that their valid agreements will be legally enforceable. However, there are three common exception situations where specific rules of law allow parties to be discharged from having to perform their contractual duties:

1. *Bankruptcy* proceedings are governed by federal law, and allow a debtor that has been granted an order of discharge to be forever excused from having to pay valid debts owed to unsecured creditors.

The philosophy of these laws is to provide a "fresh start" to a debtor who has suffered financial reverses and is now insolvent. Because of the risks involved, many creditors are reluctant to extend substantial amounts of unsecured credit in the form of open account purchases of goods and services, or make outright loans unless there is some form of collateral or other collection protection.

2. *Statutes of limitations* are legal time periods established by the laws of each state during which a plaintiff is required to file suit on a particular type of claim, including most contracts and sales transactions.

If a lawsuit is not timely filed by the plaintiff, a defendant may raise this failure as an absolute defense that will cause dismissal of the case and forever excuse the defendant from having to perform, even though the plaintiff has an otherwise successful case.

Contracting parties are presumed to know their legal rights (even though we know this is often not the case). Ignorance of the law is no defense, and a potential plaintiff must file suit within the time frames specified. For example, the UCC requires its breach of contract cases to be brought within four years from when the breach occurs, most states require medical malpractice cases to be filed no later than one year after the plaintiff is first reasonably aware of the problem sued upon, and negligence cases seeking recovery for personal injuries have limitation periods of from three to seven years, depending upon the state law where the dispute arose.

3. *Intentional contract alteration* is a little-known but very effective way for a party to be legally excused from having to perform. The alteration must be material, relating to one of the essential terms, such as subject matter, price, quantity, or terms of payment. The wrongdoer is penalized by not being allowed to enforce any part of the contract. The innocent party is given the choice to disregard the contract, enforce it under its original terms, or require enforcement per the altered terms — whichever is best.

Gertrude is a wealthy woman, but is elderly and in poor health. Her only debt is a five-year promissory note for $100,000 payable to Andrew, a private lender, which provided the investment capital three years ago for her financial holdings. She dies and Andrew, thinking she didn't keep a copy of the note, skillfully alters it to read $400,000. He then files a creditor's claim in her estate proceedings for payment of that amount. Unfortunately for Andrew, Gertrude had saved a copy of the original note in her personal papers, and her executor now claims the estate has no payment obligation whatsoever due to Andrew's unlawful conduct.

Andrew loses the entire unpaid principal of the promissory note, plus any accrued interest due. This sanction is similar in its punitive nature to the forfeiture of principal or interest in the usury cases or the NO SP + BF construction cases.

Discharge by Impossibility

Sometimes events occur after the formation of a contract that make one party's required performance impossible. These are no-fault events, usually unforeseeable and outside the control of the party who now wants to be legally excused from having to perform. If the complaining party could reasonably have prevented the problem or is the cause of it, he is legally bound under its terms.

Occasionally, one of the contracting parties seeks to be released from performance, claiming his inability to financially perform caused by circumstances beyond his control, such as bad weather or bad luck. This "I can't pay" defense is known as *subjective impossibility*," and is uniformly rejected by the courts.

In *Christy v. Pilkinton, 273 S.W.2d 533 (Ark. 1954)*, Christy agreed to purchase an apartment house from Pilkinton for $30,000 (remember, this was 1954!). When the time came to close, Christy was unable to raise enough money to complete the transaction, and Pilkinton sued for specific performance. The defense raised was that Christy's used car business had declined and he could not borrow the unpaid balance of $29,900 (only a $100 deposit was paid).

The trial court ordered Christy to perform, and on appeal, the ruling was affirmed. "Proof of this kind does not establish the type of impossibility that constitutes a defense. There is a familiar distinction between objective impossibility, which amounts to saying, 'The thing cannot be done,' and subjective impossibility – 'I cannot do it.' The latter, which is well illustrated by a promisor's financial inability to pay, does not discharge the contractual duty and is therefore not a bar to a decree of specific performance."

The situations recognized by the courts as allowing one party to be released from his contractual obligations are called *objective impossibility*, as mentioned above in the Christy case, meaning that, "the thing cannot be done," rather than the personal subjective test where the party individually chooses not to perform.

- Subsequent illegality – the required action is legal at the time of contracting, but barred afterwards by statutory or case law, or factual circumstance.

- Destruction of the subject matter – after making the contract, an outside no-fault event, such as fire or windstorm, destroys the property on which it is based, or factual circumstance also prevents its completion.
- Personal service contracts – where parties who are supposed to perform are unable to do so because of accident, illness, or other incapacity suffered through no fault of their own. In the event of death, their estate is discharged from any continuing liability, such as a party who had contracted to give a golf exhibition. If, however, the contract were just to buy the golf clubs, their estate would be liable since no unique personal services are involved.

You will recall we discussed these same scenarios in an earlier chapter as legal grounds for termination of a contract offer.

Some disputes are a bit different, but so closely related to these categories of objective impossibility that they are treated the same way:

- To resolve a prior title insurance dispute with another party, the defendant agreed to buy an easement for access to highway 95 across the plaintiff's property.

  Later the defendant claimed the easement transfer was rendered impossible because the State Department of Transportation would not approve such access. The plaintiff sued to enforce the purchase agreement, the trial court ruled in his favor, and the appellate court reversed:

  "The doctrine of impossibility operates to excuse performance when the bargained-for performance is no longer in existence or is no longer capable of being performed due to the unforeseen, supervening act of a third party." *Haessly v. Safeco Title Insurance Company of Idaho, 825 P.2d 1119 (Id. 1992)* (similar to destruction of the subject matter)

- The plaintiff, a college-educated bachelor, signed up with the defendant for a series of seventy-five dance lessons at an agreed price of $1,000, after he was told he had "exceptional potential to be a fine and accomplished dancer" during the free introductory phase of the defendant's sales plan, and signed additional contracts thereafter for a total of 2,734 hours of lessons, for which he paid in advance $24,812.80. The contract the plaintiff signed stated in bold print, "Non-Cancellable Contract: I understand that no refunds will be made under the terms of this contract."

  The plaintiff was severely injured in an auto accident that rendered him incapable of continuing his dance lessons, and he demanded return of the unused portion of his lessons based upon impossibility. The defendant declined based upon the wording of the contract. The plaintiff sued to rescind the contract.

  The trial court granted rescission and the appellate court affirmed:

  "Defendants do not deny that the doctrine of impossibility of performance is generally applicable to the case at bar. Rather they assert that . . . the contract indicates a contrary intention. Such bold type phrases as (No Refunds, etc.) manifested the party's mutual intent to waive their respective rights to invoke the doctrine of impossibility. This is a construction which we find unacceptable . . . plaintiff never contemplated that by signing a contract with such terms as 'Noncancellable' and 'No Refunds' he was waiving a remedy expressly recognized by Illinois courts." *Parker v. Arthur Murray, Inc., 295 N.E.2d 487 (Ill. App. 1973)* (similar to disability in a personal service contract)

- The plaintiff hired the defendant to install a sewer lateral for the home it was building. The defendant did not complete the job, claiming it had relied on the plaintiff's representations regarding the depth of the foundations and subsurface soil, which proved to be materially different and thus made their performance impossible.

  The plaintiff hired a new contractor to complete the job, and then sued for breach of contract. The trial court granted the plaintiff summary judgment, denying the impossibility defense, and the appellate court affirmed:

  "The record reveals that the subdivision plat which showed the actual depth of the sewer main was on file in 1994, prior to the execution of the contract. Defendant, who held itself out as an expert excavator, could have taken reasonable steps to determine the depth of the subsurface soils and sewer main . . . Impossibility excuses a party's performance only when the destruction of the subject matter of the contract or the means of performance makes performance objectively impossible. Moreover, the impossibility must be produced by an unanticipated event that could not have been foreseen or guarded against in the contract." *Comprehensive Building Contractors, Inc. v. Pollard Excavating, Inc., 674 N.Y.S.2d 869 (N.Y. App. Div. 1998)*

Another apparent form of "objective impossibility" recognized by the UCC and most states, though technically different, involves situations where, although a party could actually perform, he chooses not to do so because the no-fault events complained of have so damaged him financially he claims it is no longer economically feasible:

- Frustration of purpose – excuses performance when the contract benefits are rendered worthless by outside events, such as a lease of your vacant lot to park cars for the upcoming Super Bowl and then having the game cancelled. These cases are rarely litigated because the contract objective can no longer be attained and courts will allow the parties to be returned to the status quo.

"Under the doctrine of commercial frustration, if the happening of an event not foreseen by the parties and not caused by or under the control of either party has destroyed or nearly destroyed either the value of the performance or the object or purpose of the contract, then the parties are excused from further performance. The doctrine of commercial frustration is close to but distinct from the doctrine of impossibility of performance. Both concern the effect of supervening circumstances upon the rights and duties of the parties; but in cases of commercial frustration, performance remains possible but the expected value of performance in the party seeking to be excused has been destroyed by the fortuitous event which supervenes to cause an actual but not literal failure of consideration." *Werner v. Ashcraft Bloomquist, Inc., 10 S.W.3d 575 (Mo. App. 2000)*

In *Chase Precast corporation v. John J. Paonessa Company, Inc., 566 N.E.2d 603 (Mass. 1991)*, a case of first impression, the defendant-general contractor agreed with the Massachusetts Department of Public Works to resurface and improve portions of Route 128, and subcontracted with the plaintiff for the replacing of the grass median strip with concrete median barriers.

After the project began, angry residents objected to the removal of the grass median and its replacement with the concrete barriers. In response, the department entered into a settlement agreement with the protestors stating that no additional concrete barriers would be used, and deleted them from their contract with the defendant, who in turn notified the plaintiff to stop production.

The plaintiff sued for breach of contract. Before stopping production, the plaintiff had produced and delivered one-half of the required median barriers, and was paid in full for those items. The defendant claimed it was excused from performance by virtue of the defense of "frustration of purpose," although this argument also involved aspects of impossibility due to destruction of the subject matter and subsequent illegality.

The trial court ruled for the defendant, and the court affirmed:

"This court has long recognized and applied the doctrine of impossibility as a defense to an action for breach of contract . . . the parties shall be excused . . . (when) performance becomes impossible from the accidental perishing of the (basis of their bargain) without the fault of either party.

"On the other hand, although we have referred to the doctrine of frustration of purpose in a few decisions, we have never clearly defined it . . . when an event neither anticipated nor caused by either party, the risk of which was not allocated by the contract, destroys the object or purpose of the contract, thus destroying the value of performance, the parties are excused from further performance."

Do you think the court's ruling would have been the same if Chase had not been paid yet for its production and delivery of concrete median barriers? Should application of the "frustration of purpose" defense be limited by the amount and type of damages allegedly suffered by the plaintiff suing for breach of contract?

- Commercial impossibility is the first cousin of the "unforeseen difficulties" doctrine that we previously visited in our discussion of legal consideration, as an exception to the rule that pre-existing duty promises are legally unenforceable. It is used in this new context for cases where outside events that occur after making the contract have a serious adverse financial impact and the disadvantaged party wants to be excused from having to perform.

It is also used as a companion rule with "frustration of purpose," because its definition in the UCC is almost identical to the "frustration" definition in the Restatement of Contracts:

"Where, after a contract is made, a party's principal purpose is substantially frustrated without his fault by the occurrence of an event the non-occurrence of which was a basic assumption on which the contract was made, his remaining duties to render performance are discharged, unless the language or the circumstances indicate the contrary." (Frustration of Purpose) *Restatement of Contracts, Section 265*

"Delay in delivery or non-delivery in whole or in part by a seller . . . is not a breach of his duty under a contract for sale if performance as agreed has been made impracticable by the occurrence of a contingency the non-occurrence of which was a basic assumption on which the contract was made . . ." (Commercial Impossibility) *Uniform Commercial Code, Section 2-615*

In *Northern Corporation v. Chugach Electrical Association, 518 P.2d 76 (Alaska 1974)*, the plaintiff was the low bidder and was awarded a contract by the defendant for the repair and protection of the upstream face of the Cooper Lake Dam. It required the plaintiff to quarry and haul gravel rock from a site on the opposite end of the lake to the dam in winter, by "transport across Cooper Lake to the dam site when such lake is frozen to a sufficient depth to permit heavy vehicle traffic thereon."

During repeated attempts by the plaintiff to commence the transport beginning in December of 1966, the ice conditions were unable to support their trucks, and some equipment was damaged. When the plaintiff complained about the unsafe conditions, the defendant threatened default unless performance took place. The plaintiff continued to attempt transport, but ultimately ceased in March of 1967.

When the defendant again threatened default unless performance was completed by April 1, 1968, the plaintiff returned to Cooper Lake, and "started hauling with half-loaded trucks; but within the first few hours, two trucks with their drivers broke through the ice, resulting in the death of the drivers and loss of the trucks." The plaintiff then ceased operations and notified the defendant that it considered the contract terminated due to impossibility of performance.

The plaintiff sued for its reasonable costs in attempting performance, less sums already received. The defendant counterclaimed for damages, claiming it had overpaid. The trial court "discharged the parties from the contract on the ground of impossibility of performance."

On appeal, the decision on discharge was affirmed.

"Discharge of a party for impossibility of performance abates the severity of the old common law doctrine that not even objective impossibility excused performance; . . . the Restatement of Contracts has departed from the early common law rule by recognizing the principle of 'commercial impracticability.' Under this doctrine, a party is discharged from his contract obligations, even if it is technically possible to perform them, if the costs of performance would be so disproportionate to that reasonably contemplated by the parties as to make the contract totally impractical in a commercial sense."

But isn't there an apparent legal inconsistency in not excusing from performance a party like *Christy* who says, "I cannot do it," because his business suffers financial reverses, but excusing *Northern* who also says, "I cannot do it," because "it can only be done at an excessive and unreasonable cost"?

"Impossibility" is further defined as "not only strict impossibility but impracticability because of extreme and unreasonable difficulty, expense, injury, or loss involved" (*Restatement of Contracts, Section 454*). But how much is "extreme"? How much is "unreasonable"? How costly must the anticipated loss be? What if the amount of loss to be suffered by a small company will impact it much more severely than a greater loss to be incurred by a larger company?

A party faced with an unprofitable transaction will always answer these questions in a way that justifies being excused from performance, so the commercial impracticability doctrine as a convenient excuse from performance is difficult to properly apply, and is dangerous in the marketplace.

The *Northern* court recognized this problem of application when it said:

"The doctrine ultimately represents the ever-shifting line, drawn by courts hopefully responsive to commercial practices and mores, at which the community's interest in having contracts enforced according to their terms is outweighed by the commercial senselessness of requiring performance . . . "

The more "reasonably foreseeable" the underlying circumstances that create the commercial difficulties are, the less likely a court is to allow a party to escape its contract obligations.

Acme Oil contracts to buy 100,000 barrels of crude oil over the next six months from Saudi Arabia at a fixed price of $30 per barrel for its chain of nationwide gas stations. Thirty days after making the contract, a Middle East peace agreement is signed by all the previously warring countries, and the worldwide price of crude oil drops to $10 per barrel. Acme Oil says it will go broke if it has to pay the $30 per barrel contract price, and sues to rescind the contract based upon "commercial impossibility."

Tough luck, Acme Oil. Yes, the events that occurred after you make your contract have had a negative financial impact, but they are not unforeseeable.

There have been past hostilities in the region that caused oil shortages and higher prices, as well as peaceful periods where oil prices dropped. If it happened before, it could happen again.

Acme Oil could reasonably have protected themselves by a *force majeure* clause in the contract that would allow price adjustments in the event of specified outside events, such as Acts of God involving severe weather events and/or disruptions in oil supply or demand caused by the changing politics of the region.

Discharge by Agreement of the Parties

No matter what the provisions of their contract, the parties may mutually agree to modify them in whole or part or cancel them entirely, so long as they are executory.

- Mutual rescission – the contract is cancelled and performance is no longer required by either party.
- Waiver – one of the parties voluntarily gives up the legal right to complain and agrees to excuse the other party's non-performance.
- Modification – certain of the required performance promises of the existing contract are changed, but the basic agreement remains intact.
- Substitution – the old contract is cancelled and a new one is created which takes its place.
- Novation – by mutual agreement, one of the parties to a contract is released from performing and an outside third party is substituted in its place. This often is sought by a mortgage debtor who wants to be released from liability when he sells the encumbered property to another party with comparable financial credit who has agreed to assume the payment obligation.

"A substituted contract, or a novation, in which the sole participants are the parties to the original agreement or obligation not only creates a new agreement or obligation, but also rescinds the former one. It is not unlike the emergence of a butterfly from a chrysalis. It is the two-fold character of the transaction, that is, the rescission and substitution, which constitutes the supporting consideration for both phases of the transaction." *Dorsey v. Tisby, 234 P.2d 557 (Oregon 1951)*

Discharge in Conditional Contracts

Usually the required performances in a binding contract and the terms stating them must be clear, definite, and unequivocal. If, however, a party's required performance is dependent upon the occurrence of an uncertain, future event, the contract is conditional, and disputes arise as to when one's performance is legally required:

- Condition precedent – the legal duty to perform does not arise until the happening of a future, uncertain event. If you promise to buy a parcel of land subject to it being rezoned to allow business usage, you are not required to perform until this outside event occurs. Notice the root word is "precede," meaning to come before.

  Usually the existence of a condition precedent is based upon the wording of the contract and will be denied in questionable cases:

  - Franklin's will stated that her estate was to go to the Waltmans, "in case I die on my way to & from Jersey." Franklin made the trip safely. When she died six years later, a will contest ensued, and the trial court ruled the will contained a condition precedent – dying on the trip to New Jersey – and since she didn't, that will was ineffective and her earlier will was in effect. The appellate court reversed:

    "A conditional or contingent will is one that takes effect only upon the satisfaction of a certain condition or happening of a specified contingency.

If the condition is not satisfied, or the contingency fails, the will is rendered inoperative and void." However, courts do not regard a will as conditional when it is reasonable to infer that the testator was merely expressing a reason to make a will (because she was concerned about her pending trip). *In re Estate of Franklin, 2001 WL 896635 (Tenn. App. 2001)*

- Condition subsequent – the legal duty to perform currently exists, but may be excused in the future if the specified event occurs. If you lease a college bookstore and promise to pay monthly rental so long as the university across the street exists, you are legally obligated unless and until that future event occurs to discharge you. Notice the word "subsequent," meaning to come after.

The key to determining whether or not a contract is conditional is its specific wording, because that is the best expression of the intention of the parties. Courts will examine these disputes on a case-by-case basis since the legal effect of condition precedent (no contract obligation yet) and condition subsequent (contract currently exists with possible future discharge) are exactly opposite.

The words commonly used to indicate the existence of a conditional contract are usually conjunctions, connective words signaling something before or after the stated performance may affect its enforcement:

- Conditioned upon
- Subject to
- On condition that
- When
- If
- As soon as
- For so long as
- Provided that
- After

In *Pace Construction Corporation v. OBS Company, Inc., 531 So.2d 737 (Fla. App. 1988)*, Pace, as general contractor, agreed with Shumann Investments to construct for them a commercial building. OBS was the dry wall subcontractor, and the contract between it and the plaintiff stated, "Final payment shall not become due unless and until the following conditions precedent to Final Payment have been satisfied: . . . c) receipt of final Payment for Subcontractor's work by Contractor from Owner . . . "

After OBS completed their work, they were unable to collect payment from Pace because it had been refused payment by Shumann. OBS sued Pace for the monies due, and was granted summary judgment. On appeal, the decision was reversed and remanded, with the court agreeing that "The subcontract agreement expresses a clear intent to shift the risk of nonpayment by the owner from Pace to OBS and that, therefore, OBS is not entitled to recover final payment from Pace or pursue its claim against the payment bond until Pace receives such payment from the owner."

"In most subcontract agreements, payment by the owner to the contractor is not intended to be a condition precedent to the contractor's duty to pay the subcontractor . . . most subcontractors are not willing to assume the risk of owner nonpayment because they cannot afford to remain in business without prompt payment for their completed work . . . a subcontract agreement may nevertheless contain valid provisions which shift this risk to the subcontractor."

This was one of those cases. OBS allowed this legal time bomb to blow up in their face. Do you think they did so consciously, as part of the process of negotiating their business deal with Pace, or did they simply overlook the clear and unambiguous wording that shifted the payment risk to them?

If, however, a party is improperly prevented from performing its required condition precedent, it is excused from its contractual obligations, and the party at fault suffers the loss.

In *Barrows v. Maco, Inc., et al, 419 N.E.2d 634 (Ill. App. 1981)*, the plaintiff, a roofing contractor, hired the defendant as a commission salesperson to work a designated territory securing roofing contracts and doing public relations work with his customers.

The plaintiff's employment agreement provided that his basic commission on jobs was 26% of the net profit, and, "To qualify for payment of the commission, the Salesman must sell and supervise the job; the job must be completed and paid for; and the Salesman must have been in the continuous employment of the company during the aforementioned period . . . In such case that Salesman's employment shall be terminated for any reason prior to the complete supervision and installation of a job, the Salesman shall not be entitled to and shall not receive credit for any commission on the said job."

One of the plaintiff's roof repair contracts was with the Cook County School District, with whom the defendant had done business for many years. The plaintiff testified that he was present at the job site sixty to ninety times to help explain the job's progress to various school district personnel. After various problems between the defendant and its subcontractor on that job that caused the school to stop paying before completion of the job, the defendant notified the plaintiff that his employment was terminated and he would not receive any commissions.

The plaintiff sued the defendant to recover his commissions due under his employment contract. They denied liability on the grounds that he was not entitled to commissions because all the conditions of that provision had not been satisfied. The plaintiff claimed that the defendant's own actions prevented its subcontractor from completing the job.

The trial court entered judgment for the plaintiff, and the appellate court affirmed:

"A party to a contract may not complain of the nonperformance of the other party where that performance is prevented by his own actions. A party cannot take advantage of a condition precedent the performance of which he has rendered impossible."

The rationale for this fairness principle is similar to the rule we examined in an earlier chapter on offer, to the effect that the offeror is legally prohibited from terminating a unilateral offer (promise in exchange for an act) while the offeree is in the process of proceeding in good faith to complete the required performance.

Conditional contracts can also be used to protect parties against uncertain future events if and only if they are anticipated to the extent that a conditional clause addresses them.

The specific events may not be specified, but general areas of concern need to be anticipated as potential problems so the parties can protect themselves accordingly. Here is an actual dispute that took place:

Major league baseball teams customarily sell the exclusive broadcast rights to the highest bidder. This is done annually. The Florida Marlins entered into annual contracts with the same Miami radio station starting in the early 1990s. They became champions of major league baseball in 1997 by winning the World Series. The winning bid for the next year was much higher than previous years in anticipation of their new status as defending champions. However, to the dismay of players and fans and the broadcast station, the owner decided to dismantle the team for alleged financial reasons and not permit it to defend its title. The radio station sued to rescind its now greatly overpriced contract, but had no legal grounds to do so because the contract left no "out" for their problem, and the owner could do whatever he wanted with his team.

The radio station could have defused this time bomb if the winning bid for the broadcast rights had been:

"Conditioned upon ownership not engaging in any business practices or conduct, intentional or unintentional, that have the effect of substantially reducing the following, audience, appeal to advertisers or other broadcast of value of the broadcasts, and if such practices or conduct occurs, then the amount to be paid for the broadcast rights shall be adjusted downward (like a force majeure clause) to reflect the loss suffered by the broadcasting party."

As a practical matter, following this unique dispute, most all companies bidding for broadcast rights of sports teams now include similar condition precedent clauses in their contracts.

The Engagement Ring Cases

One of the more interesting types of disputes that involve the rules of conditional contracts are the cases to determine ownership of an engagement ring following termination of the engagement, and refusal of the donee to return it to the donor.

Some states decide these disputes based upon who is "at fault," meaning the party that broke the engagement. The other party is deemed to be "not at fault," and gets to keep the ring.

But there are inherent difficulties and unpleasantness in this process of blaming one party over another, the "he said/she said" finger-pointing argument which probably was a part of the engagement break-up in the first place.

This caused most states to now follow a no–fault approach. They treat engagement rings as conditional gifts in contemplation of marriage, which must be returned to the donor no matter who caused the end of the relationship, *if* the condition precedent of marriage does not take place.

These are the same reasons that most states have changed their domestic relations laws for the termination of a marriage from a rather complicated process of fault divorce that required the plaintiff to prove specific grounds, such as extreme cruelty, habitual intemperance, or adultery, to the simplified procedures that now exist for no-fault dissolution of marriage.

In *Meyer v. Mitnick, 2001 WL 171453 (Mich. App. 2001)*, a case of first impression, the plaintiff gave the defendant a custom-designed engagement ring he bought for $19,500 when they became engaged. Three months later the plaintiff asked the defendant to sign a prenuptial agreement, and when she refused the engagement was broken. Both parties claimed it was the "fault" of the other.

When the defendant refused to return the ring, the plaintiff sued, alleging it was a conditional gift. The defendant counterclaimed, alleging it was an unconditional gift and that, because the plaintiff broke the engagement, she was entitled to keep the ring.

The trial court granted summary judgment to the plaintiff, holding that he was entitled to return of the ring, "Because an engagement ring is given in contemplation of marriage, the marriage itself is a condition precedent to the ultimate ownership of the ring." It ignored the issue of who ended the engagement.

The appellate court affirmed, noting that, "While there is no Michigan law regarding ownership of engagement rings given in contemplation of marriage where the engagement is broken, the jurisdictions that have considered cases dealing with the gift of an engagement ring uniformly hold that marriage is an implied condition of the transfer of title and that the gift does not become absolute until the marriage occurs."

Once we recognize an engagement ring is a conditional gift, the question still remains: who gets the gift when the condition is not fulfilled?

The court than analyzed the history of how courts have handled these situations and adopted the no-fault rule:

Generally, courts have taken two divergent paths. The older one rules that when the donor has unjustifiably broken an engagement, the donor shall not recover the ring. However, if the engagement is broken by mutual agreement, or unjustifiably by the donee, the ring should be returned to the donor . . .

The other rule, the so-called "modern trend," holds that because an engagement ring is an inherently conditional gift, once the engagement has been broken the ring should be returned to the donor. Thus, the question of who broke the engagement and why, or who was "at fault," is irrelevant.

In *Lindh v. Surman, 742 A.2d 643 (Pa. 1999)*, also a case of first impression, the plaintiff proposed marriage to the defendant and presented her with a diamond engagement ring he purchased for $17,400. Two months later, the plaintiff broke the engagement and asked for the ring back. The defendant did in fact return it, the parties reconciled, and again the plaintiff proposed marriage and gave the defendant the same ring.

Five months later, the plaintiff again called off the engagement, and this time, after he requested return of the ring, the defendant refused. The plaintiff then sued, seeking recovery of the ring or a judgment for its equivalent value. The case then went to an arbitration panel that ruled for the defendant. The plaintiff appealed that decision, where a non-jury trial resulted in a judgment in his favor for $21,200, the fair market value of the ring, based upon the application of no-fault rules of law.

The Pennsylvania Supreme Court accepted final appellate jurisdiction, and affirmed the decision for the plaintiff, thus answering the two basic questions before it:

"(1) What is the condition of the gift (i.e., acceptance of the engagement or the marriage itself), and (2) Whether fault is relevant to determining return of the ring. Janis (the defendant) argues that the condition of the gift is acceptance of the marriage proposal, not the performance of the marriage ceremony. She also contends that Pennsylvania law, which treats engagement gifts as implied-in-law conditional gifts, has never recognized a right of recovery in a donor who severs the engagement.

"This theory (1) is contrary to Pennsylvania's view of the engagement ring situation . . . This court, however, has not decided the question (2) of whether the donor is entitled to return of the ring where the donor admittedly ended the engagement. In the context of our conditional gift approach to engagement rings, the issue we must resolve is whether we will follow the fault-based theory, argued by Janis, or the no-fault rule advocated by Rodger.

"A ring-return rule based on fault principles will inevitably invite acrimony and encourage parties to portray their ex-fiancées in the worst possible light, hoping to drag out the most favorable arguments to justify, or to attack, the termination of an engagement. Furthermore, it is unlikely that trial courts would be presented with situations where fault was clear and easily ascertained and, as noted earlier, determining what constitutes fault would result in a rule that would defy universal application."

Would you consider the following transfers by Rodger to Janis during their relationship as completed or conditional gifts?

- A diamond ring prior to announcing their engagement
- Additional jewelry such as rings, earrings, bracelets and necklaces given prior to announcing their engagement
- Additional jewelry items given after announcing their engagement
- Gift items such as computers, television sets, and clothing given before or after the engagement
- An automobile titled in Janis' name when the engagement is announced

The Satisfaction Contract Cases

The most difficult disputes are those that involve "satisfaction contracts." These are condition precedent contracts where the obligation of one party to pay for the specified goods or services is conditioned upon prior approval.

The most obvious practical question they raise is why any party would agree that he need not be paid unless the other is satisfied. Perhaps this was required in their negotiation, or the ego involved does not anticipate anyone could be less than thrilled with the work to be done or goods to be delivered. In any event, these cases have given rise to two legal tests used in determining their result:

- Personal satisfaction test – if the required performance involves personal taste, individual comfort, aesthetics, or similar factors the courts are subjective. No matter whether outside parties consider the required performance acceptable, it must satisfy the party involved. Examples are personal portraits, photographs, paintings, artistic creations, individual hairstyles, custom clothing, and cosmetic surgery.

  Brad, the famous actor, contracts with Salvador, the famous artist, to paint Brad's portrait, "subject to my approval," for a price of $5,000. After a number of sittings, the painting is completed. Brad goes to Salvador's studio, where ten other famous artists eagerly await the finished product. When the cover is removed from the painting, the artists all declare it to be the best work Salvador has ever done. Brad looks at it and says, "I don't like it. I'm not paying one cent for it." Salvador sues for breach of contract.

  Brad wins. The nature of the work was purely personal and should be judged by the subjective test of satisfaction. No one forced the artist to agree to a satisfaction contract. He assumed the risk if his customer was not pleased. The opinions of the third parties are immaterial.

- Industry standard test – if the required performance involves mechanical fitness, construction, and repairs, the courts are objective. If the work involved is completed reasonably well by meeting the prevailing industry standards as attested by outside expert witnesses, payment is required no matter whether or not the party involved is personally satisfied. Most basic commercial contracts for property repair, improvement, or construction fall into this category.

  Brad contracts with Salvador to paint Brad's Beverly Hills residence for an agreed price of $5,000, "subject to my approval." After several weeks, during which Brad was out of town, the job is completed. Ten other house painters that admire Salvador's work are present to view the finished product. Brad takes one look at it and says, "No way, this is not what I wanted, I won't pay." The ten house painters all say the work is excellent, exceeding industry standards. Salvador sues for breach of contract.

  Brad loses. The nature of the work to be done is outside the realm of a personal or custom artistic creation. Instead, it is commercial work and must therefore be judged objectively under that industry's standards.

What about this case, where the line between subjective and objective considerations is not so clearly drawn?

Brad, a famous actor, hires Salvador, a famous artist, to paint Brad's Beverly Hills residence for an agreed price of $5,000, "subject to my personal specifications and approval." The job consists of painting each room of the house a different color, requiring the blending of common primary colors to achieve a unique new color. In addition, Brad's swimming pool is to be painted with a laughing likeness of him on it, to achieve a visual image from his diving board of launching yourself into his face. When the job is completed, amidst much publicity and media attention, ten other area artists declare it to be fabulous and the best work of its kind. Brad doesn't like it and refuses to pay.

Pretend you are deciding this dispute. What would you argue in support of Brad's legal position? What arguments would you make in favor of Salvador? Who should win and why?

Here are some cases in which satisfaction contracts were involved and the legal principles discussed.

In *Indiana Tri-City Plaza Bowl, Inc. v. Estate of Glueck, 422 N.E.2d 670 (Ind. App. 1981)*, the parties had a lease agreement that required Glueck, as lessor, to provide the plaintiff with adequate paved parking and a building for its bowling alley.

For the first eleven years of the lease, the plaintiff used parking from the adjacent shopping center owned by Glueck. When the center went into receivership, the parties had a dispute over parking, which they attempted to resolve by a settlement agreement which required Glueck to build a parking lot after submitting the plans to plaintiff for *prior approval*.

When Glueck submitted his architect's plans to the plaintiff for approval, it failed to reply for four months and eventually responded without approval or disapproval. Glueck claimed it was acting in bad faith.

The plaintiff sued for specific performance of the lease and damages. The defendant counterclaimed for damages. The trial court ruled for the defendant, applying the "reasonable person" standard of approval, and the plaintiff appealed. The appellate court affirmed on the issue of prior approval.

"Although Indiana has not previously discussed the situation of a party to a contract having his duty of performance *conditioned upon his own satisfaction*, other jurisdictions have. A minority of jurisdictions use one standard, which gives the party to be satisfied an unqualified right of rejection in all circumstances unless he acts fraudulently. The majority of jurisdictions use two standards, reasonable person and good faith, to determine if a party has been satisfied."

- Reasonable person standard: "Satisfaction is said to have been received if a reasonable person in exactly the same circumstances would be satisfied. The reasonable person standard is employed when the contract involves commercial quality, operative fitness, or mechanical utility which other knowledgeable persons can judge."
- Good faith standard: "The recipient of the work must be genuinely satisfied; which includes a subjective satisfaction. However, the mere statement by the

recipient that he is dissatisfied is not conclusive. The majority of jurisdictions will recognize the recipient's dissatisfaction only when he is *honestly*, even though unreasonably, dissatisfied and acts in good faith. The standard of good faith is employed when the contract involves personal aesthetics or fancy."

"We conclude that Indiana should follow the majority view . . . In the case before us, the construction of the parking lot concerns commercial value and operative fitness rather than personal aesthetics. Therefore, the good faith standard is not applicable to the facts before us."

In *Beverly Way Associates v. Barham, 226 Cal. App.3d 49 (Cal. App. 1990)*, the defendant contracted to sell a residential building to the plaintiff for $3.9 million.

The agreement provided that, "Buyer's obligations to purchase the Property shall be conditioned upon approval by the buyer of a number of specified inspections and documents, and delivery of clear title and conveyance documents at the close of escrow." One of these requirements was "a certified ATLA survey of the property."

When the buyer received the survey, it did not approve it due to a perceived problem regarding the number of available parking spaces, and proposed "some alternatives to keep the deal alive." There were no further communications between the parties until the buyer advised, "We are prepared to waive our objections to such items and to proceed to close escrow within 45 days . . ." When the defendant refused to go forward with the original sales transaction, the plaintiff sued for specific performance.

The trial court ruled that "By disapproving the survey on December 12, 1988, plaintiff buyer terminated the contract and cannot sue on same." The appellate court affirmed:

"Both sides to this appeal treat the buyer's right of approval under paragraph 5 of the contract as a condition precedent in favor of the buyer. They are quite correct in that characterization . . . There can be no question but that the buyer exercised its power of disapproval in this case . . . This rejection, communicated to the seller, terminated the contract. It left the buyer with no power to create obligations against the seller by a late 'waiver' of its objections and acceptance of the proffered documentation."

In *Morin Building Products Company, Inc. v. Baystone Construction, Inc., 717 F.2d 413 (7th Cir. 1983)*, the defendant was hired by GMC to build an addition to its Chevrolet factory, and, in turn, hired the plaintiff to furnish and erect the aluminum walls for the structure for a contract price of $23,000.

The main contract required that the exterior siding of the walls be of a specific aluminum type, "with a mill finish and stucco embossed surface texture to match finish and texture of existing metal siding." It further provided "that all work shall be done subject to the final approval of the Architect or Owner's (GM's) authorized agent, and his decision in matters relating to artistic effect shall be final, . . . should any dispute arise as to the quality or fitness of materials or workmanship, the decision as to acceptability shall rest strictly with the Owner . . ."

After the plaintiff erected the walls, the exterior siding appeared in bright sunlight to lack a uniform finish and was rejected by GM's representative. The plaintiff claimed the defect was trivial, and GM's rejection was unreasonable. The defendant removed the plaintiff's siding, hired another subcontractor to replace it, and GM approved the replacement siding. The defendant then refused to pay the plaintiff for the original aluminum siding, and it sued for the balance.

The trial jury ruled for the plaintiff, and the appellate court affirmed based upon its conclusion that the governing standard should be objective rather than personal:

"The general rule applying to satisfaction in the case of contracts for the construction of commercial buildings is that the satisfaction clause must be determined by objective criteria. Under this standard, the question is not whether the owner was *satisfied in fact*, but whether the owner, as a reasonable person, *should have been satisfied* with the materials and workmanship in question.

"The building for which the aluminum siding was intended was a factory – not usually intended to be a thing of beauty. That aesthetic considerations were decidedly secondary to considerations of function and cost is suggested by the fact that the contract specified mill-finish aluminum, which is unpainted."

In concluding its opinion, the court tells us, in so many words, how the inexact wording of the approval clause by GM created the financial time bomb that blew up in their face, and also suggests how it could have easily been defused:

"We repeat that if it appeared from the language or circumstances of the contract that the parties really intended General Motors to have the right to reject Morin's work for failure to satisfy the private aesthetic taste of General Motors' representative, the rejection would have been proper even if unreasonable. But the contract is ambiguous because of the qualifications with which the terms 'artistic effect' and 'decision as to acceptability' are hedged about, and the circumstances suggest that the parties probably did not intend to subject Morin's rights to aesthetic whim."

Discussion Exercises

1. Discuss any additional situations where a contract party should be discharged by operation of law.

2. Discuss any additional situations that should constitute objective impossibility.

3. Discuss how much contemplated financial loss renders a contract commercially impracticable.

4. Discuss your preference of what rules should govern engagement ring disputes.

5. Discuss your preference of the rules governing Satisfaction Contract disputes.

The Importance of Wording "Pay-When-Paid" Clauses

In *Power & Pollution Services, Inc. v. Suburban Power Piping Corporation, 598 N.E.2d 69 (Ohio App. 1991),* Suburban was the general contractor on a construction job who contracted with the property owner, LTV Steel Corporation. Suburban had a separate subcontract with P&P Services that contained a "pay-when-paid" clause that read:

"Company (Suburban) shall not be required to pay any such monthly billing of the subcontractor prior to the date Company receives payment of its corresponding monthly billing from the Owner."

Analysis

When LTV filed for Chapter 11 Bankruptcy, Suburban claimed it was excused from having to pay P&P. P&P sued for monies due under the contract. The trial court granted summary judgment for P&P, and that decision was affirmed on appeal, rejecting Suburban's argument that the clause was a condition precedent to its obligation to pay.

Defuse Replay

"Ohio courts have not previously addressed the issue of how 'pay-when-paid' clauses should be interpreted and enforced . . . (Suburban) cites (a prior case) which held that a promise to pay 'if and when funds are available' was conditional and did not impose any obligation to pay until funds were available. The use of the conjunction 'if' in the payment provision evidenced that party's intention to condition receipt of payment by the subcontractor upon receipt of payment from the owner and is, thus, distinguishable from the present case."

Conclusion

The contract wording is absolutely critical in these cases. The more definite, clear, and unequivocal the intention of the parties is expressed, the easier it is for them to place themselves within the law's protection. Here are two additional clauses:

- For the general contractor: "The parties recognize and acknowledge the existence of a construction contract between the Property Owner and the General Contractor establishing specific rights and duties between them, including the payment of monies for work performed.

The receipt of such payment(s) by General Contractor from the Property Owner IS an absolute condition precedent and prerequisite to any payment obligation owing to Subcontractor, and must first occur before the General Contractor is required to pay the Subcontractor."

- For the subcontractor: "The parties recognize and acknowledge the existence of a construction contract between the Property Owner and the General Contractor establishing specific rights and duties between them, including the payment of monies for work performed. The receipt of such payment(s) by General Contractor from the Property Owner is NOT a condition precedent or prerequisite to the payment obligations due to Subcontractor; rather, the General Contractor shall pay the sums due hereunder to Subcontractor promptly and without regard to its receipt of payment funds from the Property Owner."

Case Exercise 8

An Ounce of Protection Works

In *Architectural Systems, Inc. v. Gilbane Building Company, 760 F. Supp. 79 (Dist. Ct. Md. 1991)*, the plaintiff entered into a construction subcontract to provide drywall and tile work on the defendant-general contractor's construction project with Carley Capital Group for conversion of their warehouses into condominiums.

The main contract and subcontract provided, "It is specifically understood and agreed that the payment to the subcontractors is dependent, as a condition precedent, upon the contractor receiving contract payments, including retainer from the Owner."

When the owner became insolvent during construction and ceased making payments to the defendant, it ceased paying the plaintiff.

Analysis

The plaintiff sued to recover the $348,155 remaining unpaid under the subcontract. The defendant claimed it had no liability due to the condition precedent clause. The trial court granted Gilbane summary judgment, and the appellate court affirmed:

"Although Gilbane acknowledges that in the construction business the general contractor incurs the owner's credit risk, it maintains that the risk of insolvency was transferred explicitly by the condition precedent in the Trade

Contract. ASI argues that it did not assume the credit risk simply by the inclusion of the statement 'as a condition precedent' in the Trade contract, and that the subcontract does not address owner insolvency specifically."

Defuse Replay

The court noted a simultaneous similar case the defendant had won that has also contained, as here, "both a pay-when-paid provision and an unambiguous precedent provision." *Gilbane Building Co. v. Brisk Waterproofing Co., 585 A.2d 248 (Md. App. 1991)*

In agreeing with the defendant that the condition precedent was a defense to its liability to ASI, the court noted that the subcontractor had assumed that business risk. "It may not be sound business practice to accept such a business proposal but that is what occurred. The provision unambiguously declares that Gilbane is not obligated to pay ASI until it first received payment by the Owner. The cause for the Owner's nonpayment is not specifically addressed and could be due to a number of causes, including insolvency."

Conclusion

The court's opinion clearly delineates the boundaries of when the general contractor may enforce a "pay-when-paid" clause, and when the subcontractor may disregard it.

Perhaps the critical wording of such clauses is part of the business negotiations between the parties, and one or the other makes a conscious decision to trade off advantages/disadvantages. More often, the parties simply are unaware of these legal distinctions and fly blindly into their agreements, hoping for the best result, but sometimes receiving the worst, like ASI.

CHAPTER 5

MANAGING SPECIFIC TYPES OF CONTRACTS

A. SPECIAL RULES FOR SELLING GOODS

"I will buy with you, sell with you, talk with you, walk with you."

—Shakespeare: *The Merchant of Venice*

"The buyer needs a hundred eyes, the seller not one."

—George Herbert

"Don't sell the stock; sell the sizzle."

—Elmer Wheeler

In our examination thus far of commercial transactions, we have been primarily concerned with the common law general rules and fairness exceptions that have been in existence for many years. They govern how business transactions are created and enforced. They are historically the main source of contract law, and govern most transactional disputes in the business marketplace, including the sale of goods and services.

We have also been introduced to specialized rules of more recent origin that pertain solely to *sales of goods*. They are codified by statutory law in the form of the Uniform Commercial Code (UCC), Article 2. It streamlines and encourages the modern flow of commerce by seeking to affirm the existence of contracts and enforce them rather than provide technical and sometimes outmoded loopholes for avoiding them.

The UCC also codifies existing law and provides an orderly framework for planning sales transactions and predicting the outcome of commercial disputes. Rather than having to face differing laws of the fifty U.S. states and adapting transaction jurisdiction to which venue would work best for buyer or seller, it provides the parties with a national forum for their transactions.

Stated in its own words, its underlying purpose and policy is "to simplify, clarify, and modernize the law governing commercial transactions" (*UCC 1-102*). All states have adopted the UCC provisions except for Louisiana, which has approved portions of the UCC, and whose laws based upon the French civil law should be separately examined for local disputes.

The UCC applies to sales of movable, tangible personal property known as goods. These are transactions where title or ownership of the items in question pass from seller to buyer. It does not apply to gifts.

It also does not apply to real property or intangibles such as money, marketable securities, and legal rights. Nor does the UCC apply to transactions whose main component is the sale of services.

Since most business transactions have mixed aspects of both goods and services, the legal test to be decided on a case-by-case basis is "What is the main or dominant aspect of the transaction?"

This distinction is critical in many disputes where the plaintiffs claim they are damaged financially or personally by defects in the "goods" they purchased, and therefore subject to warranty protection under the UCC that requires sellers of "goods" to stand behind their transactions.

While the UCC applies to all sales of goods, it also in certain cases requires higher standards of conduct from a party who has the legal status of a *merchant*, which is defined to be someone who deals primarily in the type of goods involved or is considered to be an expert regarding them.

In *Cook v. Downing, 891 P.2d 611 (Ok. App. 1994)*, the plaintiff had dentures made for her by the defendant, a dentist who devoted less than 50% of his practice to fitting and making dentures. She had resulting mouth problems that she attributed to ill-fitting dentures, and complained to the defendant. He referred her to oral surgeons, who ruled out the possibility that her sore spots were caused by denture fitting problems, and suggested a generalized condition due to allergies or autoimmune reactions.

The plaintiff sued for breach of warranty under the state's UCC law and was awarded damages by the trial court, but the appellate court reversed, holding that the UCC did not apply. The appellate court noted the dispute as a case of first impression:

"Finding no Oklahoma law on point, we . . . hold that . . . a dentist is not a merchant, and dentures, furnished by a dentist, are not goods under the UCC."

The dissenting opinion stated the applicable law in these types of transactions:

"The transaction of a patient being fitted for and purchasing dentures from a dentist is actually a hybrid. It is not purely a sale of goods by a merchant, nor is it purely the providing of a service by a health care professional. Whether implied warranties under Article 2 of the U.C.C. apply to such a transaction should depend on whether the predominant element of the transaction is the sale of goods or the rendering of services."

In *Central District Alarm, Inc. v. Hal-Tuc, Inc., 886 S.W.2d 210 (Mo. App. 1994)*, the plaintiff was in the business of selling security systems, and the defendant operated retail lingerie and novelty stores. The plaintiff sold and installed one of their systems, but it was a used instead of a new VCR as required by the contract between the parties.

When this was discovered by the defendant due to scratches on the unit, the plaintiff offered to replace it with a new unit, "as soon as one arrived, which would take one or two months." The defendant refused, and demanded return of the deposit.

The plaintiff sued for breach of contract, claiming the right to cure defects under the UCC. The defendant denied that right, and claimed it had been defrauded.

The trial court entered judgment for the defendant, and the appellate court affirmed, first stating that the transaction was a sale of goods, and therefore governed by the UCC:

"In a contract which calls for both goods to be furnished and services to be performed, the test for whether the UCC applies is whether the predominant purpose of the contract is to render services with goods incidentally involved, or to transact a sale, with labor incidentally involved. CDA supplied and installed security equipment pursuant to a 'Sales Agreement.' The contract did not include ongoing maintenance or services other than installation. Under the predominant purpose test, this was a sale of goods . . . "

Differences Between Contract Laws

In many disputes that involve a sale of goods, the result may differ depending upon which body of law applies. There may be a common law rule that favors one party and a UCC exception that favors the other. In the case of such a conflict, the UCC will govern.

There is also a body of law known as the United Nations Convention on Contracts for the International Sale of Goods, or the CISG, which is a treaty ratified by more than fifty of the countries engaged in a large proportion of the world's commercial business transactions, including the United States. It governs all non-domestic contracts for the sale of goods between parties located in different countries that have ratified the treaty.

The CISG allows treaty parties to "opt-out," or non-treaty parties to "opt-in," depending upon the strategies involved in a particular transaction and the laws that will benefit the parties most. Since a treaty is a federal law, the CISG supercedes the UCC in disputes where either could be applied.

These differences can be critical factors in planning a contractual transaction and evaluating disputes.

Though we have examined many of them in prior sections with text and case studies, here is a helpful summary of the differences between our common law rules, UCC provisions, and the CISG:

Common Law Versus UCC Versus CISG

A. Application

The common law applies to all sales transactions. This includes services, tangible personal property, intangibles such as rights of legal action, stocks and bonds and money used as a medium of exchange, and real property. The UCC applies only to sales of tangible personal property, known as goods, and can be used in products liability cases. The CISG applies to all commercial/business sales of goods, but not to consumer sales of goods for personal, family, household, and auction purposes, and is not applicable in product liability disputes.

B. Merchants

Under the common law, a merchant is generally described as a person engaged in a type of commercial activity. Under the UCC, a merchant is a person who deals in goods of the kind involved in the particular transaction, or who has special skills or expertise relating to the transaction. Under the CISG, a merchant is broadly defined as anyone who has a place of business. Thus, if the author sold you his old laptop computer at a garage sale, he would be a merchant under the CISG, but not under the UCC.

C. Terms of the Offer

Under common law rules of definiteness, if any of the essential contract terms, such as subject matter, price, terms, time, and quantity, are missing, there can be no valid offer.

The UCC will fill all the gaps created by open terms, except quantity, and declare the offer valid using an objective standard of what appears reasonable under the facts and circumstances of each case. Aside from a reasonable price, terms of payment, and time for payment, there are two other UCC rules that seek to achieve a balance between buyer and seller where gaps exist in contract terms:

- Place of delivery – seller's place of business, or if none, then seller's residence
- Assortment of goods – buyer's choice will be binding

The CISG will not fill contract gaps for either price or quantity.

D. Advertisements as Offers

The common law and UCC consider advertisements as a general rule to be invitations for offers, rather than offers, even if they describe themselves as offers. The exception is if the ad's wording is so specific that a reasonable offeree would assume the ad to be an offer. The CISG presumes that advertisements that call themselves offers are, in fact, offers, and imposes no specific wording requirements.

E. Revocation of the Offer

Under the common law, an offer may be revoked at any time before a legal acceptance occurs, even if the offeror agrees to hold it open for a stated period of time. It is up to the offeree to protect himself by creating one of the exception situations that render the offer legally irrevocable, such as an option or the detrimental reliance doctrine of promissory estoppel.

This unlimited power of revocation held by the offeror is also limited by the UCC firm offer rule. It makes the offer irrevocable for a maximum time of three months if it is in a writing that is signed or initialed by a merchant and grants an additional time for acceptance.

The CISG follows the firm offer exception to the common law revocation rule, but allows such offers stated by a merchant to be verbal, as well as written.

F. Form of Acceptance

The common law mirror-image rule requires a valid acceptance to clearly match all the terms and provisions of the offer. If the acceptance does not mirror the offer, but changes it in any material way by modification, addition, or deletion, it is only a counteroffer.

Under the UCC Battle of the Forms, the purchase order offer and the order acknowledgement acceptance usually contain different pre-printed terms tailored to benefit either the buyer or the seller. In such a case, if the parties have agreed on all the basic terms (the detailed front page of their form), thus expressing their mutual intent to be bound, there is a valid acceptance. Disputes as to which of two differing clauses in the standardized part of the form (the reverse boilerplate sections) are then usually decided in favor of the first form, so long as the changes are of a material nature.

The CISG follows the common law mirror-image rule, and deems any changes in the purported acceptance to be a counteroffer.

G. Time of Acceptance

Under the common law receipt rule, offer and revocation, counteroffer, Acceptance, and rejection are all legally effective from a communication standpoint when actually received. Acceptance also may be legally effective when sent, under the Mailbox Rule, if the acceptance is transmitted the same way as the offer (regular mail offer and regular mail acceptance).

The Mailbox Rule is used more liberally under the UCC. Acceptance is legally effective when sent, so long as it is done through any reasonable medium, properly stamped and addressed, and is sent either the same way as the offer was received, or in any other way that results in faster communication. Thus, an offer sent by fax and an acceptance sent by regular mail would not satisfy the rule.

The CISG rejects both the Mailbox Rule and the reasonable medium rule, requiring the acceptance to be actually received before it is legally effective.

H. Pre-Existing Duty

Under the common law, a contract modification based upon a new promise by one of the parties to do what he was originally legally bound to do is unenforceable due to lack of legally sufficient consideration. Under the UCC, if a merchant makes the modification payment promise, either verbally or in writing, it is enforceable. Under the CISG, the modification payment promise is enforceable whether made by a merchant or not, but it must be in writing.

I. Writing and Signing Contracts

The Statute of Frauds requires contracts for the sale of goods for the purchase price of $500 or more to be in written form. The UCC allows enforcement of these contracts in purely verbal form in certain situations:

- Sale of custom goods, where the seller has substantially started manufacture
- Partial delivery of the goods by the seller
- Partial payment for the goods by the buyer
- Admission in court by the parties that they have a contract

The basic Statute of Frauds requires written contracts to either be signed by all the parties or, if less than all, the signing party in any dispute must have been the defendant.

Under the UCC Non-Signer Rule, if there is a verbal agreement between two merchants for the sale of goods and its terms are confirmed by a written memorandum or other writing signed by one and sent or delivered to the other, the non-signing merchant is legally bound if he does not object within ten days after receiving the confirmation.

Under the CISG, there is no basic writing requirement in contracts for the sale of goods. Each dispute is governed by its own facts, and the parties involved have the burden of proving verbal agreements – a difficult task when they have conflicting agendas as to who made the better business deal.

J. Warranties

The common law has no separate rules that require sellers of goods to perform properly, other than basic breach of contract situations where the parties are legally required to perform their promises.

The UCC imposes implied warranty requirements on sellers of goods, merely from the act of selling the goods to the public. The implied warranty of merchantability requires a merchant seller to furnish goods that will perform their usual and customary purpose. The implied warranty of fitness for a particular purpose, applicable to all sellers whether they are merchants or not, requires that the goods are suitable for a special usage of the buyer.

The CISG recognizes the implied warranties, but only allows them in transactions between a merchant-seller and a merchant-buyer.

K. Seller's Breach

The seller's basic duty is to make timely delivery of conforming goods. If the buyer claims a default, the common law requires giving the seller a "timely" notice of breach, after he has inspected the shipment. The UCC requires the giving of "reasonable" notice of breach. No exact time periods are specified, and the unique facts of each case will govern. If the required notice is not given at all, or not made within the time parameters, the buyer may lose its default rights. The seller's legal right to cure defects expires, under both the common law and the UCC, once the contract delivery date arrives, unless the contract states otherwise.

The CISG allows notice of default to be given as long as two years after the goods are delivered, if the goods are not conforming and there was some reasonable explanation for the long delay in inspection. If the seller gives a "Nachfrist" notice to the buyer prior to delivery of the goods, the seller is allowed an additional grace period to cure defects after the normal cure time has expired.

Imperfect Title Cases

In the normal UCC sale of goods, the seller has legal title to what is sold to the buyer. A buyer cannot usually acquire good title if the seller's title is imperfect in any way.

But what if the buyer of the goods satisfies the legal definition of a "good faith purchaser for value" (GFP) by paying a fair price, having no knowledge of the title imperfection, and reasonably believing the seller to have good title? Does a GFP gain any special ownership rights to the goods?

A) The Void Title Rule: If the seller of the goods to the GFP was a thief or finder of stolen goods – no better title can be conveyed, and the GFP must return the goods on demand of the true owner. Since the seller has void title, no better title can pass to another, even if he is a GFP. The only recourse of the GFP is to locate the thief or finder (highly unlikely) and sue him for the return of the purchase price of the goods.

> Matty owns an expensive laptop computer with a personalized encoded security chip that emits a retrieval signal to locate the item if lost or stolen. He is working on it in his office, goes to the restroom for a few minutes, leaving his door open, and returns to find his computer missing. During his absence, Thief entered the office and took it. Thief then offers it for sale to Sammy for a fair price. Sammy knows nothing about how Thief acquired it. In the meantime, Matty activates his retrieval device, locates Sammy, and demands return of his computer. Sammy refuses.
>
> Sammy must return the computer to Matty. Sammy's seller had void title, and could not pass any better title in the transaction. The only recourse for Sammy, since he will never find Thief, is to try to find facts that will support a claim that Matty somehow voluntarily delivered the computer to Thief.

B) The Voidable Title Rule: If the goods are *voluntarily delivered* to another by the true owner under circumstances where he has assented to the transfer, even though it would constitute fraud by the recipient, such as misrepresentation, impersonation, or a dishonored check – the party in possession of the goods has voidable title, and may pass good title to a GFP.

In these cases, the true owner may not legally reclaim the goods from the GFP, and their only recourse is an action for money damages against the party to whom he delivered the goods for their fair market price or replacement value.

Max owns a large-screen projection television set that needs repair. He calls National TV Sales and Service (National) for a "pick up and repair" because they make house calls for such large items. Travis is fired by National the day Max's order comes in and decides to get his revenge. He falsifies the repair order with his own name, goes to Max's house, and picks up the TV set by impersonating the correct employee.

He then sells it to Agatha, who knows nothing about the fraud, for a fair price. When Max doesn't hear back from National, he inquires and they discover the problem and verify the sale to Agatha. Max demands the item from her and she refuses.

Agatha may keep the TV set. Travis had voidable title, since the true owner intentionally delivered it to him, and he can pass good title to her as a GFP. Max now has a claim against National for their negligent conversion of his property, and hopes they are still in business and solvent to pay his damages.

In order for Max to prevail against Agatha, he would have to find facts to prove either (1) the TV set was stolen from his possession, or (2) she was not a GFP, because she knew or should have known of the questionable circumstances due to paying a price far below fair market value.

C) The Merchant Entrustment Rule: If the true owner of the goods delivers them into the possession of a merchant (usually for repair or modification), the merchant has voidable title and can pass good title, by mistake or otherwise, to a buyer of those goods in the ordinary course of the merchant's business.

In these cases, which are the most bizarre of all, the buyer has legal title to the goods and is not required to return them to the true owner, who now has a claim for conversion of his property and damages for replacement against the merchant.

The rationale in these cases that protects the GFP is that the merchant is held to a higher standard of care. The GFP did nothing wrong. Max was in the best position to prevent the problem and failed to do so.

Changing the above case a bit, Travis is the employee of National who goes to Max's house, properly picks up the TV set, and brings it back to their shop for repair. They complete their work and place it on the floor in an area where used TV sets are sold. Agatha is a customer during regular hours who is mistakenly sold that item for a fair price by a salesperson before it is re-delivered to Max. When he finds out about the problem and contacts Agatha, she refuses to return his TV set.

Agatha wins again. She satisfies all requirements of the merchant entrustment rule. The only way for Max to recover his property would be to prove that either (1) National is not a merchant for such merchandise, and is, for example, selling these items as a hobby or (2) the sale to her was outside the ordinary course of regular business, because it was after hours or otherwise not authorized.

D) The pawnshop cases present an interesting issue of whether or not pawn shops can ever be a GFP. The legal argument is sometimes made by the true owner of goods sold under the voidable title or merchant entrustment doctrines that pawnshops are known to sometimes deal in merchandise of questionable origin, and therefore, they should not be allowed GFP status.

While a few states adhere to this extreme view, most do not, and apply the same standards of "intentional or voluntary delivery" to establish the voidable title necessary for conveyance of "good title" to a GFP. Although each of these disputes is closely evaluated on a case-by-case basis, they often are governed by statutes that require owners of stolen property to timely file police reports, and thus preserve recovery rights if the items have not yet been sold to good faith purchasers in the ordinary course of business.

The cases in this A–D section are entertaining and sometimes unusual, presenting various interpretations of the general rules of imperfect title set forth above.

VOID TITLE RULE: In *Johnny Dell, Inc. v. New York State Police, 375 N.Y.S.2d 545 (N.Y. 1975)*, a New York auto theft ring stole a car in Canada and, using stolen registration forms, transferred it ultimately to Elmer, a good faith buyer. He then sold the auto to the plaintiff, a car dealer. When that dealer attempted to transfer the vehicle to another dealer, the defendant impounded it, and the plaintiff sued for an order directing release of the vehicle.

The trial court denied the request, and the court affirmed, holding that "It would appear that Elmer purchased from a thief, thereby obtaining no title at all." The plaintiff, in turn, in purchasing from an individual, Elmer, could obtain no better title than Elmer possessed; to wit: none.

The court also noted the factual circumstances that could have defused this time bomb, but didn't. "Plaintiff, having failed to show that it purchased from a dealer in the ordinary course of business, did not obtain good title. At this point, plaintiff, being a dealer in the goods, *could have* transferred to an innocent bona fide purchaser for value good title by means of a completed sale."

The imperfect title rules of UCC 2-403 are explained: "A purchaser of goods acquires the title which the transferor had or could transfer. A person with voidable title has power to transfer a good title to a good faith purchaser for value. Entrusting of possession of goods to a merchant who deals in goods of that kind gives him power to transfer good title to a buyer in the ordinary course of business. However, absent (these circumstances), one may not obtain title from a thief, nor may such purchaser assert a claim against the true owner."

VOIDABLE TITLE RULE: In *Greater Louisville Auto Auction, Inc. v. Ogle Buick, Inc., 387 S.W.2d 17 (Ky. App. 1965)*, the defendants sold the vehicles in question to Caylor, who paid with checks totaling $12,500 that had been supplied to him by the plaintiff as advances to finance his acquisition of autos to be sold through their auction. They stopped payment on the checks, so they were returned as uncollectible, and the defendant-sellers received nothing. The defendants sued for the monies lost, the trial court ruled in their favor, and the appellate court affirmed.

The court recognized that the defendant had voluntarily delivered the vehicles to Caylor, thus passing "voidable title," which, in turn, enabled him to pass "good title" if the case fell within either: (1) the merchant entrustment rule, or (2) the good faith purchaser rule.

"Certainly Auction (was not) a 'buyer in the ordinary course of business or other good faith purchaser' from Caylor, since it did not purchase from him but merely acted as his agent in selling the cars to others . . . Auction knew that for the past two or three weeks Caylor's checks had been bouncing like rubber balls, from which it was bound to realize that other checks given by him to other people would likewise be dishonored, particularly after the stop orders."

In *Al Saud v. Fast Forward, Inc., 672 N.E.2d 568 (Mass. App. 1996)*, the plaintiff, a member of the Saudi royal family, imported into the U.S. four luxury automobiles valued at $430,000 that he had purchased in Saudi Arabia – a Ferrari, two Aston Martins, and a Lamborghini.

The vehicles were required to conform to U.S. safety and emissions standards, so the plaintiff shipped them to Pereira, who was recommended to him to do the necessary work, although he was not licensed as either an auto dealer or broker. Pereira transferred the vehicles to dealer Stoehr, who then transferred them to the defendant-dealer Fast – without either a certificate of origin or a certificate of title.

When the plaintiff saw an advertisement in an automobile magazine for his Ferrari, he realized there was a problem, hired a private investigator, and recovered three of his vehicles. The Ferrari had been sold by the defendant, a car dealer, in the ordinary course of business, and thus legally belonged to its new buyer, so the plaintiff sued for money damages.

The trial jury found that the "plaintiff had entrusted those vehicles to Pereira who was not a merchant dealing with merchandise of the type involved in the instant case, (and) that, in dealing with Pereira, Fast and Stoehr were neither buyers in the ordinary course of business of any of the vehicles nor good faith purchasers for value, and that the plaintiff was entitled to damages from Fast in the amount of $430,000."

The trial judge accepted the jury's findings, and penalized Fast by doubling the award of damages to $860,000, based upon testimony proving that Fast had knowingly purchased counterfeit certificates of origin to transfer title to the plaintiff's vehicles.

In *The Creggin Group, LTD. v. Crown Diversified Industries Corp., 682 N.E.2d 692 (Ohio App. 1996)*, a conventional dispute, the buyer from a purchaser who had voidable title qualified as a good faith purchaser for value, and was therefore accorded good title and allowed to keep the goods.

The defendant sold its Cessna aircraft to Duke, who paid with a non-certified check and delivered him possession. He advertised it for sale in a trade journal, and then sold it to the plaintiff with a forged bill of sale for a fair price. When the defendant reported the plane stolen, the FBI ultimately traced it to the plaintiff and had it returned to the defendant. The plaintiff sued to recover the plane, claiming it was a GFP for value from Duke, who had voidable title. The trial court agreed with the plaintiff, and the appellate court affirmed:

"The 'voidable title' doctrine evolved to ameliorate the harshness of the basic rule that a seller can convey no greater title than that seller has to convey. This doctrine attempts to reconcile the rights of a 'true owner' who was fraudulently induced to transfer title in goods to a 'wrongdoer' with the rights of an innocent purchaser from the wrongdoer. Title in the wrongdoer is 'voidable' because the true owner is entitled to rescind the transaction and recover the goods from that individual. The right of rescission is cut off, however, by a transaction to a 'good faith purchaser.' "

UCC 2-403(1) sets forth the voidable title doctrine, and specifically states, "A person with voidable title has power to transfer a good title to a good faith purchaser for value, when goods have been delivered under a transaction of purchase, . . . even though:

1. the transferor was deceived as to the identity of the purchaser, or
2. the delivery was in exchange for a check which is later dishonored, or
3. it was agreed that the transaction was to be a 'cash sale.' Or
4. the delivery was procured through fraud . . .

The voidable title doctrine only applies where there is a 'transaction of purchase' (as opposed to theft)."

Here are three merchant entrustment situations:

• The plaintiffs were grain farmers who delivered their grain to a trucker to take a grain elevator to the defendant for them as their agent so they could complete its sale. In the past, the trucker had also engaged in the practice of buying grain directly and reselling it to the defendant. On this occasion, the trucker improperly listed his name as the owner of the grain, and was directly paid $288,000 by the defendant. The plaintiffs never were paid by the trucker, and sued for the unlawful conversion of their property.

  The trial court entered summary judgment for the defendant, and the appellate court affirmed, holding that "The trial court properly granted summary judgment to the elevator because the undisputed facts show the farmers entrusted their grain to an independent trucker who was also a merchant, thereby empowering him to transfer ownership to the elevator as a buyer in the ordinary course of business." *Schulter v. United Farmers Elevator, 479 N.W.2d 82 (Minn. App. 1991)*

• The plaintiff owned three paintings that it displayed at the home of the artist after he declared bankruptcy and the plaintiff bought the paintings from the trustee. It allowed the artist to continue to possess and display the paintings. The artist sold them to the defendant for $50,000, after the defendant had viewed them and noted that there were no tags or labels on them to indicate in any way that the artist no longer owned them. The price paid was more than appraised value, and the defendant received a bill of sale from the artist. The plaintiff sued to recover possession of the paintings from the defendant.

  The trial court ruled for the defendant, and the appellate court affirmed. "Under (UCC 2-403), a buyer in the ordinary course of business will prevail over the claim of a party who entrusted such items to the merchant. In order for McKean to be protected by (UCC 2-403), DeWeldon, Ltd. must have allowed Felix DeWeldon to retain possession of the paintings (they did). McKean must have bought the paintings in the ordinary course of business (he did). He must have given value for the paintings, without actual or constructive notice of DeWeldon Ltd's claim of ownership to them (he did). Finally, Felix DeWeldon must have been a merchant as defined by (UCC 2-104) (he was)." *DeWeldon, LTD. V. McKean, 125 F.3d 24 (1st Cir. 1997)*

- In *Alsafi Oriental Rugs v. American Loan Company, 864 S.W.2d 41 (Tenn. App. 1993)*, the plaintiff allowed Bradley to take three of his oriental rugs out on consignment with the understanding that she would return them if her customer was not interested. She never returned, but the plaintiff did not report the rugs to the police department as stolen.

   She was really working for another rug dealer, Salaam, and turned the rugs over to him. He took them to the defendant's pawnshop, completed the necessary pawn of goods paperwork, and received $5,000. He never returned to redeem the rugs. Five months later, the plaintiff learned his rugs were in the defendant's shop, and filed suit to regain possession of them.

   The trial court ruled for the plaintiff on the basis that his rugs had been stolen, and the void title rule protected his claim of ownership. The appellate court reversed, noting one of its earlier decisions, where a tractor and blade was delivered to a buyer based upon a promise to return the next day, which never occurred. "In the present case, the plaintiff voluntarily relinquished possession to Rickman. As one commentator has pointed out, '(a) thief who wrongfully takes goods is not a purchaser ... but a swindler who fraudulently induces the victim to voluntarily deliver them is a purchaser ... '"

   The court also noted the Tennessee Pawnbrokers Act, which is a typical statute to protect owners of stolen property that winds up in such stores: "The statute gives such a person a right of recovery if he notifies the 'proper authorities' of the theft and the location of the property purported to be stolen within 30 days after acquiring such knowledge."

   The plaintiff failed to file a police report and forfeited his pawnshop recovery rights. Again, knowledge of the laws that protect or harm our business transactions enables us to anticipate potential problems and avoid them.

Risk of Loss in Regular Sales

There is a timeline in UCC sales transactions that usually starts with the creation of the contract and ends with the delivery of the goods. What if at some point while the goods are in transit in this timeline they are lost, damaged, or destroyed through no fault of either seller or buyer? As between the two contracting parties, who should bear the risk of loss? That party must pay for the goods. Usually insurance is carried by the parties to cover such losses, but what if there is none, or what if policy exclusions deny coverage?

These questions are answered by two basic types of transactions, with different rules of law:

- Two-party direct sales between seller and buyer
- Three-party shipping cases involving seller, carrier, and buyer

Two-Party Direct Sales – No-Fault Loss

The risk-of-loss rules in these transactions are different depending upon whether or not the seller is a merchant.

- A non-merchant-seller has risk of loss until "tender of delivery" to the buyer is made. This means the seller has done all he can do short of actual delivery, and he notifies the buyer he is holding the goods for him.
- A merchant-seller, being held to a higher standard, does not relinquish risk of loss until the goods are actually received by the buyer.

Andrew goes to ShopperMart to buy a freezer. He chooses the floor model he wants, pays for it at the cashier, and then is directed to the warehouse behind the showroom to pick up his purchase. When it is wheeled out for him he realizes the truck he brought is too small, and decides to return the following morning. That evening a fire of unknown origin burns the warehouse and destroys all the merchandise, including his item. Who has risk of loss?

ShopperMart retains the risk of loss. They are a merchant seller, and the no-fault loss event occurred before they completed actual delivery to their buyer.

If the freezer had been bought at a garage sale or under other circumstances where his seller was not in the primary business of selling such items, Andrew would suffer the risk of loss. The freezer was being held overnight in the seller's warehouse solely for his convenience – tender of delivery had been made.

In *Martin v. Melland's, 283 N.W.2d 76 (N.D. 1979)*, the plaintiff contracted with the defendant, a farm equipment dealer, to buy a new truck with attached haystack mover for $35,389 and trade in his old one for $17,389, leaving a balance due of $18,000. He delivered his certificate of title to the old unit, but was allowed to retain and use it until his new one was ready, which was to be in about two months due to some needed modifications. The contract was silent as to allocating risk of loss.

Fire destroyed the trade-in unit, due to no fault of the plaintiff, while it remained in his possession, and his insurance had lapsed. The plaintiff sued to require the defendant to bear the loss and it refused. The trial court ruled for the defendant, and the appellate court affirmed: "Thus, the question in this case is not answered by a determination of the location of title, but by the risk of loss provisions in (UCC 2-509) . . . It is clear that a barter or trade-in is considered a sale and is therefore subject to the Uniform Commercial Code. It is also clear that the party who owns the trade-in is considered the seller."

"It is undisputed that the contract did not require or authorize shipment by the carrier pursuant to (UCC 2-509(1)); therefore the residue section, subsection 3 is applicable: 'In any case not within subsection 1 or 2, the risk of loss passes to the buyer on his receipt of the goods if the seller is a merchant; otherwise the risk passes to the buyer on tender of delivery.' Martin admits that he is not a merchant; therefore it is necessary to determine if Martin tendered delivery of the trade-in unit to Melland's (UCC 2-503) . . . It is clear that the trade-in unit was not tendered to Melland's in any case. The parties agreed that Martin would keep the old unit 'until they had the new one ready.' "

Three-Party Indirect Sales – No-Fault Loss

These transactions are commonly known as "the shipping cases." The distance between shipping and delivery points, as well as the length of time involved in the shipment, is immaterial. The risk-of-loss rules in these transactions are different depending upon what type of legal contract is created between the parties.

- In a "shipment contract," risk of loss passes from the seller to the buyer upon completed delivery of the goods to the designated carrier. Until this occurs, the seller remains responsible for any no-fault loss events. Completion of such delivery is usually signified by a receipt issued by the carrier called a bill of lading. These contracts are more favorable to sellers.
- In a "destination contract," risk of loss remains with the seller until the goods are tendered to the buyer at the specified destination. Actual physical delivery to the buyer is not required in all cases. These contracts are more favorable to buyers.

The rule that should apply to a risk-of-loss dispute in these shipping cases may be specifically negotiated by the parties as part of their transaction and mentioned in the contract by stating, "This is a shipment contract," or "This is a destination contract."

Often however, the parties are not equally aware of their legal rights. If you are a seller, you might insert "shipment contract" into your proposed terms and the buyer might not question it, thinking, "Of course, the goods are being shipped to me." Similarly, a buyer might insert "destination contract," and an uninformed seller might let it stand, thinking, "Of course, I have to ship the goods to the stated destination." In either case, the premium, as always, is on advance knowledge of the governing rules of law.

> UCC 2-509 *Risk of Loss in the Absence of Breach* states: "(1) Where the contract requires or authorizes the seller to ship the goods by carrier (a) if it does not require him to deliver them at a particular destination (emphasis added), the risk of loss passes to the buyer when the goods are duly delivered to the carrier even though the shipment is under reservation (2-505); but (b) if it does require him to deliver them at a particular destination and the goods are there duly tendered while in the possession of the carrier, the risk of loss passes to the buyer when the goods are there so tendered as to enable the buyer to take delivery . . . (3) (In direct sales), the risk of loss passes to the buyer on his receipt of the goods if the seller is a merchant; otherwise, the risk passes to the buyer on tender of delivery."

The parties can insert any terms they choose in their proposed contract, of course, and perhaps they will gain an advantage due to the inattention or ignorance of the other party. In the best of all sellers' worlds, that clause would state,

"Risk of loss passes to the buyer at the time the contract is signed." Its counterpart for a buyer would read, "Risk of loss passes to the buyer thirty days after the goods are received, inspected, and approved."

The UCC also specifies trade terms that determine not only who is required to make transit arrangements and who pays freight charges, but also who bears risk of loss in shipping cases, the most common of which is FOB:

- FOB seller or seller's city – seller makes all arrangements and pays all costs, including risk of loss, prior to delivery of the goods to the carrier. This is a shipment contract.
- FOB buyer or buyer's city – seller makes all arrangements and pays all costs, but has risk of loss up to the time of tender of delivery to the buyer. This is a destination contract.
- Contract is silent as to these terms – it is considered a shipment contract for risk-of-loss purposes. The seller is favored.

Ashley is a New York lawyer who has an important trial in Boston. While in Boston, she contracts with Red Sox Motors (RSM) to buy a new Mercedes, "FOB Boston," for a prepaid price of $35,000. RSM hires Auto Carriage, Inc. to deliver the auto to her. After the car is delivered to them, their driver has an accident on the Massachusetts Turnpike en route to New York caused by wet weather, which totally destroys the shipment. None of the parties have insurance to cover the loss. Ashley demands the return of her money and RSM refuses.

The facts of the case identify the transaction as a three-party sale, and the FOB seller's city trade term as a shipment contract. The risk of loss passed to Ashley as soon as RSM completed delivery of the auto to the carrier. Since the loss event took place afterwards, Ashley has the risk of loss and cannot recover her money.

If the contract specified, "FOB New York," it would have been a destination contract and Ashley would have won.

In *Morauer v. Deak & Co., Inc., 26 UCC Rep. 1142 (Sup. Ct. D.C. 1979)*, the plaintiff contracted to buy investment bags of gold and silver coins for $35,000 from the defendant, a D.C. dealer. He took personal delivery of the silver coins, but chose to have the gold coins shipped to his Maryland residence to avoid the D.C. tax on the sale of gold.

The defendant shipped the gold coins in two packages, uninsured via U.S. registered mail, relying upon its own commercial insurance policy to cover any risk of loss. The plaintiff received one package and, thinking it contained the entire order, didn't open it for inspection until two years later, when he discovered a portion of the coins were missing. When he notified the defendant of the problem, it was discovered that the post office records had been destroyed and the defendant's insurance had expired.

The plaintiff sued to recover the value of the missing coins. The court ruled in favor of the defendant, holding that "The risk of loss of the gold coins in question passed from the defendant Deak to Morauer upon Deak's delivery of the coins to the Post Office for shipment to Morauer."

The agreement between the parties was silent as to the type of risk of loss contract, but the court determined that "shipment contract" rules governed:

"The fact that the parties had agreed that Deak would ship the coins to Morauer's residence in Maryland is not dispositive of this controversy. A 'ship to' term in a sales contract has no significance in determining whether the agreement is a 'shipment' or 'destination' contract. Moreover, there is a preference in the UCC for 'shipment' contracts."

Regular Sales – Loss Due to Fault

The no-fault risk of loss rules change if one of the parties breaches its duties under the sales contract. The breaching party always has risk of loss, no matter whether or not the no-fault rules would have a different result.

The required duties of the parties are:

- Seller – to deliver conforming goods. This means the completion of required actual or tendered delivery of the goods in an undamaged condition, with no material defects or deviations.
- Buyer – to accept and pay for the goods. This means receipt of the goods, inspection of them within a reasonable time, prompt notification of any material problems in type or condition, and completed payment in good funds.

Let's go back to Ashley's automobile purchase, via carrier, from RSM, "FOB Boston." In this shipment contract, since the no-fault loss occurred while the auto was in possession of the carrier, the buyer had risk of loss. But what if when the wreckage of Auto Carriage, Inc. was inspected it was discovered that the wrong auto was shipped to Ashley? This non-conformity would constitute a breach of contract by the seller, and shift risk of loss back to RSM. If it was a destination contract due to terms of "FOB New York," the seller would have retained no-fault risk of loss. But what if at the time the auto was destroyed, the buyer's check had bounced due to insufficient funds? This breach by the buyer would shift the risk of loss back to Ashley.

Risk of Loss in Conditional Sales

Many sales of goods are made in the commercial marketplace, where the buyer has the privilege of returning all or part of the items to the seller for credit or refund. What if a no-fault risk–of–loss event occurs while the goods are in the buyer's possession, before the return option has been exercised? Who bears risk of loss?

These transactions, sometimes known as trial sales, fall into two categories:

- Sale on approval – a condition precedent purchase contract based upon buyer's satisfaction, where there is a current transfer of possession of the goods to the buyer, but no transfer of ownership or obligation to pay until the buyer accepts the goods. The buyer has a return privilege until the goods are accepted. Acceptance may occur if:

a) the buyer expressly indicates acceptance verbally or in writing
b) the buyer ratifies by failing to return the goods on time
c) the buyer impliedly accepts by conveying the goods by sale or gift

Since ownership of the goods remains with the seller while the goods are in the buyer's possession, the seller retains risk of loss. The loss is also not subject to the claims of buyer's creditors, nor claimable for loss under the buyer's insurance.

Joseph wants to get those washboard stomach muscles that he sees in the television infomercials and orders the "Super Ab Cruncher" from Steel Man, Inc. for $99 "on 90-day approval." He tries it immediately, but then gives up in fifteen days because of the muscle soreness in his initial workouts. He puts it back in the box, addresses it for return to the seller, and intends to mail it the next morning. That night lightning strikes his roof, a fire starts, and his house and all its contents burn to the ground. When Joseph informs Steel Man, Inc. they demand payment and he refuses. Who has risk of loss?

Joseph does not have to pay. Ownership of the goods remained with the seller at the time of no-fault loss. They can file a claim with their insurer if they have coverage.

In *Prewitt v. Numismatic Funding Corporation, 745 F.2d 1175 (8th Cir. 1984)*, the plaintiff responded to the defendant's ad and bought Morgan silver dollar collector coins valued at $3,400 on terms that stated, "Everything is available to you on a 14-day approval basis." When the coins arrived, the plaintiff didn't like them, and since there were no specific instructions how to return unwanted items, the plaintiff returned them via Federal Express within the required time.

The plaintiff then agreed on the same terms for a second shipment of coins, valued at $20,000. They were again returned via either Federal Express or the U.S. Postal Service within the required time.

A third shipment on the same terms was made, valued at over $61,000, and they were returned on time via certified mail in two packages, with the maximum amount of insurance available – $400 per package. The defendant never received the packages, demanded payment, and the plaintiff brought a declaratory judgment suit to determine his nonliability.

The trial court ruled that the transaction was a "sale on approval," and the defendant had to bear the risk of loss. The appellate court affirmed on the basis of the UCC, section 2-327(1), which provides:

"(1) Under a sale on approval unless otherwise agreed
      (a) although the goods are identified to the contract the risk of loss and the title do not pass to the buyer until acceptance; and

   (b) use of the goods consistent with the purpose of the trial is not
      acceptance but failure seasonably to notify the seller of election to
      return the goods is acceptance, . . .
   (c) after due notification of election to return, the return is at the
      seller's risk and expense, but a merchant buyer must follow any
      reasonable instructions."

Notice how simple it would have been for the seller to avoid this liability time bomb by merely providing specific instructions for a method or manner of returning items. All the defendant had to say was, "Any returns shall be made via Federal Express, U.S. Registered Mail, or any other means whereby the shipment value as reflected by the payment invoice price enclosed is fully insured."

Also consider the fact that millions of dollars of goods are sold daily on "approval" basis, where sellers are happy to accept the potential risk of no-fault loss while the goods are in the buyer's possession, banking on the fact that most persons will never get around to returning them on time, even if they're not interested in buying.

- Sale or return – a condition subsequent contract that grants the buyer a future right to return unsold inventory for refund or credit within a specified time. There is a completed sale, where the buyer has legal title to the goods as soon as they are delivered and paid for.

  The buyer has risk of loss, an insurable interest in them, and the goods are subject to seizure by his creditors.

Sarah owns a women's clothing boutique in a local mall. She orders one hundred of the latest sports outfits from Gals R Us, for $99 each "with ninety-day right of return" and no payment due until forty-five days. After delivery and sale of one-half of the shipment in thirty days, she prepares to return the unsold items. They are boxed for mailing, but overnight her sprinkler system malfunctions and they are ruined. When she informs the seller and requests a credit for their loss, they refuse and demand full payment for the entire shipment.

Sarah owns the entire shipment as soon as they arrive and bears the risk of loss for all remaining in her possession. She must pay the full amount. Hopefully, she is insured for this type of loss.

A consignment sale, where the owner of goods (consignor) entrusts them to a merchant (consignee) for the purpose of trying to sell them, is legally treated for risk-of-loss purposes as a sale or return. If the consignee is successful, it usually receives an agreed percentage of the sales proceeds, with the balance to be paid to the consignor.

They are dangerous to parties unaware of this legal status, because the consignee is generally presumed to be the owner of goods in its possession, and subject to the claims of its creditors. These may include lenders who have liens against the contents of the consignee's store or a bankruptcy trustee, if the consignee seeks the financial protection of that court.

The UCC provides protection for the owner-consignor if he complies with state law, which usually requires that he record a security interest in the goods with his secretary of State, or otherwise mark the goods with a conspicuous notice of his ownership interest.

In *Auclair v. Jackson, 15 U.C.C. Rep. Serv.2d 1212 (B.C. Ala.1991)*, the Auclairs operated a gun shop and convenience store in Alabama, to which Jackson delivered seventy firearms for them to sell on consignment per an agreement between the parties that had an attached listing of all the guns.

The Auclairs filed for bankruptcy, Jackson removed his guns from the store without the permission of the bankruptcy trustee, and the trustee sued to have the guns returned as a part of the bankruptcy estate of the Auclairs, available for sale to pay off their creditors. The court ruled in favor of the trustee:

"(UCC 2-326(3) regarding consignments applies to the facts of this case. Under that subsection, goods delivered on consignment are 'deemed to be on sale or return.' Thus, by deeming the consignee a purchaser of the goods, the consignor is precluded from asserting an ownership claim to the goods vis-à-vis the consignee's creditors."

"Jackson is precluded from asserting his ownership of the firearms vis-a-vis the trustee. However, the subsection is not applicable to a consignor who − (a) complies with an applicable law providing for a consignor's interest or the like to be evidenced by a sign, or (b) established that the person conducting the business is generally known by his creditors to be substantially engaged in selling the goods of others, or (c) complies with the filing provisions of the article on secured transactions (UCC Article 9)."

Jackson's guns exploded here, in a financial liability sense, because he was unaware of these legal requirements. Such is usually the case, as we have seen throughout this book. How simple it would have been for him to attach small hang tags to the trigger guards of each weapon, noting his name, address, phone number, and that the items were "consignment goods − the property of Luke Jackson."

Non-Performance of Sales Contracts

As previously stated in our discussion of risk of loss, the seller must deliver conforming goods and the buyer must accept and pay for them. Failure of either party to render this performance constitutes a breach, for which the UCC provides a number of different remedies, in addition to the fact that the risk of loss remains with a party who breached its contract duties.

These remedies are based upon the fairness principle of restoring the injured party to his pre-breach position, so that the business scales are returned to a position of balance. The UCC statute of limitations is four years to file suit for an alleged breach of a sale-of-goods contract.

The usual remedies for the non-breaching party include the right of rescission to cancel the contract, the privilege of being excused from performance, and the recovery of damages:

• Compensatory − to reimburse for out-of-pocket expenses incurred as a result of the breach, and the effort to restore the status quo

- Consequential – to cover damages, like loss of future profits, that flow as a reasonable result of the breach
- Punitive – to punish the wrongdoer with additional damages in extreme cases of willful and malicious wrongdoing

Assurance of Performance

If either party to the contract is reasonably concerned that there *may be a default in performance* by the other party, he may make written demand for assurance, and the party receiving the demand must give a positive response within thirty days, or the demanding party may treat the contract as cancelled.

This is a valuable strategic tool. Perhaps the buyer who makes the demand has a legitimate concern whether a strike at the seller's plant will delay delivery. Rather than waiting for an ultimate default, which could be months later, the "assurance" procedure speeds up matters and allows the demanding party to plan accordingly to find alternate sources of goods.

It also is of practical benefit if one of the contracting parties realizes, due to a change in market conditions or by virtue of being out-negotiated, that he made a bad business deal. He would love to be legally excused from having to perform. This "assurance" procedure gives him that opportunity. It is relatively easy to give a reasonable explanation for the concern, thus satisfying the UCC requirement that the parties act in good faith. Once the demand for assurance is received, the recipient is on the clock, and has the burden of responding with a timely good faith positive answer that he will perform, or the contract may be nullified.

The Perfect Tender Rule

If the goods delivered by the seller are non-conforming *in any way*, the buyer has the right to:

- Reject the entire shipment , treat the contract as cancelled, and recover any damages sustained (especially if the buyer made a bad deal), or
- Ignore the default, accept the shipment, and proceed with the transaction, (especially if the buyer made a good business deal), or
- Accept the correct portion of the shipment, reject the part that is non-conforming, and recover any partial damages sustained.

This rule is very hard on sellers if applied literally. What if their shipment was 99% perfect and only 1% non-conforming? They would still be in violation of the rule and subject to its sanctions.

Therefore, parties to these transactions usually limit its application by inserting appropriate wording in their contract to handle these situations in a more equitable manner, relating to the seller's right to cure defects, as discussed later in this chapter. Of course, if no such limiting wording is present, the perfect tender rule will still apply, to the advantage of the buyer.

In *Moulton Cavity & Mold Inc. v. Lyn-Flex Industries, 396 A.2d 1024 (Maine 1979)*, the plaintiff agreed to manufacture and sell to the defendant twenty-six innersole molds, after the defendant had approved the sample molds. Upon delivery to the buyer, the molds were rejected because they allegedly did not "exactly" satisfy the required specifications.

The seller sued for breach of contract, alleging wrongful rejection. The buyer contended that the perfect tender rule allowed it to reject, regardless of whether or not the seller had substantially performed. After the trial court ruled for the seller, the buyer appealed and the decision was reversed in the buyer's favor.

The court first noted that the perfect tender rule has been criticized because "It allowed a dishonest buyer to avoid an unfavorable contract on the basis of an insubstantial defect in the seller's tender." But UCC Section 2-601 continues the application of the rule because it "states that, with certain exceptions not here applicable, the buyer has the right to reject 'if the goods or the tender of delivery fail *in any respect* to conform to the contract.' "

The burden is put upon the seller to limit the right of the buyer to reject nonconforming goods in the contract, and thus protect itself.

Buyer's Rights to Inspect, Reject, Accept, and Revoke

The buyer has the right/duty to make a good faith inspection of the shipment for any defects or deviations within a reasonable time after it arrives, before the legal duty to accept or reject the goods arises. The time for inspection varies with the type of goods sold – one generator in a wood carton can be unpacked and viewed at once, whereas an order of 1,000 men's suits demands much more time and attention to detail.

The good faith factor applies in situations where a buyer realizes he has made a bad business deal and decides to claim some questionable defect or deviation so that a seller's default can be declared and the contract cancelled. If the buyer acts in bad faith, he is in default and the seller's remedies apply.

If a preliminary inspection does not reveal any defects or deviations, but a later inspection does, and the problem was not easily discoverable and will substantially impair the value of the goods, the buyer may revoke a prior acceptance.

This right to revoke acceptance is especially important in C.O.D. shipments, where the buyer is required to accept and pay for the goods *before* inspecting them. In these cases. inspection is required within a reasonable time *after* arrival. If problems are revealed, the buyer has the legal right to revoke his acceptance within a reasonable time after discovery.

Acceptance occurs when the buyer expresses it in words, implies it by conduct such as reselling the goods to another, or by default if the buyer fails to reject within a reasonable time.

In *Graaf v. Bakker Brothers of Idaho, Inc., 934 P.2d 1228 (Wash. App. 1997)*, Bakker Brothers agreed to buy Graaf's onion seed crop under a contract that stated, "Deliver all the seed F.O.B. as directed . . . buyer can reject the crop if the germination rate is less that 85%, 'or if the seeds cannot be cleaned to contain less than one per cent (1%) inert (material)' . . . "

When the buyer began processing the seed and tested samples for germination, it found rates below the required 85% and told Graaf that the seeds had failed the contract requirements, were unmarketable, buyer would not pay for them, and seller should pick them up.

Graaf then sued Bakker for breach of contract, both parties moved for summary judgment, and the trial court ruled for Bakker, finding that the seller had breached the contract and the buyer had timely rejected the shipment.

On appeal, the decision was affirmed.

On risk of loss under 2-510 (1): "The seller by his individual action cannot shift risk of loss to the buyer unless his action conforms with all the conditions resting on him under the contract. Therefore, even if we assume that the contract's use of F.O.B. passed the risk of loss, the term became operative only when Mr. Graaf tendered conforming goods."

On the right to reject under 2-513(1): "A buyer has a right before acceptance to inspect delivered goods at any reasonable place and time and in any reasonable manner. The reasonableness is again a question of trade usage, past practices between the parties, and the other circumstances of the case."

The appellate court determined that Bakker acted reasonably and effectively rejected the shipment.

In *Fortin v. Ox-Bow Marina, Inc., 557 N.E.2d 1157 (Mass. 1990)*, the plaintiffs purchased a new thirty-two-foot power boat from the defendant, and there was to be work done, including "installation of the cabin top and pulpit, installation of special equipment and optional items, and electrical work."

After early delivery, the buyers inspected the boat and noted problems, including "ill-fitting engine latches, marred gel coat in the cockpit, a missing bow eye, and numerous scrapes on the hull near the water line." The defendant's sales representative assured them all the defects would be cured and the special work completed by the closing date in two weeks.

On the day of the closing, the buyers again inspected and found nothing further had been done. They were assured that the boat would be made completely ready shortly, and went ahead with the closing.

About one week later, at the defendant's request, they made a checklist of all the items to be repaired or corrected, which now included additional problems to the marine toilet.

Three weeks later, the boat was re-delivered to them for their maiden voyage, on which they had additional problems with the depth finder, marine radio, one engine, and the electronic equipment. Again, they were assured that repairs would be completed within a few days.

The buyers attempted again to use the boat and the problems persisted, to the point that they hired counsel, notified the seller they were revoking their acceptance (four months later), and sought a refund of their purchase price and related damages, including loan interest they had paid on the financed portion of the purchase price. The seller refused, suit was filed, and the trial court ruled for the buyers.

On appeal, the decision was affirmed, based upon UCC Article 2:

"There is no dispute that the Fortins, having inspected the boat on several occasions earlier and after noting a number of defects, did not reject the boat, as they would have been entitled to do under (2-602). However, a buyer may revoke an acceptance providing that he or she can show that the 'nonconformity' in the goods that the buyer has purchased 'substantially impairs (their) value to him (or her), (2-608) (1); that the buyer has accepted the goods on the 'reasonable assumption that (their) non-conformity would be cured and it has not been seasonably cured, (1) (a), and that he or she revoked acceptance 'within a reasonable time after the buyer discovers or should have discovered the ground for it.'"

As to the issue of whether or not the revocation of acceptance was made within a "reasonable time," the court said, "Many courts have held that any delay on the part of the buyer in notification of revocation of acceptance is justified where the buyer is in constant communication with the seller regarding nonconformity of the goods, and 'the seller makes repeated assurances that the defect or nonconformity will be cured and attempts to do so.'"

"Thus, the defendant errs when it looks solely at the length of time it took the Fortins to revoke acceptance – four months – in asserting that the notice of revocation was untimely. Delays of longer than four months have been held to be reasonable, when regular complaints from the buyer and assurances and repair attempts from the seller filled the gap between acceptance and revocation."

Seller's Right to Cure

After the goods arrive and the buyer's inspection reveals any defects or deviations that are properly communicated to the seller, the general rule is that the buyer may reject and cancel the transaction.

This is desirable when the buyer made a bad business deal and seeks a way to be legally excused from performance, especially by using the "out" provided by the perfect tender rule of rejection where the seller has not limited its application.

But what if the seller wants to be given an opportunity to correct the defects and complete the transaction? This is the case when the seller made a good deal and hates to lose it. The UCC Section 2-508 (1) provides an exception that limits the buyer's right of rejection, and grants the seller the *absolute* right to cure defects:

"Where any tender or delivery by the seller is rejected because non-conforming and the time for performance has not yet expired, the seller may seasonably notify the buyer of his intention to cure and may then within the contract time make a conforming delivery.

"If however, there is no advance time to cure due to delivery on the due date or late delivery, the seller's right to cure is *discretionary* on the part of the buyer and is not guaranteed."

The skillful seller should therefore always try for early delivery so as to preserve "cure" rights:

Boris buys an old hotel in South Beach and remodels it in the Art Deco style for sale as a twelve-unit condominium. He orders glass and chrome furnishings from Hialeah Manufacturing with a delivery date of October 15 so that he can have his grand opening on November 1 for the upcoming winter season. The seller delivers on October 10. Boris inspects the next day and finds that the bedroom furnishings have the wrong color upholstery.

He checks other sources and finds another local supplier who would sell him the items for less than he originally agreed to pay. When he notifies the seller of the problem, he advises he is canceling the contract. They demand the right to cure.

This case illustrates how the different agendas of the parties dictate the remedies they seek. If the seller can clearly cure and complete the corrected delivery by November 1 it has the legal right to do so. But what if the time is tight, like in our case, where although the problems were discovered before November 1, it may take a few days beyond that date to complete the cure? When should the time for performance by the seller expire?

The seller will argue that the cure can be effected within a reasonable time, and fairness requires it be allowed. The buyer will argue to the contrary and seek all default remedies. What do you think? What is reasonable? Should any cure at all be allowed after the due date? One day late? One week late?

Another "cure" possibility is available to the seller under UCC Section 2-508 (2), after the time for performance has expired, that will circumvent the requirement of getting the buyer's approval:

"Where the buyer rejects a non-conforming tender which the seller has reasonable grounds to believe would be acceptable with or without money allowance the seller may if he seasonably notifies the buyer have a further reasonable time to substitute a conforming tender."

ABC Co. orders fifty current-model 5960 laptop computers from Dell Co., to be delivered no later than July 1. They are delivered on time, but don't work properly and are rejected. Dell Co. suggests it can immediately furnish last year's model 5959, which lists for 10% less, and deliver the order at a 15% discount below the contract order price. ABC Co. first accepts the proposal, but then rejects it. Dell Co. then promptly notifies the buyer that it will re-ship conforming current model 5960s. It has a reasonable time after the July 1 deadline to do so.

Buyer's Right to Cover

If the seller fails to deliver, or it appears delivery will be delayed beyond the performance date, the buyer may protect itself by trying to purchase substitute goods in the marketplace in good faith and without delay, and thus complete the contract.

This often occurs in situations where the goods are being purchased for resale by the buyer for existing orders to its customers. The buyer, faced with competition in these situations, cannot afford to lose the potential business relationships. Often a premium must be paid in these last-minute market purchases to locate the necessary goods.

The buyer's measure of damages is the difference between the original purchase price and the amount actually paid for the replacement goods, plus additional damages such as out-of-pocket costs and loss of future profits.

The *right* to cover differs from the *duty* to mitigate damages, in that the buyer is not required to cover, while the non-breaching party must always act reasonably to try to lessen the amount of ultimate damages it suffers.

Using the "Cure" example, the facts told us that Boris had set a grand opening for his art deco hotel on November 1 so he could catch the winter season. If his seller defaulted on delivery, it would make no sense for him to just file suit for breach of contract and nothing else. He would probably seek another seller-manufacturer who would be paid a premium for expediting the order so that the hotel could open on time. Then he would determine the full extent of his damages and sue his defaulting seller.

Other common "cure" cases are seasonal goods such as Thanksgiving turkeys, Easter bunnies, July 4 fireworks, and Christmas trees:

Kayla sets up a large tent every holiday season and sells Christmas trees. She has done this for the past ten years in the same location, and her business is comprised mainly of repeat customers. She orders her trees, as usual, from Wisconsin Arbors, Inc., specifying November 15 as the delivery date. On November 17 Kayla still has no trees, so calls her seller and learns that due to a clerical error, they sent her trees to another customer. When she requests a duplicate shipment to her she is told that all the trees are sold. She locates another supplier, who fills her order at a 25% premium, which she pays, together with additional costs for shipping, insurance, and advertising.

Kayla can recover all the damages that are reasonably related to the failure of her seller to timely perform.

In *Red River Commodities, Inc. v. Eidsness, 459 N.W.2d 811 (N.D. 1990)*, the defendant agreed in two contracts to grow and sell to the plaintiff a total of 350,000 pounds of confection sunflowers at a floor price of 11.25 cents per pound. The defendant made no deliveries to the plaintiff, and it later learned he was selling sunflowers to a competitor at 22 cents per pound. The plaintiff sued for anticipatory breach of contract, and urged the defendant to perform.

When he refused, the trial court found that "in an attempt to mitigate damages (RRC) purchased 'cover' at $26.00 per hundred weight.' Implicitly, this determined that RRC's substitute purchases at 26 cents per pound were reasonable."

The trial court ruled for the plaintiff, and the court affirmed, citing UCC Section 2-712:

"Cover – Buyer's procurement of substitute goods.

1. After a breach . . . the buyer may 'cover' by making in good faith and without unreasonable delay any reasonable purchase of or contract to purchase goods in substitution for those due from the seller.
2. The buyer may recover from the seller as damages the difference between the cost of cover and the contract price together with any incidental or

consequential damages . . . , but less expenses saved in consequence of the seller's breach.
3. Failure of the buyer to effect cover within this section does not bar him from any other remedy."

Other Remedies for Breach

Aside from the basic remedies of contract cancellation, seller's cure, and buyer's cover, as well as the recovery of money damages from the breaching party, the UCC provides additional remedies to the injured party depending upon the stage of the transaction where the breach occurs.

Seller's Remedies – Buyer Defaults

- Stop processing the order, withhold delivery, and sell it for scrap.
- Withhold delivery, complete the order, and re-sell for the best available price.
- If the goods are in transit, stop delivery and reclaim the goods.
- If the goods are in buyer's possession, demand their return.

This is called the "right of reclamation" and is not a very practical remedy. The UCC requires the seller to send the defaulting buyer a ten-day written notice before being allowed to sue for return of the goods. Why bother? If the buyer has the goods and defaults by failing to properly pay the seller, that means insolvency and the buyer has already sold off his available assets.

The best procedure for a seller is to receive all or a large portion of the purchase price, or some security to assure payment, *before* releasing possession of the goods. This protects against most buyer defaults.

Buyer's Remedies – Seller Defaults

- Retain and store rejected goods awaiting seller's return instructions.
- Resell rejected goods if seller doesn't arrange their return in a reasonable time.
- Resell perishable goods as seller's agent.
- Sue for specific performance of the contract if the goods are unique.
- Recover goods from an insolvent seller.

This is the impractical buyer's counterpart of the seller's right of reclamation. The UCC provides a buyer who has made a partial payment the right to recover the goods if the seller's insolvency occurs within ten days of the first payment, and the buyer tenders the balance of the purchase price.

What buyer, in his right mind, would pay additional sums to a financially distressed seller? And what insolvent seller would voluntarily relinquish possession of partially paid goods that could be sold to others for emergency cash?

Like every other step of commercial transactions, both parties need to anticipate the potential problems that can occur and seek to plan accordingly to avoid them, or at the very least minimize their financial impact.

Discussion Exercises

1. Discuss areas of the law involving international sales of goods where you believe the UCC rules should govern rather than the CISG.

2. Discuss situations where the void title rule causes an unfair result.

3. Discuss situations where the voidable title rule causes an unfair result.

4. Discuss whether a buyer of goods from a pawnshop should ever be considered a good faith purchaser.

5. Discuss whether the shifting of risk of loss to a buyer of goods before delivery causes an unfair result.

6. Discuss whether sale on approval or sale or return is the fairer type of trial sale from the standpoint of the seller or buyer.

7. Discuss whether a seller that delivers non-conforming goods should have any right to cure defects after the required performance date.

Case Exercise 1

Can a Used Car Buyer Who Does not Receive a Certificate of Title Be Considered a GFP?

Two Cases – Two Results

In *Thorn v. Adams, 865 P.2d 417 (Ore. 1993)*, the defendant bought a car and her son-in-law took it into the car dealer for repairs. Several days later, the plaintiff saw the car on the dealer's lot next to several cars marked for sale. The dealer allowed her to take it for a test drive and later mistakenly sold it to her without also delivering to her a certificate of title.

When the defendant learned of the sale, return of the car was demanded. The plaintiff refused and filed suit to require the defendant to deliver the title to her. The defendant counterclaimed for an order requiring the plaintiff to surrender possession of the car, or pay for its fair market value. Both parties moved for summary judgment.

In *Alamo Rent-A-Car, Inc. v. Mendenhall, 937 P.2d 69 (Nev. 1997)*, Clark rented a 1994 Lexus from the plaintiff using an alias, obtained a "California quick title" using forged signatures of fictitious parties, advertised the car in a Las Vegas newspaper, and sold it to the defendants for a price of $34,000 cash. They then had it registered, licensed, and titled in their names.

After the car was seized by the Nevada Department of Motor Vehicles, the defendants sued to recover it as good faith purchasers for value from Clark, who they claimed had voidable title. Alamo was substituted as the defendant, and it claimed that Clark was a thief with void title and could not pass good title to the buyers.

Analysis

In *Thorn*, the trial court ruled for the buyer's claim of ownership, finding it was a purchaser in the ordinary course of business from a merchant with voidable title, to whom the goods were entrusted. The Oregon Supreme Court affirmed:

"Defendant argues that it is unfair to place motor vehicle owners at the mercy of the entrustment principle . . . (But) the entrustment principle promotes one of the basic goals of commerce:

"In most cases the equities between the entruster-owner and the buyer in the ordinary course are equal, and the balance is tipped in favor of the latter because that frees the marketplace and promotes commerce. This goal, called 'security of transactions,' is an ideal of the commercial law. The protection of property rights . . . is not an ideal of the commercial law . . . On the assumption that both the entruster and buyer have been equally victimized by the dishonesty of the merchant-dealer, section 2-403(2) resolves the issue so as to free the marketplace; rather than protect the original owner's property rights."

In *Alamo*, the trial court also ruled for the buyer and awarded it ownership and possession of the automobile. But the Nevada Supreme Court reversed, equating the manner and method of how Clark obtained the auto as that of a thief, and thus applying the void title rule:

"The issue of whether a thief can convey voidable title is one of first impression in Nevada. In Cooper (a prior case), an original owner/seller gave title to a buyer who purchased the car with an invalid cashier's check. Thus, the buyer had fraudulently obtained the vehicle from the owner, as did Clark; however, the owner had actually transferred the vehicle's title to the buyer . . . Because Alamo still had possession of the Lexus' title, Clark could not have had voidable title simply by fraudulently obtaining a facially valid California title."

Conclusion

Which case makes more sense? While the merchant entrustment cases sometimes cause an unfair result for the entruster-owner, possession of the certificate of title is really not relevant to the issue of whether the auto seller has a voidable title. *Thorn* recognizes the usual procedure in the purchase of an automobile, where the buyer first takes possession and then later receives the title after the necessary paperwork is completed.

Contrast the circumstances that occurred in *Alamo*. The buyer argued that the renter-owner really caused its own problems when it "did not verify the validity of Clark's driver's license." If it had, the automobile would never have been delivered to Clark, and there would have been no court dispute. In addition, before the buyers paid the cash purchase price to Clark, they verified his signatures on the California title and his driver's license, and otherwise did everything a good faith purchaser could do. Was Clark a thief with void title, as the court ruled, or did he satisfy the definition of having voidable title because the Lexus had been "voluntarily delivered" to him as a result of the fraud-like deception of Clark?

A. Do you agree with the court's final decision in either or both cases?

B. How should a court deal with the issue of possession of the certificate of title in these automobile sale cases?

C. What legal test(s) would you create for determining the difference between void and voidable title?

B. SPECIAL RULES FOR PRODUCT LIABILITY

"Consumption is the sole end and purpose of all production;
and the interest of the producer ought to be attended to only so far
as it may be necessary for promoting that of the consumer."

—Adam Smith

Legal Overview

In addition to the duties of a seller–manufacturer of goods to deliver conforming goods to the buyer, there is an additional duty owed to assure that the goods are not defective.

Product defects may cause out-of-pocket economic loss to the buyer, such as the purchase price paid, costs of replacement, loss of future profits, and the possible loss of customer relationships. If so, the seller has UCC contract liability under the law of warranty.

If product defects cause personal injuries, the seller incurs common law and statutory tort liability under the laws of negligence or strict liability.

This entire area of seller's liability for damages due to defective merchandise is aptly called "Product Liability." Often the same set of facts in a dispute may result in multiple claims of breach of warranty and damages due to negligence and/or strict liability.

The historical perspective tracks the evolution of consumer's rights in the business marketplace. Up to the late 1800s, in our agrarian, rural society, sellers-manufacturers were favored by the law. The prevalent legal doctrine was *caveat emptor* – *let the buyer beware*. Unless a seller specifically guaranteed the performance of the goods sold in a separate promise that was part of the contract, the buyer had no right to sue for damages caused by product defects.

In both contract and tort cases, a direct contractual relationship called "privity of contract" was required between the parties, due primarily to the fact that the buyer-plaintiff usually purchased the goods directly from the seller-defendant. If remote parties were damaged by product defects, they had no legal recourse.

Then, the industrial revolution that started in the early 1900s brought massive changes to society, with large segments of the population moving into the larger cities to work in factories to produce the goods demanded by the consuming public, lengthening the lines of product distribution.

Injured consumers usually did not deal directly with the seller-manufacturer responsible for defects in the products they purchased. The laws gradually changed to protect the consuming public under the new doctrine of *caveat venditor* – *let the seller beware*. Sellers of goods were better able to absorb the increased costs of doing business, and product liability claims were permitted by remote injured parties.

Negligence – Fault Liability

The largest number of civil lawsuits filed in both federal and state courts is personal injury tort claims arising from alleged negligent conduct of the defendant that results in damages suffered by the plaintiff.

Negligence is an unintentional non-contract wrong. The plaintiff is required to prove that the defendant was at fault, through these three legal elements:

1. The defendant had a duty to maintain a certain standard of care
2. The defendant breached this duty by falling below the standard
3. The plaintiff was injured as a direct result of the defendant's breach

In the usual negligence disputes there is no transactional relationship between the parties. They are usually total strangers, as often occurs in automobile collisions, plane crashes, industrial accidents, and related commercial or non-commercial involvement where the defendant has unintentionally injured the plaintiff due to conduct which meets the legal tests of elements (1) and (2) above.

On the other hand, in products liability negligence disputes, a seller and buyer have transacted for the goods in question, which prove defective in some way, injuring the buyer or others who are legally entitled to recover for their damages.

Products liability negligence claims typically involve allegations of:

- Negligent manufacture of the goods causing injury
- Negligent design of the goods causing injury
- Failure to inspect for defects causing injury
- Failure to warn of defects causing injury

The defendant in such claims will attempt to avoid liability by proving any or all of these traditional legal defenses:

- Assumption of the risk – the plaintiff's injury was caused by a known and foreseeable danger that the plaintiff exposed himself to, thereby causing his own loss:
  - The plaintiff is hit by a hockey puck or baseball
  - The plaintiff is injured skiing or skydiving
  - The plaintiff becomes ill from drinking outdated milk
  - The plaintiff is knowingly treated by an unlicensed doctor

- Product misuse – the plaintiff's inappropriate or incorrect usage of the product causes his injury (the following are actual cases, believe it or not):
  - Hammering a nail with the barrel of a loaded revolver
  - Cleaning your teeth with a steak knife
  - Drying a pet in your microwave

- Comparative negligence – the plaintiff's own negligence caused a part of the loss. Originally "contributory negligence" was an absolute bar to a plaintiff's claim even if the defendant was mostly at fault. The courts gradually recognized the unfairness of this approach and modified it so that the plaintiff's proven damages are just mathematically reduced by the percentage of the loss he caused.
- Statute of limitations – each state has laws that proscribe the time period in which negligence suits must be commenced, running from one year in professional malpractice cases to four years in some situations that involve the sale of defective merchandise. Even if the plaintiff could prove the required legal elements of negligence, his failure to sue on a timely basis is an absolute bar to recovery.

Often the alleged negligent conduct of the defendant involves more than one of these categories of claim and defense in the same factual pattern. The damages sought by a plaintiff are the usual categories found in personal injury cases:

- Compensatory – to reimburse for actual expenses or damages
- Consequential – to cover resulting damages, such as loss of wages from one's employer or lost profits from one's business
- Incidental – costs of the claim/lawsuit process
- Pain and suffering, mental anguish, and loss of companionship

An injured plaintiff also commonly seeks punitive damages, especially where the conduct of the defendant in its manufacture or sale, design, inspection, or concealment of the product defects is considered willful, malicious, reckless, or outrageous. Let's analyze the following typical dispute:

Curtis buys an electric coping saw at Sears, manufactured by Sheffield Co. Its operating instructions state, "not to be operated at speeds higher than 1,000 rpm's or used to cut metallic or other non-wood based objects."

The saw is equipped with a detachable blade guard as standard equipment, because some woodworking functions cannot be performed while it remains in place. Due to a production flaw, the bolts holding the saw blade in place are sheared in half. Curtis detaches the blade guard to do intricate wood carving with the saw, starts it, and then, when it is running at 1,100 rpm's, the blade shatters, severing two of his fingers. He sues Sears and Sheffield Co. for product liability negligence, and they raise all available defenses. Who wins and why?

Curtis would allege the negligence of Sheffield Co. in shearing the blade bolts constituted defective manufacture and design, and failure to properly inspect. If in fact Sheffield Co. knew about the problem and allowed sales to take place, they also breached their duty to warn of defects. This negligence was the proximate cause of his injury. Since privity of contract is no longer required, Curtis can sue Sheffield Co. even though he did not deal with them directly.

One of Sheffield's defenses would be that Curtis assumed the risk by detaching the blade guard. He would successfully counter by arguing the product contemplated such removal and was produced to allow it. This was not a case of him removing permanent blade protection.

Sheffield would also argue that Curtis was contributorily negligent by operating the saw in excess of the stated rpm limit and should not recover any damages. He would counter that, at best, he was only negligent to the extent of 5% to 10%, and the blade would probably have broken by prolonged use under 1,000 rpm's. Under the comparative negligence doctrine now followed by most states, his award would just be reduced by the applicable amount, rather than being barred completely. Decision for Curtis against Sheffield Co.

The claim against Sears is different. Curtis probably sues them hoping to induce a nuisance settlement. They are considered a "deep-pocket" defendant due to their financial resources, but would still have to spend large sums for attorney's fees and related expenses. (That same "deep pocket" may also cause Curtis to settle, because his financial resources are much more limited.) Let's assume they refuse to settle.

They will win and be dismissed as a defendant because they were only the retail intermediary in the chain of commerce, committed no acts of negligence, and were not at fault.

There are a large number of successful product liability negligence cases due both to the sheer volume of manufacture and sale of goods to consumers and the litigious society in which we live, where an injury from a defective product is usually the subject of a claim for damages.

There are also cases in which recovery is denied:

In *Daniell v. Ford Motor Company, 581 F. Supp. 728 (Dist. Ct. N.M. 1984)*, the plaintiff was despondent and attempted to commit suicide by locking herself inside the trunk of her Ford LTD automobile, which had been manufactured by the defendant. She promptly changed her mind about the suicide attempt once she was locked inside, but remained there for nine days until she finally was rescued.

The plaintiff sued the defendant in product liability negligence for negligent design in not having an internal trunk release, and for failure to warn consumers that the trunk could not be unlocked from inside. The defendant moved for summary judgment.

The court granted defendant's summary judgment:

"Under negligence, a manufacturer has a duty to consider only those risks of injury which are foreseeable. A risk is not foreseeable where a product is used in a manner which could not reasonably be anticipated by the manufacturer and that use is the cause of the plaintiff's injury . . . The court holds that the plaintiff's use of the trunk compartment as a means to attempt suicide was an unreasonable use as a matter of law.

"Nor did the manufacturer have a duty to warn the plaintiff of the danger of her conduct, given the plaintiff's unforeseeable use of the product . . . There is no duty to warn of known dangers."

This was an unusual case that could be criticized as nonsense litigation, but it still had a beneficial result to consumers. After it was decided, auto manufacturers tried to brainstorm factual scenarios where a different result would occur and the language of the case pointed them in the direction of a potential problem due to the possibility of children crawling into auto trunks. This is called "an attractive nuisance" in the law of negligence, and remedial design was needed.

"The design features of a trunk make it well near impossible that an *adult* intentionally would enter the trunk and close the lid. The dimensions of a trunk, the height of its sill and its load floor, and the efforts to first lower the lid and then to engage its latch, are among the design features which encourage closing and latching the trunk lid while standing outside the vehicle."

This problem could also exist for an adult. What if you lived on the ocean, where strong gusts of wind were a common occurrence? And what if your car had a large trunk? And what if your bags of groceries overturned so that you had to crawl completely into your trunk to retrieve them? Get the picture?

Since this 1984 case, all auto manufacturers have changed the design of their cars to provide an internal trunk locking mechanisms.

Now compare the following case of a successful recovery based upon failure to warn the consumer:

In *Dunne v. Wal-Mart Stores, Inc., 679 So.2d 1034 (La. App. 1996)*, the children of the plaintiff bought their 500-pound mother an Aero Cycle exercise bike to help her lose weight. The second time she used it, beyond a short trial run, it collapsed under her weight; she fell off the bike backwards and was severely injured.

Although the AeroCycle was not designed to be used by persons weighing over 250 pounds, the owner's manual and other safety information had no statement or warning regarding that weight-use limit.

The plaintiff sued Wal-Mart and the manufacturer of the bike under the Louisiana Products Liability Act that read:

"The manufacturer of a product shall be liable to a claimant for damage proximately caused by a characteristic of the product that renders the product *unreasonably dangerous* when such damage arose from *a reasonably anticipated use* of the product by the claimant or another person or entity" (emphasis added).

The trial court ruled for the defendant, holding that "The use of this exercise bike by a woman of 500 pounds was not reasonably anticipated."

The plaintiff appealed and the appellate court reversed:

"There was no issue of misuse of the product by plaintiff in this case. In fact, the record demonstrates that plaintiff used the product in a manner wholly consistent with its intended use . . . Plaintiff had no reason to know that the AeroCycle would not sustain her weight as she previously had used a similar exercise bike for several years without incident . . . Here, there is absolutely no evidence contained in the record that the danger was obvious or that plaintiff knew or should have known of the danger."

Since we are all graduates of the school of anticipatory thinking by now, it is incredible that the bike manufacturer did not include a one-sentence statement in its materials that said, "WARNING: THIS PRODUCT IS NOT TO BE USED BY ANYONE WEIGHING MORE THAN 250 POUNDS – SUCH USE MAY RESULT IN SEVERE INJURY!" If there had been such a warning, the defendant would have won the case.

Strict Liability – No-Fault Recovery

As commerce expanded and the laws changed to accommodate consumers who bought and used goods in their everyday business, product liability disputes sometimes arose where a party suffered a severe negligent injury but was unable to prove who caused it.

If this were the case, the injured parties would be unable to win a negligence claim because they could not sustain their required burden of proving the defendant was at fault.

In the 1960s, as more and more courts allowed these claims in the interest of fairness, states began to pass public policy laws recognizing the no-fault doctrine of "strict or absolute liability." They reasoned that the sellers of defective goods could best absorb the costs of litigation through insurance and increased prices for their products. Now, almost all states recognize it.

The doctrine provides that all the parties in the chain of distribution of a *dangerously defective* product, from first manufacturer to final retailer, may be sued by anyone who is injured by that product – without regard to whether or not they were at fault.

In order to recover, a plaintiff or his legal representative need only prove that (1) the seller is a merchant engaged in the business of selling such a product or in the chain of distribution, (2) it was sold to the plaintiff, and (3) it was dangerously defective because the plaintiff suffered a severe injury or died.

The Restatement, Second of Torts states strict liability will be imposed if:

"(1) the defendant was engaged in the business of selling a product such as the defective one;

(2) the defendant sold the product in a defective condition;

(3) the defective condition made the product unreasonably dangerous to the user or consumer or to his property;

(4) the defect in the product existed when it left the defendant's hands;

(5) the plaintiff sustained physical harm or property damage by using or consuming the product; and

(6) the defective condition was the proximate cause of the injury or damage."

This raises a presumption of strict liability, and shifts the burden of proof to the defendant to prove the product was not defective at the time it left its control. As hard as it would be for a plaintiff to prove the fault of the defendant, that's how hard it is for the defendant to prove non-fault. Most all such cases are ultimately settled by the defendants and their insurers in the plaintiff's favor.

The Curtis v. Sears and Sheffield Co. case we discussed in the negligence section also has facts that would allow a claim for strict liability. The electric saw was "dangerously" defective, as evidenced by Curtis's severe injury. Sheffield Co. was a merchant seller-manufacturer who sold it to Curtis. Curtis prevailed against Sheffield Co. for negligence but lost against Sears since he could not prove they were at fault. In a separate count for strict liability against them, he would win against both. Sears cannot escape liability here because they were the retail seller in the chain of distribution of the product.

Here is an example of the usual type of strict liability case, based upon an actual incident that occurred a few years ago in Miami, Florida:

Juan is a construction worker who buys a cold soda on his break at a nearby local convenience store. He drinks the soda while standing outside the store. After a few minutes, he feels ill, convulses, and collapses. The store calls 911, and Juan is rushed to the hospital emergency room and dies. His autopsy reveals a large amount of pure cocaine in his stomach, which is traced back to the can of soda. A search of the store reveals three other cans similarly tainted.

The seller of the soda received the soda from his distributor. They received it from their jobber, who received it from the importer, who received it from the manufacturer in Colombia. No one knows who put the cocaine in the soda. The executor of Juan's estate sues all the parties in the chain of commerce for strict liability.

The plaintiff will win against everybody. The burden of proving the three required elements of strict liability will be easily satisfied, and the defendants will be unable to prove where the problem arose. They will all be presumed liable to the plaintiff for all legally recoverable damages.

The unusual cases also occur in this category, causing much discussion and debate as to whether the strict liability doctrine goes too far in protecting the rights of consumers:

In *Greene v. Boddie-Noell Enterprises, Inc., 966 F. Supp. 416 (W.D. Va. 1997)*, the plaintiff purchased hot coffee at the drive-through window of a Hardee's restaurant. The cup she was holding in her hand splashed hot coffee on her legs when "the lid came off" as her vehicle hit a dip in the road as it exited the restaurant. She was treated at a hospital emergency room, missed eleven days of work, and suffered permanent scarring to her thighs.

The plaintiff sued the defendant, claiming the product she purchased was "unreasonably dangerous" as required by the Virginia statute for strict product liability. The defendant-restaurant operator moved for summary judgment, which was granted.

On appeal, the decision was affirmed:

"The plaintiff argues that the mere fact that she was burned shows that the product was dangerously defective, either by being too hot or by having a lid which came off unexpectedly. But it is settled in Virginia that the happening of an accident is not sufficient proof of liability, even in products cases."

The court also noted, somewhat critically, the famous 1984 McDonald's hot coffee case in which an eighty-one-year-old customer was burned in a similar manner as this case, sued the fast food chain for her injuries, and received a jury verdict of $160,000 in compensatory damages and $2.7 million (later reduced to $480,000) in punitive damages.

It certainly appears that this Hardee's case was a copycat of the McDonald's case. Unfortunately for the plaintiff, the result was not the same. As a practical matter, however, similar to what happened after the "attempted suicide in the automobile trunk" case, after the McDonald's and Hardee's cases, most fast-food sellers of coffee have reduced its temperature and placed "danger of burning" warnings on their cups.

Breach of Warranty

While negligence and strict liability theories of product liability are tort-based, warranty law is a contract concept. A warranty can be defined as a guarantee or assurance that the goods sold will measure up to a certain standard of quality or performance. If they do not work or are defective in some material way so that they can't be used, or if such defects cause personal injury to the buyer or end user, damages for breach of warranty may be recovered from the seller.

These damages may include:

- Refund of the purchase price and cancellation of the sale
- Repair or replacement of the defective goods, and completion of the sale
- Recovery of the value differential between the warranted and sold goods
- Money damages awardable in usual personal injury cases

The warranty sued upon by a buyer of the goods, called *basis of the bargain*, must be an important factor in his decision to buy.

The UCC does not go so far as the "detrimental reliance" test of liability in promissory estoppel contract cases, but still requires some degree of an inducing connection between the warranty and the decision to buy.

While the privity of contract defense that limited a buyer of defective goods to suing only his direct seller has been abandoned by our courts in tort actions, it remains to a limited extent in warranty cases. There are three alternatives provided by Article 2A of the UCC:

1. Most states grant warranty protection to the buyer *and* other natural persons in his family or household or who are a guest in his home.
2. Others extend it even further to include "any natural person who may reasonably be expected to use, consume, or be affected by the goods."
3. The most liberal alternative, allowed by a few states, expands coverage to all persons, both natural and corporate, who were injured either financially or physically so long as the damage was "reasonably foreseeable."

The UCC statute of limitations for filing suit for breach of warranty is four years from when the goods were delivered to the buyer.

Express Warranties

Express warranties are verbal or written factual representations by the seller that the goods will conform to a certain quality or performance standard. They can take many forms:

- Statements of fact about the goods – "This car has eight cylinders."
- Descriptions of the goods – "This is a Buick LeSabre."
- Performance promises – "This auto will give you thirty mpg."
- Advertisements/signs – factual statements, not just sales talk
- Purchases made from a sample or model of the item
- Custom or trade – relying upon past or local business practices

Sellers of goods are not legally required to furnish express warranties, but competition in the business marketplace demands it. Think of the largest shopping center in your local community. There are usually at least two stores that sell the same type of goods at the same level of prices. What if one store had a "no warranty – what you see is what you get" policy and another similar store said, "full warranties on all sales – we stand behind our goods"? Where would you shop? The consumer wants the best deal and will purchase from the seller providing it.

Disputes sometimes arise in express warranty cases when defendants deny liability on the grounds that the verbal or written statements in question were merely expressions of opinion rather than factual assertions.

Jeffrey goes to Glen's Clothiers to buy a tuxedo for his upcoming wedding. The salesperson directs him to the correct department, where there is a sign that reads, "finest Italian silk tuxedos," and tells Jeffrey, "I have been in this business for many years, and these are the best values in formal wear you could find anywhere." Jeffrey buys one of them for the sale price of $300. After the wedding he goes to clean the tux and is informed that it is made in China of a cheap synthetic material and will probably fall apart if cleaned. He claims breach of express warranty and the seller denies liability.

This looks like a fraud case and could probably be decided in Jeffrey's favor *if* he could prove the seller knew of the problem and intended to deceive him. Let's assume there is no such prior knowledge, just a mistaken assertion by the seller's agent.

Was there an express warranty? Yes, the sign had factual statements of "Italian silk" that were breached. But what if the sign only said, "finest tuxedos"? The word finest is an opinion – reasonable people might differ – normally not a warranty. The salesperson's statement was one of value – an opinion – more sales talk, and normally not a warranty.

But, like fraud cases, the UCC has a fairness exception to the "statement of fact" rule in factual circumstances like this one where the buyer would reasonably rely upon the opinion statements due to the superior knowledge or expertise of the seller. Jeffrey wins his claim for breach of warranty.

In *Felley v. Singleton, 705 N.E.2d 930 (Ill. App. 1999)*, the plaintiff purchased a used 1991 Ford Taurus with 126,000 miles on the odometer from the defendants for $5,800. After a test drive, the defendants told him the car was in good condition, answered all his questions with positive responses, and the plaintiff bought the car.

Within the first month of use, the plaintiff experienced problems with the clutch pedal and the brakes costing almost $2,500, and then sued for breach of express warranty. The trial court entered judgment for the plaintiff, and the appellate court affirmed. The issue before the court was whether the statements made by the defendants were an express warranty or just sales puffery of an as-is sale:

"Section 2-313 of the (UCC) governs the formation of express warranties by affirmation in the context of a sale of goods such as a used car. Section 2-313 provides, in relevant part:

"Express warranties by the seller are created as follows: (a) any affirmation of fact or promise made by the seller to the buyer which relates to the goods and becomes part of the basis of the bargain creates an express warranty that the goods shall conform to the affirmation or promise.

"We agree . . . that, in the context of a used car sale, representations such as the car is 'in good mechanical condition' are presumed to be affirmations of fact that become part of the basis of the bargain."

Louisiana has an unusual statutory law called "Redhibition" that allows a buyer of goods that have hidden defects to rescind the transaction and recover the purchase price paid.

In *Crow v. Laurie, 1999 WL 99069 (La. App. 1999)*, the plaintiffs bought a used seventeen-foot fishing boat and trailer for $2,500. After one use, the plaintiffs discovered that the boat's transom forming the stern of the boat was rotten and the boat should not be used. The condition was not visible under its outer layer of fiberglass.

After the plaintiffs unsuccessfully tendered the boat and trailer to the defendant, requesting a "full and complete repair or refund of the purchase price," they filed suit. The trial court ruled in favor of the defendants, ruling that the plaintiffs "had a heightened duty of inspection" as purchasers of a seventeen-year-old boat.

The appellate court reversed based upon the doctrine of Redhibition:

"Redhibition is the avoidance of a sale on account of some vice or defect in the thing sold which renders it either absolutely useless, or its use so inconvenient and imperfect, that it must be supposed that the buyer would not have purchased it, had he known of the vice."

"In a suit for redhibition, the plaintiff must prove: 1) the seller sold the thing to him and it is either absolutely useless for its intended purpose or its use is so inconvenient or imperfect that, judged by the reasonable person standard, had he known of the defect, he would never have purchased it; 2) the thing contained a non-apparent defect at the time of sale; and 3) the seller was given an opportunity to repair the defect."

Implied Warranties

In its effort to protect the consumer, the UCC grants to every buyer of goods *from a merchant* the following two implied warranties. They arise as a matter of law, without any verbal or written statements from the seller, solely from the transaction itself:

Merchantability

This implied warranty assures that the goods purchased are fit for their normal or customary purposes of use. This would mean a pen or pencil writes, a watch keeps time, an alarm clock rings, a computer will perform its standard functions, and so on.

The merchant-seller's obligations include the goods being properly contained, packaged, and labeled, as well as being of consistent quality and quantity if more than one item.

The thrust of this implied warranty is that the buyer-consumer relies upon his merchant-seller and gets what he reasonably expects to receive. It is another of our fairness rules.

> Stephen, an accountant, decides to retire and sell his electronic equipment. He has a high-quality Texas Instruments printing calculator that performs many bookkeeping functions. They include twelve-digit, three-color printing of numbers, tax calculations, and also addition, subtraction, multiplication, and division. He sells it to Smith Office Supply. They then sell it to Riley, a young auditor.
>
> When Riley puts it to use he discovers that it will only print in black and white, and while it performs all the mathematical computations, it will not do the tax rate conversions. He demands return of his money from Smith Office Supply who, in turn, demands the return of their purchase price from Stephen.

The ordinary and customary usage of the calculator in this case is to compute and color-print calculations that include tax functions. That is presumably the basis for the bargain when it was bought by Smith Office Supply, as well as by their customer, Riley. The calculator clearly fails to perform as required and is therefore considered defective.

But the key issue here is the legal status of the respective sellers. Is Stephen a merchant with respect to the goods sold to his buyer? No, he is retired and no longer engaged in his profession, so he no longer is viewed as a merchant-seller. He is not liable for breach of the warranty for that reason.

Smith Office Supply, while having no legal recourse for breach of warranty against Stephen, is a merchant actively engaged in its primary business, which includes the sale of items such as the calculator. Therefore it is liable to Riley.

Fitness for Human Consumption

The "consumables" warranty cases are an outgrowth of implied warranty of merchantability. If the goods sold by a merchant not only fail to function properly, but also have harmful side effects resulting from their use, the buyer is also legally protected. Over the years, these cases have evolved into a separate implied warranty category and are decided on a case-by-case basis. The broad category of sellers includes bars and restaurants, package stores, licensed food sellers, public vending machines, and take-out services. Whether the items are consumed on premises or off premises is immaterial.

Originally there was a factual distinction based upon only two factors:

- Foreign object test – consumer always wins – "cutting your mouth on a piece of metal in your fish chowder"
- Natural object test – seller always wins – "cutting your mouth on a fish bone in your fish chowder"

If the cause of the damage was *reasonably related* to the food or drink in which it was found, it was considered a natural object and no recovery was allowed by the consumer. This would include situations like a chicken bone in fried chicken, orange seeds in orange juice, and meat gristle in a hamburger.

As the law became more attuned to the rights and needs of the consuming public, and the ability of businesses to absorb legal risks through insurance and pricing policies, a shift in emphasis took place in a majority of states in these cases.

All states hold that damage from a foreign object subjects the merchant-seller to liability. But what about those cases where the damage is caused by what is technically a natural object, but one that the buyer-consumer did not expect to encounter?

Most states now judge these disputes based upon a *reasonable expectation* test. If the object encountered in the food or drink was normal or customary (notice the wording similar to merchantability), and thus expected by or foreseeable to the consumer, it is treated as a natural object. But if reasonable people would not expect it under the same or similar circumstances (the objective test we have used time and time again), it is treated as a foreign object and creates seller liability.

Ricky takes his girlfriend Mia to the Om Natural Eats restaurant for lunch. They both order veggie burgers. When their food arrives she takes a big bite and says, "Wow, it's delicious." He takes a big bite and says, "Ouch, I cracked my tooth on this large uncooked carrot in my burger." He sues for breach of food warranty. The seller denies liability, claiming it was just a natural object.

Certainly carrots are part of the usual veggie burgers served in health food restaurants. But would the consumer "reasonably expect" to encounter what caused Ricky's problem? If so, you could not eat a veggie burger without carefully looking through it before each bite. That is not reasonable for food in general, and especially when it comes to a hungry diner biting into a fresh, juicy burger. The burden is upon the food seller to properly prepare it. Ricky wins.

Fitness for Special Use

This warranty applies to *all* sellers of goods, whether merchants or not. It includes garage sales, barters or exchanges, and any other transfers of title to goods. This broad application of warranty protection is limited by the legal requirements for its application:

- Seller knows or reasonably should know of buyer's desired use
- Seller knows or reasonably should know buyer is relying upon him
- Buyer does rely upon seller to deliver the correct goods
- Seller breaches by failing to provide the correct goods
- Buyer suffers damage due to seller's breach

Notice how similar these five elements are to the doctrines of fraud and promissory estoppel that we have previously discussed. Their basis is fairness, and again the law is seeking to balance the scales to protect the consumer.

This warranty protection does not relate to the merchantability situations of the goods being fit for their normal usage. It only applies to a failure of the seller to meet the special needs of the buyer.

It also requires that the buyer is not on the same level of knowledge or expertise as the seller, and is thus depending upon the seller to provide what is needed. The reasonable reliance factor is missing if the buyer is able to tell at a glance whether or not the correct goods are being furnished.

"Section 2-314 of the (UCC) provides that every sale of goods by a merchant includes an implied warranty that the goods are fit for the ordinary purposes for which they are used unless the warranty is modified or excluded. Section 2-315 of the code states that a sale of goods also includes an implied warranty of fitness for a particular purpose if a seller knows of the buyer's particular purpose for the goods and the buyer relies upon the seller's skill or judgment to select suitable goods. However, 2-316 of the code states that no implied warranties apply when a buyer examines the goods or a sample as fully as he desires, or refuses to examine the goods, prior to the purchase." *Trans-Aire International, Inc. v. Northern Adhesive Co., Inc., 882 F.2d 1254 (7th Cir. 1989)*

Zachary is a first-time scuba diver who seeks to find the wreck of an old Spanish galleon off the Florida coast. He needs a pen that will write on land, in the water, and at pressure depth so he can make notes on his dives. He goes to DEF Stationers and tells the salesperson he wants a good pen, "that will write in all kinds of weather." He buys the pen provided. On his next dive trip, it is raining and the pen writes fine, but it won't write underwater, and he is unable to record important location coordinates. As a result, he loses his salvage and sues DEF Stationers for breach of warranty.

It appears that the pen Zachary bought was merchantable, since it did function properly in "all kinds of weather," rain or shine. His problem was underwater writing, not just being able to work when wet. There are special pens that divers use for this purpose, but since he was a first-timer, he would not notice whether or not he had received the right model. If he were experienced, he would be aware of any discrepancy and could correct it.

The seller gave him what he asked for. Zachary is at fault because he didn't specify his special needs and particular usage. The seller was not a mind-reader, and therefore is not at fault.

But what if Zachary walked into the store wearing a scuba diving t-shirt, or was carrying some of his apparatus, so that it would reasonably appear what he needed the pen for? Then we would have a different result, because he could successfully argue that the seller "should have known" his special use.

Here are four implied warranty cases:

MERCHANTABILITY: In *Denny v. Ford Motor Company, 639 N.Y.S.2d 250 (N.Y. App. 1995)*, the plaintiff purchased a Ford Bronco II SUV manufactured by the defendant for her everyday use. It was advertised in their marketing manual as being "considered fashionable" for suburban driving and "particularly appealing to women who may be concerned about driving in snow and ice with their children."

While driving on a standard road, she slammed on the brakes to avoid a deer and the vehicle rolled over, severely injuring her. She sued for breach of implied warranty of merchantability, claiming the vehicle's high center of gravity, short wheelbase, and suspension design created a higher risk of rollover accidents than customary passenger vehicles. Ford claimed the car was an off-road vehicle, not designed for use as a conventional passenger automobile on paved streets.

The trial court ruled for the plaintiff and awarded damages of $1.2 million. On appeal, the decision was affirmed:

"The law implies a warranty by a manufacturer that places its product on the market that the product is reasonably fit for the ordinary purpose for which it was intended. If it is, in fact, defective and not reasonably fit to be used for its intended purpose, the warranty is breached . . . routine highway and street driving was the 'ordinary purpose' for which the Bronco II was sold and that it was not 'fit' – or safe – for that purpose."

FITNESS FOR HUMAN CONSUMPTION: In *Yong Cha Hong v. Marriott Corporation, 3 UCC Rep. Serv.2d 83 (D. Md. 1987)*, the plaintiff purchased take-out fried chicken from a Roy Rogers Family Restaurant owned by the defendant.

While eating a chicken wing, she bit into an object she thought was a worm and became ill. She sued the deep-pocket defendant for $500,000, claiming breach of implied warranty of merchantability.

After the defendant introduced evidence that the object in the chicken wing was a worm-like part of the chicken's aorta or trachea, it moved for summary judgment based upon the natural object test.

The court denied the defendant's motion:

"The reasonable expectation test has largely displaced the foreign-natural test adverted to by Marriott . . . The court cannot conclude that the presence of a trachea or an aorta in a fast food fried chicken wing is so reasonably to be expected as to render it merchantable, as a matter of law . . . Thus, a question is presented that precludes the grant of summary judgment."

In *Goodman v. Wendy's Foods, Inc., 142 S.E.2d 444 (N.C. 1992)*, the plaintiff bought a double hamburger sandwich at a Wendy's restaurant and bit into a small bone that broke three of his teeth. He sued for breach of the implied warranty of fitness for human consumption.

The plaintiff claimed the "expectation test" was the basis for recovery. The defendant claimed that the "natural object test" precluded recovery. The trial court directed a verdict for the defendant, and the plaintiff appealed.

The court reversed based on the fact that "A consumer should not reasonably have anticipated the substance's presence . . . notwithstanding the injury-causing substance's naturalness to the food . . . "

"Surely it is within the expectation of the consumer to find a bone in a T-bone steak; but just as certainly it is reasonable for a consumer not to expect to find a bone in a package of hamburger meat."

As an interesting sidelight to this case, a story in the news last year mentioned an unreported case where a Wendy's customer sued for breach of implied food warranty when he allegedly became ill when he saw that one of the chicken wings in his order looked like the head of a chicken. If you were the judge, how would you rule? Hint – the customer certainly did not reasonably expect this, but he never "consumed" anything.

FITNESS FOR SPECIAL USE: In *Mack Massey Motors, Inc. v. Garnica, 814 S.W.2d 167 (Tex. App. 1991)*, the plaintiff desired to buy a vehicle that was able to tow the twenty-three-foot Airstream trailer she had ordered. When she went to the defendant to inquire about buying a Jeep Cherokee, the sales manager investigated the Airstream's specifications and recommended the Jeep "as being suitable for the purposes Mrs. Garnica was seeking – that of towing the Airstream trailer she had on order."

After she bought the vehicle she had difficulty with slipping transmission when pulling the trailer, and eventually the drive shaft on the Jeep twisted apart. She then sued for breach of the implied warranty of fitness for a particular purpose. The jury returned a verdict in her favor and the defendant appealed.

The appellate court affirmed:

"A claim of warranty of fitness requires that the goods serve their particular purpose. The evidence supported the jury determination that the Jeep Cherokee simply was exceeding its towing capacity and that Massey Motors had misrepresented the fact that this was the proper vehicle suitable for towing the Airstream trailer."

The purchase of motor vehicles, which creates a large number of sales transactions and an equally large number of products liability claims, has an alternative warranty remedy provided by the statutory "lemon laws" of most states.

These laws provide procedures and remedies for consumers that have recurring problems with their vehicles, so that litigation can be avoided and their disputes decided by an administrative panel established for that particular purpose. The remedies can include refund of repair costs, reimbursement of expenses and incidental damages, rescission of the transaction and return of the purchase price, and in some cases the requirement that the dealer substitute a new vehicle.

Florida's *Chapter 681 Motor Vehicle Sales Warranties* is representative:

"Consumer means the purchaser, other than for purposes of resale, or the lessee of a motor vehicle primarily used for personal, family or household purposes.

"Lemon Law rights means the period ending 1 year after the date of the original delivery of a motor vehicle to a consumer or the first 12,000 miles of operation, whichever occurs first.

"Motor vehicle means a new vehicle, . . . and includes a vehicle used as a demonstrator or leased vehicle, . . . but does not include vehicles run only upon tracks, off-road vehicles, trucks over 10,000 pounds gross vehicle weight, the living facilities of recreational vehicles, motorcycles, or mopeds.

"After three attempts have been made to repair the same nonconformity or a motor vehicle has been out of service by reason of repair of one or more nonconformities for 20 cumulative calendar days, the consumer shall give written notification, by registered or express mail to the manufacturer, of the need for repair . . . in order to allow the manufacturer a final attempt to cure the nonconformity or nonconformities.

"If the manufacturer, or its authorized service agent, cannot conform the motor vehicle to the warranty by repairing or correcting any nonconformity after a reasonable number of attempts, the manufacturer, within 40 calendar days, shall, in consideration of its receipt of payment of a reasonable offset for use, replace the motor vehicle with a replacement motor vehicle acceptable to the consumer, or repurchase the motor vehicle from the consumer and refund to the consumer the full purchase price, including all reasonably incurred collateral and incidental charges, less a reasonable offset for use. However, the consumer has an unconditional right to choose a refund rather than a replacement."

Seller's Disclaimers of Liability

A full product liability disclaimer is a contract clause that the seller inserts to release it from any liability. It is a form of exculpatory clause, similar to the "not responsible for loss or damage . . ." cases we looked at in the chapter on illegality. A partial disclaimer limits the amount, procedures, and type of recovery.

When we buy new merchandise, especially appliances, we find inside the carton a cellophane-enclosed package of papers containing the product warranty. We rarely open it, but know it should be saved. We usually throw it in a kitchen drawer and never look at it again unless we have a problem with a product defect.

One of my class exercises involves the students each bringing in one of these warranty cards. They usually cover a wide spectrum of small, low-priced items to large, expensive ones. They often include household appliances, home furnishings, sporting goods, apparel, jewelry, and computer products. They may even include automobiles, with the booklet on "lemon law" protection provided by the State Department of Motor Vehicles.

They are all express warranties of one form or another, but upon inspection most talk about *limitations* on how they are applicable and the seller's duties to repair or refund or pay damages.

Sellers of goods in today's commercial marketplace realize that their customers expect some form of express warranty, so they give it to them. But as they giveth, they taketh away in the limitations they impose. Consumers either don't mind or more probably don't even notice because these warranty cards are rarely read.

These disclaimers of liability by the seller usually impose certain requirements on the buyer to notify of defects and return goods within a specified time. They also list common exclusionary situations of nonliability:

• Product misuse or abuse
• Acts of God or other accidental damage
• Failure to follow instructions
• Improper installation
• Cosmetic damage
• Unauthorized repairs
• Costs of product removal or re-installation

Since competition requires these express warranties and buyers expect them, sellers often protect themselves by limiting the express warranties by time and type and exclusions. But sellers also usually completely disclaim any legal responsibility for the implied warranties.

The UCC allows such disclaimers of liability for implied warranties so long as they are conspicuous and easy to understand, but imposes certain legal requirements:

• Merchantability – may be verbal or written, but must contain the word "merchantability"
• Fitness for special use – must be written, but no specific wording is required so long as its intent is clearly expressed

Do you think non-merchant-sellers of goods should have any implied warranty liability? Do you think merchant-sellers should be allowed to disclaim legal responsibility for implied warranties? Are the scales of justice evenly balanced with our current warranty laws?

Discussion Exercises

1. Discuss where you would draw the liability dividing line of foreseeability in the four areas of products negligence.

2. Discuss areas where "caveat emptor" should be the governing law.

3. Discuss areas where "caveat venditor" should be the governing law.

4. Discuss the arguments pro and con regarding the doctrine of strict liability.

5. Discuss types of "natural objects" found in consumables that should and should not result in seller's liability.

Case Exercise 2

The Little Engine that Couldn't

In *Leavitt v. Monaco Coach Corporation, 616 N.W.2d 175 (Mich. App. 2000)*, the plaintiff bought a new motor home from the defendant. While shopping for it he "informed defendant of his plans to use the coach extensively for travel in mountainous areas and of his wish to avoid problems he had experienced with rented vehicles that lacked sufficient engine and braking power."

"Almost immediately upon receiving the vehicle, and for the years leading up to this lawsuit, plaintiff complained that his coach could not maintain ordinary highway speeds going up steep hills and that the brakes were prone to overheating while going down."

Despite many warranty repairs, the plaintiff concluded that the engine and brakes were not suitable and he sued for breach of implied warranty of fitness for a particular purpose.

Analysis

The trial jury found for the plaintiff and awarded damages of $33,730, after the judge denied the defendant's motion for directed verdict. The appellate court affirmed, rejecting as not supported by the evidence the defendant's arguments that the "plaintiff did not explain his special needs for engine power with sufficient particularity to establish a warranty of fit-ness for a particular purpose."

"Where the seller at the time of contracting has reason to know any particu-lar purpose for which the goods are required and that the buyer is relying on the seller's skill or judgment to select or furnish suitable goods, there is . . . an implied warranty that the goods shall be fit for such purpose."

Defuse Replay

Sellers of goods have a continuing problem of when non-actionable pre-liminary sales talk becomes possible warranty liability. Most of the cases for breach of either express or implied warranty are caused by an overzealous seller trying to close the deal.

Because of the litigation risks when problems result from the goods that are sold, many sellers are now using disclaimers to protect themselves. If the defendant in this case had inserted the following clause in the sales contract with the plaintiff, the case of the plaintiff would probably not have survived a motion to dismiss:

"SELLER MAKES NO WARRANTY, EXPRESS OR IMPLIED, CONCERNING THE PRODUCT OR THE MERCHANTABILITY OR FITNESS THEREOF FOR ANY PURPOSE CONCERNING THE ACCURACY OF ANY INFORMATION PROVIDED BY THE SELLER."

Conclusion

Consider the multitude of legal principles that now protect the consumer-purchaser of defective goods. Alternate counts in the lawsuit could include:

1. Breach of contract

2. Breach of express warranty

3. Breach of implied warranty of merchantability

4. Breach of implied warranty of fitness for human consumption

5. Breach of implied warranty of fitness for a particular purpose

6. Strict liability

7. Product negligence

It is no wonder that the sales price of goods in this country has to factor in the potential liability expenses of damage claims, and that defendant-sellers lobby for tort reform while plaintiff-buyers seek even broader judicial protection.

C.   SPECIAL RULES FOR E-COMMERCE/CYBERLAW

"Microsoft holds monopoly power with its Windows operating system, and it used its power to harm both consumers and competitors."

—U.S. v. Microsoft Corp., 65 F. Supp.2d 1 (D.D.C. 1999)

Legal Overview

We have experienced dramatic technological advancements during the last century in every area of human involvement, including but not limited to population movement (rural to urban), transportation (trains, planes, and automobiles), basic communications (telephone, radio, television, and movies), life comforts (air conditioning, paper copiers, faxes, cell phones), medicine (antibiotics, surgical techniques, organ transplants), alternative medicine (holistic health), nutrition (vitamins, food supplements), food supply (agribusiness), and many others.

As these innovations changed the structure of our society, the legal system slowly responded with laws, rules, and regulations adapted to the areas where disputes occurred so as to try to maintain the orderly framework of legally permissible, predictable, and enforceable acts, usage, and behavior.

But nothing prepared us, our legislators, or the judicial system for the way our lives and our need for governing laws have changed due to the Internet revolution.

Seemingly isolated technology links resulted in our current computerized world. It is an interesting story of how the wheels of progress were set in motion:

- In the late 1960s the U.S. Defense Department researched military communication using massive computers in their DARPA network.
- In the early 1980s they joined with the National Science Foundation to extend this capability to the scientific community, resulting in the NSFNET that joined the scientific and academic communities.
- These two networks merged in the late 1980s, and we had the earliest version of the Internet.
- Then in mid-1990 Congress authorized use of this network for commercial purposes.
- In the early 1990s a Swiss scientist designed the technical protocols, coding languages, and hyperlinks necessary for creation and linkage of informational and commercial websites, thus giving birth to the World Wide Web.

This chain of events led in the late 1990s to an explosion of usage, resulting in our current global and instantaneous method of communication and commerce, which is accessible to everyone through a network of millions of computers. It is truly mind-boggling!

We call it the Internet (interrelated network), and it operates in an area we call Cyberspace. It is the superhighway of electronic communication and information gathering and dispersal. It is the worldwide office for merchants and non-merchants to conduct their business, and the marketplace of the world for electronic commerce.

"The Internet is the world's largest computer network (a network consisting of two or more computers linked together to share electronic mail and files). The Internet is actually a network of thousands of independent networks, containing several million 'host' computers that provide information services. An estimated 25 million individuals have some form of Internet access, and this audience is doubling each year. The Internet is a cooperative venture, owned by no one, but regulated by several volunteer agencies." *MTV Networks v. Curry, 867 F.Supp. 202 (S.D.N.Y. 1994)*

With the advent of the Internet, our legal system found itself totally unprepared for its unique needs. Our existing laws on contracts and sales, though refined over the years and usually effective in normal transactions, were inadequate in many areas of this new way of doing business electronically. New laws were needed and, as e-commerce disputes began to be litigated, court decisions were rendered in many areas that change the old rules.

In addition, the unique domain of Cyberspace required a uniform set of laws to govern nationwide, rather than a series of inconsistent state laws. This also took time and effort.

Many disputes also arose because the business community is historically slow to react to technological advances such as paper copiers, fax transmission of documents, office computerization, and especially the potential opportunities for paperless contracts, continuous worldwide selling, and marketplace presence through websites.

Internet law alone could be the current subject of an entire book, running the gamut of legal issues from business torts to intellectual property rights to electronic speech rights to consumer protection to securities, taxation, and Cybercrime.

It is in a process of early evolution, as rules of law for offline transactions are gradually adapted to its needs, and new technologies are frequent.

Therefore, the purpose of this chapter is to highlight some of the main areas of electronic commerce and Cyberlaw that relate to our focus on contracts and sales laws. Since Internet laws and court decisions are so new, the examples used in this chapter will be based upon current legislation and recently decided cases, rather than hypothetical situations.

Recent Origin of Cyberlaw

Reno v. ACLU, 521 U.S. 844 (1997), was the first case to be heard by the U.S. Supreme Court that tested governmental limits to regulate the Internet. The legal question before it was whether the Communications Decency Act, which created criminal liability for the online transmission of "indecent" and "offensive" material to minors, violated First Amendment free speech protection.

The act created a defense if defendants took effective action to block the offensive material. The practical problem that resulted in this test case was that available technology was unable to differentiate between filtering out the material to minors and providing it to adults, so that the law restricted both proper and improper transmissions.

246 PREVENTATIVE LAW FOR BUSINESS PROFESSIONALS

The trial court found the act unconstitutional under the First Amendment. The Court affirmed the lower court, and in the process accurately predicted what had proved to be the Internet revolution:

"(T)he Internet . . . provides a relatively unlimited, low-cost capacity for communication of all kinds. The Government estimates that 'as many as 40 million people use the Internet today, and that figure is expected to grow to 200 million by 1999.' This dynamic, multifaceted category of communications includes not only traditional print and news services, but also audio, video, and still images, as well as interactive, real-time dialogue. Through the use of chat rooms, any person with a phone line can become a town crier with a voice that resonates farther then it could from any soapbox. Through the use of Web pages, mail exploders, and newsgroups, the same individual can become a pamphleteer."

Surfing the Net

Internet addresses are constructed using a domain name system (DNS) that allows users to enter an electronic name, or alias, that has been previously licensed to an individual or a company, and be forwarded to that specific numeric Internet address.

We navigate the web by first "going online." This requires the user to register with one of the many Internet service providers (ISP).

This provides the opportunity for electronic mail communications (e-mail) of a personal or business nature between the individual addresses created by the parties, coded to their ISP.

Companies and individuals can also create their own websites, which are their commercial stores or personal offices located in Cyberspace, and are accessible 24-7 throughout the world. The websites consist of web pages created by the parties that may also contain links to other web pages and websites, thus creating a continual subnetwork of flowing information and commerce within the World Wide Web.

We can access information and visit web locations by entering the information category or desired domain name in one of the commercial search engines, or entering the specific hyperlink address in our computer browser.

Domain Names

Website names are called domain names, which identify the names of particular users or, more importantly in the world of commerce, their commonly used business name. The domain name is how the public identifies and finds the user on the World Wide Web.

The objective of domain name licensing is to register the prefix name most easily recognizable to the public, such as ge (general electric), gm (general motors), or ibm (international business machines). This is accomplished through various domain registries created for this purpose that have identifying suffixes such as .com and .net (commercial/individual use), .edu (educational/research facilities), and .gov (governmental facilities).

Since the Internet began as a governmental project, the assigning of domain names was originally under federal control. However, in the late 1990s, the assigning and management of domain names was privatized to the Internet Corporation for Assigned Names and Numbers (ICANN), which oversees the entire system even though there are many private registries for licensing domain names.

Domain Names must Comply with Registry Standards

In the case of *National A-1 Advertising, Inc. v. Network Solutions, Inc., 2000 WL 1513791 (2000)*, the plaintiff (National) sought to register thirty domain names with the defendant (Network), then the sole domain registry company. Network had a decency policy for these second-level domain names that prohibited the usage of the profanity that comedian George Carlin made famous – the seven words banned by the FCC in broadcast media. Their registration process automatically filtered out and rejected these "disapproved names" submitted by National because they contained the restricted strings of letters.

National claimed they were entitled to First Amendment rights of free speech because Network was performing a "governmental" action. Network countered, claiming its actions were purely as a private business and thus valid.

Analysis

The court first presented a detailed historical analysis of the Internet and how it works under headings of "I. Government's role in the Evolution of the Internet," "II. The Cooperative Agreement and Network Solutions' Authority," and "III. Navigating the Internet."

It then attempted to apply legal tests from traditional disputes:

"Because of the relative novelty of the Internet, there is very little precedent applying traditional and familiar legal principles to its operation." The court ruled in favor of Network, allowing it to reject the registration applications, notwithstanding the fact that the rejection might adversely affect the business of the applicant.

"Standing alone, however, the mere fact that plaintiffs might, as a result of Network Solutions' conduct, realize less Internet traffic to their sites by people typing in assumed domain names, does not convert an otherwise invalid claim into one of constitutional significance . . . the First Amendment does not guarantee anyone a profit."

The court also noted how the government's role in the Internet was intentionally being reduced and turned over to private businesses, so that under this current trend of how the business is conducted, Network was not a government actor and not subject to the claims made by the plaintiff.

Defuse Replay

When National was advised of the rejection of their application, what did they do? They reacted with a "let's sue them" approach, and spent thousands of dollars in lawyer's fees and countless hours of their own time, not to mention the stress and bad publicity surrounding the matter, in misguided constitutional litigation.

They should have just changed the wording of their domain names a bit – enough to avoid the rejection filters of Network, but still leave the phonetic name intact. For example, the offending s-h-i-t could be s-h-m-i-t, the prohibited f-u-c-k could be f-o-r-k, and so on. A play on words is often more effective than the actual words, anyway. They could have accomplished indirectly what they failed to do directly, with just a little bit of creative thought.

The registration procedure is simple. With an online visit to a domain registry, name availability, cost and duration information, and completion of the process is a click of the mouse away. The cost is so nominal now (as low as $3.95 for one year per assigned name) that anyone can register one or more names.

The timing of the emerging technology and the realization by mainstream business that this was the new commerce created business opportunities for a number of enterprising young entrepreneurs, who literally made millions of dollars in the 1990s by registering the names of the most well-known businesses, famous personalities, and common business categories.

These people were called Cybersquatters because they were not doing anything with the names except sitting on them, waiting for the real parties in interest to notice and pay up. There were no legal prohibitions on what they were doing because the non-existent Internet laws lagged far behind the emerging world of high-tech. Registered trademark names were researched and then used as a basis for domain name registrations.

Registrant-owners of exxon.com, jerryseinfeld.com, and others, such as wallstreetjournal.com, were delighted to assign their names for large sales prices. These young geniuses registered most of the Fortune 500 companies and the Hollywood star list before the parties directly involved realized what was happening in their marketplace. The result was financial windfalls to the registrants.

In late 1999, Congress finally addressed the problem by passing the Anti-Cybersquatting Consumer Protection Act, which legally prevents registration of well-known names of companies or persons if done in *bad faith*. That aspect of the intention of the registrant reflects the view of the legislators that the prohibited parties were Cybercriminals who were extorting money in order to free the names that they had kidnapped.

Factors tending to show bad faith are:

- Multiple registrations by one registrant
- Solicitation of sale or assignment by the registrant for an inflated price
- Lack of name similarity with the name registered
- Lack of an active related business or personal connection

The legal sanctions imposed by the act included money damages and injunctive relief, but questions then arose as to the problems of civil lawsuits that would be public, time-consuming, and very costly. A Uniform Dispute Resolution Policy (UDRP) was adopted by ICANN limiting the legal recourse of all its domain name registrants to arbitration before the World Intellectual Property Organization (WIPO), an agency of the United Nations, and several private dispute resolution companies.

First Registration of a Domain Name May not Be Binding

In its first ruling under the UDRP, styled *World Wrestling Federation v. Bosman*, the WIPO heard a complaint filed by the WWF claiming that the defendant had registered "worldwrestlingfederation.com" in bad faith as a Cybersquatter, and solicited its sale to them. The WWF owned a prior registered trademark for that name under federal law for a number of years before Bosman's domain name registration. WWF demanded cancellation of Bosman's rights in the name and its transfer to them.

Analysis

The arbitrator ruled in favor of the WWF, stating that no legal ownership rights existed in the plaintiff, and assigned the name to them, citing the various factual indicia of bad faith that included the solicitation and the fact that the defendant had no personal or family connection to the registered name. He was merely trying to take advantage of the economics of the situation.

Defuse Replay

Interestingly enough, had Bosman registered prior to passage of the act he would have faced no legal impediment to his scheme, and the WWF would no doubt have paid his price. Bosman would have won under the priority doctrine of "first in time, first in right." After the act, a domain name registration that is valid on its face may still be cancelled on grounds of Cybersquatting, but the complaining party must prove the required legal aspects of bad faith.

But there still appears to be a loophole in the act. While it clearly protects names of well-known persons and companies, there is no prohibition on using generic names. If each time a specific name is registered, its class or category name were also registered, there would be an effective back-up position. Examples are kraft.com with cheese.com, pepsi.com with soda.com, and budweiser.com with beer.com. If Bosman would have registered "wrestling.com" with his specific domain name, he might have been counting profits instead of losses.

Some recent cases reflect a jurisdictional loophole that exists in the Anticybersquatting Consumer Protection Act of 1999:

In *Harrods Ltd. v. Sixty Internet Domain Names, No. 00-2414 (4th Cir. 2000),* the plaintiff sued under the act, alleging that the defendant, an Argentinean company, registered with Virginia-based Network Solution, Inc. (now VeriSign) sixty domain names such as "harrodsbank," harrodsshopping," and "harrodsvirtual" in bad faith, infringing upon and diluting its U.S. registered Harrods trademark.

The trial court found that fifty-four of the names were registered in bad faith, and ruled they were therefore forfeited and must be returned to the plaintiff.

The appellate court affirmed and expanded the lower court's ruling, so that now the act's jurisdiction provisions may be used not only to stop bad faith Internet domain name registration, but also to combat trademark infringement.

Rather than having to obtain personal jurisdiction over the offending party in Argentina, the court allowed the in-rem filing of infringement and dilution claims by going to the U.S. jurisdiction where they were registered.

In *Mattel, Inc. v. Barbie-Club.com, 310 F.3d 293 (2nd Cir. 2002)*, the plaintiff sued to cancel fifty-seven Internet sites that allegedly sought to Cybersquat on their Barbie trademarks. Because it could not obtain personal jurisdiction over the defendants, it sought (similar to the Harrods case) to invoke the act's in-rem jurisdiction in the U.S. venue of New York, where it had deposited its trademark registration certificates.

The trial court and appellate court dismissed the suit, and ruled that individual lawsuits would have to be filed in each jurisdiction where the registering domain-name authority was located. In this case, unlike the Harrods case, most of the contested domain names were registered in states other than New York.

"Rather, it is the presence of the domain name itself . . . in the judicial district in which the registry or registrar is located that anchors the in rem action and satisfies due process and international comity."

The loophole that needs to be closed in utilizing in-rem jurisdiction to avoid the necessity of acquiring personal jurisdiction is that of multi-state domain name registries. Since separate lawsuits have to be brought in each state of registration, the economics of that litigation prevents effective action.

Why not amend the act to state, "In cases of multiple domain name registrations, suit for claims of bad-faith domain name registration and/or trademark infringement/dilution may be properly filed in any one of the registry jurisdictions and be binding upon all registrations that are found to have violated the Act."

The anti-Cybersquatting law applies only to disputes that occur after its enactment in 1999. However, it was recently deemed to have retroactive application in the unusual Pennsylvania case of *Schmidheiny v. Weber, 319 F.3d 581 (3rd Cir. 2003)*, where a billionaire sued an alleged Cybersquatter who offered to sell him the Internet domain with the billionaire's name followed by .com.

The trial court dismissed the lawsuit because the offending name had been registered by Weber more than nine months before the law took effect. But the appellate court reversed due to the fact that Weber had re-registered the name in June 2000, "an action within the purview of the Anti-Cybersquatting Act."

Another prohibited domain name practice is typo-squatting. This involves the intentional misspelling of words in domain names to siphon off Internet traffic from its intended destination to another site.

In *National Association of Professional Baseball Leagues, Inc. v. Zuccarini (WIPO 2003)*, the defendant intentionally registered "minorleaugebaseball.com," and the commonly made misspelling caused Internet traffic for the correct site (professional baseball's farm clubs in U.S. and Canada) to be directed to the defendant's pornographic website. The plaintiff had registered "minorleaguebaseball.com" and "minorleaguebaseball.org" in 1996 and 2000, respectively, and received various trademark registrations in 2001.

The defendant had a lengthy history of registering domain names using the trademarks of others with slight misspellings to increase Internet traffic to his sites.

A WIPO arbitration panel ruled for the plaintiff, and directed that the defendant transfer the disputed domain name back to the plaintiff.

"Typosquatting is inherently parasitic and of itself bad faith" because the intent is to "siphon off traffic from its intended destination, by preying on Internauts who make common typing errors."

The panel also noted that bad faith was further reinforced by the directing of traffic to a pornographic site and the past pattern of such activity by the defendant.

Internet Statutes and Contract Law

There are two uniform statutory laws, created in 1999, that govern the formation, performance, and enforcement of certain aspects of electronic contracts:

- UCITA (Uniform Computer Information Transactions Act of 1999) – regulates agreements to create, transfer, or license computer information and software.
- UETA (Uniform Electronic Transactions Act of 1999) – accords electronic signatures and electronic records the same status as written signatures and paper contracts.
- E-SIGN (Electronic Signatures in Global and National Commerce Act of 2000) upgrades UETA so that e-contracts cannot be denied legal enforceability because of electronic delivery or signatures, and so that electronic signatures can be legally notarized.

The first two statutes do not actually replace existing contract law and do not officially become the law of a state until formally adopted. (UCITA has been approved in 5 states, UETA in 38 states.)

But they nevertheless are guidelines that may be followed on a case-by-case basis, similar to the Restatement of Contracts and the UCC before it achieved statewide adoption. E-SIGN is a federal law that has nationwide application.

While they usually follow the common law or the UCC rules for offline contract transactions, the main differences in the Internet statutes are:

- Electronic acceptance of an offer is not effective until received – the reasonable medium rule is not applicable.
- Counteroffers are not effective against electronic agents' offers, which include voice mail and web page order systems. A contract is formed upon placing the basic order, and any additional conditions imposed are to be disregarded.
- Electronic records of a transaction may be clarified by prior dealings or trade usage and are not restricted by the parol evidence rule.
- Electronic records of a transaction are in compliance with the Statute of Frauds's writing and signing requirements.
- Transactions for $5,000 or more (and licenses for one year or more) must be electronically authenticated – less than the Statute of Frauds's dollar limit of $500 or more.
- Tender of performance of an electronic document occurs when it is available for download from the licensor's website.
- Unilateral electronic contracting mistakes do not bind the consumer if there is prompt notification to the other party of the error – contrary to the

non-cancellation of such offline contracts. But this does not apply to relieving consumers if the other party requires a click-on or similar method to confirm the order before it is finalized, and the consumer erroneously approves.

- Electronic self-help stated in the agreement can be used after fifteen days' prior notice in the event of a licensee breach in the usage or payment of licensed information or software, through the activation of embedded disabling commands.

    But if software is improperly disabled, the licensor may be liable for damages. The judicial remedies are mandatory in non-electronic commercial transactions.

- The statute of limitations for breach of a licensing agreement is one year from discovery, but not more than five years from the actual breach event – most UCC limitation periods are shorter.
- Warranties of non-infringement, non-interference, and informational accuracy apply to a license of informational rights – in addition to the implied warranties of non-electronic transactions.
- Disclaimer of electronic warranties is allowed by the licensor-seller if it specifies by individual name, or collectively by using the words, "as-is," "with all faults," or similar language.
- The licensor's breach of a software licensing agreement may be "cured" without the licensee's consent:

    1. Before expiration of time for contract performance
    2. After expiration, if completable within a reasonable time
    3. If completed before licensee cancels the contract

    Notice that (1) above is the same rule as the UCC, so long as the cure can be completed before the expiration date. (2) and (3) differ from the UCC cure after the required date that requires the buyer's permission whether or not the seller actually completes the cure.

- Licensee has the right to "cover" the licensor's breach by entering into a substitute electronic transaction, and recover as damages the value of the promised performance, or the difference between it and the cover cost – this is essentially the same protection as the UCC.

Click-Wrap/Shrink-Wrap Contracts

Computer software programs are an essential part of today's e-commerce. They have been created for most all aspects of everyday business and are customarily offered for sale and usage with a requirement that the customer first accept and agree to the terms of their licensing agreement.

When retail software is purchased and delivered, the licensing agreement is usually referred to on the exterior carton and enclosed with the software disks inside a plastic or cellophane package – a shrink-wrap license.

This license is also encoded on the software disks and scrolls out on the user's screen when the program is opened, requiring a mouse click on "I accept" before usage is allowed. The acceptance click creates the legal contract and "wraps" around all the terms, and the user is legally bound whether or not he has read or understood.

License agreements customarily include the common contract dispute clauses for (1) forum selection (where to sue), (2) choice of law (what rules that court must apply), (3) choice of remedy (arbitration rather than litigation), and (4) disclaimers of liability (no warranties or money damages).

Even if the user is able to add additional requests, instructions, or conditions, under UCITA they do not create a counteroffer, as would be the case under the UCC in non-electronic contracts.

All Terms in Shrink-Wrap Licenses Are Binding

In the case of *ProCD Inc. v. Zeidenberg, 86 F.3d 1447 (7th Cir. 1996)*, the plaintiff compiled information from more than 3,000 telephone directories into a computer database that it sold on CD-ROM. It spent considerable sums to create and maintain this product, which was sold at a high price to commercial users. It marketed a low-price version to the general public for personal, non-commercial usage only, as specified in the use restrictions encoded and detailed in its shrink-wrapped disks, which appeared on the computer screen every time the program ran.

"The database in SelectPhone (trademark) cost more than $10 million to compile and is expensive to keep current." The product package stated the software was subject to restrictions included in the enclosed license. The license terms were in the printed manual inside the product box as well as encoded on the disks.

The defendant bought the consumer product but then violated the restrictions by forming a company and reselling the information to the public on the Internet at a price below what the plaintiff charged its commercial customers. ProCD sought an injunction to prevent the illegal usage. Zeidenberg defended, saying he was not bound by the license since the product was sold to him without requiring his specific acceptance.

Analysis

"The 'shrinkwrap license' gets its name from the fact that retail software packages are covered in plastic or cellophane 'shrinkwrap,' and some vendors, though not ProCD, have written licenses that become effective as soon as the customer tears the wrapping from the package."

The court ruled in favor of the plaintiff, based upon principles of basic contract law, stating that the defendant's conduct in using the product knowing it was subject to some license restrictions bound him to its terms. This was acceptance by conduct.

The defendant's argument was rejected by the court, which mentioned by analogy other common purchases of consumer goods like computers, where the buyer makes the purchase, brings the merchandise home, and then reads the enclosed shrink-wrapped information for the first time.

"Transactions in which the exchange of money precedes the communication of detailed terms are common (insurance, airline tickets, concert tickets, drugs, consumer goods). To use the ticket is to accept the terms, even terms that in retrospect are disadvantageous . . . And that is what happened. ProCD proposed a contract that a buyer would accept by *using* the software after having an opportunity to read the license at leisure. This Zeidenberg did. He had no choice, because the software splashed the license on the screen and would not let him proceed without indicating acceptance."

Note that this case did not involve a click-wrap, "I accept" situation, and was decided pre-UCITA. Most computer software is now coded so that the opening of the program accesses a license agreement that must be scrolled from beginning to end and clicked on for acceptance before it will function. This is a more direct expression of acceptance of all the terms, and the user is bound. Read the terms, and if they are not acceptable, don't click your approval.

Defuse Replay

Let's update this case to post-UCITA, and change the facts to include a click-wrap acceptance feature that does not require the user to first scroll through all the terms. Under these modified facts, Zeidenberg could win, arguing that UCITA's requirement for these types of contracts that the user "manifest his assent" requires a *knowing acceptance of the terms*. He could argue that since the software seller allowed usage without scrolling through the terms, he never assented to them, and the seller had waived its rights. He could also claim that the "acceptance by conduct" rules for offline contracts were not applicable under UCITA.

Most Internet license disputes involving "click-wrap" and "shrink-wrap" licenses seem to uniformly enforce the agreements in question:

- A forum selection clause contained in the online subscriber contract of MSN was enforceable, where the plaintiffs clicked on the "I agree" prompt at the end of the scrolled agreement. *Caspi, et al v. Microsoft, 732 A.2d 528 (N.J. 1999)*
- The purchaser's use of the defendant's software, which contained a limitation of recoverable damages to only the purchase price, which was enclosed in a shrink-wrap license accompanying the software, was acceptance of the limitation and it was enforceable against the purchaser. *Mortenson v. Timberline Software Corporation, 998 P.2d 305 (Wash. 2000)*

The following recent case is, however, reminiscent of the ProCD Inc. case in its use of "browse-wrap" rather than "shrink-wrap" or "click-wrap" licenses, and its result favoring the customer.

In *Specht v. Netscape Communications Corp, 2002 WL 31166784 (2d Cir. 2002)*, the plaintiff and others sued Netscape and its parent company, America Online, Inc., alleging that usage of its free SmartDownload plug-in software transmits private information about the user's file transfer activity. The plaintiffs claimed this transmission, which included other downloads made from the Internet, violated federal laws, including the Electronic Communications Act and the Computer Fraud and Abuse Act.

The defendants moved to compel arbitration pursuant to a binding arbitration clause in their license agreement that also required the losing party to pay all court costs. They asserted that "the mere act of downloading" indicated assent, because the user was not required to click on or view the license to proceed.

The trial court ruled for the plaintiffs on the arbitration issue and the appellate court affirmed. It found the license to be more like a "browse-wrap" license, in which only an icon notice appears on the website for download, and this could be accomplished without viewing or even being aware of the existence of the license.

"Where consumers are urged to download free software at the immediate click of a button, a reference to the existence of license terms on a submerged screen is not sufficient to place consumers on inquiry or constructive notice of those terms.

"We disagree with the proposition that a reasonably prudent offeree in plaintiff's position would necessarily have known or learned of the existence of the SmartDownload license agreement prior to acting . . . Reasonably conspicuous notice of the existence of contract terms and unambiguous manifestation of assent to those terms by consumers is essential if electronic bargaining is to have integrity and credibility."

Notice how this ruling tracks the rationale we examined earlier in the chapter on contract acceptance regarding the "fine-print" cases.

Spam

Spam on the Internet has become a major problem. It is estimated that these bulk junk mails, generated by e-marketers through computer programs that randomly generate millions of e-mail addresses, now comprise over 50% of our daily e-messages. The problem has become so acute that three of the nation's largest e-mail account providers – AOL, MSN, and Yahoo – in response to complaints from their more than 200 million account holders, formed an alliance in April 2003 to try to develop technology to hunt down spammers and build evidence files of improper mailings that could be used to assist state and federal prosecutors.

They were criticized by anti-spam activists, who claimed they were part of the problem because of the ease with which spammers were able to use their systems as a platform for transmissions using their free e-mail services. The companies are trying to develop technical means to digitally mark spam mail so that it can be identified more readily by users and spam filters. A major part of the problem has been the lack of a visible distinction between legitimate e-mail messages and spam.

Microsoft chairman Bill Gates presented the annual address at the November 2003 Comdex technology convention and announced that his company would soon unveil beefed-up anti-spam software designed to:

(a) Weed out suspicious messages before delivery to in boxes by programs that run on back-end computer servers
(b) Help identify, separate, and delete junk mail through separate programs that run on individual PCs and laptops
(c) Boost security by blocking computer viruses

It did and is currently one of the most active litigants against illegal spammers.

Finally, state legislators became involved and created some anti-spam laws in response to the public outcry. The state laws place the burden of reducing spam directly upon the offenders. California's law is the first, effective January 1, 2004. It requires spammers to seek the permission of computer users to send them the e-mails (opt-in) and imposes sanctions that allow lawsuits for unwanted solicitations against violating spammers for $1,000 per unwanted e-mail up to a maximum recovery per spammer of $1 million. Delaware's law is similar. Utah's is even tougher, allowing consumers to sue for $25,000 for each day they receive unwanted spam. Virginia's law is also considered one of the most severe. It prohibits falsifying information that would allow bulk e-mailers to be identified, and sets felony numerical limits for spam volume. Almost thirty states have enacted anti-spam laws. Florida is one state that has not.

Federal legislation was also discussed and actively debated, culminating in the nation's first federal anti-spam law, called the "Can Spam Act of 2003," which was enacted December 16, 2003.

This legislation preempts state laws but is being criticized as not strong enough on spammers. It denies consumers the right to independently sue spammers, but allows suit by the FTC, state attorneys general, and Internet service providers. Spam is still allowed so long as the e-mails include a postal address for the sender and a working link for the recipient to opt out. It thus places upon the recipient the affirmative duty and laborious task of replying to each unwanted message with a request to be left alone. The law carries fines of $250 per e-mail violation with a cap of $2 million and a maximum five-year prison sentence.

But the law allows a "carve-out" for states with tougher laws to pursue criminal charges independently against spammers.

What do you think? If you were in charge of policy, how would you deal with the problem of spam?

Cookies

"Cookies" are used by website operators to gather personal information about their users. Often this information is shared for a fee with businesses interested in sending sales solicitations to these potential customers. The federal Electronic Communications Privacy Act (ECPA) was passed to prohibit this practice, except where the affected party consents.

In the recent case of *In re: Pharmatak, Inc., 329 F.3d 9 (1st Cir. 2003)*, drug companies invited users to their websites to learn about their products and obtain rebates, and Pharmatak sold the companies a service that accessed and collected this information so they could do intra-industry comparisons of website traffic. Pharmatak retained this information in its computers, and they were sued by the Internet users whose data was collected without prior consent.

After the trial court ruled against the plaintiffs, the appellate court reversed because, "Neither the drug companies nor the Internet users consented to the interception of private information."

Invasion of Privacy

Whether or not an employer commits an invasion of privacy by searching a worker's e-mails is a frequent legal problem. Some courts have decided these disputes in the employer's favor if the search was to monitor status of pending business matters, protect trade secrets, or otherwise serve a legitimate business purpose.

The employer-employee sensitivities in this area led to passage of the Electronic Communications Privacy Act, which bans "interception" of messages at the time of transmission, but otherwise allows the employer to dig through an employee's e-mails in computer storage.

It exempts the owner of the e-mail system from a claim of "illegal seizure" of stored e-mails, according to the recent case of *Fraser v. Nationwide Mutual Insurance Co., #01-2921 LEXIS 24856 (3rd Cir. 2003).*

In that case Fraser was terminated by Nationwide because he "blew the whistle" in letters to public agencies that alleged illegal conduct by his employer. When it learned of the letters, Nationwide was concerned Fraser might be revealing company secrets to its competitors and decided to search its main file server.

Fraser lost his claim for damages because there was no "live intercept" violation, and federal whistleblower laws only protect public, not private employees.

Personal Jurisdiction in Cyberspace

The filing of a lawsuit against a non-resident defendant invariably results in a motion to dismiss filed on grounds that the court lacks jurisdiction over the person of the defendant. This is especially true when the defendant is a corporation formed in a foreign state and doing business nationwide. Courts try to determine if there is a physical presence of some kind within the forum state.

If the defendant loses, it must incur the time, expense, and inconvenience of defending itself in a foreign court. Often this risk of non-local court jurisdiction will induce the defendant to settle on terms favorable to the plaintiff.

If, however, the motion is granted, and the plaintiff must bring suit in the defendant's home court, settlement will often occur in the defendant's favor.

The minimum contacts test of doing business that is used to determine if a non-resident defendant is subject to the jurisdiction of a local court is complicated when the business contacts involve a website presence in the state. Distinctions are made depending upon the type of business conducted:

- Active website – sales of goods are offered and can be completed online
- Partially active website – interactive usage with password access
- Passive website – the user is a viewer/listener of information content posted on a site with unlimited access

The more active the web presence in the state, the easier it is for a court to allow jurisdiction over the person of the defendant. Operating a website for profit, whether it be via direct sales or links to other websites, will subject the site owner to jurisdiction in the home state of a plaintiff-customer. However, there are still conflicting court decisions on these issues. Try to differentiate the following cases of Zippo and Bensusan.

In *Zippo Manufacturing Company v. Zippo Dot Com, Inc., 952 F.Supp 1119 (W.D.PA. 1997)*, the plaintiff-maker of the famous Zippo lighters was a Pennsylvania corporation that sued a California corporation protesting its sale of domain names using the word "zippo." Suit was filed in Pennsylvania, and the defendant argued that personal jurisdiction was lacking because they owned no property, had no employees, and maintained no physical presence in that state.

The court ruled that it had personal jurisdiction over the defendant, using a "sliding scale test" of the extent of contacts with Pennsylvania (active to passive) that resulted from the activities of the defendant.

It noted that "The likelihood that personal jurisdiction can be constitutionally exercised is directly proportionate to the nature and quality of commercial activity that an entity conducts over the Internet."

"At one end of the spectrum are situations where a defendant clearly does business over the Internet (personal jurisdiction granted) . . . At the opposite end are situations where a defendant has simply posted information on an Internet Web site which is accessible to users in foreign jurisdictions (personal jurisdiction denied) . . . The middle ground is occupied by interactive Web sites where a user can exchange information with the host computer. In these cases, the exercise of jurisdiction is determined by examining the level of interactivity and commercial nature of the exchange of information that occurs on the Web site."

In reaching its decision that the defendant was clearly operating an active website, the court noted, "It is undisputed that Dot Com contracted to supply Internet news services to approximately 3,000 Pennsylvania residents and also entered into agreements with seven Internet access providers in Pennsylvania."

The trend of the courts in offline and Internet cases is to confer jurisdiction under the "sufficient minimum contacts with the forum state test" with as little as a single significant advertising or sales contact within the state. As technology becomes more sophisticated, this problem can be minimized for Internet usage by the development of websites that will target a more localized customer base in particular selected locations, rather than the broader contacts currently in Cyberspace.

In *Bensusan Restaurant Corporation v. King & The Blue Note, 937 F.Supp. 295 (S.D.N.Y. 1996)*, the case involved two blues clubs that both used the name "The Blue Note." The defendant used it first in 1980 in Missouri when he opened his small club. The plaintiff used it in 1985 when it opened its much larger New York club and registered the name as a federal trademark. Both parties maintained websites.

The defendant's site was posted on a computer server in Missouri to promote his club. It had a disclaimer that stated, "The Blue Note's Cyberspot should not be confused with one of the world's finest jazz clubs, the Blue Note, located in the heart of New York's Greenwich Village." It also had a hyperlink to the New York site.

The plaintiff sued in New York for trademark infringement, and the defendant moved to dismiss for lack of personal jurisdiction. The trial court granted the defendant's motion, and the appellate court affirmed on the grounds that the defendant did not conduct business in New York.

"An act of infringement (if one existed) would have occurred in Missouri, not New York. The mere fact that a person can gain information on the allegedly infringing product is not the equivalent of a person advertising, promoting, selling or otherwise making an effort to target its product in New York.

"King, like numerous others, simply created a Web site and permitted anyone who could find it to access it. Creating a site, like placing a product into the stream of commerce, may be felt nationwide – or even worldwide – but, without more, it is not an act purposefully directed toward the forum state . . . There is in fact no suggestion that King has any presence of any kind in New York other than the Web site that can be accessed worldwide."

The court also distinguished the case of *Compuserve, Inc. v. Patterson, 89 F.3d 1257 (6th Cir. 1996)*, in which the court found personal jurisdiction proper in Ohio over an Internet user from Texas who subscribed to an Ohio-based network service.

The user had "reached out" from Texas by entering into a separate agreement with the Ohio service to sell his software over the Internet, and filled a number of orders there.

This personal jurisdiction test of being active in soliciting business was also used in *Minnesota v. Granite Gate Resorts, 568 N.W.2d 715 (Minn. App. 1997)*, where a Nevada Internet gaming company was subject to in personam jurisdiction in Minnesota in a lawsuit for consumer fraud. Its website claimed to "provide sports fans with a legal way to bet on sporting events from anywhere in the world, 24 hours a day!" and listed a toll-free phone number to call for information which, when accessed, confirmed to the caller that it was legal to place bets in Minnesota. The court ruled that the defendant's active solicitation of local consumers furnished sufficient minimum contacts for in personam jurisdiction.

Online Service Provider Liability

Companies providing Internet access to customers, such as AOL, Bell South, MSN, Juno, and the like, are financial "deep pockets." In the early days of the Internet, they were traditionally targeted by plaintiffs who alleged that defamatory statements, infringement of trademarks, and unlawful domain name use were legally attributed to the ISP that provided the information platform. The fact that the guilty parties could usually not be located in Cyberspace caused such vicarious claims to be numerous and potentially disastrous.

Congress responded in 1996 by passing the Communications Decency Act, to provide federal immunity from such lawsuits, and many states have enacted similar legislation. The act provides in section 230:

"No provider or user of an interactive computer service shall be treated as the publisher or speaker of any information provided by another information content provider."

Courts consider the ISPs to have a qualified privilege that protects them from liability, so long as they did not know of the offending transmissions.

Once a customer goes online, there is normally no control over message content, and therefore no corresponding liability.

Cases are still filed, however, seeking to impose ISP liability:

- Crank e-mail falsely attributed to the plaintiff is sent through the Prodigy e-mail server. The plaintiff's defamation suit is dismissed due to qualified privilege, with the court saying, "Just as the phone companies are not responsible for defamatory messages sent over phone lines, e-mail servers are not responsible for the content of messages they do not control." *Lunney v. Prodigy Services, Co., 683 N.Y.S.2d 557 (Sup.Ct.App.Div N.Y. 1998)*
- False message posted on AOL bulletin board advertising offensive Oklahoma City bombing t-shirts with the plaintiff's name and phone number. His suit was dismissed under the Communications Decency Act. *Zeran v. America Online, Inc., 129 F.3d 327 (4th Cir. 1997)*
- Negative comments about the plaintiff's books were posted on Amazon's site. Suit was dismissed under the act. *Schneicer v. Amazon.com, Inc., 31 P.3d 37 (Wash. App. 2001)*
- NSI, the main registrar of domain names, does not monitor them as to whether or not they infringe registered trademarks. The plaintiff contended that its registration of offending marks violated the Anticybersquatting Act of 1999. The suit was dismissed. Only the infringer is liable. *Lockheed Martin Corp. v. Network Solutions, Inc., 141 F.Supp.2d (N.D.Tex. 2001)*
- Gucci sued the offending website and its ISP for alleged trademark infringement. They had notified Mindspring on several occasions of the problem but it did nothing to stop the infringement. The court ruled the ISP was not protected by the act under these facts. *Gucci America, Inc. v. Hall & Associates, 2001 WL 253255 (S.D.N.Y. 2001)*
- The plaintiff's copyrighted clip art was posted on a website for free download. It sued the provider of the host computer for infringement. The court indicated that while the ISP could not be sued for direct or vicarious infringement, possible contributory infringement could be proven if the ISP had prior knowledge of the violation. *Marobie-FL, Inc. v. Nat'l. Assn. of Fire Equipment Distributors, 983 F.Supp. 1167 (N.D. Ill. 1997)*

The Future of Internet Law

We are only a few years into the era of litigating and legislating Cyberspace disputes. UCITA and UETA are being modified and updated by adopting states to reflect current disputes. More federal laws will be passed to address Internet issues. Input from other countries will result in their own versions of laws. Cases will be decided at all court levels to add layers of precedent to various concepts.

Many questions remain to be answered regarding Internet contracts and sales transactions, and how our traditional concepts of the law and the legal system will be changed by technology. These influences are being felt with ever-increasing frequency as more and more Cyberlaw disputes are being decided.

Some questions of practical daily importance to the consumer are:

- If licensed software is installed in the computer you sell, does its "no sale or transfer" restriction apply to you? Does it apply to the buyer? Does the software have to be removed from the desktop before sale?
- Do license restrictions apply to used software purchases? Is there a legal difference between offline retail purchases from computer stores or garage sale purchases and online website transactions?
- Can licensed material be copied or quoted for scholarly or academic purposes by the licensee, even though prohibited by terms of the license agreement?

Of broader application are the types of current cases, of which the following are a representative sample:

- State taxing authorities that are seeking increased revenue sources are now trying to tap into the Internet revenue stream by trying to collect use taxes from online sellers of goods that are delivered in their jurisdictions. The California Sales and Use Tax Department has claimed that Barnesandnoble.com's distribution of promotional coupons in California makes them a retailer engaged in business in the state, and therefore subject to use taxes. Barnes & Noble asserts they are advertising, not selling, and therefore not liable for the taxes. The dispute is pending.
- Alternate dispute resolution is strongly urged for Internet-related disputes. One option is to mediate a dispute online through the Online Ombuds Office. Another is negotiation through ClickNSettle or similar online companies.

  Insurance claims can be settled online through Cybersettle, the first company of this kind and the exclusive grantee of the Computerized Dispute Resolution System and Method Patent, through which over 475 insurance companies have settled over $80 million in claims in the last few years.
- Courts are adopting electronic case filing in civil matters to allow 24-hour access to case files from any location, remote document filing, immediate e-mail notification of case activity, and electronic service of court filings. Most courts are also creating their own websites.

  Once a judge designates that a case can be handled electronically, attorneys can file documents over the Internet and bring a diskette to the clerk's office for entry into the system. The public will have access to most of the systems, except for sealed documents. Criminal cases are currently excluded because of issues of privacy.

  Electronic data discovery (EDD) is the wave of the future in our technology-oriented business environment. More than 90% of documents produced since 1999 were created in digital form. Information technology specialists will be used to ease the burdens of production of documents and related factual discovery.

  Federal courts are beginning to install technology courtrooms where monitors, screens, and digitized evidence are projected to dramatically reduce the length and cost of trials. This project is expected to spread to state courtrooms and eventually be a modern way of conducting trials.

But critics point to "jammiesurfers," those nosey souls who could check out the details of divorces and other highly personal cases anonymously from their home desktop. The balancing of the public's right to access versus the litigant's right to privacy is still to be resolved.

- Under the Sarbanes-Oxley Act of 2002, the deadline for SEC filings of insider transaction has been reduced from forty to two business days, and all companies now have to electronically report.

- Mistrials are being sought in cases where jurors are doing Internet research on legal terminology and other factors involved in their lawsuits, contrary to the judge's instruction when he charges them with the law they are supposed to use in their deliberations. This is occurring in both civil and criminal cases.

  The traditional sanctions for juror misconduct, such as being held in contempt of court, are not easily applied because it is almost impossible to monitor their conduct outside the courtroom as a case progresses to its conclusion. Attorneys faced with an adverse verdict now routinely question the jurors about Internet usage.

- The Children's Internet Protection Act of 1999 allowed federal funding for computers and Internet access to be denied to all public and school libraries that fail to install "filtering" software to block sexually explicit websites. It is being legally tested with claims of various groups that it is so narrowly drawn that it violates First Amendment free speech because the filtering software currently available blocks a huge amount of protected material along with prohibited material. In 2001, the two funding programs governed by the law gave more than $200 million to public and school libraries for Internet access costs. The U.S. Supreme Court will hear arguments on the matter.

- The Federal Trade Commission's Mail or Telephone Order Merchandise Rule has been held to also apply to orders by computer. The rule spells out the ground rules for sellers of goods making promises about shipments, notifying customers about unexpected delays, and refunding consumers' money. Time for shipping must have a reasonable basis. If the shipping time is not specified, delivery must be made within thirty days. If that time cannot be met, the customer must be promptly notified and given the opportunity to cancel and receive a full refund. For delays up to thirty days, the customer's silence is consent, but for longer delays the customer's consent is required. If orders can't be filled in a timely manner, the seller may cancel if the customer is promptly notified and given a refund.

- The sending of unsolicited advertising faxes and unsolicited prerecorded phone advertisements, both of which violate the Telephone Consumer Protection Act of 1991, are increasingly being monitored and numerous lawsuits have been filed to claim allowable statutory damages.

Overview

The initial phase of Internet Law growth that started in the early 1990's was marked by frenzied activity of legislators and courts to update the legal system to the needs and potentialities of this new age of information technology and online business, as well as its perils and pitfalls.

The Internet became a new frontier for personal and business usage. The idea that instantaneous global communication and transactional activity was available for everyone, easy and effective, free of charge, did not require anyone's permission, and was free of governmental regulation was Utopia!

But like all such concepts, this global and unified sovereignty has now entered a much more problematical phase after fifteen to twenty years of unprecedented enthusiasm and rapid growth.

There is a growing concern that the Internet may fragment into separate cyberspace universes that divide along commercial and territorial boundaries.

Its early success as a unifying open source environment may now lead to commercial border wars between governments, big business, and the public. Here are a few potential problem areas:

A. Government enforcement of their own digital sovereignty, like the great online firewall of China that attempts to censor its citizen's usage of search engines and erect cyber borders.

B. Countries that start their own Domain Name Systems to locate, identify and control what their citizens can see.

C. IP numbers that are manipulated by using scripts other than the original Latin alphabet to nationalize available Internet content.

D. Social networking systems, like Facebook and other semi-open platforms, that are Cyber–Universes with their own membership and usage rules, regulations, and enforcement procedures.

E. Apple has created its own controlled high technology World with its generations of iDevices, as well as its platform of thousands of company controlled Apps. Google and Amazon are not far behind in doing the same, as well as in the rapid growth of online advertising and "cloud" platforms.

F. Dynamic growth in mobile device, android, and smart phone platforms.

G. Internet neutrality rules to be established by the Federal Communication Commission and tested in the courts as to whether broadband companies may charge for faster delivery of content with pay-for-priority transactions.

Discussion Exercises

1. Discuss the five main areas of your company's Internet usage.

2. Discuss the amount of time you spend daily in Cyberspace.

3. Discuss the types of purchases or sales you and your company have made on the Internet and any business law problems you have encountered.

4. Discuss the consumer liability rules you would create for click-wrap, shrink-wrap, and browse-wrap software licenses.

5. How would you deal with the problems of spam and cookies?

6. What rules would you create for personal jurisdiction in Internet disputes?

7. What areas of Internet law do you think will be created, enlarged, or reduced?

CHAPTER 6

HOW THE LEGAL SYSTEM WORKS

A.   THE PURPOSE OF LAWS

"We are a government of laws, and not of men."

—John Adams

*"Laws are generally found to be nets of such a texture, as the little creep through,
the great break through, and the middle-sized are alone entangled in."*

—William Shenstone

Laws Provide Our Framework of Society

Laws are the rules of conduct that govern our everyday lives. They tell us what we can and cannot do. They set the permissible boundaries of our individual, corporate, and governmental behavior.

Every day there are literally hundreds of them we obey and hundreds that we disobey, some with full knowledge of their existence, many others in ignorance until after the fact. The threat of enforcement of laws and the consequence of violating them is one of the threads that hold the fabric of our society together.

Many laws act as a deterrent to criminal behavior. "If you can't do the time, don't do the crime," says the jailhouse adage.

Equally as many laws deter personal or corporate civil misconduct. If one's private actions or non-actions violate certain laws, one's behavior may be adapted accordingly due to our judicial system. If a large company is inclined to abuse its powers of size, influence, and financial strength, it may refrain due in large part to the possibility of lawsuits that protect and compensate the affected parties with large damage awards.

The contracts and sales laws of the commercial marketplace are the heart of transactional business:

- The parties make an agreement to buy or sell goods or services
- One party believes it made a bad business deal and seeks a way to legally be excused from having to perform
- The other party believes it made a good business deal and seeks to legally enforce the agreement
- This dispute is ultimately resolved based upon the governing rules of law

If the game is baseball or basketball, soccer or squash, we can't be skilled players unless we know the rules of the game.

The same applies to the game of business. Knowledge of the laws helps us to plan proposed transactions, evaluate their advantages and disadvantages, consider alternate courses of action, negotiate terms, and avoid disputes. If disputes do occur, the laws assist in predicting their probable outcome and provide a basis to negotiate compromises. In totality, they provide the framework of acceptable conduct in both personal and business interactions.

Laws Help to Predict the Outcome of Disputes

Since life in our busy world invariably leads to disputes of one kind or another, some being simple misunderstandings and others having more far-reaching legal implications – it would be very helpful to be able to predict their probable outcome.

We are not talking about something so imprecise as intuition or psychic skills. Our laws, whether they be legislative statutes, judicial court decisions, or executive orders, are created as a result of disputes of one kind or another that have ripened into lawsuits, or raised sufficient public attention to be the subject of laws passed by our political bodies to help protect our perceived health, safety, and general welfare.

The past is the best predictor of the future. When a new dispute arises, judges look to prior cases, legislative enactments, administrative orders, or other sources of law to guide them. We can do the same thing in evaluating a current dispute and making our best management decisions.

For some disputes, the available authorities are so clear and pervasive that an answer can be stated with reasonable assurance. For others, the law on the subject may be confused or inconsistent. For some disputes, the situations are so novel and unique that no governing laws exist. This sliding scale of predictability leads us into another aspect of laws – their ability to change to meet necessary challenges.

In *American Heart Association, et al v. County of Greenville, 489 S.E.2d 921 (Sup. Ct. S.C. 1997)*, the dispute involved conflicting claims of ownership to the will of the infamous "Shoeless Joe Jackson," a member of the Chicago "Black" Sox baseball team accused of throwing the 1919 World Series. The original will contained a rare example of his original signature, worth approximately $100,000 to autograph collectors.

That will was in possession of his wife until she died in 1959, when it was filed with the defendant as required by law as a part of the probate of her estate. Her will devised it to the plaintiff charities. They and the defendant brought a declaratory judgment action to determine legal ownership of the will document.

The trial court granted summary judgment declaring the defendant owner of the original will, and the decision was affirmed on appeal.

The plaintiffs asserted, "A will is a person's personal property since individuals may during their lifetime own, possess, use, enjoy, and dispose of their will any way they see fit and upon death, the will becomes part of one's estate, passing directly to the personal representative."

The courts disagreed. "The trial court ruled that the Jackson will is a public record and must remain in the care, custody and control of the Probate Court . . . original wills, which are required by state law to be filed with the Probate court, constitute 'public records.' . . . the probate code neither intends nor provides that the deliverer of a will, even if a devisee under it, gain ownership in the actual document."

Laws Change to Meet Changing Social Conditions

"If our existing case law is inadequate to accommodate the business transactions made in today's business world, and if, as the Court's opinion concedes, our law is not in accord with that in a majority of jurisdictions, it simply does not do to continue to decide 1980 controversies based on what in 1912 was thought to be the better law to follow." *Hoffman v. S V Company, Inc., 628 P.2d 218 (Idaho 1981)*

Contrary to the layperson's view of the law, it is flexible and in a constant state of flux on a delayed basis, as it tries to respond to the ever-changing needs of society. The process of change is slow, but sure. Once a certain critical mass of events is reached, combined with media attention and public outcry, the wheels of change begin to turn and eventually a landmark case or legislative enactment occurs that completes the process.

We have seen this happen in landmark cases such as *Brown v. Board of Education of Topeka, 347 U.S. 483 (1954)* (school integration), *Bakke v. Regents of the University of California, 483 U.S. 265 (1978)* (reverse discrimination), *Roe v. Wade, 410 U.S. 113 (1973)* (abortion rights), and *Miranda v. Arizona, 384 U.S. 436 (1966)* (right to criminal counsel).

We have seen it happen in laws passed to abolish slavery, grant women the right to vote, prohibit child labor and unsafe working conditions, end discrimination and job harassment, establish a minimum wage, grant social security, provide social assistance such as medicare and medicaid, assist the consumer, protect the environment, and so on.

We have also seen the pendulum swing back and forth. Alcohol sale and consumption was prohibited by the Volstead Act and 18th Amendment on moral and religious grounds.

It was then repealed by the 21st Amendment when the growth of organized crime and the public's thirst combined to end that experiment in legislating morality. "Right to Life" versus "Pro-Choice" signals the uncertain legal future of abortion. Muhammad Ali was a "draft-dodger" in the eyes of the law when he refused to serve in the Vietnam War, and then was later considered a hero for his courage in opposing it.

Our immigration laws, which at the turn of the century resulted in populating many of the major industrial areas of the country with a work force, were ostensibly passed in the spirit of freedom and liberty. But some had originally been passed as exclusionary protection against certain "undesirables." These laws are still in a state of flux, depending upon where local pressures exist.

We have seen our laws change recently in the evolution of lawsuits for money damages by cigarette smokers against tobacco companies.

For many years these lawsuits were routinely dismissed at the trial court level. The U.S. Supreme Court routinely affirmed the lower court rulings on appeal by a unanimous 9-0 vote. Gradually similar cases were heard where the tobacco companies prevailed, but the votes began to change as some justices wrote dissenting opinions.

Then a lifelong smoker, who began smoking as a teenager before mandatory health warnings and continued until her diagnosis of terminal lung cancer, brought a lawsuit. She claimed her permanent injuries were caused by a combination of the defendant's deceptive advertising, fraudulent concealment of health risks, and their industry-wide conspiracy to "hook" smokers and maintain their nicotine addiction.

That landmark 1992 case, styled *Cipollone v. Liggett Group, Inc., 505 U.S. 504 (1992)*, was heard by the U.S. Supreme Court after it slowly traveled the trial court-appellate court route, with majority opinions in favor of the defendant and dissenting opinions in favor of the plaintiff, until the Court ruled for the first time that the Federal Cigarette Labeling Act did not bar such lawsuits against tobacco companies.

Following *Cipollone*, more and more lawsuits were heard by trial courts around the country, and eventually juries began to enter large damage awards against the defendants in both individual actions and the much larger class actions filed on behalf of smokers within a particular state or nationwide. The law in this area had come full cycle from no recovery to full recovery, with most plaintiffs' verdicts carrying hefty awards of punitive damages, as mentioned in the chapter on remedies.

But the law in this area continued to evolve as states successfully sued the tobacco companies and recovered hundreds of millions of dollars in settlements for the large sums they were forced to pay to medicare and medicaid patients suffering from smoking-related ailments.

Success in these typical cigarette smoker cases then led to class action litigation on behalf of flight attendants for damages caused by direct and secondhand smoke. Now, another type of tobacco lawsuit is being filed on behalf of users of smokeless tobacco products, based upon the same arguments that proved successful in the tobacco smoking cases – concealing smoking dangers, failing to warn consumers of true risks, and manipulating nicotine levels to make the products more addictive.

Once the tobacco company litigation began to emerge as a viable plaintiff's source of recovery, similar lawsuits were filed as test cases against alcohol manufacturers and sellers for a variety of alcohol-related personal injuries, as well as the same type of Medicare and Medicaid reimbursements requested in the tobacco cases.

The results were different, however, with few if any recoveries allowed. While similarities between alcohol and tobacco exist in that neither activity is prohibited by law, there are far less instances in the alcohol cases of corporate misconduct such as misleading advertising, hidden data on harmful effects to health and safety, and enhancements of addictive contents of the products.

Another area of litigation that followed the tobacco cases was lawsuits against manufacturers and distributors of inexpensive small handguns known as "Saturday Night Specials," on the theory that there was a link of negligence liability between the proliferation of their availability and the resulting violence in their usage that resulted in damage to the public.

The gun companies made the same arguments about lawful sale, but ingenious counterarguments were made by the plaintiffs that the defendants were "negligent" in their failure to properly safeguard the guns against intended or accidental usage by minors, and in allowing such cheap, easily concealable weapons to be available.

Such arguments did not lead to any successful court cases, but created enough congressional pressure to result in many of the largest gun manufacturers voluntarily agreeing to create and provide gun-locking devices so that handguns legally in one's home for protection could be protected against accidental or unauthorized use by juveniles and intruders.

A new trend in the gun cases may now be emerging due to the recent unreported West Palm Beach, Florida, court case of *Grunow v. Valor Corp.*

In this case, for the first time in U.S. judicial history, a jury found a major handgun distributor contributorily negligent for 5% of the damages suffered when a thirteen-year-old boy took one of their small guns, manufactured without a safety mechanism, from a family friend to his high school and shot and killed one of his teachers. The widow brought a wrongful death action that named the gun distributor as one of the defendants.

The jury verdict in *Grunow* was subsequently overturned, but additional test cases will no doubt be filed to test the judicial limits of recovery in the gun cases.

Our society has always been preoccupied with physical appearance, and court disputes have inevitably followed. In the late 1800s, the "full figure" was considered attractive and healthful. We have now come full circle, from "big is beautiful" to "thin is in." But more people than ever suffer from obesity and its related ailments, burdening individual and governmental pocketbooks. We are a fast-food, sugarholic society.

This is now reflected in obesity lawsuits being filed against deep-pocket fast food chains like McDonald's and Burger King. Though few survived early dismissal, large dollar settlements have been recently announced based on allegations of false advertising of fat content of foods sold and other deceptive trade practices. Like the gun cases, a litigation trend may emerge.

Another drastic change has occurred in how lawyers may attract new business. Every state has statutory provisions that disallow improper solicitation. Advertising of any kind by lawyers was strictly prohibited. Terms like "ambulance chasing" have crept into our vocabulary to signify unlawful conduct by lawyers or their agents, who sought to sign up new clients, literally while they were being treated for their personal injuries. There were also common law protective doctrines to prevent abusive attorney-client practices.

Then the tables turned when lawyers were allowed to advertise, subsequent to the landmark case of *Bates v. State Bar of Arizona, 433 U.S. 350 (1977).* In the years that have elapsed since that decision, lawyer advertising is now the norm rather than the exception. Lawyers and law firms, large and small, have now remade themselves as service industries to meet increased competition and make fees affordable. Larger firms, innovations such as isolated tasks done by lower-paid assistants, standardized forms, office automation, and increased use of technology have all become a part of this revolution.

In *Saladini v. Righellis, 687 N.E.2d 1224 (Mass. 1997),* the Massachusetts Supreme Court recognized this new trend, and struck down the old common law rules of champerty (selling an interest in a lawsuit) and barratry (bringing frivolous lawsuits), leaving it up to judges in individual cases to determine the fairness of contractual payment arrangements made to finance litigation.

Sometimes events, such as the death of the Lindbergh baby in the 1930s, cause a legislative or judicial response, and new laws result. That particular event resulted in federal kidnapping laws. The explosion of a Union Carbide chemical plant in Bhopal, the Three Mile Island Nuclear disaster, and the Exxon Valdez oil spill led to stronger rules to protect the environment. The Justice Clarence Thomas judicial confirmation hearings raised the national sensitivity to workplace sexual harassment. The accounting scandals at Enron and World Com will lead to greater corporate accountability. Our society often cannot know where legal protection is needed until situations arise which make such needs evident.

Laws Try to Achieve a Balance of Fairness

Contrary to popular belief, in addition to hundreds of general laws that govern our personal and business relationships, there are just as many exceptions to these rules designed to prevent one party from taking unfair advantage of the other. Visualize the scales of justice. They appear as the governing image in courtrooms throughout the land. Their motto is, "We who labor here seek only truth." It is usually achieved by the presentation of conflicting points of view. Our legal system tries to achieve this balance.

In *Flagiello v. Pennsylvania Hospital, 208 A.2d 193 (Pa. 1965)*, the plaintiff was injured in a fall that broke her ankle while she was a patient at the defendant's non-profit hospital for an unrelated ailment.

She claimed the the defendant was negligent, and sued for money damages. The defendant claimed that the legal rule of charitable immunity established in prior cases insulated it from liability. After the trial court granted judgment based on this general rule of law, the Supreme Court reversed, citing the following fundamental rule of legal fairness:

> "From the earliest days of organized society it became apparent to man that society could never become a success unless the collectivity of mankind guaranteed to every member of society a remedy for a palpable wrong inflicted on him by another member of that society."

Our legal system is based upon a system of checks and balances. The plaintiff and the defendant have a dispute. They both determine their legal rights by consulting a lawyer, who researches the sources of law and evaluates their respective positions. Let us assume they both believe they are right, are unable to mutually settle their differences, and the dispute becomes a lawsuit. Both sides are bound by the same sets of rules for when to sue, where to sue, and how to sue.

Even the conduct of a lawsuit resembles a pendulum as the parties alternate in their trial presentations. The plaintiff files complaint, the defendant answers, both sides discover all surrounding facts and circumstances. If either party objects to anything, the other presents counterarguments. The plaintiff presents its case, and then the defendant does the same. They may cross-examine each other. They argue their cases to the jury, first the plaintiff and then the defendant. Point-counterpoint.

Both sides request a decision in their favor. But it is an adversarial process, and there can only be one winner. When the trial court decision is rendered, the loser has the right to appeal. Again, point-counterpoint. Ultimately a point of finality is reached. In the process, both sides have been allowed a full presentation of their conflicting positions.

Our governmental structure is also based upon checks and balances. The framers of our Constitution implemented the scales of justice concept by devising the structure of our government. The executive branch cannot usually do anything without the advice and consent of Congress. Congress cannot usually legislate unless both the House and Senate concur. The lower court decisions are subject to review by higher courts until one final decision is made.

We have two judicial systems operating simultaneously to cover the wide spectrum of human and business relationships: criminal law and civil law.

Criminal laws are offenses against society, and are enforced by the governmental authority. Sanctions may be warnings, license suspensions, fines, probation, imprisonment, and loss of life.

The more serious the offense, the more severe the penalty. The criminal law system acts as a deterrent to criminal conduct, assuming we know the rules and don't break them, and also keeps the peace by enforcing with appropriate judicial action those laws that are broken.

Notice these ten significant characteristics of the criminal law system:

- Cases are heard in separate criminal courts
- The state or other governing authority is the complainant
- The party who violated the law is the defendant
- If there is an injured party, he may be a witness, but not one of the main parties to the proceeding
- The defendant is not required to testify due to our constitutional privilege against self-incrimination
- Jury decisions are called verdicts, and must be unanimous decisions of guilty or not guilty. Otherwise there is a hung jury and the case will either be retried or the defendant will be acquitted
- Criminal juries are usually nine to twelve persons
- The state may not appeal a verdict in favor of the defendant
- The state must prove its case "beyond and to the exclusion of every reasonable doubt"
- If the state wins its case, the guilty defendant may face imprisonment

Civil laws are the rules of conduct that relate to all areas other than criminal matters, and they govern commercial business transactions. The usual legal remedy in a civil action is money damages. They may include many different kinds of monetary recovery, including actual losses (compensatory), projected losses (consequential), special aspects of personal injury cases (pain and suffering, mental anguish, and loss of consortium), and monetary punishment of a defendant to deter egregious conduct (punitive).

There are also non-monetary remedies available in appropriate cases. The most common are specific performance (the defendant is required to honor his contract to sell you his unique one-of-a-kind painting), injunctive relief (the defendant is legally restrained from a specific unlawful act, such as stalking a former spouse), child custody, and adoption.

Notice these ten significant differences of the civil law system:

- The disputes are between private parties
- The complaining party, called the plaintiff, sues the defendant
- The plaintiff may file a civil lawsuit without an attorney
- The defendant can be interrogated and must testify at trial
- The defendant must provide full discovery of material information, including pertinent documents, experts reports, and lists of witnesses
- Cases may be decided by the judge alone or be heard by a jury. Either party may request a jury trial. The jury's decision is called a judgment, and need not be unanimous.
- Most civil juries consist of six persons
- In most cases, the losing party has the right to appeal the adverse decision
- The plaintiff's burden of proof is much less than in a criminal case. It must prove its case "by the greater weight of the evidence"
- The winning plaintiff usually recovers money damages from the defendant and can collect them, if not voluntarily paid, by having the court seize the defendant's assets and sell them at public sale

One of the most graphic examples of the differences between the criminal and civil law systems was the O.J. Simpson legal drama that took place in 1999. In *State of California v. Simpson*, he was acquitted by a jury of murdering his former wife, Nicole, and her friend, Ron Goldman. In *Goldman v. Simpson*, he was ruled responsible by the jury for the wrongful death of Ron Goldman and liable for money damages, under the same facts.

The identical facts of each case produced different results due to the basic differences between the two legal systems under which they were presented.

Laws Solve Problems in Different Ways

Strict constructionists are judges who exercise judicial restraint and won't change laws on their own, even if they think they are bad laws. They take a narrow view of their role in the legal system. They refuse to function as legislators.

Judicial activists do not wait for what they consider bad laws to be repealed or good laws passed, and sometimes attempt to meet the current needs of the culture with their court decisions. Their decisions may even rewrite statutory laws that they feel no longer serve the needs of society.

In *Flood v. Kuhn, 407 U.S. 258 (1971)*, the major league baseball player Curt Flood challenged professional baseball's reserve clause, which considered players to be the property of their ball clubs and allowed them to be traded from one club to another without their consent. He claimed this violated federal antitrust laws in that it restricted fair competition, and sought a ruling overturning the long-established antitrust exemption for baseball. He demanded to be made a free agent to make his own bargain with any other team of his choice.

The high court ruled against him, as it had in other cases brought over the years. Justice Blackmun said, "In view of all this, it seems appropriate now to say that with its reserve system enjoying exemption from federal antitrust laws, baseball is, in a very distinct sense, an exception and an anomaly . . . And what the Court said (in 1922), and what it said (in 1953), we say again here in 1972: the remedy, if any is indicated, is for congressional, and not judicial, action."

Interestingly, as a result of this case and the refusal of the Court to allow free agency, the baseball players's labor union ultimately won this right in its collective bargaining agreement, resulting in the huge salaries baseball players receive today. This, in turn, has led to more labor turmoil and another assault on baseball's antitrust exemption as the baseball owners claim they cannot operate profitably, threaten contraction of certain small market teams, and seek to implement a salary cap on the players.

In *Kreimer v. Bureau of Police, 765 F.Supp. 181 (N.J. Dist. 1991)*, a homeless person was ejected and barred from a local public library because of its policy of nuisance exclusion based upon "annoyance of other persons" or "offensive personal hygiene." The policy also stated that patrons who are not actively "using library materials shall be asked to leave the building."

In holding this library policy unconstitutional, Judge Sarokin took a judicial stance of social consciousness in saying, "Society has survived not banning books which it finds offensive from its libraries; it will survive not banning persons whom it likewise finds offensive from its libraries. The greatness of our country lies in tolerating speech with which we do not agree; the same toleration must extend to people, particularly where the cause of revulsion may be of our own making. If we wish to shield our eyes and noses from the homeless, we should revoke their condition, not their library cards."

In *Bush v. Gore, 531 U.S. 98 (2000)*, the 2000 presidential election brought into play both strict construction of the federal Constitution by the five majority justices and the attempt to mold a fairness remedy to a unique problem by the four dissenting justices.

The presidential election held November 7, 2000, resulted in an unprecedented constitutional crisis. Mr. Gore won the popular vote. But under our laws, presidents are elected by a majority of the electoral votes apportioned to each state. The winner of the election hinged on the Florida vote. Mr. Bush had an original victory margin of 1,784 votes, which was later reduced by machine and manual recounts to a winning of 537 votes, which was certified by Florida's secretary of state as required by law.

Mr. Gore contested the results and demanded a full manual recount, based upon various allegations of error and impropriety. At Mr. Bush's request, the U.S. Supreme Court agreed to consider the situation. The Florida Supreme Court twice invoked its equitable powers to create a remedy to meet this unique problem, and sided with Mr. Gore by requiring the counting of various previously identified votes, a manual recount of other undervotes, and "such other orders as were necessary to add any legal votes to the total statewide certifications."

The U.S. Supreme Court reversed the Florida Supreme Court by a 5-4 vote, and Mr. Bush was officially declared president. The majority ruled that any recount would be unconstitutional because it violated the equal protection clause of the federal Constitution's 14th Amendment. Their ruling stated, " . . . there was no recount procedure in place (under the Florida ruling) that comported with minimal standards required under the Fourteenth Amendment . . . for the recount could not be conducted in compliance (with the 14th Amendment) without substantial additional work." This represents an example of the "strict construction" aspect of the judicial restraint approach.

The dissenters argued that "This was not an occasion which required federal judicial intervention in a state election." They were also concerned that the majority's "concern about the December 12 deadline was misplaced, and (the majority's conclusion that) a constitutionally adequate recount was impractical was a prophecy which the Court's own judgment would not allow to be tested."

Rather than being concerned with what was technically incorrect, inconvenient, or impractical, the dissenters focused on the fact that "Under the very special circumstances of the case at hand, basic principles of fairness might have counseled adoption of a uniform and specific standard to guide the manual recount ordered by the Florida Supreme Court."

The dissenters, as well as the Florida Supreme Court, followed a judicial activism approach to try and solve the unique problem facing them.

Discussion Exercises

1. Discuss any other situations where laws may provide a societal framework.

2. Discuss any other situations where laws may help predict the outcome of disputes.

3. Discuss any other situations where laws were created to meet changing social conditions.

4. Discuss any other situations where laws try to balance fairness.

5. Discuss how laws may impact your business marketplace to:

- Encourage existing business activity

- Restrict existing business activity

- Create new business opportunities

Case Exercise 1

John Lennon's Long and Winding Road to Stay in the U.S.

Lennon v. INS, 527 F.2d 187 (1975), tells this story. In 1968 police officers from Scotland Yard made a warantless search of John Lennon's London apartment, found one-half ounce of hashish, and placed him under arrest. He claimed he was unaware of its presence, but pleaded guilty to possession of cannabis resin and was fined 150 pounds.

In 1971, John and his wife Yoko arrived in the U.S. to seek custody of his daughter by a former marriage to a U.S. citizen. Since his conviction rendered him excludable under the U.S. Immigration Act ("any alien who has been convicted of . . . any law or regulation relating to the illicit possession of . . . marijuana"), he and his wife were issued temporary visas. Under the law, when the visa expired they were required to leave the U.S. or face deportation.

When the visa expired, the INS notified the Lennons that they had to leave the country. They applied for and received 3rd preference immigrant visas, which are given to "qualified immigrants who . . . because of their exceptional ability in the sciences or the arts will substantially benefit prospectively the national economy, cultural interests, or welfare of the United States." This status was a prerequisite to petitioning for permanent residency.

Deportation hearings were held by INS, and ten days after approval of their immigrant status, the Lennons applied for permanent residence.

Yoko Ono's petition was granted because she had previously gained permanent residence status in 1964 while married to her first husband, but John Lennon's was denied and he was ordered deported.

Analysis

The order of the immigration judge was based upon the belief that Lennon's 1968 conviction made him excludable under the Immigration Act, and was upheld by the Board of Immigration Appeals.

The board conceded that the Immigration Act "does not exclude aliens convicted of possession under laws which make knowledge immaterial to the offense."

However, they concluded that "A person who was entirely unaware that he possessed any illicit substance would not have been convicted under the British Dangerous Drugs Act."

Lennon argued that he was not excludable because "He had not been convicted of violating a law forbidding *illicit* possession." He urged that, under British law, guilty knowledge was not an element of the offense, and therefore his possession could not have been illicit.

That act states, "A person shall not be in possession of a drug unless . . . authorized."

The U.S. Court of Appeals ruled in favor of Lennon, agreeing with his contention that the British law made guilty knowledge irrelevant. They said:

"Under British law, a person found with tablets which he reasonably believed were aspirin would be convicted if the tablets proved to be heroin. And a man given a sealed package filled with heroin would, if he had any opportunity to open the parcel, suffer the same fate – even if he firmly believed the package contained perfume."

The court also noted that the purpose of the Immigration Act's exclusionary clause was to bar undesirable aliens.

"There is also, we note, some indication that Congress, in enacting (the Law) was far more concerned with the trafficker of drugs than with the possessor."

There was a dissenting opinion that suggested the Immigration Act's exclusionary language was very clear in that it would, "exclude any alien who has been convicted of a violation of any law or regulation relating to the illicit possession of narcotic drugs or marijuana."

"Since the statute applies to any alien, it makes no difference whether he be John Lennon, John Doe or Johann Sebastian Bach.

"The undisputed fact, however is that Lennon did plead guilty to the possession of cannabis resin, and while this may have been convenient or expedient because of his wife's pregnancy and his disinclination to have her testify in court, it is elementary that we cannot go behind the plea."

Defuse Replay

The majority decision brought into its reasoning many factors outside the limited issue of comparing the wording of the British and U.S. laws that seemed to justify their ruling as being the right and proper thing to do.

They noted after reviewing INS records of over 1,800 deportable aliens against whom no proceedings had been instituted that "Many aliens granted such status had criminal records far more serious than Lennon's. Some were convicted of murder or rape, and one was described in his file as 'an admitted heroin addict' who was reputedly on of the largest suppliers of marijuana and narcotics in the area."

They also took note of Lennon's argument that he was being singled out for deportation because the INS "instituted deportation proceedings because they feared he might participate in demonstrations that would be highly embarrassing to the then-existing administration."

The dissenting opinion refused to consider any such matters they deemed extraneous to the real issue at hand, that Lennon was an alien convicted by his own guilty plea of possessing a banned substance. The argument that the U.S. law required criminal intent and the British law did not was disregarded.

"It is the unusual case where contraband such as this is surreptitiously planted in one's reticule or blue jeans pocket. Yet by disregarding convictions under the British Statute or any other foreign counterpart, the majority would admit to the United States those who knowingly possessed any illicit drugs."

Conclusion

This case is a fine example of the different points of view involved in judicial activism (majority opinion) and judicial restraint (dissenting opinion).

The majority goes outside the narrow confines of the legal issue before it to recommend changes in the immigration laws and their interpretation, and in effect attempts to rewrite certain provisions.

The minority takes a more rigid view of strict construction to maintain the separation between the functions of the judicial and legislative branches of government and refuses to bend or modify the existing law.

The majority also considered social justice and how our immigration laws should be viewed under current times:

"We have come a long way from the days when fear and prejudice toward alien races were the guiding forces behind our immigration laws . . . Deportation is not, of course, a penal sanction. But in severity it surpasses all but the most Draconian criminal penalties. We therefore cannot deem wholly irrelevant the long unbroken tradition of the criminal law that harsh sanctions should not be imposed where moral culpability is lacking."

"The excludable aliens statute is but an exception, albeit necessary, to the traditional tolerance of a nation founded and built by immigrants. If, in our two hundred years of independence, we have in some measure realized our ideals, it is in large part because we have always found a place for those committed to the spirit of liberty and willing to help implement it. Lennon's four-year battle to remain in our country is testimony to his faith in this American dream."

A. Do you agree with the court's final decision?

B. How do you think a current court would rule on this dispute after the terrorist attacks of September 11, 2001?

C. What changes in our immigration laws, if any, do you think are currently necessary?

D. Discuss what part, if any, you believe Lennon's substantial financial resources played in permitting him to maintain the four-year legal proceedings and to ultimately prevail.

Case Exercise 2

"Modern Vulgarism" Undercuts Sexual Harassment Laws

In *Breda v. Wolf Camera, 222 F.3d 890 (11th Cir. 2002)*, the plaintiff was hired as a full-time sales associate in the defendant's camera and film store in Savannah, Georgia. She alleged that she was subjected to sexual harassment throughout her employment and resigned approximately fourteen months later.

She then filed suit under Title VII of the Civil Rights Act, claiming her employer knew or should have known of the harassment, and failed, as required by law, to take remedial action.

The defendant had a clear and established policy regarding suspected harassment that stated, "Anyone who believes that he or she is being subjected to harassment or who has witnessed such harassment must immediately notify his or her manager."

The plaintiff followed this procedure and complained on at least four or five occasions to her store manager of the conduct of a fellow employee. The manager insisted her complaints did not constitute sexual harassment, but were "only general animosity between co-workers."

The trial court granted summary judgment to the employer, which was reversed on appeal (222 F.3d 886) and remanded back to the trial court, "to allow the district court to resolve factual disputes regarding the timing, extent, and nature of Appellant's complaints."

The behavior complained of by the plaintiff included allegations that her co-workers used sexual epithets and obscenities, waited for her outside the restroom and berated her for taking so long, told her that she made sales because male customers wanted to have sex with her, and used the store's telephoto lenses to ogle her.

Analysis

The trial court, after the remand, ruled again in favor of the employer and dismissed the plaintiff's complaint, basing its ruling in part on the view that the conduct complained of was not sufficiently severe to violate her civil rights.

"The modern notion of acceptable behavior – as corroded by instant-gratification driven cultural influences (e.g. lewd music, videos and computer games, perversity-programming broadcast standards, White House internal affairs and perjurious coverups of same, etc.) has been coarsening over time . . .

"Today, a victim may have to accept a certain amount of boorish behavior or workplace vulgarity as normal rather than a civil violation in today's 'Slouch Toward Gomorrah' society."

In finding the alleged behavior not legally actionable, the court said:

"The conduct is juvenile, offensive, and at times even mean-spirited, but merely inserting every last rude or sexualized comment/gesture/joke into a lengthy list accumulated over the years of employment does not a Title VII claim make."

Defuse Replay

Title VII liability for hostile work environment sexual harassment requires a plaintiff to establish:

1. she is a member of a protected group,

2. she received unwelcome sexual harassment,

3. the harassment was because of her sex, and

4. the harassment was *sufficiently severe* to alter her employment conditions.

The trial court's own words highlight the opposing points of view:

"Sensitive judges might find a case laden with sexually crude jokes and behavior sufficient to send the case to a jury, if not support a jury's 'hostile environment' determination.

"In contrast, judges desensitized by contemporaneous, 'Vulgarians-at-the-Gate' cultural standards might find the same facts insufficiently severe, then grant the defendant summary judgment."

Conclusion

This case demonstrates a number of our concepts about the purpose of laws. First, it is a fine example of how changing social conditions will influence not only changes in the law, but how existing laws are interpreted by courts hearing disputes. Had this case been decided at the time of passage of Title VII in the 1960s or even through the 1980s – when the terms "obscenity" and "pornography" had a workable legal framework that defined and limited one's actions – the plaintiff would probably have been a clear winner.

However, any lines of acceptable behavior that previously existed have certainly been blurred by the times in which we now live.

Second, the trial judge interestingly labels himself as being "desensitized" by current standards of our culture, and rules for the employer. His approach is a form of reverse judicial activism, because while he considers all external factors, his ruling is against the party seeking relief.

A ruling for the plaintiff would therefore be made by a "sensitive" court that limited its analysis just to the specific acts, rather than the surrounding social arena. Such a decision would fall within judicial restraint, because it is limited in focus to the specific acts, rather than the times in which they occur.

A. Do you agree with the court's final decision?

B. What arguments would you make in support of judicial restraint? What arguments would you make in support of judicial activism?

C. How should judges interpret pre-existing laws that were created in different social times?

B.   THE SOURCES OF LAW

"The chess board is the world, the pieces are the phenomena of the universe, the rules of the game are what we call the laws of Nature."

—Thomas Henry Huxley

If we are to learn to use the Anticipatory Thinking Approach to preventative law, it is essential to identify the particular rules of law that may govern our business transaction.

We cannot realistically plan anything until we know the legal constraints that we are operating under. Once we plug the factual aspects of our proposed transaction into the legal rules that apply to it, we will have a much better picture of our prospects for success.

Perhaps we will receive confirmation that allows us to proceed exactly as planned. Maybe we need a substantial reworking of our ideas to circumvent a potentially explosive legal time bomb or two, and proceed down a different road. At worst, we may be forced to abandon the proposed transaction entirely, but even if this occurs, we know we have located a potentially fatal problem and avoided its financially deadly consequences. Our finances remain intact and we have preserved our financial ability to find another deal on another day.

We are presumed to know the laws that pertain to our transaction. We may not raise "ignorance of the law" as a legal defense in the event of a dispute. And we know to a certainty that it is impossible to be aware of those laws relevant to our proposed deal unless they are researched properly. All the more reason to learn how to find them and become familiar with those that apply to our intended course of conduct *before* it is finalized, so that we may weigh all the possible alternatives and choose wisely.

Knowledge is power, and in the marketplace of commercial transactions advance knowledge usually results in wise decisions. In our legal system, the laws that govern our everyday lives are found in these sources:

- COURT CASES – When a factual dispute between the parties becomes a lawsuit, brought in the appropriate federal, state, or municipal court jurisdiction, and is concluded with a final judgment in favor of either the plaintiff or the defendant, we have legal precedent created by the judicial branch of government.

  Notice the root word, "precede," meaning that which comes before. This ruling may be used as persuasive authority in a future dispute involving similar facts.

  This source of law began in this country as the English common law, and has evolved on a case-by-case basis.

  The public usually becomes aware of cases when an appellate court decision is published by the court, becomes a matter of public record, and is then a part of the information superhighway available through services such as Westlaw, Lexis-Nexis, and the main Internet search engines. Trial court decisions and results of arbitration proceedings are not automatically reported, although they may be the subjects of news stories when they involve disputes of interest.

- STATUTES – These are formal laws adopted by the legislative branches of government in their formal law-making sessions. These laws are usually enacted by the U.S. Congress on the federal level, as well as the state legislatures, and may also include laws of local governments, called ordinances, covering a variety of areas including building codes, zoning regulations, and traffic laws.

  Sometimes laws on a given subject are codified by recognized authorities such as the Restatement of Contracts, which seeks to review and analyze various conflicting laws on the subject from various states and present one recommended legal view. Though not binding on the parties as governing law, it nevertheless is often cited as persuasive authority on the subject.

The Uniform Commercial Code, which applies to sales of goods, is a body of statutory law that has been adopted in whole or part by all states. It governs these transactions unless the parties provide otherwise, and overrides local laws or common law rules that may be conflicting. It is binding on the parties as a primary source of law.

All state laws also include "statutes of limitations," which are laws that specify time limits for filing lawsuits. No matter how strong the plaintiff's case, the defendant may raise its untimely filing as a defense, and the matter will be legally dismissed.

There are different time periods for each type of legal action. For example, in malpractice cases, parties usually have one year from their first reasonable opportunity to discover the alleged negligent act to sue. In contracts and sales cases, the limitation periods range from three to seven years from the date of breach, depending upon the state in which the contract or transaction was finalized.

- ADMINISTRATIVE REGULATIONS – As society has become more complex and government has expanded, a large group of regulatory agencies have been created on all levels of government to enact and oversee the enforcement of certain types of laws that seek to protect the public. These agencies include the Internal Revenue Service (taxes), Securities Exchange Commission (investments), Food and Drug Administration (consumables), Environmental Protection Agency (pollution), and many others.
- CONSTITUTIONS – They establish the structure of our federal and state governments. There is one U.S. Constitution, the supreme law of the land, and fifty different state constitutions. The federal and state constitutions are similar in their creation of the basic three branches of government:

  - Judicial (courts) to enforce the laws
  - Legislative (congress/legislatures) to enact the laws
  - Executive (president/governors) to interpret the laws

  While similar in format to the U.S. Constitution, state constitutions may differ significantly, and court disputes sometimes result from these conflicts.
- BILL OF RIGHTS – It guarantees to each citizen certain fundamental rights and privileges, such as freedom of religion, freedom of speech, and freedom of the press. It consists of constitutional amendments that have been approved over the years for the benefit of the public. They are a form of governmental commandments, the "thou shalt not" duties having been replaced with a form of "thou shalt" have certain guaranteed rights.

These sources of law have an enforcement priority in the event of a dispute. The U.S. Constitution takes precedence over all other laws. Federal laws govern over state laws. State laws prevail over local laws. Statutes have a higher priority than administrative regulations.

Contracting parties may also negotiate specific clauses in their agreements that designate (1) where disputes must be decided (forum selection), (2) the rules of law to be applied (choice of law), and (3) whether or not lawsuits or arbitration will be the means of dispute resolution (choice of remedy).

Before any domestic transaction is finalized, the parties must be aware of and analyze the federal and state laws that may be involved, as well as the laws of foreign countries if the proposed transaction is international. This strategic advance planning could be critical to the successful outcome of a dispute.

Triton, Inc., a New York corporation, discusses the sale of $1,000,000 worth of computer parts to Vailtronic Co., a Colorado corporation. (All buyers of goods prefer full seller warranties in the event of any product defects, and all sellers of goods prefer to sell without warranties.)

In its negotiations, the buyer is firm in requiring any disputes to be heard in Colorado rather than New York. The seller huffs and puffs, but finally gives in on this if the law of Japan will apply to the transaction. The buyer assumes that Japanese and U.S. law are similar, since both countries are very active in the sale of goods. (Japan has no warranty laws!)

The contract is finalized, the goods are shipped, one-half of the agreed price is paid upon shipment, and the buyer refuses to pay the balance when it discovers the goods are defective after they arrive.

The seller sues buyer in Colorado (forum selection) and wins the case, because that court must use the Japanese law agreed upon by the parties (choice of law).

Where can we find these sources of law, so that they can be reviewed in detail and analyzed, hopefully prior to completing the agreement, so that we may know the particular rules of law that may pertain to our particular transaction?

- A lawyer's initial consultation – explain your problem or proposed transaction and learn the basic legal rules that govern. This is traditionally done by contacting an attorney, making an appointment, and discussing your matter in the law office.

  Newer innovations also exist, such as being able to speak directly to an attorney in your state over the telephone for a fixed fee per inquiry ("ask an attorney" service of lawexpress.com), and having a lawyer available for you at any time for unlimited calls by paying an annual fee ("retainer service" of amerilawyer.com).
- Go to the law library of any law school – ask for help from the librarian or a law student. They often are more skilled at research than the practicing lawyer because it is a daily part of their academic life.
- Use the Internet information highway – you can surf your way through Cyberspace and find all levels of the rules of law. Every major browser, such as Netscape and Internet Explorer, as well as search engines such as Lycos, Yahoo, and Google, to name a few, have a separate "Law" link that will speed you to your goal. Some helpful Internet addresses are *www.law.com*, *www.findlaw.com*, and *www.westbuslaw.com*.

There are legal research databases such as Westlaw and Lexis-Nexis where any case that has ever been decided by an appellate court can be accessed. Legal forms are available at *www.lawguru.com*. Legislative information is presented at *http://thomas.loc.gov*. *www.law.cornell.edu* provides a spotlight on legal events, as does *http://jurist.law.pitt.edu*. Even Court TV, which has raised the level of awareness of the legal system for millions of viewers, has a web page at *www.courttv.com*.

In the case of *Whirlpool Financial Corporation v. GN Holdings, Inc., 67 F.3d 605 (7th Cir. 1995)*, Whirlpool had made a $10 million loan to GN based upon certain false and misleading financial projections contained in a private placement memorandum. (Does this sound familiar in the era of Enron, World Com, and the Arthur Andersen accountants?)

Whirlpool sued for securities fraud three years after making the loan, GN defended based upon the one-year statute of limitations in federal securities law, and both the trial court and appellate court agreed that Whirlpool's claim was barred.

Whirlpool had contended that certain industry trends were concealed from them, extending their time to sue. The court disagreed on the basis that this information was in the public domain and readily available through the Internet. "In today's society, with the advent of the 'information superhighway,' federal and state legislation and regulations, as well as information regarding industry trends, are easily accessed."

Discussion Exercises

1. Discuss any other sources of law that may be available.

2. Discuss any other helpful Internet law sites.

3. Discuss a situation where a court case resulted in a statute.

4. Discuss a situation where a statute resulted in a court case.

5. Discuss your opinions as to which is most important in contract negotiations:

a. Forum selection

b. Choice of law

c. Choice of remedy

Forum Selection Clause Upheld

The case of *Carnival Cruise Lines, Inc. v. Shute, 499 U.S. 585 (1991)*, involved a dispute regarding whether or not a forum selection clause in cruise tickets was legally enforceable in a ticket holder's personal injury lawsuit.

Mr. and Mrs. Shute, residents of the state of Washington, were passengers on a cruise between California and Mexico, operated by Carnival, whose principal place of business was Miami, Florida. "The 'passage contract tickets' received by the couple contained a clause (standard in the industry) designating courts located in the state of Florida as the agreed-upon exclusive venue for litigating any disputes arising under the contract between passenger and carrier."

During the cruise, the wife fell and was injured. She claimed the negligence of the cruise line and its employees was the cause, and sued in Washington federal court to recover damages. Carnival successfully moved to dismiss based upon the forum selection clause.

The appellate court, however, reversed, on the grounds that "it would be unreasonable to apply the forum-selection clause of the ticket contract" because of their concerns that it was not freely bargained for, it had not been read prior to the voyage, even if it had been reviewed its legalities would not have been understood, and "there was evidence in the record to indicate that the couple were physically and financially incapable of pursuing the litigation in Florida."

Carnival appealed to the U.S. Supreme Court, which accepted the case and decided it in Carnival's favor.

Analysis

The U.S. Supreme Court majority decision in favor of Carnival created a standard for the cruise industry, and similar types of service providers, to specify a forum for suit in their contracts, even though it is not the subject of bargaining between the parties:

"1. a cruise line, which typically carries passengers from many locales, has a special interest in limiting the fora in which the line could be subject to suit,

2. such a clause has the salutary effect of dispelling any confusion about where suits arising under the contract must be brought and defended, thus sparing litigants and courts the time and expense of litigating those issues, and

3. cruise line passengers benefit in the form of reduced fares reflecting the savings which the line enjoys by limiting the fora where it may be sued."

Two justices dissented. They felt the forum-selection clause was unreasonable, "because only the most meticulous passengers would be likely to become aware of it in the fine print on their tickets . . . the forum-selection clause in question lessened or weakened the couple's ability to recover . . . because it was safe to assume that any witnesses could be assembled with less expense and inconvenience at a west coast forum than thousands of miles away in Florida."

Defuse Replay

From the viewpoint of the passenger, what could have been done to defuse the time bomb created by the forum selection clause?

The majority decision suggests that the couple "presumably had the option of rejecting" the clause. As a practical matter, only lawyers, business law professors and their students, and readers of this book would even be aware of the potential problem.

If the clause was removed, the issue of the proper forum to hear the case would have been determined by the "most closely related contact" legal test. Since the injured party was a Washington resident who boarded the cruise in California, the West Coast aspect of the case mentioned in the dissent would point to a Washington forum. Florida would be viewed as a "remote alien forum." If that had occurred, the plaintiff may well have been able to induce a favorable settlement in her favor.

If the clause was not removed, the couple could still have continued with their cruise and been faced with the result of this case. The majority and dissenters both recognized that this would probably have removed any leverage they had to settle the dispute, since once rebuffed in Washington they would probably never have filed suit in Florida.

However, a third scenario exists. When the couple bought their ticket, presumably from a travel agent, their demand for a Washington forum could easily have been legally accomplished by inserting it in their reservation and invoice. After all, the agent wants to sell a ticket and would probably let customers write in anything they want as long as the deal is closed.

Neither the agent (whose acts bind Carnival under the laws of agency) nor Carnival would probably have noticed it or appreciated its legal import. By doing this, the pre-printed forum-selection clause in the ticket would have been revoked.

Conclusion

This case has far-reaching effects because it may have become a legal precedent for the entire cruise line industry or other types of customer carriage.

The Court's wording was not limited to legal pronouncements for Carnival alone. In fact, nowhere in its opinion does it refer to Carnival. Rather, it makes continued references to "a cruise line" (rather the "the" cruise line), and by so doing seems to broaden its impact industry-wide.

The same result would no doubt apply for choice of law and choice of remedy clauses, since the specific terms of the contract between the parties will govern any disputes – absent fraud or unfair advantage being taken.

The case also has the effect of putting prospective customers on notice that they should be aware in advance of the contract clauses in their tickets, which can be easily accomplished by requesting a copy of the standard ticket in advance for review from one's travel agent. If Internet booking is the method of purchase, some carriers are now making their ticket forms available online for review and questions.

A. Do you agree with the Court's final decision?

B. How can consumers be protected from adverse forum selection?

C. Should this decision be given industry-wide application?

C.   To Sue or Not to Sue?

"We were not born to sue, but to command."

—Shakespeare: *King Richard II*

Had Hamlet revealed his thoughts in the current commercial marketplace, his famous soliloquy ("to be or not to be") would have been altered from questioning his existence to trying to decide whether or not to institute litigation ("to sue or not to sue").

Hopefully, you will structure your commercial transaction so skillfully that everything works perfectly. This book will certainly help you. But it is a rare occurrence when a business transaction completes without a dispute. Even the apparently successful ones usually encounter a business law time bomb or two, but the parties are either unaware of the danger or consciously choose to ignore it because the deal is too good to question.

The objective is always to end the dispute by inducing the other side to accept a resolution favorable to us, hopefully through skillful use of anticipatory thinking. The faster, cheaper, and less damaging to future business relationships we can accomplish this, the better. But we live in a litigious society.

The basic equation of business success is *Gross Revenue − Expenses = Net Profits*. Legal costs are a significant expense item for most businesses, because when businesses are confronted with the inevitable dispute, most managers are knee-jerk reactive, full-speed ahead, and damn the torpedoes.

But the best executive decisions are made not in the heat of anger, but in the calmer mindset of responding to the predicament and weighing the relative advantages and disadvantages before making a final decision.

Litigation, although sometimes necessary, should be the remedy of last resort after a thoughtful risk-reward analysis of a possible lawsuit. Some of the important factors to consider are:

- The desired result, considering present and future consequences
- The strength of the case based upon applicable rules of law
- The history of court decisions in similar cases
- The monetary amount of damages recoverable
- The type of monetary or non-monetary relief available
- The available non-litigation choices

Some of the negative aspects are:

- The costs of litigation, including time spent and legal expenses
- The stress involved in the adversarial process
- The possibility of damaging business relationships
- The public nature of the proceedings
- The time to resolve the dispute on crowded court dockets
- The uncertainty of the appellate process
- The uncertainty of collecting a winning judgment
- The negative perception as a litigious party
- The possibility of an opposing countersuit

Some of the positive aspects are:

- Winning the case and recovering money damages
- Winning the case and receiving a non-monetary remedy
- The public nature of the proceedings can be informative and educational
- The possibility of establishing a legal precedent
- The possibility of clarifying confusing legal issues
- The possibility of setting an example of activism
- The possibility of deterring future improper or unlawful acts
- The power of the right to subpoena witnesses
- The power of discovery of otherwise unavailable information
- The power to prevent imbalances of corporate or governmental power

Sometimes a party to a business dispute is faced with a weak case, either because of adverse rules of law or unfavorable facts. Nevertheless, even marginal cases may have "nuisance value." The filing of a lawsuit in these situations, or the threat of doing so, may be an effective way to induce the other party to settle on a more favorable basis than had previously been available just through verbal or written demands.

One word of caution, however. The filing of a completely frivolous lawsuit or sham pleading is frowned upon by the courts, and may result in an award of damages against the filing party for "abuse of process."

Most people think the winning party automatically recovers its reasonable attorney's fees. But this is not so in most states. While a judge may award such fees in the unusual cases where the plaintiff has filed a purely groundless lawsuit, fee reimbursement will usually only be allowed if the lawsuit is based upon a written agreement or a statute that allows such a recovery.

Sometimes the most skillful response to a dispute is to walk away, even though you have legal grounds to sue. What if the defendant, against whom you have a valid claim, is your sole supplier of critical goods? While you might win the lawsuit, you probably would jeopardize your future business. What if your potential expenses of litigation would far exceed the amount due you? What if your lawsuit subjects you to a counterclaim for abuse of process? The best decision in such a case would be not to sue.

The parties themselves, without lawsuits or lawyers, resolve most disputes. This is the broad category called settlement. Trial lawyers will tell you that "a bad settlement is often better than a good lawsuit," due to the many disadvantages of suing. But it takes two to tango, as the song goes.

Many lawyers express displeasure with the current adversarial system, and are seeking more and more to assume a role as "counselors at law" who evaluate potential disputes and try to find ways to enable their clients to reach acceptable compromises.

If one of the parties refuses to agree, there can be no settlement, no matter how reasonable the other party's proposals. If that occurs, and the claimant party refuses to let the matter go and walk away, a lawsuit will be filed. Often, however, this will be the needed impetus to complete the settlement. The mere threat of litigation may not do the trick, but when legal papers are physically served on you, the possibly expensive message is much louder and clearer.

Against the backdrop in this country of too many lawsuits brought by too many combative lawyers, there has emerged a strong opposition movement called ADR – Alternate Dispute Resolution, where the parties agree, guided by their attorneys, to try to find a way to resolve their differences outside a courtroom.

And what is most interesting is that the legal profession, which itself helped to create the runaway train of litigation through the use of legal advertising, contingency fee arrangements, liberalized discovery rules, and use of graphic evidence creating large awards of money damages by juries, is at the forefront of this ADR movement.

The main types of Alternate Dispute Resolution are:

- Arbitration – the parties choose a neutral third party to hear their evidence and decide the dispute. It can be non-binding, but usually is agreed to be final. Binding arbitration is commonly used for disputes in labor agreements, building construction, and professional malpractice actions.

Advantages include skilled experts who hear and decide the disputes, which are resolved faster, less expensively, and with less animosity than the combat of litigation, and the privacy of the proceedings.

Disadvantages are lower awards than would be available with jury trials and the lack of any appellate remedies in the event of erroneous decisions. But recent decisions reflect growing court frustration with rubber-stamping these awards and a developing trend to review their amounts using judicial tests.

Arbitration is the usual remedy to resolve international disputes. Our Congress enacted the Federal Arbitration Act way back in 1925, but in recent times its usage has greatly increased. It validates arbitration-only clauses in the contracts of parties in interstate commerce. Similarly, many states have adopted the Uniform Arbitration Act for intrastate commerce, which allows the contracting parties to agree in advance that any disputes must be submitted to arbitration.

Typical disputes resolved by arbitration are labor and employment disagreements, breach of contract cases, tort claims, securities law cases, and consumer complaints.

A typical clause reads, "In the event of default, the parties agree to resolve any disputes exclusively by final and binding arbitration, and waive all rights or remedies to sue in a court of law."

The current trend is toward more, rather than less, usage of arbitration to resolve disputes, as evidenced by these cases:

- Arbitration may be required as a condition to employment. *Johnson v. Circuit City Stores, 148 F.3d 373 (4th Cir. 1998)*
- Deposition discovery does not violate the right to arbitrate. *Merrill Lynch v. Adams, 2001 WL 331976 (Fla. App. 2001)*
- Cost-sharing renders an arbitration clause void. *Perez v. Globe Airport Security Services, 2001 WL 649497 (11th Cir. 2001)*
- Employment arbitration form is binding even though unread by the employee. *Haskins v. Prudential Ins. Co., 230 F.3d 231 (6th Cir. 2000).*
- Contract allowing judicial review of arbitration award is upheld. *LaPine Technology v. Kyocera, 139 F.3d 884 (8th Cir. 1997)*
- Employment contract limiting arbitration remedy to back wages is ruled unconscionable. *Armendariz v. Foundation Health Psychcare Services, 80 Cal.Rptr.2d 235 (Cal. App. 1998)*
- People's Court's Judge Ed Koch has arbitral immunity for alleged slanderous remarks made during court proceedings. *Kabia v. Koch, 2000 WL 1341941 (N.Y. Civ. Ct. 2000)*

Other ADR methods are:

- Mediation – the parties choose a disinterested third party to act as an intermediary between their intractable positions and try to lead them to a settlement of their dispute. If the go-between is an interested third party, the proceedings are called conciliation. No binding decisions in either are made without the mutual consent of the parties. The purpose is just to listen and act as an impartial buffer between the conflicting positions of the parties.

- Med-Arb – this is a combination of the two main forms of ADR, tailored by the parties to their specific needs.
- Minitrial or Rent-a-Judge – this is usually a non-binding lawsuit, where the parties, through their lawyers, agree to a private trial and present their evidentiary case before a retired judge or experienced trial lawyer, who advises them of his informal decision and then encourages them to settle.
- Summary Jury Trial – this is usually a non-bonding mock trial in which the parties, represented by their lawyers, present their opposing positions before a typical civil jury of six persons, and are able to get the reactions to their witnesses and evidence. The reaction of the sample jury may enable the parties to better evaluate their cases and settle their differences.
- Negotiation – the informal give-and-take bargaining process between the transaction parties that occurs at many stages of planning, creating, performing, and enforcing contracts.

Even if the mutually agreed ADR procedures are non-binding on the combatants, their ability to be present and communicate their conflicting positions to an impartial intermediary in each other's presence often softens their conflict and ends the dispute.

The resolution process is assisted by the private and confidential nature of ADR. No dirty laundry is washed in public, unlike most court files, which are open for inspection by the public and the media.

Other countries have long recognized the value of avoiding lawsuits. They note our "sue as a first resort" mentality is reminiscent of the gunslinger battles of the old West. Suing someone is often frowned upon as being dishonorable or uncivilized. And if a lawsuit is necessary, one of the main remedies in a number of Asian countries is a public apology rather than money damages.

Our legal system is also criticized for allowing contingency fee hiring of lawyers, the large awards of our juries in personal injury cases, use of graphic demonstrative evidence, and money damages that can include such nebulous concepts as pain and suffering, mental anguish, and loss of consortium.

The remedy of punitive damages, allowed in extreme cases to punish a defendant and often limited only by the net worth of the defendant, is unique in the United States and is also viewed by outsiders as a flawed concept. The tort reform movement, seeking to place monetary caps on certain types of legal action and damage awards, is a reaction to its excesses.

While the ADR movement and settlement mentality is growing in this country, and someday may result in markedly lower levels of litigation, that day has not yet arrived. Our commercial marketplace, with all its potential business law time bombs, produces numerous business disputes that cannot be amicably resolved and require the services of lawyers to evaluate them and file the many lawsuits that often result.

As one of my students so astutely noted after a class discussion of one's choices in resolving a dispute – "suing sucks, but sometimes you have to do it."

Discussion Exercises

1. Discuss any other advantages or disadvantages of suing.

2. Discuss any other advantages or disadvantages of ADR procedures.

3. Are there other types of alternate dispute resolution that you think could be effective in resolving the disputes typical to your business?

4. Discuss any positive experiences of your company with lawsuits/ADR.

5. Discuss any negative experiences of your company with lawsuits/ADR.

Case Exercise 4

You Are Bound to the Terms of the Contract You Sign Whether You Read It or Not

In the Matter of the Arbitration between Mostek Corporation and North American Foreign Trading Corporation, 502 N.Y.S.2d 181 (N.Y.App.Div. 1986), was a contract dispute between a seller (Mostek) and a buyer (NAFTC) of microchips regarding whether or not its arbitration clause was binding.

The parties negotiated the terms of their transaction at the offices of the buyer, and then a purchase order was prepared and signed by both.

The front of the purchase order stated that the order was placed under certain conditions set forth on its reverse side. One such condition stated, "Any dispute arising out of this order shall be submitted to arbitration as provided in the terms set forth on the back of this order."

That clause was never specifically discussed by the parties, and the seller's agent claimed he never even read the reverse side of the purchase order before signing it. He also claimed that the procedure in the electronics industry was that his order had to be accompanied by a home office sales order confirmation to be binding.

Analysis

The trial court ruled for the seller, holding that the arbitration clause was not binding. The appellate court reversed, ordering the parties to proceed with arbitration. It noted that the contract was signed by each of the parties in the presence of each other, and that "buyer and seller are sophisticated corporate entities," and "the intention of the parties can be gathered from the four corners of the signed agreement itself."

The court also noted that the Federal Arbitration Act governed the transaction because the two parties were involved in interstate commerce, (seller – Texas/buyer – New York), that there was a federal policy favoring arbitration, and that the act specifically provides, "a written provision in a contract (for interstate commerce) to settle by arbitration a controversy thereafter arising . . . shall be valid, irrevocable and enforceable."

Defuse Replay

The two-sided form contract is the standard method of doing business in the commercial marketplace. It is completed in one of two ways in the usual transaction:

1. After the parties have completed their negotiations for the basic terms of their transaction, the buyer submits its preprinted purchase order form. The mutually agreed terms are filled in on the front, and the reverse contains the standard clauses, commonly called "boilerplate provisions," which are most favorable to and commonly used by the buyer. The seller then sends its preprinted order acknowledgement form, which also agrees to the basic terms on the front, and contains on the reverse the seller's clauses.

2. After the parties have completed their negotiations for the basic terms of the transaction, they both sign the same preprinted form, inserting on the front the specifics of their deal and becoming legally bound to the clauses on the reverse.

Because of the obvious dangers of becoming bound by terms and conditions you have not read, usually due to the lack of time to go over every single word and line of preprinted forms, contracting parties usually protect themselves by inserting clauses such as:

1. "In the event of a dispute regarding differing terms of the purchase order and the order acknowledgement, the _____ (p/o or o/a) shall govern." This is what is known as the contract exception to the "Battle of the Forms" rule of the Uniform Commercial Code, which is discussed in the chapter on acceptance of offers.

2. "The parties are only bound by the terms and provisions appearing on the front page of the contract, and reserve the right to object to boilerplate terms on the reverse side of the contract in the event of a dispute relating to them."

Conclusion

One of the fundamental principles of contracts is that you are legally bound by the agreements you sign. Whether or not you read or understand them is immaterial. The exceptions that provide valid defenses to enforcement are the fairness situations where one of the signing parties was coerced, mistaken, or deceived. The two universal contract admonitions are "put it in writing" and "read it before you sign it."

A. Do you agree with the court's final decision?

B. Do you usually read the items that you sign? What types? What parts?

C. Have you or your company ever had a legal dispute regarding a contract you signed?

Case Exercise 5

Lawsuit Permitted for Injuries Suffered by a Pro Football Player in a Regular Season Game

Hackbart v. Cincinnati Bengals, Inc. and Clark, 601 F.2d 516 (10th Cir. 1977), raised the legal question of whether an injury from an intentional blow inflicted by one professional football player on another in a regular season game can create tort liability for the offending player and the team that employs him.

The injury occurred after an interception of a Cincinnati Bengal's pass, The Denver Bronco's defensive back, Dale Hackbart, became an offensive player and attempted to block opposing player, Charles "Booby" Clark.

While Hackbart lay on the ground after the block, Clark, "acting out of anger and frustration, but without a specific intent to injure . . . stepped forward and struck a blow with his right forearm to the back of the kneeling plaintiff's head and neck with sufficient force to cause both players to fall forward to the ground."

The officials didn't see the incident and no penalty was called. However, the game film showed very clearly what had happened. The plaintiff did not report the incident immediately or seek medical treatment, but he did by the next day when he was in pain. He was treated by the team trainer and cleared to play. He participated in two more Sunday games before he consulted a doctor and it was discovered he had a serious neck fracture.

Analysis

The trial court rejected the plaintiff's claim on legal grounds that he had assumed the risk of known dangers by signing on as a professional football player. It said, "Professional football is a species of warfare and that so much physical force is tolerated and the magnitude of the force exerted is so great that it renders injuries not actionable in court."

The trial court suggested the non-legal remedies available for such offenses were a penalty, expulsion from the game, and/or suspension for future games. There was also an implied suggestion that future retaliation by or on behalf of the injured player would also probably occur.

The appellate court reversed and ordered a new trial on the evidence relating to the act that caused the injury. It said, "The game of football is not on trial, but rather, the trial involves a particular act in one game."

It directed the new trial not consider previously introduced evidence of whether or not the plaintiff or the defendant were dirty players, or other acts of violence between other players and other teams.

It further pointed out that the rules of the game prohibit the intentional striking of blows. "All players are prohibited from striking on the head, face or neck with the heel, back or side of the hand, wrist, forearm, elbow or clasped hands."

"Therefore, the notion is not correct that all reason has been abandoned . . . whereby the only possible remedy for the person who has been the victim of an unlawful blow is retaliation."

Defuse Replay

Although the trial court treated the case as if the plaintiff had no legal right to seek money damages, the rules of the game had no such prohibition.

Under the rules of professional football in effect at the time of the injury, there was no limiting clause or exclusionary provision that limited the legal remedies of a player physically injured by their violation.

Such a waiver of remedy clause could be in both the game rules and the player's standard employment contract. It could read:

"The undersigned player does hereby agree that professional football is, by definition, a violent contact sport similar to armed combat, and it may be reasonably anticipated and assumed that injuries will occur within the scope of player's employment, including but not limited to regular season games, exhibition games, and team practices. Player acknowledges and agrees that there shall be no legal remedies for such injuries in any court of law, alternate dispute resolution proceeding, or otherwise, and player's sole compensation remedy is any insurance carried by employer and/or employee."

Conclusion

Subsequent revisions to the game rules and provisions in the collective bargaining agreement between pro football players and management have addressed the potential legal problem illustrated in this case by limiting the legal remedies of injured players.

The court's ruling also revealed one of the important purposes of our system of laws, as discussed in that chapter:

"The potential threat of legal liability has a significant deterrent effect. Private civil actions constitute an important mechanism for societal control of human conduct."

A. Do you agree with the court's final decision?

B. Should the ruling in this case extend to all sporting events?

C. What if Hackbart had retaliated and Clark had sued him for damages?

D.   LEGAL REMEDIES AVAILABLE

"He that will not apply new remedies must expect new evils;
for time is the greatest innovator."

—Francis Bacon

There are two basic issues in every civil legal dispute – liability and damages. Liability depends upon whether or not there has been a breach of some legal duty owed by one party to the other. The damages suffered make a breach actionable, creating a necessity to redress the civil wrong by providing an appropriate remedy.

Money Damages

The most common civil remedy to the aggrieved party is a claim for money damages. They are commonly classified as follows:

- Compensatory damages – direct amounts necessary to reimburse the injured party for out-of-pocket expenses, such as medical charges, property repairs, value losses, and other harms. Also known as reimbursement damages, they are intended to restore the status quo, give back the benefit of the bargain made, and otherwise place the non-breaching party back in the position that would have existed if there had been no breach of duty.

Stella contracts to sell an antique vase to Herbert for $10,000. Herbert refuses to perform, and as a result of his breach, Stella, despite her best efforts, is only able to sell the vase for $6,000. Her compensatory damages for loss of her bargain are $4,000.

The incidental expenses that are incurred by a non-breaching party are also recoverable, and include monies spent to maintain the status quo or avoid additional loss, additional costs for salvage, liquidation, or advertising, and court costs if litigation is required. Note, however, that attorneys' fees as a general rule are NOT automatically recoverable by the prevailing party in a lawsuit, unless based upon a statute awarding them or a written contract clause, such as the following:

"In the event of a dispute requiring the services of an attorney, the prevailing party agrees to pay all reasonable legal expenses and attorneys' fees incurred."

In *Jordan v. CCH Inc., 2002 U.S. Dist. LEXIS 19104 (2002)*, a top sales employee who was suddenly fired when he reached age fifty-seven and replaced by a thirty-year-old with minimal experience sued for violation of the Federal Age Discrimination Employment Act (ADEA). He was awarded damages by the jury of $90,000 for contract monies earned, $260,000 in lost future earnings, and $33,000 to equalize for the "negative tax consequences" of receiving his lost pay in a single tax year.

- Consequential damages – special or indirect amounts to compensate for losses suffered that flow as a foreseeable result of the breach, such as loss of wages, loss of profits, and incidental extra amounts spent after the breach to avoid further losses.
- Personal injury damages – have both compensatory and consequential aspects, but, unlike basic contract and sales commercial disputes, include additional categories such as pain and suffering, mental anguish, and loss of sexual consortium.

In a recent case, a paralyzed snowboarder who claimed a ski jump had been negligently designed requested pain and suffering damages of $10 million, the jury awarded $713,000, and then the judge made a post-trial addition of another $5.3 million to that award, claiming it was inadequate. That additur is now on appeal. *Vine v. Bear Valley Ski Co., Cal.Sup.Ct. Case no. 317766 (2002)*

- Nominal damages – token monetary awards of $1 or $2 made as a matter of principle, when there has been a technical breach of duty creating liability, but little or no corresponding economic loss.

The late comedian Rodney Dangerfield based his humor upon the statement "I don't get no respect." *Star* magazine published a false article about him, headlined, "Vegas Casino Accused Caddyshack Funnyman: Rodney Dangerfield Swills Vodka by the Tumblerful, Smokes Pot All Day and Uses Cocaine." He filed suit for libel, requesting damages to his reputation of $1 million. The trial court found liability against the defendant and awarded "actual damages in the nominal amount of one dollar." It reasoned that the acts complained of, rather than cause him economic loss, conferred a monetary benefit since he now could use it as a real-life example of how he "don't get no respect." *Dangerfield v. Star Editorial, Inc. v. 1996 U.S. App. Lexis 23401 (9th Cir. 1996)*

• Punitive damages – exemplary damages awarded in addition to base damages in tort cases and some contracts cases where the defendant's conduct is so willful, malicious, reckless, and outrageous that an expensive financial lesson is needed to deter any such future conduct. So long as there are even nominal direct damages, an award of punitive damages is possible, though they must be somewhat proportional.

"Although compensatory damages and punitive damages are typically awarded at the same time by the same decision maker, they serve distinct purposes. The former are intended to redress the concrete loss that the plaintiff has suffered by reason of the defendant's wrongful conduct. The latter, which have been described as 'quasi-criminal,' operate as private fines intended to punish the defendant and to deter future wrongdoing." *Copper Industries, Inc. v. Leatherman Tool Group, Inc., 532 U.S. 424 (2001)*

They are only awarded under the American legal system. They also are used as a potent bargaining strategy to gain immediate attention to one's potential claim, and will often induce the opposing party to settle when they are claimed.

Originally, in most states, the amount of punitives recoverable was only limited by the net worth of the defendant. "The bigger their pocketbooks, the harder they will be hit," said plaintiffs' lawyers. But as the jury awards continued to escalate, some legislatures passed tort reform laws as a reaction to large punitive awards, capping them to various multiples of actual damages suffered in an effort to stem the trend toward ever larger awards. There was no judicial uniformity from state to state, awaiting some definitive legal guidelines.

Proponents of punitive damages argued that they were an effective deterrent to corporate misconduct. The size and financial impact of modern corporations gives them tremendous power in the business marketplace that they often abuse. Cases in point have been chemical pollution, dangerous drugs, automobile defects, and the tobacco lawsuits. Class action lawsuits provide relief for plaintiffs whose individual claims are too small to litigate in a separate suit. The fear of large punitive damage awards may work better than legislation to keep products safe. In addition, many products have been improved after juries tagged their makers with large damage awards.

Opponents argue that our juries are suffering from punitive damage inflation. Large damage awards that would have been totally off the charts a few years ago are now viewed as commonplace with the use of modern trial techniques, demonstrative evidence, and the electronic courtroom. These awards are often viewed as a windfall for plaintiffs' lawyers, who receive contingency fees, often have cases with numerous plaintiffs certified into one huge class action, and take their fees and run, leaving their hundreds or thousands of clients with a relatively small per-person recovery. Products never get to the marketplace, they say, because of the risk of these damages.

The opponents seem to have gained an advantage, as many of the larger awards of punitives that were on appeal were reversed or lowered. Then came *State Farm v. Campbell, 538 U.S. 408 (2003)*, where the U.S. Supreme Court set forth definitive guidelines for the first time. The Court ruled that "The ratio of punitive damages to compensatory damages almost never should exceed single digits," creating a maximum punitive multiplier of nine times actual damages. That ruling overturned a jury award of $1 million compensatory damages and $145 million punitive damages.

The court also said, "A defendant should be punished for the conduct that harmed the plaintiff, not for being an unsavory individual or business ... The wealth of a defendant cannot justify an otherwise unconstitutional punitive damage award."

Before the *Campbell* decision, the main punitive damages case was Florida's 1994 *Engle* case in which plaintiffs sued the large tobacco companies in a class action on behalf of 700,000 other Florida smokers, claiming they were unable to stop smoking and developed various serious health problems due to nicotine addiction. Their jury award of punitive damages of $145 billion, the largest in U.S. history, was roughly eighteen times more than the defendant's proven net worth and it may have given the U.S. Supreme Court the impetus to create its punitive damage guidelines.

The verdict was overturned in *Liggett Group v. Engle, 853 So.2d 434 (Fla. App. 2003)*, and the class was decertified as being "too unique and specialized to be tried collectively in a class action." The court also said, "The amount awarded should be large enough to provide retribution and deterrence, but cannot be so great as to result in bankruptcy." The case may still be reviewed, however, by the Florida Supreme Court.

Legislation has recently been passed by Congress to eliminate or restrict the use of class actions in mass torts and related cases. The Class Action Fairness Act of 2005 requires all class actions over $5 million where two-thirds of the plaintiffs are out-of-state to be tried only in federal courts. State legislatures are also setting dollar limits on medical malpractice awards, and some states are recommending that winning plaintiffs only receive a percentage of punitive awards, with the remainder going to the state for education and related public purposes.

Oregon has an unusual statute, passed in 1995, which awards 60 percent of any punitive awards to a state fund benefiting crime victims. It was recently legally challenged by a plaintiff who recovered $550,000 in punitive damages in an action for fraudulent transfer of real property against his former attorney, and was declared constitutional. The effect was that $330,000 of the plaintiff's share now belongs to the state. *DeMendoza v. Huffman, Oregon Supreme Ct. Case no. SC S48430 (2002)*

Despite tort reform and the Campbell case, the threat of punitive damages is still a potent bargaining tool to induce favorable settlement of disputes, and juries are still making large awards in appropriate case.

In *X-IT Products, L.L.C. v. Walter Kidde Portable Equipment, Inc., 155 F.Supp.2d 577 (E.D. Va. 2001)*, two young Harvard Business School students had invented a lightweight folding emergency escape ladder for a classroom assignment.

They entered negotiations with the defendant to sell the rights to their creation, but were unable to reach an agreement. Then the defendant introduced and marketed the same product as its own. The plaintiff sued for infringement of intellectual property rights, theft of trade secrets, and breach of implied contract. The trial jury ruled for the plaintiff, awarding $21 million in compensatory damages and $95 million in punitive damages. The appellate court reduced the awards to $3.1 million compensatory and $9.4 million punitive. Both parties threatened a further appeal. Then they settled out of court for a total award to the plaintiff of $17.4 million.

There are also judicial limits to awarding punitive damages, even though the large awards get most of the media headlines.

Legal Limitations

Damages have to be reasonably ascertainable in amount. The more speculative or conjectural the type and amount of damages, the less likely is a court to grant such a damage award. This is known as the certainty requirement of damages.

Damages also have to be "reasonably foreseeable." If the damages sued upon by a plaintiff are such that a reasonable defendant, in the same or similar factual situation, would not have anticipated them, recovery will be denied or minimized. The loss suffered by the plaintiff must be a "proximate" or foreseeable result of the defendant's wrong, not "remote" or unforeseeable.

In the landmark case *Palsgraf v. Long Island Railroad Company, 162 N.E. 99 (N.Y. App. 1928)*, taught in all law schools in the land to illustrate the negligence doctrine of causation, Mrs. Palsgraf was standing on a platform in the defendant's railroad waiting for a passenger train. On another platform at the opposite side, a train stopped and two men ran forward to board it while it was starting to move away. One man jumped aboard, and the other man, who was carrying a small package covered by a newspaper, seemed unsteady. The defendant's employee, in an effort to assist the man, negligently knocked the package from his hands.

The package, which contained hidden fireworks, exploded, and the shock of the blast threw down some large scales at the opposite end of the platform, which struck and injured Mrs. Palsgraf. She sued the defendant railroad for negligence.

After a trial court verdict for the plaintiff, the appellate division affirmed, and then this appeal was made to the court of appeals, where the renowned Justice Benjamin Cardozo, writing for the majority of the court, reversed:

"What the plaintiff must show is 'a wrong' to herself, *i.e.*, a violation of her own right, and not merely a wrong to some one else, nor conduct 'wrongful' because unsocial, but not 'a wrong' to any one. . . Here, by concession, there was nothing in the situation to suggest to the most cautious mind that the parcel wrapped in newspaper would spread wreckage through the station. If the guard had thrown it down knowingly and willfully, he would not have threatened the plaintiff's safety, so far as appearances could warn him. His conduct would not have involved, even then, an unreasonable probability of invasion of her bodily security. Liability can be no greater where the act is inadvertent."

There is also a doctrine called "mitigation of damages." It requires the non-breaching party to use his best efforts to do what is necessary to reasonably lessen the amount of potential damages.

Kevin signs a one-year lease to rent an apartment from Stanley. At the end of the third month, Kevin's plans change and he vacates the apartment. Stanley may not automatically claim damages of unpaid rent for the unexpired term. He is legally required to try to re-let the premises. If he is successful and the rental paid will be less, his contract damages are the difference between Kevin's lease and the amount received, plus expenses. If he is unable to find a new tenant, he can recover the full unpaid rent plus expenses. If he somehow is able to rent for more than required by Kevin's lease, a few states would require him to refund the excess to Kevin, and most others allow him to retain this "found money" as damages for his trouble.

Often, the concepts of remedies for breach of contract and mitigation of damages are interconnected in disputes before the courts:

"Upon the breach of a contract, the party seeking relief has the choice of three remedies: rescind the contract, refuse to treat the breach as a termination of the contract and request that the court compel performance under the contract, or consider the breach to be a termination.

"A basic principle of the law of damages is that one who claims to have been injured by a breach of contract must use reasonable means to avoid or minimize the damages resulting from the breach . . . although the injured party is often spoken of as having a 'duty' to mitigate damages, the term is misleading because there is no liability for failing to take such steps; the party is merely precluded from recovering for avoidable damages." *West Pinal Family Health Center, Inc. v. McBryde, 785 P.2d 66 (Az. App. 1989)*

Non-Monetary Remedies

There are also equitable remedies available in those disputes where the non-breaching party cannot be adequately compensated by monetary damages:

- Suppose the parties enter into a contract to perform specialized personal services or to buy or sell unique, one-of-a-kind personal property items such as works of art, custom jewelry, personal heirlooms, real property, or other special items whose loss could not be replaced by an award of money. The remedy for breach of such an agreement is *specific performance*, in which the judge orders the contract promise(s) to be performed.

In *Okun v. Morton, 203 Cal. App.3d 805 (Cal. App. 1988)*, the litigation concerned a contract dispute for development of the restaurant and commercial enterprises known as the Hard Rock Café. The plaintiff had been operating a local restaurant and tourist attraction by that name in England, contacted the defendant about investing, and ultimately the parties agreed to open the first U.S. operation in Los Angeles, California. The parties signed an agreement in 1982 whereby the plaintiff paid $100,000 to the investing limited partnership in exchange for a 20% share in the operating general partnership, including the future right to participate in "all business opportunities which arise in connection with the business of HRC."

After the initial success of the HRC concept, the defendant planned expansion to a number of other cities, but advised the plaintiff he could not financially participate, and rejected the plaintiff's renewed offer to accept his 20% share.

The plaintiff sued for specific performance of the 1982 agreement. The trial court ruled for the plaintiff. On appeal the defendant claimed, "Specific performance should not have been granted because enforcement of the contract will require continuous and protracted judicial supervision."

The appellate court rejected this argument, and affirmed the specific enforcement of the rather unique agreement of the parties.

"Defendant retains the discretion under the terms of the judgment to structure each venture as he pleases so long as he maintains the 20/80 ratio and does nothing to interfere with or burden plaintiff's right to participate in the deal."

Specific performance will not usually be granted, however, in cases of alleged breach of contracts to require performance of personal services, because it is against public policy to force one party to work for another against its will.

But the breaching party can be legally ordered *not* to do so by injunctive relief, as explained below.

Here is a case for you boxing historians. In *Madison Square Garden Corp. v. Carnera, 52 F.2d 47 (2nd Cir. 1931)*, the defendant, a professional prize fighter, contracted in his next bout to box the winner of the Max Schmeling-Young Stribling fight for the world heavyweight championship. The agreement prohibited him from any prior fights without the plaintiff's permission. He breached it by agreeing to fight Jack Sharkey, and the plaintiff sued for an injunction to prohibit the contemplated bout.

The trial court granted the injunction and the appellate court affirmed. "Defendant's services are unique and extraordinary. A negative covenant in a contract for such personal services is enforceable by injunction where the damages are incapable of ascertainment."

- Suppose the parties have entered into a contract and then one of the parties wants to avoid its legal consequences, (probably because he realized he made a bad business deal), and alleges a legally sustainable ground for non-enforcement such as incapacity, illegality, fraud, or duress. The remedy to cancel such an agreement is *rescission*.
- The party allowed to legally withdraw is often required to return any benefits received (*restitution*). Notice these four situations:

  Carlton agrees to sell his custom car to Lucy for $15,000. After she makes a partial payment of $5,000, he refuses to complete the sale. She may sue for her deposit instead of seeking money damages for breach of contract or suing for specific performance.

  Carlton agrees to sell his custom car to Lucy for $15,000, she makes a partial payment of $5,000, and then she defaults. Carlton then sells the car to Trent for $12,500. Lucy can recover her $5,000 deposit less Carlton's $2,500 loss of bargain damages. If Carlton had been unable or unwilling to sell the car, he could have retained the $5,000 as agreed default damages, so long as his agreement permitted him to do so.

Carlton agrees to sell his custom car to Lucy for $15,000, she pays the full purchase price, and then he successfully disaffirms the contract on legal grounds of lack of real consent. He may cancel the transaction, but must return any benefits received. He receives his auto back, but must return the money paid by Lucy.

Carlton agrees to sell his custom car to Lucy for $15,000 under a verbal agreement that is not legally enforceable under the statute of frauds. She improves the car with his permission prior to the closing. If he decides to cancel, she must be paid the reasonable value of the services she rendered.

- Courts may not make new contracts for the parties, but may in certain situations rewrite them to more accurately reflect their agreement. Suppose there is a significant drafting error in the terms of a contract, or a clerical miscalculation in sales computations that are not the result of a breach by either party. The remedy to correctly rewrite the contract is *reformation*.
- Suppose you reside in a city that has a local law requiring the adjoining local bar to close no later than 2 a.m., and they fail to comply, disrupting your sleep and general peace of mind. Monetary damages won't help you, but a legal action requesting an *injunction* to stop the prohibited conduct will, such as was the Carnera case, *supra*. This is also the common remedy in domestic disturbances, where the aggrieved party legally requests a *restraining order*.

In *Beverly Glen Music, Inc. v. Warner* Communications, *Inc., 178 Cal.App.3d 1142 (Cal. App. 1986)*, there was an unusual attempt to use the injunction remedy. Then-unknown singer Anita Baker signed a recording contract with the plaintiff. She later breached that contract by signing with the defendant. The plaintiff sued to enjoin the defendant from hiring her rather than suing her directly. The trial court and appellate court ruled against the plaintiff, saying:

"While there are numerous cases on the general inability of an employer to enjoin his former employee from performing services somewhere else, apparently no one has previously thought of enjoining the new employer from accepting the services of the breaching employee."

- Suppose you are unsure of your legal rights relating to a particular situation or contractual provision, and need a judicial ruling so you can know whether or not, or how, to proceed. If you have this legal requirement of bona fide doubt and no other remedy at law, the remedy is called *declaratory judgment*.
- There are many other civil remedies that may or may not include money damages, a few of which are paternity, adoption, divorce, and custodial rights, immigration matters, and restorations of legal rights.

Contract Tort of Bad Faith

A "tort" is usually defined as a non-contract civil wrong. In the broad category of civil disputes, all must fall in categories of either contract or tort matters. The traditional torts that affect business and the commercial marketplace include, but are not limited to, the following:

1. Theft of trade secrets, formulas, and valuable technology – also known as industrial espionage
2. Infringement of intellectual property rights – patents, copyrights, and trademarks
3. Invasion of privacy – unauthorized viewing of one's files, confidential data, or electronic mail
4. Defamation – false publication of verbal (slander) or written (libel) matters that injure one's reputation
5. False imprisonment – unauthorized detention of falsely accused shoplifters
6. Right of publicity – unauthorized use of one's name, likeness, voice, or other personal characteristics, for financial gain
7. Products liability negligence

With the advent of the Uniform Commercial Code being adopted statewide, thus achieving a uniformity of contract laws and the resultant predictability for planning transactions and resolving disputes involving a "sale of goods," a new form of contract tort has arisen under section 1-203 whereby the transacting parties owe each other a *duty of good faith.*

This has been interpreted by courts and expanded into the *implied covenant of good faith and fair dealing,* which is a broad duty imposed by law on contracting parties, irrespective of the terms of their contract, to assure that they will not take unfair advantage of each other by impeding or preventing the benefits reasonably anticipated from the contractual relationship of the parties.

"It is well settled that, in California, the law implies in *every* contract a covenant of good faith and fair dealing. Broadly stated, that covenant requires that neither party do anything, which will deprive the other of the benefits of the agreement.

"Although the precise contours of the covenant depend upon the nature of the contract, where a contract confers on one party a discretionary power affecting the rights of the other, a duty is imposed to exercise that discretion in good faith and in accordance with fair dealing." *Okun v. Morton, supra*

Breach of this duty to act in good faith and deal fairly with each other creates a remedy additional to the traditional breach of contract, and is treated as a tort.

This is significant, because tort actions traditionally result in an award of damages larger than contract actions, and since the essence of this tort is unfairness and misconduct, substantial damages are often awarded.

Areas where the tort of bad faith are applied may be as broad as any contract dispute where one party takes unfair advantage of the other, as well as specific situations such as borrower-lender disputes, employee firings, and failure of insurers to properly service the policies of their customers, including failure to settle within policy limits or promptly pay benefits that are due.

In *Gourley v. State Farm Mutual Automobile Insurance Company, 227 Cal. App.3d 1099 (Cal. App. 1990)*, the plaintiff was a passenger in an automobile struck by an uninsured drunk driver. She was not wearing a seat belt, suffered serious injuries that resulted in permanent disability, and filed a claim for uninsured motorist coverage under her automobile insurance policy with the defendant, demanding the policy liability limit of $100,000.

The defendant advised the plaintiff, their policyholder, that they would contest her claim due to her failure to wear a seat belt, although that was not really a valid defense under California law. In addition, the defendant only offered a maximum settlement of $25,000. When an arbitrator awarded the plaintiff $88,137, the defendant paid the plaintiff, and she sued for breach of the implied covenant of good faith and fair dealing.

The trial jury awarded the plaintiff $15,765 in actual damages for emotional distress and one hundred times that amount for punitive damages of $1,576,500. On appeal, the verdict was affirmed. The appellate court decision set forth the law applicable to the tort of bad faith:

"The gist of the bad faith action is to compensate the insured for the angst caused when the insurer willfully refuses to pay under the policy. The primary focus of the tort is the personal wrong done. If it were merely pecuniary, a contract cause of action would suffice . . .

"There is an implied covenant in every insurance contract that the insurer will do nothing to impair the insured's right to receive the benefit of the contractual bargain that the insurer will promptly pay to the insured all sums due under the contract. A major motivation for the purchase of insurance is the peace of mind that claims will be paid promptly. When an insurer unreasonably refuses to pay benefits due, it frustrates that motivation and a cause of action in tort arises."

The appellate court then explained the legal criteria for an award of punitive damages (similar to the U.S. Supreme Court guidelines set forth in the *BMW case, supra*):

"In making our determination, we look to three factors: (1) whether the amount of the award reasonably reflects the reprehensibility of the defendant's conduct; (2) whether the punitive damages bear a reasonable relationship to the actual damages; and (3) whether the award will have a deterrent effect without crippling the financial existence of the defendant."

In *Dalton v. Educational Testing Service, 663 N.E.2d 289 (N.Y. App. 1995)*, the plaintiff, a high school student, took the SAT, administered by the defendant. When he did so, he signed a statement which reserved to the defendant, "the right to cancel any test score . . . if ETS believes that there is reason to question the score's validity."

The plaintiff took the test twice. Because his score on the second test increased by more than 350 points, his score was considered "discrepant" and the defendant, after a finding that the handwriting differed, notified the plaintiff of their intention to cancel his score, stating, "The evidence suggests that someone else may have completed your answer sheet and that the questioned scores may be invalid."

When the plaintiff was given the opportunity to provide additional information in his defense, he presented evidence that he had mononucleosis for the first test, evidence that his preparatory test scores were consistent with his results on the second test, statements of other students confirmed that he was in the classroom during the second test, and handwriting certification verified that we has the author of both tests.

ETS submitted the handwriting to a new document examiner, who again suggested that the tests were in different handwritings. They did not, however, "make even rudimentary efforts to evaluate or investigate the information" submitted by the plaintiff.

The plaintiff sued, and the trial court ruled in his favor, finding that ETS had breached its duty of good faith. On appeal the case was affirmed:

"Implicit in all contracts is a covenant of good faith and fair dealing in the course of contract performance ... This embraces a pledge that neither party shall do anything, which will have the effect of destroying or injuring the right of the other party to receive the fruits of the contract. Where the contract contemplates the exercise of discretion, this pledge includes a promise not to act arbitrarily or irrationally in exercising that discretion."

In *Sons of Thunder, Inc. v. Borden, 690 A.2d 575 (Sup. Ct. N.J. 1997)*, the defendant, a leading producer of clam products, hired DeMusz to be the captain of one of its four boats used to harvest clams. Later, in order to implement their business project for fishermen to shuck the clams on the boats and thus provide a larger haul, they decided to buy a larger boat for their "Shuck-at-Sea" project.

With the defendant's approval, DeMusz formed a company to implement the proposal, bought the boat, and leased the necessary equipment for the project.

Then the defendant orally agreed with DeMusz to assure a long-term supply so that he could buy a second boat, which he did under the name of the plaintiff. This oral contract was for one year, with automatic renewals up to five years, allowing either party to cancel by giving ninety days' written notice. The plaintiff was unable to buy the boat on its own credit until the defendant intervened with assurances that "they expected the contract to run for five years," and that revenues produced would be sufficient to support the loan.

Soon after the boat was ready, the defendant's management changed and they refused to honor the plaintiff's contract. They also refused to purchase from the plaintiff, acquired a different fishing boat company to perform their clam project, and invoked the ninety-day termination clause in the contract. The plaintiff sued for breach of contract and breach of the covenant of good faith and fair dealing.

DeMusz and a Borden executive testified at trial that the ninety-day termination clause was only to apply after one year. The jury found for the plaintiff, awarding $363,292 for lost income during the four months Borden refused to honor the contract, and $412,000 for one year's lost profits.

On appeal, the verdict was affirmed. "A party to a contract may breach the implied covenant of good faith and fair dealing in performing its obligations even when it exercises an express and unconditional right to terminate and the trial court correctly determined that the jury could have reasonably found that Borden breached its obligation to perform its duties in good faith."

"Although the Uniform Commercial code (UCC) governs this case, the obligation to perform in good faith found in the common law exists in every contract, including those with express termination clauses."

Intentional Interference with Contract

This is an intentional tort that has come more into legal usage as the commercial marketplace has grown and become more competitive. It is applicable in situations where there is an existing financially advantageous contract, and an outside third party such as a disgruntled bidder for a construction project or business takeover wrongfully induces one of the contracting parties to cancel. Often, the breaching party then enters into a new contract involving the same subject matter with the inducer.

The five traditional elements of this tort, which is sometimes described as "intentional interference with contract" if there is a specific contractual relationship, and "intentional interference with prospective economic advantage" if there is a non-contractual business relationship, are:

1. Existence of a legally enforceable contract involving the plaintiff
2. The contract is current, in good standing, and not in default
3. The defendant is aware of the contract's existence
4. The defendant unlawfully induces a contracting party not to perform
5. The plaintiff suffers financial damage

Dane and Trent are competing bidders on the chalk and eraser contract with the university. The bid specifications provide that "All bidders represent and warrant that they are U.S. citizens; if not their bid may be disregarded and this contract will be privately reassigned." This provision is necessary to assure continued federal funding for the university. Dane's bid is lowest and he is awarded the $75,000 contract. Trent is furious, and gives the university forged documents that indicate Dane is an illegal alien, following which they cancel his contract and award it to Trent.

Notice we have all the required elements of the tort reflected in the facts. Element 4 has been clarified by most court decisions to require the inducement to be a separate actionable tort or breach of contract. In this case, providing false written information that damages Dane's reputation is the tort of libel, and supports the "unlawful inducement" requirement.

In *Buckaloo v. Johnson,et al, 537 P.2d 865 (Cal. 1975)*, the plaintiff was a licensed real estate broker who had an exclusive real estate listing on a piece of waterfront property owned by Benioff. Four years after it had expired, she put a sales sign on the property that created an "open listing," whereby any broker who furnished a buyer would receive a commission, unless the owner made a direct sale to an independent buyer not furnished by the broker.

The plaintiff was approached by the defendants, who expressed an interest in that property. He informed them what he knew about the property and they left, promising to return the next day since he had secured accommodations for them.

When they did not return, the plaintiff registered their names with Benioff, informing her he was the "procuring cause" of any later purchase by the defendant, thus attempting to protect himself regarding the right to a commission.

Later, the plaintiff learned the property had been sold to the defendants and his request for a commission was refused. He then sued the seller and the defendants for damages for breach of an implied contract, and for intentional interference with prospective advantage. The trial court dismissed the plaintiff's complaint based upon lack of a written agreement required by the statute of frauds.

On appeal, the court reversed, stating, "Even at this late date defendants fail to comprehend that plaintiff is not alleging interference with contract but interference with prospective advantage. The protected area of activity is not a contractual relationship but an economic relationship with the potential to ripen into contract. Whether the relationship is of sufficient depth to support the tort is a factual question which plaintiff will be put to the burden of proving at trial."

(These proofs include evidence that the defendants conspired, after being made aware of the benefits of a purchase by the plaintiff, to purchase directly and secretly, thus eliminating his entitlement to a real estate commission.)

The court explained the distinction between the two types of tort:

"The great weight of authority is that the tort of interference with contract is merely a species of the broader tort of interference with prospective advantage. Thus while the elements of the two actions are similar, the existence of a legally binding agreement is not a *sine qua non* to the maintenance of a suit based on the more inclusive wrong.

"(Contracts) which are voidable by reason of the statute of frauds, formal defects, lack of consideration, lack of mutuality, or even uncertainty of terms, still afford a basis for a tort action when the defendant interferes with their performance."

Discussion Exercises

1. Discuss other types of monetary remedies.

2. Discuss other types of non-monetary remedies.

3. Discuss other types of equitable remedies.

4. Discuss limitations, if any, you would put on actual damages.

5. Discuss limitations, if any, you would put on punitive damages.

Case Exercise 6

Zsa Zsa Loses/Wins a Dispute for Her Cancelled Movies

In *Hollywood Fantasy Corporation v. Zsa Zsa Gabor, 151 F.3d 203 (5th Cir. 1998)*, the plaintiff company was in the business of providing fantasy vacation packages that would allow participants to make a movie with a Hollywood personality and imagine themselves movie stars for one week, for a stated fee. They contracted with the defendant to be one of two celebrities at the event, but she cancelled two weeks before it was to occur.

The plaintiff tried unsuccessfully to replace the defendant, and then had to cancel the event, refunding their ticket purchases to the few customers that existed. Shortly thereafter, the plaintiff went out of business and brought this action in a Texas federal trial court against the defendant for breach of contract and fraud.

Analysis

When the defendant failed to appear at the call of the trial docket, the judge entered a default judgment on the issue of liability and the jury awarded damages of $3 million.

She moved to set aside the default judgment on grounds she had not been properly notified. The court granted her motion and ordered a new trial. At trial, the jury awarded the plaintiff $100,000 in damages on its breach of contract claim and $100,000 on its fraud claim. In a post-trial order, the court set aside the fraud verdict as being not supported by the evidence, but upheld the contract claim verdict.

The defendant appealed, claiming that there was no valid contract because she had not accepted the plaintiff's offer to perform, but had instead made material changes to it, resulting only in a counteroffer, rather than a legal acceptance of the offer.

The appellate court disagreed with her, and affirmed the trial court judgment, stating, "We find that the modifications Ms. Gabor sought were not material because they did not significantly increase Hollywood Fantasy's financial obligations or significantly reduce Ms. Gabor's performance obligations . . ."

The appellate court then addressed the issue of money damages awarded, and ruled, "The $100,000 damages award cannot be supported as the recovery of lost profits."

It reviewed testimony of the plaintiff to the effect that he "estimated" he would have lost $250,000 from future fantasy vacation events and $1 million in future profits from bloopers and outtakes from videotapes of clients acting with the personalities, and found that it was too imprecise and not based upon factual data.

The court discussed the legal requirements for a recovery of consequential damages in the form of lost profits:

"Lost profits must be proved with reasonable certainty . . . at a minimum, opinions or estimates of lost profits must be based on objective facts, figures or data from which the amount of lost profits may be ascertained. Mere speculation of the amount of lost profits is insufficient."

The court then reduced the jury award to $57,500, the defendant's evidentiary out-of-pocket expenses for the celebrity event, which included printing, advertising, film preparation, and travel expenses. "The general rule is that the non-breaching party may only recover out-of-pocket expenses incurred after the contract was formed."

Defuse Replay

Did Zsa Zsa win the battle but lose the war, or vice-versa? The roller-coaster aspects of this case are a real-life movie worthy of the publicity she always craved as an actress.

The plaintiff originally received a $3 million default judgment. When it was set aside, as judges routinely do if the defendant can furnish evidence of lack of notice or excusable neglect, it was a clear signal to the plaintiff that its case needed to be able to support the burden of proof for both liability and damages. It appears it did its homework on liability, but was not prepared to properly prove any damages beyond actual expenses incurred.

The defendant, on the other hand, having survived the default judgment, should have paid attention to the potential damage award she would incur, and settled the case. The ideal time would have been immediately after the trial judge set aside the plaintiff's default judgment. At that moment, the defendant had maximum bargaining leverage.

Conclusion

According to the many news articles about her, Zsa Zsa Gabor never met a rich man she didn't like, and she was equally enamored with publicity. Give her a forum where she was the center of attention, and she was at her best.

In this case, she was again in the spotlight. She parried questions and answers with the lawyers as well as the judge, and there was a daily pre- and post-trial news conference for good measure.

Perhaps the reason she allowed the case to continue to its inevitable conclusion was how important it was to her to be in the bright lights of publicity.

The pendency of this case was her last real opportunity to play a starring role. If viewed from that perspective, she was successful.

A. Do you agree with the court's final decision?

B. Do you think courts apply different standards for celebrities?

C. Does this case warrant punitive damages?

E.   DIFFERENT COURTS AVAILABLE

"Scholars dispute and the case is still before the courts."

—Horace

More than 90% of transactional disputes are resolved without lawyers, more than 90% of those are settled without a lawsuit being filed, and in 90% of those that are litigated the matters are resolved before there is any final decision by judge or jury.

Yet, there are still an abundance of lawsuits in our knee-jerk "sue 'em" reactivity to the challenge of matters not seeming to go our way. So, our focus now turns to the assumption that we will be faced with litigation after we have moved through these events in the typical business transaction:

- Preliminary negotiations between the parties
- Mutual agreement is reached either verbally or in writing
- A material dispute arises
- The parties are unable or unwilling to resolve their differences or invoke formal settlement procedures such as arbitration or mediation
- Threats of legal action are made
- Lawyers are hired
- A lawsuit is filed by one party in a chosen state or federal court

The strategic planning of a lawsuit has been compared to a military campaign. At the very least, it certainly resembles a challenging game of chess. The successful player is usually able to stay one step ahead of his opponent.

Of course, the lawsuit itself is just a final stage of the typical progression of events that has culminated in a business transaction gone bad. At any stage, one of the parties will usually try to induce the other to accept a favorable settlement of some kind. And the deciding factor in such inducement may be, for the purposes of this chapter, the court location where the lawsuit can be brought by the plaintiff or resisted by the defendant.

The litigation game is all about leverage. Which party has gained a perceived advantage at any given time? Choosing a particular court in which to sue or defend is a strategic chess match that goes on behind the scenes in most cases.

Legal Overview

But where should the plaintiff file suit? What are the choices available? Where must the case be defended? What are the defendant's choices? What strategies are available at this level of the dispute?

Forum Selection

If the contract between the parties has a "forum selection clause," it determines in advance by mutual agreement where and in what court any disputes will be heard. It is a part of the advance planning strategy in negotiating commercial transactions.

As we previously discussed in the chapter on sources of law, "choice-of-law clauses" can be agreed upon in advance by the parties to govern what laws will apply in the event of a dispute.

If, for example, in a contract for sale of goods, a seller has successfully inserted a requirement that Japanese law will govern (all sales are as-is with no guarantee of performance) rather than the usual UCC law applicable throughout U.S. courts (all sales of goods have warranty protection), the buyer who successfully requires that any disputes be brought in a New York federal court will still be faced with the foreign law being applied by the local forum. The seller would have the advantage in a dispute that occurs, and could probably induce a favorable settlement.

If, however, there were no choice-of-law clause in the contract, a New York forum selection clause would assure that the buyer had UCC warranty protection because the designated court would be duty bound to apply local law. The buyer would have the settlement advantage if a dispute occurred.

Forum Non Conveniens

If there is no forum selection by mutual agreement of the parties, the plaintiff, as the complainant in the lawsuit, will choose where to sue. Sometimes the defendant objects on the grounds that it does not have sufficient legal contacts with the chosen forum to be fairly required to defend there, as required by the due process clause of the U.S. Constitution.

Sometimes the defendant's request for dismissal is based upon the doctrine of *forum non conveniens*. It is a procedural remedy of fairness, derived from eighteenth-century English law, that allows a court to reject jurisdiction over a case if the result would be "vexatious and works unnecessary hardship on the defendant."

This usually occurs in situations where the defendant is a financial "deep pocket," the dispute involves personal injures or large contract damages, important events have primarily occurred outside the United States, but the plaintiff files suit in a U.S. court. The defendant claims the plaintiff is "forum shopping," by using our courts to hope for the unique aspects of our judicial system not available outside the U.S. – large jury awards, unlimited trial discovery, contingent fee hiring of lawyers, punitive damages for extreme conduct, and appellate remedies.

If the parties had agreed upon a forum selection clause in their contract, there could be no "forum shopping" in the event of a contract dispute. But such advance planning often does not occur in contracts, and is not possible in non-contract cases such as alleged negligence of the defendant causing personal injuries to the plaintiff.

In modern times, courts have become wary of the motivations of some foreign plaintiffs in seeking judicial relief in U.S. courts, and have often expressed these concerns:

"(Without this) procedural tool ... Texas will become an irresistible forum for all mass disaster lawsuits. 'Bhopal'-type litigation, with little or no connection to Texas, will add to our already crowded dockets, forcing our residents to wait in the corridors of our courthouses while foreign causes of action are tried." *Dow Chemical v. Alfaro, 786 S.W.2d 674 (Tex. 1990) (dissent)*

The reference to "Bhopal" comes from probably the most famous application of the forum non conveniens doctrine to reject the plaintiffs' choice of a U.S. forum. Union Carbide owned 51% of its Bhopal, India subsidiary, and due to alleged negligence at its chemical plant in 1984, lethal gas was released which killed or severely injured thousands of persons. It was the most devastating industrial disaster in history.

Suit was filed by the government of India against the "deep pocket" parent company in New York federal court. Union Carbide contended that the case should be heard in India. The court dismissed the U.S. action, requiring that it be litigated in India. The court's decision was based upon the almost exclusively India-based aspects of the dispute:

- All witnesses were in India
- All documents were in India
- Transportation and translation problems would ensue if it were held in the U.S.
- Plant managed entirely by Indian citizens
- Plant operation regulated by Indian agencies
- No Americans employed at time of accident
- No Americans visited prior to one year before accident
- No communications for five years between plant and U.S.

The court said, "The doctrine of forum non conveniens is a rule of U.S. law, which states that where a case is properly heard in more than one court, the one that is most convenient should hear it. Given the facts of this case, the courts of India are the more convenient forums."

Union Carbide settled the case in India before trial, in 1989, for $470 million, which was estimated to be one-half of what a jury award would have been in the U.S. *In Re Union Carbide Corporation Gas Plant Disaster at Bhopal, 809 F.2d 195 (2d Cir. 1987)*

Notice how the settlement value of this lawsuit changed depending upon where the plaintiff was legally permitted to litigate.

Federal or State Court

If there is no such advance selection of the forum, we must examine the applicable rules of law governing jurisdiction of courts. It can be critically important to the outcome of the case but is seldom understood by the general public as a strategic opportunity for advance planning.

Our judicial system is actually dual layers of courts that operate concurrently. There is one federal system and fifty separate systems within each state. All have three basic levels. While state court judges are usually elected for limited terms, federal court judges are appointed for life.

The trial court level is where the case is initially presented, and is presided by a judge as to matters of law and, if either party requests it, heard by a jury that evaluates the factual evidence. At this level, there is presented the testimony of the actual parties and their witnesses, all documentary evidence is introduced, and a final judgment is entered. State trial courts are numerous, usually being located within each county. There is at least one federal trial court in each state, but there may be more than one since they are located in major population centers.

The appellate level is usually an automatic right of the losing party to try to convince a higher court that there were substantial errors of law in the trial. While there is only one judge on the trial level, there are usually three or more that hear appellate cases. There is no new evidence presented at this level. The judges are limited to the "record" of the lower court. State appellate courts are located according to each state's population needs, while federal appellate courts are less numerous, there being only thirteen to serve all fifty states.

The supreme court of each state and the U.S. Supreme Court are the highest levels of the court system. These are the "courts of last resort," whose legal decisions are final. Unlike the appellate level, there is no absolute right to appeal a civil case. Whether or not this highest court decides to hear a case usually depends upon its importance to the public and impact on society. Applications to be heard are by "writ of certiorari."

The decision of the higher courts may either be to affirm and leave the trial judgment intact, reverse it, modify it in some manner, or grant a new trial. Unanimous or majority vote determines the appellate decision. Often, majority decisions will include dissenting opinions, which can signal critical times when the law may change in a particular area as new cases arise with similar facts.

The typical appellate evolutionary process starts with a case where the trial court decision is unanimously affirmed. Then in a later similar case, there is a majority affirm with one dissenting vote, and later another similar affirm with a smaller majority and more dissents. Finally, another related case is decided where the majority vote swings over to the reversal side and we have come full cycle, with a new legal precedent.

There are significant practical reasons for a plaintiff to choose to file suit in either the federal or state court system.

Some of the major advantages and disadvantages are:

FEDERAL

- Judges free from local politics
- Judges more experienced
- Better suited for complex cases
- More time-consuming procedures
- More expensive to complete

STATE

- Local interests may prevail
- Judges less experienced
- Uneven levels of judicial expertise
- More flexibility
- Faster resolution of disputes

Jurisdiction over the Subject Matter

Federal courts have concurrent jurisdiction with state courts, so that a plaintiff has the choice of suing in either place, depending upon its jurisdictional requirements.

Federal courts have exclusive jurisdiction to hear disputes involving certain federal laws, including immigration, admiralty, bankruptcy, antitrust, and intellectual property rights.

Federal court jurisdiction requires that (1) the dollar amount sued for must exceed $75,000, AND (2) there must be "diversity of citizenship." Diversity legally means that the litigants are both permanent resident citizens of two different U.S. states, that one litigant is a U.S. citizen and one is a sovereign foreign country, or litigation between U.S. citizens and foreign nationals. For purposes of corporate parties, "diversity" is governed by their state of incorporation.

If the dispute involves the interpretation or constitutionality of a federal law, suit must be filed in a federal court, but no minimum dollar amount or diversity of citizenship requirements is enforced.

If the federal court jurisdictional requirements are not met, the plaintiff may be required to sue in the appropriate state court.

Notice how intricate these disputes can be. If the plaintiff files suit in federal court and meets the jurisdictional requirements, the federal procedural law will apply, but the court must use state substantive law, absent a choice-of-law clause in the contract sued upon. This is the famous *Erie Doctrine*.

But the defendant may still successfully raise an issue of what state law to use depending upon where it is really doing business under the minimum contacts legal test, which in turn depends upon the choice-of-law rules applied by the court, as we see in the next case.

Lazard Freres & Co. v. Protective Life Insurance Company, 108 F.3d 1531 (2nd Cir. 1997), involved a dispute between two large and sophisticated bank debt traders regarding the sale of $10 million face value of bank debt.

The plaintiff, a New York investment bank and broker-dealer, agreed to purchase the bank debt of MCC, and attempted to turn around and sell it to the defendant, a Tennessee corporation whose principal place of business was in Alabama. After a number of conversations, the transaction was agreed, and reduced to a written "Scheme Report." The defendant had required in the verbal negotiations that "twenty percent of the face amount of the debt was going to be paid (within 60 days), and there were no outstanding litigations against MCC that would reduce the value of the debt." The written document, unread by the defendant before signing, did not contain these assurances.

The defendant discovered the problem when the price of the MCC bank debt dropped substantially, and refused to close the deal. The plaintiff sued for breach of contract, and the defendant asserted fraud as its defense. The trial court granted the plaintiff's motion for summary judgment and the defendant appealed. On appeal, the summary judgment was vacated, and the case remanded for a trial on the issues raised.

One of the areas of dispute was what law to apply because, "A federal court sitting in diversity must apply the choice of law rules of the forum state," in this case New York.

"Until the latter part of this century, New York courts employed a traditional, 'territorially oriented' approach to choice-of-law issues which applied the law of the geographical place where one key event occurred, such as the place of the wrong in tort cases or where an agreement was entered into or performed in contract cases.

"In contract cases, New York courts now apply a 'center of gravity' or 'grouping of contacts' approach. Under this approach, courts may consider a spectrum of significant contacts, including the place of contracting, the places of negotiation and performance, the location of the subject matter, and the domicile or place of business of the contracting parties . . . The traditional choice of law factors, the places of contracting and performance, are given the heaviest weight in this analysis . . . Under New York conflicts rules, the center of gravity of the MCC transaction was New York."

A number of recent federal court cases reflect disputes as to how the jurisdictional amount required for a case to be heard in federal court is computed.

The disputes take two different forms: (1) the plaintiff files suit in state court, the defendant requests removal to federal court, and the plaintiff files motion to remand back to state court, or (2) the plaintiff files suit in federal court and the defendant moves to remand.

- Punitive damage claims cannot be added to basic damages to meet the $75,000 jurisdictional amount requirement. *Kirkland v. Midland Mortgage Co., 2001 WL 224776 (11th Cir. 2001)*
- Counterclaim amounts are properly includible in determining jurisdictional amount. *Spectator Mgt. Group v. Brown, 131 F.3d 131 (3rd Cir. 1997)*
- Each diversity plaintiff must have $75,000 at stake. *Leonhardt v. Western Sugar Co., 160 F.3d 631 (10th Cir. 1998)*

- Choice-of-law rules are based upon a five-point weighing test. *Hughes v. Wal-Mart Stores, Inc., 250 F.3d 618 (8th Cir. 2001)*
- Multiple plaintiffs may not add up the dollar amounts of their claims in order to meet the federal minimum jurisdictional amount. *Sdregas v. Home Depot, 2002 U.S. Lexis 12159 (E.D. PA. 2002)*

State court jurisdiction has no such limitations, other than the fact that different levels of state courts hear cases in different dollar levels, like small claims courts, which usually have a jurisdictional ceiling of $5,000.

Once the plaintiff completes court jurisdictional strategy on either the state or federal level, the venue issue arises. It is a procedural rule that requires the plaintiff to file suit in a state or federal court located nearest to:

1. where the defendant legally resides (primary residence of at least six months plus one day, not summer/winter homes or vacation residences), OR
2. where the dispute legally arose (where contract was signed, transaction was completed, or injuries occurred)

Notice how the legal system again tries to level the scales of justice by directing venue toward the defendant's home base.

The plaintiff chooses to sue, chooses a legal remedy, and chooses where to sue – but that "where" involves a requirement that tries to balance any "home cooking" that might benefit the plaintiff.

If the plaintiff chooses an improper venue, the defendant may demand a change of venue to the proper court location. This is a mandatory venue change, granted by the court when the defendant files a motion to change venue.

There is also a discretionary venue change rule, whereby a defendant sometimes alleges that a fair trial is impossible due to adverse prejudicial publicity. This rarely is granted by the court in civil business cases, unless a media circus directly impacts the specific issues being litigated.

Now let's play the chess game with a common dispute, and use the rules of proper court jurisdiction and venue to illustrate situations where both of the parties might be able to strategically induce a favorable settlement.

Jack and Jill, who respectively reside in Miami, Florida, and Philadelphia, Pennsylvania, both decide to visit Disneyworld in Orlando, Florida. Jill drives south on I-95, Jack drives north on I-95, and just as they go up a hill in the Orlando city limits, Jill rear-ends Jack. Jack suffers severe injuries and decides to sue Jill for $76,000 in damages. It just so happens that Jack's family has a long history in Miami, streets are named after them, and they know a lot of important local people, so he sues Jill in Miami state court.

1. Is Jack allowed to sue in Miami federal court? Yes – he satisfies the two jurisdictional requirements of the required amount in dispute (more than $75,000) AND diversity of citizenship (Florida and Pennsylvania). But he could also choose the state court level, since they operate concurrently.

2. Is Jack allowed to sue in Miami state court? Yes – because there are no specific requirements like those imposed by the federal system.

3. Did Jack choose the proper court venue? No – he chose not to file suit where Jill resides (Philadelphia) for obvious strategic reasons. Nor did he sue, as required, where the accident occurred (Orlando). But unless Jill is aware of these venue requirements, and files a "motion to change venue" with the state court judge, nothing will change and she will have to defend in Miami state court. The case will probably settle in Jack's favor shortly thereafter. (Note: A motion is an application to the judge requesting some type of relief. If no request is made, judges don't do the work of the parties and correct their errors for them.)

4. If Jill filed a "motion to change venue" would she win? Yes – she could have the case moved within the state system to either Orlando or, more likely, to the Philadelphia state court, where she resides. The case will probably settle in Jill's favor as soon as her motion is granted.

5. If Jack had chosen the proper venue and sued in Orlando, could Jill still win on a requested venue change on the grounds that she couldn't get a fair trial due to the well-known status in Florida of Jack's family? No – we don't have a media circus here and, like most civil cases, there is not the potential for a lot of prejudicial publicity.

    However, what if our dispute in question was a suit for damages brought in Miami federal court by the family of Elian Gonzalez against the U.S. Immigration Department for the famous seizing of him by the government swat team and his return to his father for travel back to Cuba? There would have been a three-ring circus in Miami, and the venue would probably have been changed to another less volatile location.

6. If Jack had chosen the proper venue and sued in Orlando, does Jill have any other recourse? Yes – Jill can properly request the case be removed to a federal court having proper venue – a Philadelphia federal court, and she will no doubt have his case settled as soon as his request is granted. This is due to the "removal rule" of court jurisdiction, which states that a defendant who is sued in state court may remove his case to the federal level if the two federal jurisdiction requirements can be satisfied. Here we have both the required amount in dispute and diversity of citizenship, so Jill would win.

7. Are there ways that Jack can "checkmate" Jill and require her to defend in Orlando state court? Yes: (A) if Jack sues for a jurisdictional amount under $75,000 ($74,999) he will legally prevent Jill from achieving removal to federal court, even with diversity of citizenship, or (B) if Jack could also add, in good faith, another Miami defendant, he would destroy diversity and keep the case in state court, even though it met the federal jurisdictional amount threshold.

    Notice how the plot thickens as each party to the dispute plans strategy and counters the anticipated moves of the other. Whenever you see a lawsuit that is being heard in either state or federal court, it probably has gone through a similar journey.

Jurisdiction over the Person

Even when the issue of the court's subject matter jurisdiction is resolved, there is another jurisdictional question. Does this court have proper "jurisdiction over the person" of the defendant? In other words, is the defendant properly "in court" so that any rulings are legally binding?

Disputes often arise where a non-resident defendant, especially a corporation, seeks to dismiss the action based upon lack of required "minimum contacts" to constitute it "doing business" in the forum jurisdiction. This is a case-by-case analysis, but the current trend is to allow jurisdiction for most nominal local contacts such as advertisements, phone calls, and business trips.

These cases illustrate such disputes:

- Legal communications between Germany and Texas establish Texas personal jurisdiction. *Wien Air Alaska, Inc. v. Brandt, 195 F.3d 208 (5th Cir. 1999)*
- 40% ownership of Kentucky motel by French corporation not sufficient grounds for personal jurisdiction. *Dean v. Motel 6 Operating L.P., 134 F.3d 1269 (6th Cir. 1998)*
- One phone call not enough to establish minimum contacts. *Watertronics, Inc. v. Flanagans, Inc., 2001 WL 942639 (Wisc. App. 2001)*

Jurisdiction over the person usually occurs when an officer of the court delivers the legal papers to the defendant. This is called achieving "in personam" jurisdiction by "service of process," and the persons who do this are process servers:

A) When a lawsuit is filed in state or federal court, a summons is issued by the court clerk, and copies of both must be legally delivered to the defendant.

   In most states, if the individual defendant cannot be personally served, the papers may be legally delivered to any adult member of the defendant's household. This blunts the games defendants sometimes play to evade service of process. Sooner or later the court papers will properly arrive, so why delay the inevitable? Stop hiding under the bed, Mr. Defendant, accept the papers, hire a good lawyer, and get on with it.

B) When the defendant is a corporation or similar legal person, the laws of each state require it to designate a natural person as its registered agent to receive the court papers. Service of process on that person legally binds the corporate defendant.

C) Most states also have adopted "long-arm" statutes that allow non-resident defendants to be legally served if they:

   - Own real estate in the state that is the subject matter of the lawsuit
   - Commit a tort within the state, like automobile negligence
   - Made the contract sued upon within the state
   - Were "doing business" within the state (minimum contacts test)
   - Maintained an "active" website selling goods or services

D) Sometimes, the dispute concerns a piece of land, and "in rem" jurisdiction is obtained by merely posting the legal notice on the property. Landlord and tenant, mortgage foreclosures, and mechanic's lien disputes fall within this category.

So we now have a dispute that has ripened into full-blown litigation. Attorneys have been hired, the law has been researched, the lawsuit has been filed in a state or federal court of the plaintiff's choosing, and the papers have been served upon the defendant. Let the typical civil lawsuit begin.

Discussion Exercises

1. Discuss/create a case in which you as plaintiff would sue in federal court.

2. Discuss/create a case in which you as plaintiff would sue in state court.

3. Discuss/create a case in which you as defendant would remove from state to federal court.

4. Discuss arguments you would make to change the venue of a civil case.

5. Discuss any other jurisdictional strategies to induce a favorable settlement.

Case Exercise 7

Lack of Complete Diversity Prevents Federal Court Removal

In *Cheskiewicz v. Aventis Pasteur, Inc., 2002 U.S. Dist. LEXIS 15339 (E.D.Pa. 2002)*, a strict liability suit over a child's allegedly adverse reactions to vaccinations manufactured by the defendants was originally filed in Pennsylvania state court.

The plaintiffs were citizens of Pennsylvania, and the named defendants were citizens of other states, except for two Pennsylvania corporate defendants, who were allegedly involved in the chain of commerce for production of the allegedly dangerously defective product.

The defendants attempted to transfer the case to Pennsylvania federal court based upon removal jurisdiction, claiming the two Pennsylvania corporations were "sham defendants," joined solely for the purpose of defeating the diversity requirement. They requested those two defendants be dismissed.

The plaintiffs claimed that the non-diverse parties were properly joined as manufacturers of the vaccines or adulterants that allegedly caused the injuries sued upon, and therefore no required diversity existed and the case would have to be heard in state court. They filed a motion to remand back to state court.

Analysis

The appellate court granted the plaintiff's motion to remand for lack of diversity jurisdiction.

"Removal premised on diversity of citizenship fails where one of the remaining defendants is non-diverse unless: (1) there is a federal question; or (2) the non-diverse defendant was joined fraudulently.

"As there is no federal question, the defendants must show that . . . the non-diverse defendants have been fraudulently joined."

The legal test of fraudulent joinder was stated to be, "where there is no reasonable basis in fact or colorable ground supporting the claim against the joined defendant, or no real intention in good faith to prosecute the action against the defendants or seek a joint judgment."

The court found that the plaintiff's complaint stated allegations against the non-diverse defendants which raised the required "colorable claims," and therefore their joinder, which defeated removal jurisdiction, was not improper.

Defuse Replay

This case illustrates an interesting strategy to prevent a defendant from exercising the right to remove to federal court.

If removal was successful, the defendants would have had a distinct advantage simply because they could prevent the plaintiffs from suing where they wanted. By denying removal, the plaintiffs now hold the strategic advantage.

Plaintiffs often employ a checkmate strategy, as stated before, to prevent their defendant(s) from removing to federal court in one of two ways:

- Sue for less than $75,000 in cases where the damages sought are close to that jurisdictional threshold, or

- Join an additional defendant from the same state as one or more of the main defendants.

The latter strategy of creating non-diversity must pass the good faith test, but the path to accomplish this is suggested by this language from the appellate court:

"In deciding whether the non-diverse defendants were properly joined, the court must concentrate on the plaintiff's complaint at the time the petition for removal was filed."

The legal sufficiency of a complaint is whether or not it states a legal cause of action against the defendant(s). This is determined on a motion to dismiss the complaint, by assuming the truth of all its allegations.

Conclusion

The appellate court said, "If there is even a possibility that a state court would find that the complaint states a cause of action against any one of the resident defendants, the federal court must find that joinder was proper and remand the case to state court."

Whether or not the plaintiff can later prove the allegations against the added non-diverse defendants is immaterial in questions of proper removal jurisdiction. All that need be done is the stating of facts, which, *if true*, would create reasonable grounds for recovery.

This 2002 case clarifies some of the strategy questions that have previously been raised without any legal confirmation of what can or cannot be done. It will serve as a guide for the drafting of future complaints and the joinder of non-diverse defendants to thwart issues of removal.

A. Do you agree with the court's final decision?

B. Do you think the creation of non-diversity to prevent removal jurisdiction is an effective strategy? Advantages? Disadvantages?

C. Do you think it is ethical to create non-diversity if the added defendants are not really an important part of the case?

F.   STEPS OF A TYPICAL LAWSUIT

"I was never ruined but twice; once when I lost a lawsuit, and once when I won one."

—Voltaire

The plaintiff dictates the pace of a civil dispute. Always the moving party, the plaintiff has decided to sue after getting input from counsel as to the governing rules of law and the realistic prospects for success. A lawyer has been hired. A legal remedy has been selected, which usually is money damages in the typical contracts or sales case. The plaintiff, either in a state or federal court, has also chosen the jurisdiction of the lawsuit.

Let's understand a few more litigation terms:

A) "Filed the lawsuit" We hear the phrase all the time, but what does it really mean? It is deceptively simple. The plaintiff goes to the appropriate courthouse jurisdiction and presents to the clerk's office the necessary legal papers to start the proceedings, together with the required filing fee. The clerk opens a court file with the names of the parties, gives it a court file number, and assigns the case to a judge using a blind rotating file designation system. Every court document thereafter is docket stamped and goes into this file.

B) "The parties" This refers to the principals in the lawsuit, the plaintiff and the defendant. They can be he (male), she (female), or it (a legal entity, such as a corporation). Others who participate in the giving of testimony or presentation of evidence are called "witnesses." If an appeal is filed from an adverse court ruling or jury decision, the losing party who seeks appellate relief is the "appellant," and the winning party defending the appeal is the "appellee."

C) "Reported cases" Appellate court and supreme court decisions are transcribed and regularly published in various reporting services, such as West Publishing or Lexis-Nexis. Trial court proceedings are not usually reported, although some services exist strictly for that purpose. Case citation formats are keyed to the various regional legal reporting services so that any appeal of a lower court case is readily available in a law library that carries those reporter volumes, or more practically, with a simple computer keystroke.

When reading a reported case, there is a distinct pattern to the presentation. First there usually is a summary of the action taken by the reporting appellate court, followed by a review of the facts that created the dispute.

Then the rules of law pertaining to that type of problem are stated, often with citations of authority to prior cases.

(The most persuasive authority is recent cases with the same or similar facts decided in the same state.) Finally, the court does its reasoning by applying the facts of the dispute to the governing rules of law so that the necessary decision can be made.

D) "Represented by counsel" Since court proceedings are so specialized, the litigants are usually represented by their respective attorneys, and they speak and act through their lawyers. If, however, a party wishes to self-represent, it is permissible, but tantamount to judicial suicide. How can a layperson, no matter how smart, know all the ins and outs of a courtroom? It's like waking up one morning with a rotten tooth and deciding to just take care of matters ourselves with our trusty old pliers.

E) "The pleadings" All the major court documents that the parties to the lawsuit file are called the "pleadings."

F) "The evidence" This consists of all the testimony of the parties and their witnesses and all the documents they are allowed to introduce into evidence.

G) "Burden of proof" The plaintiff-complainants are always the moving party in a civil dispute, and must satisfy the legal proof test, whereby they establish their case by the "greater weight" or "preponderance" of the evidence. Visualize the scales of justice. If they are tipped, even slightly, in the plaintiff's favor, the burden of proof is satisfied.

H) "Heard by judge or jury" In most civil cases, either party may have a jury trial by simply requesting it in the initial pleading. If this occurs, the judge is in charge of the law and all necessary legal rulings. The judge is also known as "the court" or "your honor." The jury is in charge of the facts, deciding what or who to believe, and how much weight to give the factual evidence.

This is another area where strategy may induce a favorable settlement. Civil juries are usually composed of individuals, just like you and me, chosen at random from the local pool of names for jury service. Jurors are not corporations or other business organizations, and are often hostile to larger organizations, since they often are the cause of one's daily problems. So if the lawsuit is a David v. Goliath type dispute, a jury will probably be more receptive to the plight of "the little person."

If ABC, Corp. sues Mr. and Mrs. Macgillicuddy and does not ask for a jury trial, this is a clear signal and opportunity for the defendants to request it. By doing so, they have increased their bargaining leverage and will hopefully achieve a favorable settlement. Again, the judge won't do this for the parties; they have to make the chess moves themselves.

The author was a civil trial lawyer early in his career and spent many a day and night inside courtrooms, and has a special appreciation for the trial process. The scales of justice are a graphic visual metaphor for the ebb and flow of first one party and then the other trying to persuade the decision-maker to rule in their favor. The trial is like a fencing contest, a flowing back and forth of thrust and parry, point and counterpoint between the plaintiff and the defendant. At any stage of a trial, one of the parties may decide to surrender, or the judge/jury may seize upon a key aspect of the evidence presented by the plaintiff or the defendant to turn the scales in that party's favor.

Following are the chronological steps in a typical civil lawsuit. (Remember, whatever the plaintiff or the defendant allege in their pleadings must be proven by the greater weight of the evidence.)

1. The lawsuit starts with the filing of the plaintiff's COMPLAINT, which summarizes the ultimate facts of the dispute, alleges that the defendant is at fault, and requests appropriate court relief.
2. The SUMMONS accompanies the complaint, directing the defendant to appear in court or otherwise respond, usually within twenty days. The court clerk issues it, and then the summons and complaint are served by an officer of the court to achieve jurisdiction over the person of the defendant. Service may be made upon resident or non-resident defendants. If the latter, they will often try to resist the disadvantage of having to defend in the plaintiff's backyard by claiming they were not "doing business" within the forum state.

   If the defendant ignores the legal papers served and fails to respond within the required time, a default judgment may be entered by the court in favor of the plaintiff.
3. JURISDICTIONAL MOTIONS are filed by the defendant within the twenty-day response time if there is to be a contest of the court's jurisdiction. If they are granted as to improper service of process, faulty venue, or removal to a different court, the case may also be settled at this stage.

4. The ANSWER is filed by the defendant after the jurisdictional motions have been decided, or if none were filed, again within the initial twenty-day period, or later if permitted by the court. The answer summarizes the defendant's case, admits or denies specific allegation of the complaint, and states affirmative defenses claimed by the defendant. These defenses are any legal grounds that would bar the plaintiff's lawsuit.

   For example, if Car A is rear-ended by Car B, the law of negligence presumes that Car B is at fault. Car A files a complaint, which alleges that Car B struck it from the rear.

   In the answer filed by Car B, the collision is admitted but liability may be denied based upon allegations that Car A made a sudden stop, which raises the affirmative defense of contributory negligence.

   Another common affirmative defense raised by defendants is the "statute of limitations." Every state has laws that specify the period of time within which the plaintiff must bring a lawsuit. Even if a complaining party has a good case based upon the facts and applicable law, it may be dismissed if not filed in time. Here's an actual case:

   In July 1991, Whirlpool Financial Corp. (Whirlpool) loaned $10 million to GN Holdings, Inc. (GN) to help it acquire another company. To secure this financing, GN furnished to Whirlpool a private placement memorandum with certain financial projections. Three years later, GN defaulted and Whirlpool sued for securities fraud. GN raised the one-year statute of limitations in federal securities laws as an affirmative defense and won the case. The claim of Whirlpool was time-barred. *Whirlpool Financial Corp. v. GN Holdings, Inc., 67 F.3d 605 (7th Cir. 1995)*

5. COUNTERCLAIMS are sometimes filed by a defendant as a part of his answer, if he claims a legal injury arising from the same set of facts. This reverses the roles of the parties, whereby the defendant is the cross-plaintiff, the plaintiff is now the cross-defendant, and the original plaintiff must now file an answer (called a reply) to the counterclaim.

6. DISCOVERY is unique to the American legal system, and is the stage of the proceedings where most settlements are reached. This is due to the fact that now the parties can find out all the details of what really took place in the dispute, rather than the preliminary pleadings, which have just been summaries of events. Additional benefits are that once full disclosures have been made, even if the case continues, there will be no surprises.

   • Production of Documents – lists of witnesses, reports of experts, all the relevant correspondence, files, contracts, memorandums, and other items, including e-mail messages and other electronic evidence.
   • Mental or Physical Examinations – can be ordered in cases where the parties may claim damages for personal injuries or emotional distress, or their physical and mental conditions are at issue.
   • Interrogatories – written questions submitted by the parties which must be answered under oath, and to which documents may need to be

attached. This usually elicits information as to who knows about important facts, and where further information might be found.

- Depositions – oral interrogations of parties and witnesses in the presence of their lawyers, transcribed by a court reporter, and often videotaped to preserve evidence for future usage at trial if necessary, or for impeachment purposes to protect against a deponent's story being changed at trial.

7. PRETRIAL CONFERENCE is theoretically where the parties appear before the judge in an informal setting to discuss their respective positions, identify the major areas of dispute, agree upon witnesses and documentary evidence, estimate how long it will take to complete their cases, and have the judge set the actual trial date. In actuality, this is used more and more by judges to try and convince the parties to settle their differences, by subtle and not-so-subtle persuasion. Court dockets are filled to overflowing in our litigious society, and a success from the judge's standpoint is one less open case.

8. PRETRIAL MOTIONS are usually made by the parties once a court date has been set (although they can be made at any stage of the proceedings), in which they try to convince the judge that (a) they should win because the complaint or counterclaim fails to state a cause of action (Motion to Dismiss), or (b) they should win based solely upon the pleadings filed (motion for judgment on the pleadings), or (c) they should win because there are no real issues of fact to be litigated based upon all the evidence and they should win based upon the applicable rules of law (motion for summary judgment).

9. THE TRIAL is non-jury if neither party requested a jury trial. The judge then decides all issues of fact and law. In a jury trial, the judge rules on issues of the law and the jury determines issues of the facts, including the importance of the evidence and believability of the witnesses.

Let's assume that the plaintiff or the defendant has made a jury demand and we will have a jury trial. Notice the symmetry of the trial process in the following steps of a typical jury trial, where the plaintiff initiates and the defendant responds, as each side tries to tip the scales of justice in his favor. (Remember, when we refer to the "parties," their attorneys will really be performing.)

- Jury Selection – *voire dire* is the process of selecting potential jurors from the pool of voters who are called for jury duty.

   They are assembled at the courthouse, assigned to a courtroom, seated in groups usually of six, and then asked questions by the judge and both parties to determine if they are unbiased and can make a fair and impartial decision. Each party has a number of "challenges," where they can excuse a juror they feel is biased. New potential jurors are then seated in the jury box. The process continues until both sides "accept the panel."

- Opening Statements – this is a preview of their respective cases presented by the parties. The seated jury is told what the parties intend to prove, what witnesses they will hear, what evidence they will see, and what their desired ruling should be.

- The Plaintiff's Case – the entire case is presented through the testimony of the plaintiff and witnesses, and all supporting documents are introduced into evidence. As the plaintiff and witnesses "take the witness stand," they are sworn in by the court clerk, they "swear to tell the whole truth and nothing but the truth," and are then questioned by the plaintiff's counsel on direct examination. The defendant can then cross-examine about statements and documents covered in direct examination. The plaintiff's task is to satisfy its burden of proof and convince the jury to decide in its favor. The end of the plaintiff's case is signified by stating, "the plaintiff rests."

  The defendant usually moves for a directed verdict in his favor at this point, based upon the plaintiff's alleged failure to satisfy the required burden of proof. It is routinely denied if there is any evidence at all on which the jury might rule for the plaintiff.

- The Defendant's Case – the same process occurs as previously, just in reverse order, where the entire defense case is presented, and then the plaintiff can cross-examine. The defendant's task is to rebut the plaintiff's case, prove any affirmative defenses raised, and otherwise convince the jury to vote in its favor. When finished, "the defendant rests."

  Now the plaintiff usually moves for a directed verdict based upon the defendant's alleged failure to prove his case, and again it will routinely be denied. Courts are reluctant to take a case away from the jury if there is any evidence in the record upon which they could rule for the non-moving party.

- Rebuttal – if the plaintiff feels the need to counter or clarify some of the defendant's case, the judge may allow additional related testimony or documents. In most current jury trials, however, all necessary evidence is usually presented in the main cases.

- Charging Conference – this is the least understood aspect of the jury trial process. Since the jury needs to know what rules of law to apply to the facts they have heard from testimony and seen through the documents in evidence, each party confers with the judge in private chambers while the jury is in recess. The plaintiff and the defendant offer the rules of law they believe should apply to the case, called "jury instructions," the judge decides which one or parts of each one to use, and then the judge convenes the jury and presents these rules to them for use in their deliberations.

- Closing Statements – the parties summarize to the jury what they have seen and heard in the main cases, and try to convince them one last time to rule in their favor. The jurors will be reminded of what the parties promised to do in their opening statements and then be assured that those promises were kept. The jurors are also told what rules of law the judge will require them to use in deciding the case.

- Jury Instructions – the judge reads to the jurors the rules of law they will be using in this case that he has chosen from the charging conference, and then sends them to the jury room to make their decision.
- Jury Deliberations – the jurors retire to the jury room, where they appoint a foreperson to be in charge of organizing their decision-making process. They are provided with all the items that have been introduced into evidence as well as the written jury instructions. They take a pre-liminary vote, have discussions, which are sometimes quite heated, and ultimately reach a majority decision.
- The Judgment – the decision of the jury is written, handed to the court bailiff who is on call, and then the judge is informed. The court proceedings are reconvened and the judge reads the decision to the parties, and enters judgment in favor of the plaintiff or the defendant accordingly. If the judgment is for the plaintiff, it usually is a two-part award, which declares the (1) *liability* of the defendant and (2) awards a stated dollar amount of money *damages*.

10. POST-TRIAL PROCEDURES:

- The judge may hear post-trial motions of either party. If the losing party feels the amount of damages is excessive it requests a remittitur. If the winning party feels damages are too low it requests an additur.
- If the losing party claims misconduct or bias by the jurors, the attorneys or, in the rare instance, the presiding judge, file a motion for a new trial.

  In *Minichiello v. The Supper Club, et al, 745 N.Y.S.2d 24 (N.Y. App. Div. 2002),* the plaintiff alleged he was verbally and physically abused by the defendants because of his sexual orientation, and then wrongfully fired when he refused to quit his position as late night manager of the restaurant-cabaret owned by the defendants.

  The jury awarded him compensatory and punitive damages exceed-ing $20 million. The defendants appealed, contending that the damages were grossly excessive, based upon misconduct of both the plaintiff's counsel and the trial judge, including counsel's analogy references of the plaintiff's German boss to Nazi Germany and the Holocaust, as well as other inappropriate comments about African-Americans, Lati-nos, and Jews. The judge also made demeaning remarks in the jury's presence.

  The appellate court reversed and ordered a new trial, saying, "The cumulative effect of the many irrelevant and highly prejudicial com-ments made by plaintiff's counsel in the course of the trial only served to incite the jury's passion and sympathy and effectively prevented a fair and dispassionate consideration of the evidence."
- The loser may also file a motion for judgment in its favor, notwith-standing the jury decision, called a judgment n.o.v., which is similar to a motion for directed verdict filed before the jury deliberates. It asserts

that no "reasonable" jury could have ruled in favor of the winning party. It is rare when this motion will be granted, because it nullifies the jury's verdict.

- The jury is commonly polled by the losing party to verify that its announced judgment is correct. The winning party may also question the jurors as to the reasons for their decision, as a learning experience for future trial technique.

11. COLLECTING THE JUDGMENT:
This area is the subject of much public confusion as to how and when a winning plaintiff gets paid. Contrary to what most people think, you don't automatically get paid when you win a money judgment. At the same time, most winning judgments are paid by the defendants within ten days of entry. Why?

Simply because the compulsion to pay is prompted by the fact that all assets in the name of the defendant are at risk and can be legally seized and sold at auction.

If the judgment is not paid within the required time, which varies from state to state, the plaintiff files a request for issuance of a "writ of execution" and the court then orders its civil collection office to enforce the judgment.

What if the defendant becomes judgment-proof by transferring assets out of his name? Since the same court that entered the judgment retains jurisdiction to collect it, and since there is always a paper trail of transfers to evade the claims of judgment creditors, the judge can invalidate them and order the assets back into the name of the defendant so that they are now available for collection by the plaintiff.

What if the defendant really has no collectible assets? The issue here is time. A judgment is legally enforceable, state-to-state, for anywhere from five to twenty years, and interest accrues on the balance due like any other indebtedness. Judgment creditors have the right to periodically interrogate defendants under oath as to their current finances. This is called a "deposition in aid of execution." Once assets are discovered, the collection process can be completed. (Note: Before you sue someone, you usually do a preliminary investigation of their financial condition. If they don't have assets, why bother to sue?)

For example, suppose Able sues Baker and recovers a money judgment for $100,000. Able is unable to locate any assets in Baker's name at the present time. The state law provides that money judgments are valid for ten years. Five years later Able reads in the local paper that Baker just won the lottery. Guess what? Able can now complete the collection process and have the judgment satisfied.

12. APPEAL is the right of any losing party in most civil cases. Usually a pleading called a "Notice of Appeal" has to be filed within thirty to ninety days after the adverse judgment has been entered. But what most people

don't realize is that the mere filing of this notice does NOT automatically stay the process of collection of the judgment. The winning party can still seize and sell any assets found in the defendant's name.

The only way this can be prevented is by the defendant posting an "Appeal Bond" to assure that the plaintiff will be paid if the defendant loses the appeal.

No new evidence or testimony may be presented on appeal. The appellate court reviews the record of the trial proceedings to determine if there were any substantial errors of law. (Remember, the appellate court can affirm the lower court decision, reverse it, or remand and order a new trial.)

A practical problem that often arises in the appellate process is the delay in collection it can cause. Suppose a jury has just awarded $10 million and the losing party immediately announces they will appeal. A defense strategy of dragging out a case as long as possible, especially in the small versus large litigant cases, will often result in a settlement favorable to the losing party, because many plaintiffs and their attorneys cannot afford to wait the year or more it takes for an appeal to be finalized.

Or suppose the losing party at the trial court level wants to appeal, but lacks the necessary funds. Again, this lack often will prevent an otherwise meritorious appeal, and induce a settlement advantageous to the winning party.

There are, however, alternatives available to the parties. They can try to finance their appeal with banks or other conventional lenders, although they often are refused due to the speculative nature of such matters. Or, they can go to a number of private investment companies that specialize in financing appeals on a contingent basis by purchasing for cash a participation in the expected final recovery. They make money by buying at a discount, and provide the needed funds for an appellant to hire an appellate specialist or otherwise be able to complete the appeal. Often, the fact that the appeal will be financed leads to a settlement of the entire matter.

Discussion Exercises

1. Discuss in what types of cases, as a plaintiff, you would want a jury trial. In what types would you want a non-jury trial?

2. Discuss in what types of cases, as a defendant, you would want a jury trial. In what types would you want a non-jury trial?

3. Discuss what jurisdictional motions you think most effective.

4. Discuss what pre- and post-trial motions you think most effective.

Case Exercise 8

Judgment N.O.V. Granted against Winning Plaintiffs

In *Ferlito v. Johnson & Johnson, 983 F.2d 1066 (6th Cir. 1992)*, the plaintiffs filed a products liability action, based upon a failure to warn theory, for injuries suffered by Mr. Ferlito when his Halloween sheep costume made from his long underwear, glue, and the defendant's cotton batting suddenly ignited as he lit a cigarette.

He was engulfed in flames and suffered burns over one-third of his body and underwent several surgeries due to the fire.

The cotton batting is marketed and sold by the defendant to clean wounds, to apply medication, and for infant care. There were no product use warnings on the product box.

Analysis

Based upon a failure to warn theory, the jury awarded Mr. Ferlito $550,000 and Mrs. Ferlito $70,000 after finding both the plaintiffs and the defendant equally at fault under comparative negligence for causing the fire.

After the jury returned its verdict, the defendant moved for judgment n.o.v., which was granted by the trial court, setting aside the jury verdict because the plaintiffs "failed to produce any evidence that the failure to warn would have dissuaded them from using the product."

The appellate court affirmed, noting, "When suing under a failure to warn theory, Michigan law requires the plaintiff to prove that if a proper warning had been given, the plaintiff would have taken precautions to prevent injury."

The court did not have to decide if a warning was necessary, but noted the facts of the case appeared to fall within the principle that, "If the risk is obvious from the characteristics of the product, the product itself telegraphs the precise warning."

Defuse Replay

This case is a rare instance when the trial judge disregards a jury verdict. Judgment n.o.v. is an extreme remedy because the court's granting of the motion takes the case away from the jury and denies the usual appellate review of their verdict.

"A judgment notwithstanding the verdict may not be granted unless reasonable minds could not differ as to the conclusions to be drawn from the evidence."

All the plaintiffs had to do was testify, as the court points out, "how their conduct would have differed if there had been a warning on the box of cotton material."

Conclusion

As the court points out, "Neither plaintiff testified that they would not have used the cotton had they been warned." Incredible, but true.

Their case was based upon a failure to warn theory, but its essential legal elements were ignored in their presentation.

No questions were asked of them by their counsel to elicit this simple and logical response, so no such evidence was in the court record. Therefore, the jury verdict was clearly unsupported and was set aside by the trial judge. This apparent fundamental error of the plaintiff's attorney comes very close to professional malpractice.

This case result is still unusual. Trial judges rarely take cases away from the jury, and even less frequently disturb their verdict once it is rendered. Let the appellate court decide, say most judges, since that is their job and not ours.

An appellate court, if it finds substantial error in the trial proceedings, will usually remand the case to the court below for further proceedings. However, it is also legally authorized to directly enter judgment against a jury-verdict winner, if it determines that the verdict was clearly erroneous.

"Courts of appeal should be constantly alert to the trial judge's firsthand knowledge of witnesses, testimony, and issues; in other words, appellate courts should give due consideration to the first-instance decision maker's 'feel' for the overall case. But the court of appeals has authority to render the final decision." *Weisgram v. Marley Company, 528 U.S. 440 (2000)*

A. Do you agree with the court's final decision?

B. If you were the presiding judge, would you have coached the plaintiff's counsel to ask the crucial questions?

C. Should judges take such a hand-on approach to cases where it appears mistakes are being made?

Case Exercise 9

Don't Mess With Shirley Maclaine

The case of *Parker v. Twentieth Century Fox Film Corporation, 474 P.2d 689 (Cal. 1970)*, involved a dispute between actress Shirley Maclaine (Parker) and her movie studio.

She had contracted to play the female lead in a musical to be shot in Los Angeles, exhibiting her singing and dancing skills, for a fixed fee of $750,000.

The studio decided against making that film, and offered her another film at the same compensation, but it was a dramatic western to be shot in Australia. She declined, and sued to recover the agreed contract price. The studio admitted it breached her contract, but defended, claiming she failed to mitigate damages by accepting the part in the substitute film. She moved for summary judgment.

Analysis

The trial court granted the plaintiff's motion for summary judgment on the basis that there were no genuine issues as to any material facts and she was entitled to judgment as a matter of law. It awarded her $750,000 plus interest.

On appeal by the defendant, the California Supreme Court affirmed, stating, "Defendant has raised no issue of reasonableness of efforts by plaintiff to obtain other employment; the sole issue is whether plaintiff's refusal of defendant's substitute offer of 'Big Country' may be used in mitigation . . . the offer of the 'Big Country' lead was of employment both different and inferior, and that no factual dispute was presented on that issue."

Defuse Replay

Since a motion for summary judgment requires the judge to assume that all facts in the pleadings are true, the key to prevention is making the necessary factual allegations in the complaint or answer. Whether they can be proved at trial is another issue, but at least their inclusion will thwart summary judgment.

Conclusion

Part of the anticipatory thinking in the judicial process is strategic defensive maneuvering. Filing a complaint that is summary judgment-proof may well advance the case to the point of meaningful settlement negotiations. Similarly, an answer that raises, for the purpose of that pleading, significant factual issues may well push the negotiating scales in the defendant's favor.

A. Do you agree with the court's final decision?

B. Should the plaintiff be paid the full contract price even if she does nothing?

C. Is it ethical to create factual issues that may never be proven solely to prevent the granting of summary judgment?

G.   WORKING WITH LAWYERS

"The First Thing we do, Let's Kill all the Lawyers"

—Shakespeare: King Henry IV

It is no surprise that our society holds the legal profession in less than high esteem. Think about the task lawyers are usually hired to do in civil business disputes. Their respective clients have reached a point of disagreement where they both think they are right, and then must have their problems resolved by a legal system which is adversarial, combative, and can have only one winner. In the middle of this warfare is the lawyer, advocating the position of his client and seeking to downplay that of his opponent, while seeking to persuade the decision-maker to rule in his favor.

Lawyers also serve a very useful function in our business marketplace, aside from their more visible roles in the courtroom. Their main function is not suing or defending lawsuits. Many practicing attorneys never participate in a trial. Their value, equally as important as trial advocacy, is in using their persuasive skills to:

- counsel you as to the real issues in your problem and help solve them
- prioritize your matters where they are not receiving necessary attention
- avoid disputes by advance planning of strategy and techniques
- induce a favorable settlement of a pending dispute
- assist in choosing your best legal remedy if suit may be necessary

These valuable functions are in the lawyers' actions as counselors at law, educating their clients in what rules of law govern their particular factual dispute, how their unique facts fit into the applicable law, and then evaluating a probable result.

And while we send a bit of praise to the legal profession, a rare occurrence in our lawyer-bashing society, mention should also be made of the important role of lawyers in providing legal services for the poor.

This is known as pro-bono work, where no fees are charged, or expected to be received. The bar associations of most states have implemented these programs to fill the gaps left by cuts in governmental funding for social assistance programs for the financially disadvantaged. They need legal help as much as anyone, yet cannot afford to hire an attorney.

In criminal proceedings, the legal system provides an indigent defendant the right to legal counsel through the public defender's office, paid for by the local governmental authority that is bringing the charges.

In civil cases, organizations such as "legal services for the poor" are staffed by lawyers and law firms in each community, who provide this public service with funding provided from a portion of the state bar dues of attorney members, cash assessments provided by lawyers who are unable to handle indigent matters, and the IOTA (interest on trust account) program.

One's pending legal dispute is a major drama. It takes center stage in our daily soap operas. It is also like a poker hand being played. Before you place your financial bet on its outcome, you need to know if you are holding four aces or a pair of fives.

What are the rules of the game itself? Which are the winning hands? And you need to know how much is the ante you must pay to get the game started.

In most contracts for the sale of goods or services, one of the parties has negotiated a better deal than the other side, or subsequent market conditions now make it the better deal.

The advantaged party is holding the high cards now and wants to enforce the contract. The disadvantaged party holds a losing hand and wants to be extricated from it. They both turn to their respective lawyers to accomplish this.

You can represent yourself in court if you wish, but if you do so you have a fool for a client. The legal arena is highly specialized. Lawyers must graduate from an accredited three-year law school where they receive a doctoral degree, take and pass a rigorous state bar examination, and then maintain a licensed status in their state by satisfying continuing legal education requirements. They are subject to malpractice actions and state disciplinary proceedings for negligent or criminal conduct.

So, the better procedure if legal problems arise is of course to hire a lawyer. This can be done in a variety of ways, limited only by your imagination, ingenuity, and bargaining skills, depending upon what action is needed.

What will it take to end the dispute? How can we induce a favorable settlement? E-mail, a phone call, a fax, a lawyer's letter, the filing of a lawsuit, and service of the summons on the defendant? Maybe a full-blown lawsuit, and the stubborn adversary won't yield until the jury is on the verge of its decision. Or we might have to reach the point of seizing the judgment debtor-defendant's assets and schedule their sale at auction before it is over. In all these situations, the lawyer is at the center of the action.

Attorneys are uniquely equipped by training and experience to analyze a hopelessly jumbled set of facts and cut to the heart of the legal problems involved. This is a valuable skill, because lawyers will tell you that one of their most difficult tasks is to get a prospective client to explain in some clear fashion what their problem is. Most people when asked, "What time is it?" will try to tell you how to make a watch.

Legal training enables attorneys to identify the legal issues in a dispute, research the governing rules of law, evaluate whether this particular factual situation will present a strong or weak case, and suggest appropriate action.

The first step is to choose a lawyer to interview. If you have ever used a lawyer in the past, ask for advice regarding your current problem. If you have never dealt with a lawyer, get recommendations from family and friends, talk to business associates, contact your local bar association for referrals, and consult the Yellow Pages. Lawyers are now allowed to advertise, and often list their specific experience and specialties in all types of media, including websites. There is even a reference source in many public libraries called "Martindale-Hubbell" that digests local laws and presents biographical sketches of attorneys listed by state, specialty, expertise, and rankings by their peers.

Don't limit yourself by just speaking to one lawyer. Be a good shopper before you make this important choice. The initial interview with a lawyer is customarily free of charge. Clarify this before making an appointment to discuss your problem.

Your Initial Interview

For the initial interview, bring with you all pertinent information. Write out ahead of time as brief a summary of your drama as possible, as if you were writing a newspaper story and were limited in space. Try to remove extraneous facts and get down to the heart of the matter.

Ask the necessary questions at the interview, after you have explained your situation:

1. Do they regularly communicate, promptly return phone calls, and meet deadlines?
2. What is their estimated time frame for your matter?
3. Will you be consulted regarding any settlement negotiations?
4. Will they be sufficiently aggressive for your needs?
5. What is their prior experience in the area of your particular matter?
6. Will they do the work personally or delegate it to associates?
7. Do they have any potential conflicts of interest with other clients?
8. What are the capabilities of support staff and office technology?
9. How your funds will be handled?
10. What is their reputation in the legal community?
11. Qualifications aside, do you feel a rapport with this person? Would you trust him or her to be in charge of your important business decisions?

The lawyer should now be able to advise you:

1. The strengths and weaknesses of your case and reasons why
2. An estimate of the probability of a successful outcome. This should include a summary of what legal papers will be filed, the court procedures, and the anticipated defenses to the action.
3. An estimate of the time it will take to complete the matter
4. A suggestion as to the type of fee arrangement, and an estimate of fees
5. The amount of cost deposit or retainer required

Evaluate the lawyer's responses after the initial interview. Don't make up your mind immediately. Discuss the interview with trusted or experienced family or friends, and then decide.

Finalizing the Hiring

After you decide to hire, you should finalize the possible financial arrangements. Again, remember you are in the driver's seat as the buyer of these services. We automatically inquire as to the price of the car, clothing, or consumables we are considering buying, but when it comes to our purchase of professional services, most of us are reluctant to ask in advance "how much?"

And the idea that, after we are told the projected cost of the desired services, we can negotiate and structure fee arrangements to suit our needs is equally foreign to our experience.

But that is what we can and should do, especially when we need legal advice. We have many alternatives, and much power as consumers of legal services. The hiring can be structured in any mutually acceptable way. The customary arrangements include the following:

- The free initial consultation – almost all practitioners will give you this if you ask for it. Many use it as an integral part of their advertising. It can let you know whether or not you are holding the high cards in your dispute and should go forward, or just need to let the matter go and walk away.
- The flat fee – matters that require a basic task like drafting a lease, preparing a purchase or sale contract, or resolving a traffic offense are customarily quoted to a prospective client as a fixed amount. Sometimes there is a combination of flat fee for initial work plus time charges thereafter.
- The annual retainer – these fees are agreed in advance to guarantee the availability of legal advice, usually for regular clients with a going business or repetitive legal problems.

  The amount payable is usually adjusted annually, based upon the prior year's expenditure of necessary legal time. It is also known as the "eyeball" method.
- The hourly rate – the basic method of lawyer compensation. What attorneys have to sell is their time. Rates may vary depending upon a variety of factors that include the matter's complexity, the lawyer's general level of experience and special expertise, the rates usually charged in the locale, and the big firm/small firm cost factors of the law office you may hire.
- The contingency fee – the no win, no pay arrangement – is common in the United States. It is the main form of attorney engagement in personal injury tort lawsuits. It is also prevalent in malpractice actions, social security benefit disputes, patent litigation, real estate tax appeals, corporate mergers and acquisitions, and public offerings of securities.

  Unique to the American legal system, it enables the financially disadvantaged to have proper access to the courts, and makes the lawyer one's partner in a successful result. The lawyer usually fronts most or all out-of-pocket expenses for investigation, experts, and legal preparation no matter how costly or time consuming.

  These fees have also been criticized as being financial incentives that encourage lawyers to file unnecessary, unwarranted, or unmeritorious lawsuits. There is also the possibility a lawyer will be more inclined to accept the first settlement offer and collect the usual one-third contingent fee, than work harder and go to court for the usual forty percent fee. It really all comes down to properly evaluating the person you hire.
- The equity participation – this usually occurs in start-up businesses or new ventures, where there is little capital but great expectations for future profits. The lawyer is gambling that his current investment of time and effort will be rewarded in the future.
- The barter arrangement – sometimes there is a lack of available cash for fees, but both lawyer and client have products or other services of mutual benefit that can be traded.

- The combination fee – any or all of the possible fee arrangements mentioned are used, combining various aspects depending upon the negotiation between lawyer and potential client.
- The hybrid fee – creativity of prospective client and lawyer is the key, limited only by their imagination and mutual willingness to make a deal.

Whatever fee arrangement is finally negotiated, it should be put in writing and signed by both parties. It should also cover the possibility of additional work due to an appeal from an adverse decision. Read it like any other binding contract and make sure you understand it and that it accurately reflects your prior discussions.

If a retainer/cost deposit is required, clarify how and when it will be used. If the fee arrangement involves any component of time charges, make sure you will receive regular billing statements that include a detailed listing of legal services rendered, who did the work, and the applicable hourly rates. These are computer generated as standard office procedure and should be readily available.

Settling Your Case

Trial lawyers will tell you that, in most cases, "even a bad settlement is better than a good lawsuit." Due to all the potential challenges in suing, as reflected in the prior chapter, over 90% of all disputes are settled in various stages of their existence. There are advantages and disadvantages to be considered:

- Disputes may not be finally resolved for years. A fair settlement produces instant cash that is available now, and removes the possibility of losing the case at arbitration, court trial, or on appeal.
- Proceeding to arbitration or court trial may result in a much larger award.
- Settlement timing is critical. Sometimes the first offer is the best. Often, waiting until the final moment and "settling on the courthouse steps" is the most effective bargaining strategy. Many disputes are even settled after a court decision or jury award, due to the uncertainties of the appellate process.
- The legal effect of a settlement should be clearly explained: What will be its effect on past disputes between the parties, if any, or similar pending claims against others? Will it affect future business transactions?

Communication with the lawyer and active participation in settlement negotiations is important. All settlement offers should be made in writing, and copies should be furnished the client.

Appealing Your Case

In almost all civil court cases, the losing party has an absolute right to appeal the decision to an appropriate state or federal appellate court. (Normally no such appellate rights exist in alternate dispute resolution procedures such as binding arbitration.)

The notice of appeal must usually be filed within thirty days of the adverse decision of the trial court. Aside from the additional expense involved in an appeal, there is no guarantee of a favorable outcome. Less than 30% of civil cases are reversed on appeal. The trial court decision comes to the appellate court with a presumption of correctness. It can only be overturned if there were substantial errors of law. No new facts or evidence may be presented on appeal. The appellate court is limited to a review of the record of the lower court proceedings.

However, your case may be one of the lucky ones. The more time and expense you have already incurred, one more shot at winning may be your best course of action. Since appellate practice is a legal specialty, it may also be necessary to hire a new attorney and make a new written financial arrangement.

Changing Your Lawyer

Clients have an absolute legal right to change lawyers at any time. The hiring of a lawyer is like any other employment relationship. Most clients forget this. The attorney is working for you, not the other way around.

Whether the reason for a desired change is a personality conflict, difference of opinion in strategy, unhappiness with the progress of the case, or any other reason, sometimes a change is best for all concerned.

There are, of course, advantages and disadvantages. Bringing in a new lawyer will require a duplication of time and effort, and slow down the progress of the case. Also, any progress made by prior counsel, rapport with other witnesses, parties, insurance persons, judges, arbitrators, etc. will be lost. Finally, changing lawyers is perceived to be a sign of weakness by the other side.

Sometime a breath of fresh air in the form of new counsel will revitalize a stagnant case. A different approach with different parties makes a positive difference in the progress of the matter.

If the reason for a desired change is a concern about your lawyer's professional conduct, another attorney should be consulted for an opinion. Since law is such a specialized profession, what may appear to you as an impropriety may be nothing more than a tactical approach. If, however, there are grounds for legal malpractice, your new lawyer will inform you as to your options. In any event, if you are uncomfortable or dissatisfied, by all means consider making a change.

But no matter what your reasons, DO NOT even discuss firing your lawyer until you have found a replacement. Let the lawyers handle all the details between themselves. They are the experts and are familiar with such situations. Do not get involved other than to verify, when asked, that you do in fact want to make a change.

The usual procedure is for you to send a written request that your former attorney forward all your files and related information to your new attorney. If you owe any balances for costs or fees, they must be paid in full. A lawyer has a "charging lien" on client files, and is not required to release them to a new attorney until all pending balances are paid.

So shop wisely before you finalize your lawyer hiring. Combine a prudent Whom to Hire? with your wise choices of How to Hire? and When to Hire? and you will greatly improve your chances for a positive outcome to your problem.

Discussion Exercises

1. Can you think of any other arrangements to hire a lawyer?

2. For each, what are the advantages and disadvantages?

3. Match the various hiring methods with the types of disputes that would best be suited for each. Discuss your choices.

4. Discuss your personal experiences with lawyers. What was positive? What was negative?

5. Does your company use outside lawyers or in-house counsel, or is there some other hiring arrangement for legal assistance?

Case Exercise 10

In *Gisbrecht v. Barnhart, 122 S.Ct. 1817 (2002)*, the U.S. Supreme Court was presented with the legal question of whether or not contingent fee agreements made by social security benefit claimants with their attorneys to recover 25% of the past-due benefits recovered were legally enforceable.

Three claimants, each represented by the same attorneys, brought separate actions in federal court for social security disability benefits under the Social Security Act. They won, and their attorneys sought their fee awards to be paid from their clients' gross proceeds, per their fee agreements.

The act provides that "Attorneys who successfully represent Social Security benefits claimants in court may be awarded a 'reasonable fee,' not in excess of 25 percent of the past-due benefits recovered, that is payable only out of those benefits."

The trial court and the appellate court, which consolidated the three cases, refused to honor the contingent fee agreements, ruling that they were replaced under the act by the "lodestar" method of calculating fees. It's a computation in each case of a reasonable fee based upon the number of lawyer hours spent multiplied by a reasonable hourly rate.

Using the "lodestar" method would have yielded fees of approximately 10% to 50% lower for the attorneys than their agreed 25% contingency.

Analysis

On certiorari review, the majority U.S. Supreme Court reversed, ruling that the act did not displace contingent-fee agreements as the primary means for representation in such cases, but rather required the amount of fee awards under such agreements be measured on a case-by-base basis by using the "lodestar" test of reasonableness.

One justice dissented on the basis that the act merely required the "lodestar" test of reasonableness to be used to evaluate fee awards. "I conclude that a 'reasonable fee' means not the reasonableness of the agreed-upon contingent fee, but a reasonable recompense for the work actually done."

The majority noted the following points:

"Social Security representation operates largely on a contingent-fee basis."

"The agreements entered into usually specify that, 'the attorney's fee will be 25 percent of any past-due benefits to which the claimant becomes entitled.' "

Congress authorized contingent-fee agreements for agency-level representation in 1990, and "It would be anomalous if contract-based fees expressly authorized at the administrative level were disallowed for court representation."

"The lodestar method (not developed and used until some years after the act) was designed to govern imposition of fees on the losing party . . . But (the section of the act applicable here) governs the total fee a successful Social Security claimant's attorney may receive for court representation. Nothing more may be demanded or received."

Defuse Replay

The practical effect of the majority decision is to make a contingent fee agreement of not more than 25% of the past-due benefits presumptively reasonable in these cases. No proofs by the attorneys seeking such fees need be presented. The agreement will stand by itself.

But what if the contingent fee agreed upon by attorney and client exceeds 25%? Here the "lodestar" test would be used to determine the reasonableness *of the excess* only. Such agreements, no matter how high the contingency, would not be automatically excluded.

Assuming the attorney used a fair hourly rate, a higher fee than the 25% would certainly be justified in the more difficult, time-intensive cases.

Conclusion

This case points practitioners to the important practice of keeping current, accurate, and complete time records. As a former managing partner of a law firm, the author can attest to their value, as well as the importance of establishing a workable procedure to complete them on a daily basis.

The "lodestar" test, which gained a firm foothold in the 1970s as the basis for calculating most attorneys' fee awards, requires lawyers to provide evidence of the time they spent on legal matters. And this same criterion of legal time spent versus hourly rate compared with the cost of business overhead is the basis for analyzing whether or not a lawyer is operating on a profitable basis.

Yet for many law firms, one of the biggest internal problems is recording billable time. "Out of sight, out of mind," the saying goes, and nothing is more difficult than to try and reconstruct billable hours after the fact. Many are invariably lost in the process, and income suffers accordingly.

Another common saying that applies is, "You can't teach an old dog new tricks." One of the author's hardest tasks managing the law firm, and one common to the industry, was to get certain law partners to keep any time records at all. Once they became used to billing by a "seat-of-the-pants" method, flattery, threats, promises of reward, and threats of punishment were used at various times to try to get them to change.

Keeping time records is much easier in our age of technology. Rather than manual entries in one's appointment book or time diary, a computer terminal attached to the phone, copier, or fax machine will automatically register billable time, pre-programmed for whatever is the local "reasonable hourly rate." Other time spent on research, court appearances, and client conferences can be electronically entered by the support staff or legal associates, should the lead attorney be one of the reluctant old guard.

A. Do you agree with the Court's majority decision, or the dissent?

B. Can you create a hybrid decision that combines both?

C. When do you think contingent fee agreements should be used?

D. What criteria would you use in determining the "reasonableness" of an award of attorneys' fees?

E. What hiring arrangement would you seek if your company needed legal assistance?

INDEX

U

UCC 2-509 Risk of Loss in the Absence of Breach states, 210
Unconditional approval of all terms, 37
Unconscionable amount, 59–60
Unconscionable contracts, 83, 96–99, 103
Underinsured motorist coverage, 4–5
Undue influence, 112–117
Unfair advantage, 68
Unfair benefit, 19
Uniform Commercial Code, Section, 2-615, 182
Uniform Commercial Code (UCC), 15, 25, 197
battle of the forms, 42–44
Uniform Computer Information Transactions Act of 1999 (UCITA), 251
Uniform Dispute Resolution Policy (UDRP), 248
Uniform Electronic Transactions Act of 1999 (UETA), 251
Unilateral contract, 17, 175
offers, 31–32
Union Carbide Corporation v. Oscar Mayer Foods Corporation, 947 F.2d 1333 (7th Cir. 1991), 45–47
United Nations Convention on Contracts for the International Sale of Goods (CISG), 199
Unreasonably dangerous product, 230
U.S. v Microsoft Corp., 65 F.Supp.2d 1 (D.D.C. 1999), 244

V

Vaceat emptor, 226
Valid acceptance, 37–47
legal requirements, 37–41
Valid contract, 18
Valid offer, 23–47
Varsity Gold, Inc. v. Porzio, 45 P.3d 352 (Az. App. 2002), 93–94
Verbal agreement, 148
Verbal promise, 148
Verner v. Mosely, 127 So. 527 (Ala. 1930), 113
Vine v. Bear Valley Ski Co., Cal.Sup.Ct.Case no. 317766 (2002), 296
Violenti non fit injuria, 95
Void ab initio, 69
Voidable contract, 18, 66, 71, 82
Voidable Title Rule, 204–205
Void and unenforceable, 68
Void contract, 18
Vokes v. Arthur Murray, Inc., 212 So.2d 906 (Fla. App. 1968), 122–123
Voting issues, 348

W

Wagering agreements, 86–88
Warranty recovery, 15
Watertronics, Inc. v. Flanagans, Inc., 2001 WL 942639 (Wisc. App. 2001), 318
Weese, et al v. Davis County Commission, 834 P.2d 1 (Utah 1992), 100
Wells Fargo Credit Corporation v. Martin, 605 So.2d 531 (Fla. App. 1992), 120
Werner v. Ashcraft Bloomquist, Inc., 10 S.W.3d 575 (Mo. App. 2000), 181
West Pinal Family Health Center, Inc. v. McBryde, 785 P.2d 66 (Az. App. 1989), 300
Whirlpool Financial Corp. v. GN Holdings, Inc. 67 F.3d 605 (7th Cir. 1995), 324
Whirlpool financial Corporation v. GN Holdings, Inc., 67 F.3d 605 (7th Cir. 1995), 283
Whitman, Heffernan, Rhein & Co., Inc. v. Griffin Company, 557 N.Y.S.2d 342 (N.Y. App. 1990), 131
Wien Air Alaska, Inc. v. Brandt, 195 F.3d 208 (5th Cir. 1999), 318
Wilkin v. 1st Source Bank, 548 N.E.2d 170 (Ind. App. 1990), 119–120
Williams v. Walker-Thomas Furniture Company, 350 F.2d 445 (D.C. Dist. 1965), 97
Wilson v. Kealakekua Ranch, Ltd., 551 P.2d 525 (Hawaii 1976), 5–6
World Intellectual Property Organization (WIPO), 248
World wide web, 246–247
World Wrestling Federation v. Bosman, 249
Written Form, 14
Written form requirement, 130–156

X

X-IT Products, L.L.C. v. Walter Kidde Portable Equipment, Inc., 155 F.Supp.2d 577 (E.D. Va. 2001), 298

Y

Yong Cha Hong v. Marriott Corporation, 3 UCC Rep. Serv.2d 83 (D.Md. 1987), 238–239
Ypsilanti v. General Motors Corporation, 506 N.W. 2d 556 (Mich. App. 1993), 21–22

Z

Zean v. America Online, Inc. 129 F.3d 327 (4th Cir. 1997), 260
Zippo Manufacturing Company v. Zippo Dot Com, Inc., 952 F.Supp 1119 (W.D.PA. 1997), 257